Enactments

EDITED BY RICHARD SCHECHNER

To perform is to imagine, represent, live and enact present
circumstances, past events and future possibilities. Performance takes place across
a very broad range of venues from city streets to the countryside, in theatres and in offices,
on battlefields and in hospital operating rooms. The genres of performance are many,
from the arts to the myriad performances of everyday life, from courtrooms to
legislative chambers, from theatres to wars to circuses.

ENACTMENTS will encompass performance in as many of its aspects and realities
as there are authors able to write about them.

ENACTMENTS will include active scholarship, readable thought
and engaged analysis across the broad spectrum of performance studies.

Festive Devils of the Americas

Edited by
MILLA COZART RIGGIO
ANGELA MARINO
PAOLO VIGNOLO

Seagull
BOOKS
LONDON NEW YORK CALCUTTA

Seagull Books, 2015

Essays © Individual authors
Photographs © Individual photographers
This compilation © Seagull Books, 2015

ISBN   978 0 8574 2 179 1

British Library Cataloguing-in-Publication Data
A catalogue record for this book is available from the British Library

Typeset by Seagull Books, Calcutta, India
Printed and bound by Maple Press, York, Pennsylvania, USA

Contents

Acknowledgements

The Festive Devils project began as a collaborative proposal of a new born international research group 'Play, *Fiesta* and Power' initiated by Angela Marino (now at UC Berkeley), Paolo Vignolo(National University of Colombia, Bogotá), and ZecaLigièro, (UNI-RIO) to form a tri-lingual working group on the devil figure in popular fiesta, carnival and religious manifestations throughout the Americas. Having expanded to include Milla Cozart Riggio (Trinity College), and Rachel Bowditch (Arizona State University), among others, this group has now created a research collective that has met together in six different international gatherings: (1) The exploratory meeting centered on 'Fiesta, Politics and Nation', Bogotá, Colombia, spring, 2008; (2) a mini-Encuentro and Board meeting of the Hemispheric Institute of Performance and Politics (Hemi), Chicago, October, 2008; (3) the Latin American Studies Association annual meeting, Rio de Janeiro, June, 2009; (4) The Hemi bi-annual Encuentro, Bogotá, August, 2009; (5) The American Society for Theater Research (ASTR) annual meeting, San Juan, November, 2009, and (6) the Hemi Encuentro in Montreal, Canada, June, 2014. In August, 2010 Angela Marino convened an editorial retreat to read and comment on submitted essays in Chiapas, Mexico. At that time Silvia Rivera Cusicanqui (Bolivia) and Rawle Gibbons (Trinidad) were added to Ligièro, Marino, Vignolo and Riggio as members of the Editorial Board for the Festive Devils project. Their ideas and contributions to the book, including Marino's doctoral research on festive devils, helped to conceptually center this book on the many ways in which the figure of the devil in popular performance unfolds histories, practices, belief systems and epistemologies of Indigenous, Afro- and Asian-descendant communities and subalterity. In 2010, a website, designed by David Ayala and curated by Marino was launched in its first phase to provide an ongoing site for recording and illustrating a growing number of festive devil traditions throughout the Americas.

We are greatly indebted to the Hemispheric Institute of Performance and Politics (Hemi, headquartered at NYU), under whose auspices the project has developed, and who funded the Chiapas retreat, helped to fund the creation of the website, and has provided partial funding for the translation of the book into Spanish. We are particularly grateful to Diana Taylor, Founding Director of the Hemispheric Institute and to Marcial Godoy-Anativia, Associate Director, Marlène Ramìrez-Cancio, Associate Director (Arts and Media), and Niki Kekos, former Assistant Director (Administration) for their unflagging support and enthusiasm for the project. We look forward to the development of other projects of this kind under the umbrella provided by Hemi. We also wish to thank the Allan K. Smith endowment of the Trinity College, Hartford, CT English Department for its financial support. Organized, efficient, gracious and patient under pressure, Raquel Mendoza was an extraordinary editorial assistant for the English book. We congratulate her on her graduation from Trinity College with a double major in English and Theater and Dance.

Dealing with language usage and translation across a broad range of regions and traditions was important in the process of this book. Some essays were written in Spanish, some in English, one in Portuguese. Andy Klatt and Morelia Portillo Rivas translated from Spanish to English. Randy Ferrufino assisted with Spanish-English translation. Ligièro translated his own essay from Portuguese to English. Silvia Rivera Cusicanqui translated all the English essays for a Spanish edition of the book, to be published in Colombia under the lead editorship of Paolo Vignolo. Seagull Books, whose commitment to the project has been invaluable, further required translation from American English to British English norms. We are indebted to the team at Seagull Books for seeing this book through, as well as to Richard Schechner for including *Festive Devils of the Americas* in the Enactments Series, distributed in the US by the University of Chicago Press. This network tells its own story of the multi-directional global circuits involved in tracing Festive Devils along their crisscrossing paths.

Milla Cozart Riggio, Angela Marino, Paolo Vignolo
May 2015

Foreword

This wonderful volume brings together varied approaches and examples of 'festive devils' in the Americas. These devils dance, play pranks, provoke, taunt spectators, turn the tables on their adversaries, forge unlikely alliances and laugh at authority figures. Yet most devils tremble before the Virgin. For centuries, the devils have embodied contradiction—they are mocking yet reverent; unruly but they uphold their own law; domineering yet doomed to subservience. These devils perform a history of asymmetrical and unstable power relations throughout the western hemisphere from the fifteenth century to our own.

The Catholic friars that accompanied the conquerors to the Americas in the fifteenth century both brought and discovered the Devil. The Devil 'our enemy planted, in this land, a forest or a thorny thicket filled with very dense brambles, to perform his works therefrom and to hide himself therein in order not to be discovered' (Sahagún 1577: 45). The Devil epitomized excessive visibility and invisibility simultaneously—he was ubiquitous but hard to pin down. He lurked in the dense brambles, and in all the daily practices the Amerindians performed. He sowed confusion and disorder. He tormented the Europeans with everything they did not know. The native peoples' songs and dances, according to the sixteenth-century friar Berdardino de Sahagún, were 'hiding places in order to perform his works [...]. Said songs contain so much guile that they say anything and proclaim that which he commands. But only those he addresses understand them' (ibid.: 58). Invisible, the Devil posed a permanent threat. He embodied the dangers of uncertainty and indecipherability. 'And [these songs] are sung to him without its being understood what they are about, other than by those who are natives and versed in this language [...] without being understood by others' (ibid.). The Devil and the native peoples understood each other and communicated through all manner of acts. The Catholic newcomers, watching from the outside, simply could not understand the workings of their archenemy. The Devil danced rings around them. He exposed their limited access. The Amerindians, whom the Europeans considered ignorant, were in the know. The friars, meanwhile, felt powerless and mystified. The European, Catholic worldview was turned inside out and upside down.

The Devil, as we see from the writings of the early chroniclers, condensed a number of paradoxical and competing forces for the Catholics. Whatever they could not understand, the indigenous dances and songs, for example, they labelled 'diabolic'. Whatever they feared appeared before them as devil's work. They thus constructed an image of the Devil (the shape of all that was incomprehensible) and then they tried to destroy it/him. The Devil mirrored the Europeans' terror in the new, bewildering world. The Devil proved both the symptom and the embodiment of their non-understanding. The Devil was a/the/their double, part of a closed-circuit system in which it enacted both their anxiety and the object of anxiety.

For Amerindians, of course, the Devil at first meant nothing. It's not clear when they shifted from being labelled 'diabolic' and 'devil worshippers' to actively donning the role of the Devil for their own festive purposes. The doubling increased exponentially. The mirroring now included the natives' parodic reflection of European fear, mimetic projections of colonial anxiety. This too was interpreted as the work of the Devil. Friar Diego Durán speculated that 'our cursed adversary forced the Indians to imitate the ceremonies of the Christian Catholic religion in his own service' (1994: 95). The Europeans soon started thinking of indigenous people as perpetual performers, engaged in 'idolatrous dissembling', 'go[ing] about like monkeys, looking at everything, so as to imitate whatever they see people do' (Motolinía 1950: 104). The early colonists' apprehensions and anxieties were made visible through native 'imitation' and 'dissembling', themselves destabilizing practices.

This collection of essays explores many of the contradictions, power plays, mimetic gestures and liberating ambiguities posed by the many festive devils throughout the Americas. The multifaced devils are resistant figures, morphing through the centuries and the landscapes, as well as figures of resistance, always agile in eluding colonial masters and their precepts. As an ongoing festive presence with an enormous hemispheric significance, the devils continue to tease, entertain and dance rings around those of us who would define or fix them. But they engage productively with those who recognize their multivocality and their communicative potential, with those who accept the challenge of participation. The festive devils have interested an important group of academics that came together through the Hemispheric Institute of Performance and Politics to produce the essays offered here. The scholars made up a working group at the Institute's biennial Encuentros and engaged in a week-long retreat at its Centro hemisférico/FOMMA in San Cristóbal de las Casas, Chiapas. The group leaders, Milla Riggio, Angela Marino and Paolo Vignolo have been inspired in their choice of interlocutors and seeing the project to completion. This book captures the energy, the fierce interventions and the political force that are the festive devils. I, for one, accept their invitation to dance.

Diana Taylor

PART 1

Introduction

The Work of the (Festive) Devil

ANGELA MARINO

In 2006, Venezuelan president Hugo Chávez Frias, protecting himself with the sign of the cross, announced to the General Assembly of the United Nations that 'the devil came here yesterday, right here, and still today it smells of sulfur.' In this speech that captured world attention, Chávez openly defied US president George W. Bush, claiming that 'as the spokesman of imperialism [el Diablo/Bush] came [. . .] to promote the current pattern of domination, exploitation and pillage of the peoples of the world.'[1] Mirroring back a central strategy of imperialism, Chávez effectively reversed the roles with Bush as the demonic dragon and the 'peoples of the world' as the contemporary St George. The iconic St James 'matamoros' (Moor-slayer) for an instance anyway, became St James 'matayankee'.[2]

While the weapon of the devil in this case was a stone slung against a Goliath, in many ways Chávez picked up a tool bearing a long history. Since at least the second century BCE, the devil carried meanings of an adversary or opponent of war. As Gerald Messadié writes, '[T]he devil is indeed a political invention' (1997: 87). The word 'Satan' (har-Shatan) in the Old Testament translates literally as 'an opponent'. In centuries to follow, the apocalyptic turn in the Judaeo-Christian tradition further developed this notion of the devil as 'an enemy of humanity' associated with race and gender. Mediaeval texts continue to wield the devil figure against Muslims and Jews, those accused of witchcraft, intellectuals, and others deemed 'pagan'. In the early modern period of the sixteenth century, persecution intensified, where the devil became a strategic weapon for both Catholics and Puritans in colonizing the Americas (Cañizares-Esguerra 2006).[3] If this is a dance with the devil, it was choreographed, ritualized and scripted by political interests for centuries.

Acts of demonization were not only central as a strategy of 'conquest' of the Americas; they were the very basis of imperialism that *depended* on devil beliefs for land occupation and juridical claims of all kinds.[4] Undoubtedly, the devil fulfilled a fantastical and illusory role as avatar of colonizing fears and desires. Yet, for Europeans of the time, as Jorge Cañizares-Esguerra points out, 'demons were real, everyday physical forces, not figments of the imagination or metaphors standing for the hardships of colonization, as we might condescendingly be prone to assume' (ibid.: 12). It was a short step from believing in the reality of the devil to imagining that these regions were in effect devil lands and those in them were literally chained to the will of Satan.

As Enrique Lamadrid quotes in his essay in this volume, in the words of an early Franciscan: '[W]hen Prince Lucifer [. . .] was banished from heaven, he landed in the Americas where he established his dominions unopposed' (Campagne 2004: 7). Ubiquitously present, from the European perspective, the devil was lord and master of the 'new world'.

In this harrowing view of gaping hell mouths, the devil and popular fiesta may seem strangely paired. Publically staged Christian rituals (autos de fé) aimed at rooting out idolatry or exorcizing so-called devil beliefs were as infamously barbarous as the depictions of hell in fiesta plays—replete with penitent shaming, torture and immolation. Take for example, the play *Final Judgment* (1531) in which Lucia, a woman who refuses marriage, is swallowed up in flames with a serpent around her neck, condemned forevermore to hell (Olmos 2008: 54–6). With trapdoors leading down to Satan, and Christ guiding the faithful up a ladder that was rigged onto the set, the friars went to great pains to ensure that Good and Evil had their separate places within a cosmological map of ascension to heaven and an underworld of doom.[5] It may be hard to imagine much festivity, especially when a staged play such as *Final Judgment* so clearly represented the actual auto-da-fé trials of the Inquisition. Yet, these outdoor plaza events—in the case of *Final Judgment*, as performed in several locations near present-day Mexico City—typically included feasting, fireworks, music and elaborately decorated streets and archways.[6]

Moreover, as Diana Taylor points out, *Final Judgment* seemed to operate on at least two different registers, where in the end, little was actually final (2008: 51). Produced by Mexica actors and crews, elements written into the script such as fire, snakes and the dead that 'rise' may well have pointed to non-Christian deities, renewal, a continuum of life-death, and ancestral presence (ibid.). Multiple devils move in and out of the underworld, carrying the renewal fire.[7] Lucia wears a second fire snake (evoking the fire-serpent god Quetzalcóatl) that encircles her waist, which she says symbolizes 'the pleasure with which I enjoyed myself on earth', that which came from 'the heart of the house of hell' (Olmos 2008: 57). Given that hell was translated in Nahua as *temazcalli*, or steam baths that people went to for healing, it's quite conceivable that the 'house of hell' suggested not so much a bad place as one of transformation and renewal. One might therefore imagine a very different ending than the friars likely intended when the devils carry Lucia away, exclaiming, 'Now we shall give you pleasure in the nethermost hell!' (ibid.).[8]

Particularly in fiestas that appropriated Nazca, Chichimeca and Lucumí-Yoruban performances, to name a few, the points of contact between the indefatigable Christian devil and regenerative and multidimensional figures of death, the underworld, healing and renewal radically transformed the meanings of the devil and the very concept of the demonic. Sometimes the imposed Christian Devil was rejected outright. Other performances absorbed some aspects of the Christian Devil by adopting or altering the placement of horns or capes in costumes, altering the mythology of fallen angels or the embodiment of sin and evil. Figures that move between worlds and at gateways, 'tricksters' such as Saci, Kokopelli and Coyote, produce altogether different paradigms of conflict, creation/destruction and healing, and ideas around chance, virtue and skill that further mess up the schematic binary of good versus evil, and the assigned mapping of heaven–hell that missionaries worked so hard to instill. What then did these concepts of hell and the devil become? How did these various encounters of demonology and fiesta combine in performances that for so many centuries have been spun by various producers, actors and audiences? The festive devil plays out this confrontation in its performances resulting in a constantly changing and mutable figure that has remained ubiquitous, playful and perilous, in a sense, emblematic of the very nature of fiesta and carnival.

First, the devils that initially arrived in the Americas were hardly unidimensional. From the onset, the Judaeo-Christian devil echoed Persian, Egyptian and Graeco-Roman gods with regenerative powers or who served as messengers to the dead, functions defined as 'pagan' and, thus, profane (see Russell 1977: 55–121; Link 1996; Messadié 1997). By the time of the European invasion of this hemisphere, the devil figure had already morphed in several directions: linked, on the one hand, partly through the popularity of Dante's *Inferno*, to a taxonomy of dragons and beasts, and on the other, to a comic figure, one of mischief and buffoonery. Though often portrayed as a horrifying beast, the Christian Devil was also known to be irrepressible, sly, irreverent and outrageously funny. Cervantes, who wrote at the outset of the seventeenth century, predicted the tenacity of the festive devil to triumph through its antic energy. As Max Harris references in his essay in this volume, when Don Quixote and his steadfast companion Sancho Panza had a run in with a 'demon dancer' with 'bladders' (in Spanish: *vejigas*)[9] and his band of Corpus Christi players, he begrudgingly withdrew his sword. As wise-headed Sancho reminded him, better to leave the actors alone, since 'your grace should know that since they are good natured and give pleasure to people, everyone favours them' (Cervantes de Saavedra 2003: 525). Despite the attempts of missionaries in the new world to convert people into Devil-fearing Christians, fiestas and festivals—a product of the transatlantic exchange over centuries—carried levity, humour and play alongside burning effigies, snarling devil masks and stories of sin and its consequence.

Second, both fiestas and the devil, while frequently wielded as tools of oppression, are slippery and not easily controlled. Regulating officials sought in vain to maintain their power through popular fiestas. Yet, by virtue of the insistent campaign by officials to prohibit and censure these events, we have some indication that their laws went largely unheeded. Even when performances were produced under the auspices of the Church, in reality a system of patronage and local customs would often surpass any attempt to regulate these practices from city centres or Spain (Ramos Smith 2010). It was not uncommon even for members of the clergy to actively promote alternative representations of Satanas and its acolytes.

At the same time, rituals, objects, people and beliefs that were deemed non-Christian or pagan by Catholic authorities were regularly conflated with the work of devils and, in some cases, recast in festive embodiments. We know from Felix Baez-Jorge and Luis Millones that Andean and Mesoamerican pueblos responded to the persecution of their deities by strategically 'inserting them into the images and rituals of the hegemonic faith' (Baez-Jorge and Millones 2014, location 139 of 3989). Especially those expressions that deified the forces of the underworld, were connected to the earth or the ancestors or were figures of transition or travel were assimilated so long as they were labelled diabolical. As Silvia Rivera Cusicanqui, sociologist, historian and Aymara activist, writes in the context of the Andes:

> The solar deities, as much as the fish goddesses, and the chthonic forces of the earth, were hurled unto the *manqhapacha*: the space-time of the ancestors that the early ecclesiastic interpreters mistranslated into 'hell'. The consequence was even more problematic than the diagnosis. The devil was incorporated into the autochthonous pantheon and is today a fundamental sacred force—at the same time generous and risky—in Andean religiosity (2014).

Thus altered in the 'active recombination of opposed worlds', the devil in fiestas became a much more complex figure than the friars and other missionaries might have ever presumed (ibid.). A result of zealous extirpation, violence and displaced meanings, the devil figure proliferated through thousands of religious practices in the Americas. Thus, protected under the misnomer of the 'devil', this figure in popular fiesta and carnival may be the single most important receptacle into which non-conforming spiritual and religious practice and worldviews survive today.

With some irony perhaps, the more the friars tried to contain what they considered pagan, the more powerful this figure became. In popular fiestas and carnivals, festive devil performances open what amounts to an enormous capacity for play, contestation and transformation. Nefarious but mischievous and usually light of foot, festive devils at times directly threaten Church, State or other forms of organized order. Sometimes they are allowed periods of free play or danger before being reined in by existing authorities. At other times, they sustain a disciplining role with an alternative set of rules. Yet when repeatedly performed in the middle of local plazas, on streets and neighbourhoods, especially by aunts and uncles, friends and parents, the devil is brought, so to speak, home. Almost always, by adding a comic note, festive devils render the monstrous familiar. Though they can still raise fears, they become figures with their own stories attached, appropriated and owned by the communities that make them. In this way, even when a devil is a 40-foot effigy, it is a monster made visible, expressive and exposed as an object or character both produced and then destroyed by human hands.

This view of production lends itself also to the ways devil dance repertoires tell a history of migration and diaspora. Recently, the people of Perico, Cuba, identified their common lineage of Gangá-Longobá with relatives in their ancestral home of Mokpangumba in the Sierra Leone despite hundreds of years of severance by the transatlantic slave trade.[10] Dance, masks, song lyrics and music, including those associated with 'devil dances', revealed these sustained ties. From the reunion ceremonies held in Sierra Leone, one account recalls, 'So as the drums of celebration are readied, so too is the "devil," the costumed dancer wearing head-to-foot raffia with wooden panels on his back, who represents all of the ancestors. Because the ancestors are, at last, dancing with joy' (Christopher 2013). As more connections are made in this study of festive devils, comparing the choreographies, masks and music in these performances may further disentangle and reveal ancestors and histories that have been buried within.

In other cases, festive devils ultimately confound purists seeking deeply inscribed national or nativist pasts. Devil dances and customs assumed to be 'originary' in pre-Christian traditions are constantly undergoing revision and thus reflect as much of modernity as any authentic past.[11] Devil dances lapse, or are revived by new interests and agency, such as illustrated in this volume by Monica Rojas' role in renewing the Son de los Diablos in Lima, Peru. Rose Cano (Ese Teatro and the African ConeXion Project) and others have now introduced this street devil dance in a new home in Seattle, Washington. In all their forms, these devils symbolically embody, as many of the essays in this volume reveal, a method of contestation, the idea of renewal and restored energies, and the ongoing stories of diaspora and migrations. Whatever their ultimate source, we found that festive devils are continuously shaped by the edges of modernity.

Thus, what we see in this volume is that the festive devil has been as much a symbol of that which is outcast as it is a symbol of the response and effort to build anew. When this book was in the early planning stages at two different conference events in Colombia (2008, 2009), the image of the devil was everywhere on shirts and caps for a soccer club from Cali, perhaps fittingly named América. One slogan next to its trademark mascot of a red devil with a pitchfork read, '¡El que tiene más gente!, América son cosas del corazón' (The one who has more people! América are matters of the heart). Whether by sheer numbers of population, or as an affect of the heart, something of América and devils caught on—at least it did on the T-shirt. Perhaps it tells another history, one of both the trauma and the force of renewal of a hemisphere. Reading through these essays, and seeing Amiel Cayo's images that reflect the multiple overlapping influences and variations of devil masks, or considering the crisis of monopoly capitalism that comes crashing into the figure of the Burning Man (see Rachel Bowditch's essay), or when the *cofradías* of the Caribbean and the Pacific Coast dance the devils with families and communal attributes (see essays by Anita Gonzalez, Benito Irady and Rafael Salvatore in this volume), the devil appears, in all of its reconfigured ways, as a response to the new world order from which it came.

There is another step to this argument though, since I don't think any of us ended up seeing these festive devil figures as merely negation, fighting an adversarial war. Festive devils challenge and contest where they also establish and demand an alternative basis of order and value. To consider this additional step of the festive devil working within an alternative order and not as mere negation, prompted us in the discussions over this volume to revisit some of the premises of fiesta and carnival theory, and to further a reconfiguration of the carnivalesque based on the festive devil as follows in the next section.

The Festive World View: Whose Devil? Whose God?

> MIRANDA. If I weren't afraid of blaspheming, I'd say he was a devil rather than a god.
>
> ESHU (*laughing*). You are not mistaken, fair lady. God to my friends, the Devil to my enemies! And lots of laughs for *all*!
>
> Aimé Césaire, A Tempest (1969)

Scripted into Aimé Césaire's masterpiece play *A Tempest* is the festive devil Eshu, who effectively turns the devil-god paradigm on its end by revealing its dependency on the question: Whose devil, whose god? His enemies, the colonizers, will call him the devil, while friends recognize him as the Yoruba and Candomblé Orisha god Eshu. Yet, rather than merely an ambiguous and dialectical figure, Eshu steps outside the dialectic with 'laughs for all', a laughter reminiscent of carnival. As Rawle Gibbons says, 'Carnival does not assert superiority of any culture over another; on the contrary, by accepting all, it shows the folly and futility of any such notion' (personal communication with Milla Cozart Riggio). Césaire's festive devil contributes in no small way to this festive world.

There is a folly and futility in Eshu's laughter, but no less an assertion of liberation and the remaking of the island. Both Eshu as an African-Caribbean god and Caliban (whom Prospero calls a 'born devil' of his Algerian mother Sycorax in Shakespeare's play; and who is identified as a 'black slave' in Césaire's) combine liberation on the basis of two assertions: rejecting white colonialism *and* being free to create and recreate in the island space. Claiming the island as initially his own, Césaire's Caliban spits out the 'works and pomps' of 'white magic', not as a negative gesture but as a gesture of affirmation:

> PROSPERO. And what would you do all alone here on this
>   island, haunted by the devil, tempest tossed?
>
> CALIBAN. First of all, I'd get rid of you! I'd spit you out, all
>   your works and pomps! Your 'white' magic!
>
> PROSPERO. That's a fairly negative program . . .
>
> CALIBAN. You don't understand it . . . I say I'm going to spit
>   you out, and that's very positive.
>
> PROSPERO. Well, the world is really upside down (Césaire 2002: 63).

Again, as with Eshu, it is a matter of perspective where the upside-down world as conceived by Prospero is more an indication of his own disorientation. Yet from the perspective of Caliban, the island space without him is an alternative order, 'and that's very positive'.[12] To position oneself positively aligned against an upside-down world of colonialism does what Joaquín Torres García's map of the inversion of America does to the hemispheric order of north to south. Torres García's map reschematizes the primacy of the north, where the festive devil diverts the colonial logic of 'white is right.' At the same time, just as Rufino and the Qolla in Grupo Cultural Yuyachkani's play *Santiago* (2000) refuse to merely switch places with the conquering crusader atop the charging horse, this figure of the festive devil spins the horse (read: map, method and means) as a refusal to accept the primacy of a one-way view, a refusal of a dysfunctional binary altogether.

Gibbons proposes that fiesta and carnival are a response to the demonization and dehumanizing effects of this colonial order:

> Blackness is at the centre of the carnival phenomenon, and likewise, carnival
> is at the centre of blackness. That is, carnival is our existential response to
> the historical dehumanization of the black race through enslavement. It is
> our critical intervention (outside of all forms of revolt and revolution) into

a discourse, which started when the idea of enslaving Africans was proposed by [Bartolomé] de las Casas nearly 500 years ago.[13] If the term still disturbs, it is because the issue of blackness remains to this day, unresolved. Anyone observing Trinidad Carnival would see that the issue is at the root of the creative/social/economic tensions within and outside the festival today (personal communication to Milla Cozart Riggio, 2014).

Blackness is at the heart of the carnival experience, accompanied by what many note as bountiful colours, including a myriad of red, blue, green and yellow. Some discussed in this book, such as the Devil of Cumaná (see David Guss) and the Jab Molassi (Milla Cozart Riggio and Rawle Gibbons), are painted black. Yet others that dance in Corpus Christi fiestas are red or have costumes in astonishingly bright rainbow colours (see Lowell Fiet, Anita Gonzalez, Max Harris, Angela Marino, Milla Cozart Riggio and Rawle Gibbons, Monica Rojas among others in this volume).[14] Even the 'blue devils' of Trinidad can paint themselves white or green. Yet, the 'darkening' of the devil is as symbolic as it is literal, inscribed in the linguistic, judicial and political systems of colonial order. For instance, as recorded by Paolo Vignolo in this volume, a devil dressed in white in the Carnival of the Devil in Riosucio, portrayed by historian and actor Misael 'Misa' Torres, sarcastically retorts: 'A white devil? Never seen such a thing! I dress in white because I am about to celebrate my First Holy Communion.' Some devil dancers, such as the 'judíos or Jews' of La Judea de Cora, performed by Nayeri communities in the Sierra Madre mountains in Mexico, first paint themselves patterned in black and white, later changing into full, vibrant coloured dress and paint for the public procession. If blackness is at the centre of carnival, then it is also the source from which these many colours emerge. Through festive devils performing with colour, and as black and white representations of these devil figures and images of the festive devil, these fiestas undo the imperialist paradigms that shaped the devil from the early demonization of 'Moors' to the continued racialized depictions of devils in contemporary media. While Bush was clearly not the first white man to be called a devil, Chávez was playing against a much more deeply entrenched cultural order that festive devils in many ways are breaking apart.

The festive devil's body itself is central to this analysis as an embodied epistemology. Within the Christian context, as Vignolo observes, the 'festival body' is one of the very few—if not the only—joyous bodies available. Catholicism in particular glorified the bleeding, suffering body. Nudity was the condition not for pleasure but for revealing the tortured, emaciated, redemptive body of Christ. Only the Devil and his forces offered a joyously celebratory counter-concept of the body.[15] Riggio added that in Christianity, such freedom is manifested primarily by festive devils as the antithesis of the martyrized, bleeding and motionless body that rewards submission and self-abasement.

Festive devils, on the other hand, tend to revel not only in the pleasures of the body but also in its excesses, at times linking profanity with obscenity. In the parodic festive context, devils often evoke the scatological, at times with enormous phallic emblems, blood or flatulence. Such devices impudently flaunt what is disguised in 'polite' society, thus unmasking society's pretensions. But profanity in these perform-ances of devils has a larger and more complex function. What we saw in much of the contemporary literature around popular uses of the devil figure describes devils as mediators in the relationship between profanity and community through their embodiment. By taking on that which has been prohibited, shunned and denounced as abject, festive devils assume 'profanities' (the unclean, the negated as marginal, in some cases 'dirty', or more centrally 'demonic'), thereby making them visible in col-lective acts in order to rework them, reconfigure their meanings and create a con-frontation and an adjustment towards that which has been disavowed.[16]

There is also an important critical intervention of the festive devil as a cultural fetish. As David H. Brown writes in the context of early-twentieth-century Cuba: 'It seems that Christians historically have required primitive, dark or grotesque media-tors—fetishized embodiments of social contradiction and its "terrors"—in order to ritually "cure themselves of their ills"'(2003: 51).[17] Indeed, the festive forms of devils in many ways hold up a mirror to spectatorship, invented by depravities and desires that would denounce these performances as 'vulgar' and 'disorderly' while simulta-neously taking part in them as 'deliciously devilish' (ibid).[18] Raising the question of gaze, inherent to an economy of race, social norms and the policing of those norms, may well put the contemporary bourgeoisie along with Friar Motolinía and a long line of persecuting governors in the reflection of that same mirror.

In *The Devil and Commodity Fetishism* (1983), Michael Taussig describes the devil pact and other devil beliefs as a dynamic mediation between pre-capitalist and capitalist modes of production. He argues that this tension of the devil as 'he who resists the cosmic process' ultimately gives the demonic a protective role, a kind of guardian devil, as situated in Oruro, Bolivia and the mainly Afrodescendant commu-nity of Cauca, Colombia (ibid.: 18). Devil beliefs flourished, for example, as Bolivian miners pray to el Tío, a so-called devil-god of the mountain, for safety and produc-tivity. While the devil appears to aid or reward production, in another way 'the devil is the mediator of the clash between two very different systems of production and exchange' (ibid.: 37). Thus in addition to being mirrors to the social, economic and political lines of spectatorship that produce them, these devils are also mediators or regulators of unequal relations and economic conditions.

Given this role as mediator, what kinds of new devils are invented in, for example, popular media and film, and how might those devils serve as fetish or even as a measure for the cultural and social tensions in contemporary society? Devils offer a means to expose these fetishizing acts of consumption from the outside while holding a mirror to a kind of 'devil within', as in the Colombian carnival of Riosucio (see Vignolo's essay in Part 2 of this volume). Again, the devil moves between insider and outsider systems of production, somewhat uncontrolled by either.

Festive devils are ultimately cultural operators constantly working to redraw the line on these 'final judgements'. They do so by claiming the act of penance, communal responsibility and as agents to produce and renew the rules in battles of good versus evil. Festive devils re-mark the moral boundaries within the social body that defines them. Like many carnivalesque figures, at times they invert structural order by taking charge; sometimes they emerge briefly, only to fall back into an existing order. More subtly, festive devils subvert existing orders and assumptions by questioning their validity or by countering them with alternatives. They emerge as resisting but also assimilating voices that simultaneously defy and work within the Christian paradigm. Within this palimpsest, however, good and evil become porous concepts that overflow and ultimately lose their power to exist as one without the other. In this sense, the festive devil creates its own enduring (and perhaps flexible) strategy and practice to contest cultural and political forms of oppression, its own epistemological response to the conditions of being demonized.

The devil figure and devil beliefs are thus continuously adapting to the new anxieties and conditions of the present day. Yet what is significant to point out is that festive devils are almost always allied with and affirm the community from which they are born. Often, devil dances are produced collectively by a large network of people, sometimes as *cofradías* or other groups, with only a few exceptions of lone devils that perform singly or are burnt in effigy. Thus, devil dances, like other fiesta and carnival practices, are ways of practicing community belonging and identity. What Anita Gonzalez describes of festive devils on the Mexican Costa Chica illustrates this well:

> The process of staging the dance reaffirms local alliances within the community and effectively articulates Afro-Mexican identities as something different from dominant *mestizo* and Catholic ideologies. Because the dance is often performed on the Day of the Dead (*c.*31 October–2 November), it represents an alternative community response to both Native American celebrations of Indigenous ancestors and Catholic celebrations

of the Resurrection. At the same time, the corporeal procession of unified black bodies creates a fraternity of the like-minded (p. 260 in this volume; see also Rojas' essay in this volume).

In performances such as the devils of Costa Chica, the kind of communal affirmation of the devil dancers that Gonzalez observes radically differs from the spectacle of shame of the auto-de-fé performances in centuries past, in which penitents in devil's hats were marched to the confessionals or the *quemadero*.

Perhaps as an extreme example of this transformation within the fiesta itself, Miguel Rubio's essay in this volume talks about the Army of Devils in Puno, Peru— the actual Peruvian army that now has been enlisted into the fiesta of the Virgen of Candelaria, soldiers who dance for miles, with spectators not letting them rest, in a festive parody of the brutal exercizes of corporal discipline that the indigenous of Puno are subjected to when they do their military service. Festive devils are not only avatars of colonization/consumption, they have also literally appropriated the armed forces into the new fiesta state.[19] The festive devils do much more: they teach a performed tradition of change and renewal. As we see the new devils appear as orks, metal-plated serpent-beasts and various kinds of insects, this history and ongoing remaking of the devil reminds us of the forces that wish to aggrandize new evil in new guises. Whose devil and whose god is at play? Who becomes the villain in these various theatres and in what ways do they turn the saint and the dragon? While reworking these battlefields into local hands of production, resignifying their practice in a festive form, fiestas also make new armies—from *diablos armados* (armed devils) to *diablos amados* (beloved devils); from devils that hang upside down to those that stand and dance; from devils that move through time portals and air waves to those that carry histories for generations in towns they now claim. As a recent production at the Hemispheric Institute's 2014 Encuentro in Montreal by the Bread & Puppet Theater said, 'Hell is ever more at hand than heaven,' which, given the transformational work of these devils through festive performance, might in the end be a better place to be.

The Structure of the Book

A long collaborative project with hundreds of points of engagement is impossible to contain in one volume. Likewise, with thousands of festive devils, there is no intention here to represent them all, nor claim even to have gathered the 'most important' in the hemisphere. We have attempted to structure this book, however, to make the most of this fact, to allow expansiveness and further input through different media available to us. We also wish to reflect the collaborative and transnational approach from which this project emerged from both scholars and practitioners from across the hemisphere by publishing in at least two major languages—Spanish and English.

Today, devils are likely to appear wherever masqueraders take to the streets. Wearing horns, rattling tins, brandishing pitchforks or whips, masked or muddied, sometimes elegantly infernal, festive devils are common throughout the hemisphere, retaining and generating their own particularities from region to region. The essays in this volume reflect these particularities; they are also the heart of this project, collectively representing the range and depth of this material, with overlapping ideas around the devil as a symbol, character and actor/activator in popular culture, fiesta and carnival performances.

The main body of this volume is divided into three regional sections: the Andes, the Caribbean and Atlantic, and Greater Mexico of the north. Section 1, Andean and Pacific Coast Devils, includes essays on the *diabla* in the Riosucio Carnival in Colombia (Paolo Vignolo); the Puno devil's dance in the Festival of the Candelaria in Peru (Miguel Rubio of Grupo Cultural Yuyachkani); a photographic essay by mask maker Amiel Cayo (also of Yuyachkani); Oruro's carnival devils of Bolivia (Thomas Abercrombie); and a photographic essay on the *diablada* of Oruro (Miguel Gandert). Artist, activist and scholar Monica Rojas closes this section with a first-person account of the revival of the Lima-based Son de los Diablos. While clearly differences exist, the majority of these essays share the example of Indigenous- and/or African-based popular remaking of these events in the wake of contemporary migrations and struggles over territorial-cultural rights. At the time of writing this book, Colombia has one of the highest numbers of displaced people within its borders of any country in the world, with Mexico appearing to be fast on its heels.[20] In the meantime, gentrification displaces thousands of Latino and African American families in urban neighbourhoods in the United States, forcing entire communities to vacate, along with their festivals, to find new homes and, in many cases, to fight back.

In the Caribbean and Atlantic section, essays are written on the Cajuas of the Dominican Republic (Max Harris); Brazil's 'everyday' devils, including Candomblé and in popular stories (Zeca Ligiéro); the *vejigantes* of Loíza, Puerto Rico (Lowell Fiet); and Trinidad Carnival devils (Milla Cozart Riggio and Rawle Gibbons with Raviji); the Devil of Cumaná in Venezuela, (David Guss), with photos by Rafael Salvatore; in Venezuela, an essay on the producing organizations (*cofradías*) of Corpus Christi (Benito Irady) with photos of the major cofradías in Venezuela by Rafael Salvatore; and the Corpus Christi devil dances of Ocumare de la Costa (Angela Marino). The essays in this section predominantly deal with the influence of the African diaspora; the events are mainly produced by Afro-descendant co-fraternal and neighbourhood networks or smaller intergenerational networks.

Essays in the third section of Part 2 include examples from northern regions, including the Costa Chica devils of the Mexican Pacific Coast (Anita Gonzalez); the devil in popular cultural manifestations in New Mexico (Enrique Lamadrid); and the Burning Man festival of Nevada (Rachel Bowditch). These devils of the north are striking for their radical reconfiguration in the context of capital expansion, as in the devil characters that appear in stories and songs of New Mexico and the monstrous effigy of the capitalist Satan in Burning Man. They also reveal the ways migrations influence the manifestations, for example, of Afro-descendant devil dances on the pacific coast of Mexico where the devil dances tell this history.

Given the potential to draw these regional stories together, each section opens with a map identifying the specific towns, cities and islands discussed in the essays of that section.[21] After many discussions and back and forth on placing these maps, it was decided that to locate what amounts to a dozen or more manifestations of festive devils would be helpful to readers. Though the maps contain national boundary lines, they are meant to be merely referents, since one of the premises of this study is the dynamic, moving and transnational practice of these dances. They are bound to people that produce them and thus, in many ways, mark territories of their own through practice.

One of the fruitful challenges we encountered over the years of collaboration on this project was the sheer abundance of themes and approaches. Although to study a singular 'character' of the fiesta and carnival may seem narrow in focus, we found that the range of festive devils far exceeded the parameters of any one story. Our first project was that of a bilingual website.[22] The website is now a complement to and expansion of this volume, interfacing with this book and with the ongoing projects of the Festive Devils work group. The format provides a way to include full colour images, video and links to articles of interest. It also includes an interactive map of some of the devil dances that are featured in this volume, along with a few more.

We also realized at the beginning of this project that we wanted to structure the book slightly differently in order to adequately integrate the many contributions and how they were interwoven thematically. One 'introduction' would simply not suffice. We decided to point to some of the overarching themes in this introduction you are reading now, and then to create a special section at the conclusion called *Encrucijadas* or 'Crossings', dedicated to a fuller integration of the essays in Part 2 of this volume. Each in the end could serve as introduction as much as conclusion, potentially making the book readable from more than one direction. The aim, for us, has been to more fully draw from this important material towards two thematic areas that stood out—the religious and spiritual implications of the festive devil, and that of its economic, political and social functions.

Performances of festive devils have taken place over centuries and have developed networks that contribute to the identity and collective action of people in local and global communities. We are grateful for their example, and we hope that, in its own way, this volume contributes to the work of a very different devil, perhaps one that will turn the tables more than a few times and, with all its trickery, continue to be a force of transformation.

Notes

I wish to acknowledge Milla Cozart Riggio, Trinity College, and Paolo Vignolo, Universidad Nacional de Colombia-Bogotá, for their role in supporting this essay which developed over many of our collaborative engagements, earlier collective drafts and ongoing exchange.

1   Hugo Chávez Frías' speech to the United Nations 61st session of the General Assembly, 20 September 2006 (available at: http://www.un.org/webcast/ga/61/-gastatement20.shtml; last accessed on 4 January 2015).

2   St James the Matamoros (Moor-slayer), was the iconic symbol of Christian conquest in the Crusades. When this figure transferred to the Americas, it became Santiago Mataindios (Indian-slayer) as recorded in a seventeenth-century painting of the same name in the Museo de Cuzco, Perú.

3   See Fernando Cervantes (1994) for a more detailed study that shows variances in how and when demonization was deployed. Most agree that diabolism took hold more intensely in the sixteenth century, and through the Inquisition was most punitive towards black Africans and their descendants. See also Rafael Strauss (2004) and Arturo Rodríguez-Bobb (2004).

4   See Steven T. Newcomb (2008); Jorge Cañizares-Esguerra (2006); Rafael Strauss (2004); Jaime Humberto Borja Gómez (1998) and Fernando Cervantes (1997).

5   When asked by a priest before being burnt at the stake whether he wanted to go to heaven or hell, Taíno Cacique Hatuey responded: 'If heaven above is where those who call themselves Christians end up, then I'll willingly go to hell' (recorded by Dominican priest Bartolomé de las Casas).

6   *Final Judgment* was performed several times in Tlatelolco and Mexico City between 1531 and 1539 (see Mosquera 2004). For full play text in English translation and discussion of *Final Judgment*, see Taylor and Townsend, *Stages of Conflict* (2008).

7   There are actually several different kinds of devils in this play: Satan in Nahua is *tlacatecolotl* that suggests necromancy or communicating with the dead and the underworld; and the devils are as *tzitzimime* or diving bird-like creatures that 'consume from above' (see Mosquera 2004).

8   Diana Taylor discusses the friars missing the point of these double meanings (2008). See also Diana Taylor and Sarah J. Townsend (2008); and Mosquera (2004) for more on the play *Final Judgment*.

9   Referring to the custom of inflating cow or goat bladders and painting them for fiestas, such as festive devils in Loíza, Puerto Rico, known as *vejigantes* (see Lowell Fiet's essay in this volume, pp. 168–88).

10 See the story in the documentary film *They Are We* by Emma Christopher of Sydney University (available at: http://theyarewe.com/; last accessed on 6 August 2014).

11 See Silvia Rivera Cusicanqui (2009).

12 See the generation(s) of Afro-Caribbean writers, artists and activists who have written on this play, including but not limited to Kamau Brathwaite, Édouard Glissant, C. L. R. James, George Lamming and Sylvia Wynter. See also a feminist reading as expansion of this conversation in May Joseph and Irene Lara.

13 Here Gibbons refers to Bartolomé de las Casas, a noted humanist who in 1542 wrote *A Short Account of the Destruction of the Indies* (published in 1552), in which, among the damning accounts of Spanish brutality of the Americas, he refers to Spanish conquistadors as 'white devils', while in other correspondence suggests that in order to protect Indigenous people from decimation, African people should take their place as forced slave labour in the Americas.

14 Red is also associated with some saints, such as St John the Baptist. Moreover, Carolyn Dean (1999) describes this transference of the colour red in a discussion of how Incan rulers conquered by the Spanish wore red slips on their heads, or pieces of material that were first attached to figures that were conquered, and later onto those victorious, emblematically represented, for instance, in the depictions of St James.

15 From at least the ninth century onwards, the demons who tempted Christ, or were expelled from heaven, were mostly portrayed not only as dark but also naked, compared to the long clothing of Christ or of the 'good' angels. See Luther Link (1996).

16 In her essay, Riggio points to Mary Douglas (1966) as a way of getting at established cultural values defined by what a society calls dirt.

17 See also Michael Taussig (1983).

18 See also Paul Scolieri (2011) on the idea of dances in the 'new world' being invented by colonial missionaries.

19 For this term, see David Guss (1980).

20 A 2012 report by independent firm Parametria estimated that 1.6 million people were internally displaced in Mexico over a period of five years from 2006 to 2011 (see Ferris 2012: n.p.).

21 Designed by editorial assistant Raquel Mendoza.

22 The Festive Devils of the Americas website is edited and curated by Angela Marino and designed by artist, activist and scholar David Ayala. The Festive Devils project is articulated there as 'dedicated to the research, participation and continuation of fiestas, religious manifestations, and carnivals of devils dances in the Americas. Their appearances help to untangle one of the most charged figures in history; a figure highly symbolic that carries the charge of "evil" and "play" along with honour,

faith and collective action that simultaneously center and diffuse the binary of good and evil' (available at: http://www.diablosfestivos.org/diablos/; last accessed on 6 August 2014).

PART 2

Essays
Andean and Pacific Coast Devils

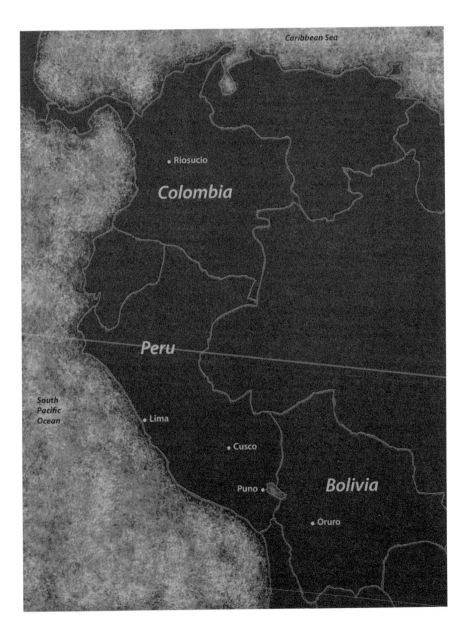

Via Crucis and the Passion of a Diabla
Public Space, Historical Memory and Cultural Rights
at the Carnival of Riosucio

PAOLO VIGNOLO

Translated from the Spanish by Andy Klatt and Morelia Portillo Rivas

The Devil is the great protagonist of the carnival of Riosucio, Colombia, from his triumphant entrance that initiates the fiesta to the closing bonfire when his effigy is set ablaze in the main plaza directly in front of the cathedral. A new icon has emerged in recent years, though—the Diabla, built and carried through the streets in a procession by a group of persons at the margins of the public sphere (street artists and artisans, but also prostitutes, alcoholics, addicts and petty criminals). The Diabla has become a symbol of recovery and participation for city dwellers at the margins. In contrast to other initiatives to promote a variety of cultural traditions, such as attempts to generate an 'Indian carnival' similar to the carnival of the Devil but in a nearby rural area, the appearance of the Diabla in the town's public space has been a successful exercise in active citizenship, reclaiming the right to popular participation in the festive performance.

Carnival Geographies

The carnival of Riosucio always begins and ends with a funeral. The ritual act that initiates the festivities pays homage to deceased *carnavaleros* or carnival makers. The procession slowly descends the path to the cemetery accompanied by a melancholy rhythm played on a traditional ensemble known as a *chirimía*. At the head of the procession is Abelardo, the old flag-bearer, carrying the green-white-and-gold flag of Riosucio with an image of a devil at its centre. The devil is portrayed carrying a gourd of the type used to ferment *guarapo*, the Indigenous sugarcane beverage that is a symbol of the carnival. Next comes the organizing committee known as the Junta del Carnaval, comprised of the town's notables dressed entirely in black. Behind them are the crowds of people who participate in the procession. Devils and masked figures move forward to the rhythm of the music, blending in with the rest of the procession. Even the hymn of the carnival has its own funereal version.

In a paradox more apparent than real, the fiesta opens in mourning in order to commemorate the *carnavaleros* and matachines of the past. Indeed, the carnival is forever a play on death. It is a collective exorcism of *la negra señora* (a female personification of death), an unbridled dance whose steps cross the subtle threshold between here and the great beyond. During carnival, the border between the world of the living and the world of the dead becomes more porous. As the procession descends to the cemetery to the slow rhythm of the euphonium and snare drums, Beto Guerrero points out:

> We live in carnival and we die in carnival . . . . The burial of a *matachín* is accompanied by music, drinking, fireworks and the carnival hymn. And it's like a parade to the cemetery—it's like a parade, as though it were a carnival parade. I've been to various burials where we've come in costume, we've painted our faces, put on make-up, all of that . . . . At the wake, we talk about the person who has passed, but in a relaxed way, you know what I mean? The nice things that happened in life, the good things that happened, that's why it's a cheerful wake and a cheerful burial. So I think that's why I say that for us carnival is life and also its death (personal interview 2007).[1]

The cortege starts in front of the bar called La Escarcha, on the northern side of the Plaza San Sebastián (the upper plaza), and it heads down to the Plaza Candelaria (the lower plaza). At the church there is a Mass in memory of those who once were carnival celebrants. Then the procession leaves the church, passes through the Curramba neighbourhood and heads down a steep street to the cemetery at the outskirts of town on the road to Sipirra.

This is a highly symbolic route which has been forged through practices that involve many families, generation after generation. The story of the town is written there in the complex cartography of carnival movements. And conversely, the steps of the carnival-goers through the streets—their legends, their poetry and their songs—are the hieroglyphs that contain the cultural memory[2] of these lands.

Groups of friends, families and neighbours called *cuadrillas* show up wearing masks, telling new stories with each carnival through song, words and dance. They expand the celebrations and spread them to local patios and living rooms. After parading through the streets and plazas of town on what is perhaps the most animated day of carnival, each group makes a visit to every one of the *casas cuadrilleras*, homes where some of the most traditional families in Riosucio provide food and alcohol to visitors until the early morning hours.

But the carnival is more than just *cuadrillas, matachines* and the members of the Junta. Every stratum and social group is represented in some way, based on where it is situated on the festive calendar and in the social spaces of carnival. Just before the beginning of carnival, for example, cattle ranchers fill the town on their horses. The wealthiest people of the region—landowners, merchants, sometimes even drug traffickers—parade through both plazas, flaunting horses that may be worth millions of dollars, alongside their relatives, their closest collaborators, their bodyguards and even their farm or ranch employees.

Similarly, Indigenous peoples of neighbouring *resguardos*,[3] who for years have felt marginalized by the carnival, may burst in suddenly with *chirimías* and costumes in a gesture of festive defiance that can be quite charged with tension.

There is also a day dedicated to a parade of *colonias*, where those who now live outside Riosucio take centre stage, carnival-style. On this day, carnival becomes above all a reunion of families and those who have gone to live elsewhere. This is why carnival is a date—a date with the Devil.

All of the characteristic dramaturgy revolves around the figure of the Devil. The party begins with the unveiling of his effigy, which has been zealously concealed in the preceding months. With his triumphant entrance through the streets of the town, the multitudes who have gathered to welcome him are possessed, which is to say, they conjure up their own devils within, break through the barriers of manners and social mores to strengthen their identities at the same time as they risk them in the dizzyingly ludic atmosphere of the fiesta. 'You must lose yourself in order to find yourself again,' carnival mask maker Hugo 'Chory' Ladino would say, 'The mask is to forget yourself. You put on the mask to forget yourself.'

Upon arriving at the Plaza San Sebastián at the top of the hill, the Devil delivers a ritual speech that is loaded with references to local events and national and international politics. From that point on, he is ubiquitous at the festivities over the course of the days that follow, while the *colonias* and *cuadrillas*, the *chirimías* and groups of musicians stir people up all across Riosucio.

Under the protection of the king of the celebration—His Majesty the Devil—carnival-goers partake of small rituals, spells and jokes. Women who want to get pregnant rub their bellies after having touched the Devil's testicles, symbols of fertility. Candles are placed all around drunken men who fall asleep on the street, so that upon waking they won't know if they are alive or dead, if they are still on earth or if they have reached hell. Then some minor, private and invisible rituals are enacted to deal with the inevitable hangovers: home remedies, prayers, ointments, gestures and spells. Carnival penetrates upward from beneath the social fabric. It seeps into the entrails of society, of homes, of families and of the subject himself.

On the last day of carnival, a funeral cortege of devils and other masked characters accompanies an effigy of the Devil for an ultimate farewell amid much weeping and farcical lamentation. At the lower plaza, directly in front of the cathedral, the Devil is solemnly burnt in effigy, to emerge out of his ashes for the next carnival.

Above all this is a fiesta of the word, where the lyrical, critical and satirical potential of language is celebrated, *matachines* and poets compete with verses and stanzas
so their Satan will soon re-emerge among his followers:

My beloved Lucifer
It is for you that I have come.
And I share this with my people
What joy it is to see you again.
The people I represent,
Devil, blessed Satan,
They ask, they cry out.
We are bursting inside.
So, please, come back soon.[4]

Foundational Myths

The festive performance is built upon a precise geography whose axis leads from the
cemetery to the two plazas, with their spacious churches, until it reaches the Vía
Crucis and climbs up Ingrumá, guardian hill of the town.[5] The rituals of death (the
funeral) and of birth (baptism), public life (in the two plazas) and private life (in the
patios of homes), the staging of pleasure (carnival parades) and of pain (the Vía
Crucis of Holy Week), the spectacles of martyrdom (the passion of Christ on the
cross and of the carnival Devil burnt at the stake) are followed by resurrection. The
fiesta journeys through the places of the town's collective memory, and through the
fiesta the town recalls its own individual and collective history. As with any history,
this one is marked by conflicts and disputes brought to light within the very festive
spaces of carnival.

Nancy Appelbaum, whose doctoral dissertation focuses on the history of this
municipality located on the eastern slope of the western range of the Colombian
Andes, underscores how Riosucio, unique in the region, was developed not around
a single central plaza but around two: the upper plaza of San Sebastián, traditionally
associated with the white and mestizo elites of the town, and the lower plaza of La
Candelaria, associated with the Indigenous population and other marginalized groups
(2003: 1).

The tale [. . .] begins in the early nineteenth century, at the very end of the
colonial era. Several groups of Indians lived the area, which was richly
endowed in gold. The biggest Indian Community was La Montaña, which
was ruled benevolently by a maverick republican priest, Father José
Bonifacio Bonafont. Northwest of La Montaña was a Spanish settlement

known as Quiebralomo, where African slaves worked the mines. Father Bonafont had enlisted the priest of Quiebralomo, one father Bueno, to help him put an end to the acrimonious disputes between the two communities by uniting them as one. On 7 August 1819, Riosuceños say, the two priests founded the new town at a site that had long been known as 'Riosucio' [...]. The villagers of La Montaña and Quiebralomo carried their respective patron saints in processions from their village chapels to the new town, and the priests ordered their old chapels burned to the ground so that they would not return (ibid.: 5).

The official version regarding Riosucio's history appeared recently on the town's official web page, stating that:

August 7, 1819, traditionally understood as our foundation date, can be seen as the day when the transfer of Quiebralomo was officially finalized, thereby fulfilling the basic elements of the city's urban consolidation. The districts of Quiebralomo and La Montaña were fused into one and given the name Riosucio [...]. This, then, is the date of Riosucio's establishment as a municipality.[6]

The exact date would be an insignificant detail were it not for the fact that it coincides with the date when the army of Simón Bolívar won the decisive battle of Boyacá against Spanish colonial troops elsewhere in what would become Colombia. It is a suspicious coincidence that conveniently allows local festivities to take precedence over a Colombian national holiday and permits a small town to be portrayed as a microcosm of the country (Ortiz 2007). In a letter addressed to Riosucio writer Otto Morales Benítez, the famous historian Germán Arciniegas wrote:

Why my enthusiasm for Riosucio? Simply because in some way, it is the image of the country. It is the city that was born on the day when the independent life of Colombia truly began. It is no small matter that the year of its foundation by Father José Bonifacio happens to be the same year when upon General Santander's engagement at the bridge in Boyacá the Republic began to function and to trample the ashes of the Spanish government... This land of so many charms emerged as an El Dorado from the mines of Marmato and has become a coffee plantation with beans brought by Father José Bonifacio (1990: n.p.).

The growth of coffee production and gold mining, the influx of settlers from the departments (provinces) of Antioquia and Cauca, the presence of European, Indigenous and African peoples, and above all the existence of an exuberant festivity able to function as a melting pot of all of these components seem to strengthen the town's candidacy as a living representation of the country. It is inconsequential that this history is a simple rhetorical device. When Riosucio researcher Álvaro Gärtner Posada (1994) dared to publicly unmask this false history, raging controversies followed. When a myth has established itself in ritual practices and in collectively shared representations, it can no longer be easily refuted via 'mere' documentary evidence. 'But the story does not end with Independence,' continues Applebaum: 'The fragmented republic still had to become a nation, just as the dual town still had to become one. The Indians of La Montaña and the villagers of Quiebralomo still did not get along and refused to attend the same church. Each group maintained its own parish and its own plaza [...]. A fence divided them' (2003: 5).

Riosucio was left severed in two by a bamboo wall over the course of more than 20 years as fratricidal wars between Liberal and Conservative Party members repeatedly submerged the new republic in bloodshed between 1819 and 1847. The wall, whose existence is documented, marked the physical and symbolic border between miners and settlers, between respectable neighbours and Indigenous peoples, those known as *memes* the 'rabble'. It was built as a marker of dispute at a time that saw the emergence of labour exploitation in the mines and the establishment of new national laws governing the partition and sale of *resguardo* lands.

One day, and here history is once again tainted by legend, the two priests agreed to place an effigy of the Devil at the centre of the wall, so that those who so desired could approach it in order to express their grievances and demands. 'If God can't unite the town,' they said, 'then let the Devil do so!' Thus emerged the figure of the Devil, who would soon thereafter become the protagonist of the local carnival. Alfredo Molano Bravo, the most important chronicler of settlement processes in Colombia, describes the origin of carnival:

> The Spanish crown conceded four resguardos to Indigenous peoples to protect the Indigenous population from extermination, and of course, to prevent miners from going hungry. The people in the upper town and the people in the lower town were physically separated by a wall built at the beginning of the nineteenth century for the purpose of preventing young girls above from coming down below and young boys below from coming up above. But business interests were stronger than racist moralism and social conflict, and this is how the fiestas of the Devil came to be, days when everyone dressed up as each other, anything could be spoken about openly, and the Devil was in charge. By some miracle, peace came to town and down came the wall. From that time on, the town has celebrated the Devil's Carnival (2008: n.p.).

Figure 1. Old effigy of the Devil. Undated.

From that moment until the present day, vox populi on the streets has elaborated on the basic structure of the carnival's foundational myth with endless variations, producing mixed and superimposed versions at divergent historical moments. In some stories, the wall separates Liberals and Conservatives. In another version, it separates Indians and conquistadors. Some attribute the wall to the conflict between independence forces and Spanish loyalists or, in another version, even between modern guerrillas and paramilitaries! Playwright and stage actor Misael 'Misa' Torres Pérez synthesizes the meaning that ultimately underlies the legend in this way:

> This is one of the most unique towns in Colombia, in Latin America, and in the world. It was created out of the dispute between two territories. There were those up above and those down below, and they were separated by a wall. The wall was removed, and those at the top and those at the bottom remained, constituted now as one. That's why Riosucio is the only town that has two cathedrals—and it's dedicated to the Devil! (1998: 11)

Metaphors of Mestizaje and the Rhetoric of Reconciliation

Notwithstanding the variations, incoherencies and contradictions inherent in all foundational myths, the narrative structure that describe the origins of carnival always outlines the same thing—there is a fratricidal struggle that puts the *communitas* at risk but salvation comes in the figure of a good Devil, invented by a churchman, that allows for the festive reconciliation of different social classes by means of a sacrificial rite. As René Girard (1972) aptly explains, the sacred ritual of the feast is always based on a symbolic sacrifice. The communion banquet is celebrated with the flesh and blood of a sacrificial animal, the Catholic Eucharist with the transubstantiation of bread and wine and, in its carnivalesque parody, the victim is the king of the carnival—in our case, the Devil himself. However, the communitas simultaneously generates a type of immunitas since the mechanisms that strengthen one's belonging to the in-group of the fiesta also function as a symbolic expulsion of the other, the outsider, and the foreigner (Esposito 2009).

The cultural and sexual promiscuity among white settlers, Indigenous *campesinos* and, to a lesser degree, black miners is consummated with the complicity of the licentious festival Devil. Under his ephemeral reign, one is allowed—in the guise of masked play—to say what would otherwise be unsayable, giving way to the reconciliation, albeit momentary, of two sides in an interminable civil war.

But the same Devil also reminds us of the existence of external danger represented as alien to the social body, from which it must be expelled (not only the terrorist, the guerrilla, but also the Indigenous person, the *campesino*, the homosexual, the queer, etc.). It is the Devil, in short, who rules over the two great discourses that underlie the construction of a national identity in Colombia: ethnic *mestizaje*[7] and the search for peace. Processes of both inclusion and the most brutal exclusion are enacted in his name.

As Appelbaum points out, three versions of Riosucio's history are in contention with one another—each with its own narrative, ideological position and imagined community. On the one hand, there is the version of the white elites, especially those with their origins in Antioquia, who implicitly or explicitly defend a historiographical reading exalting Riosucio's belonging to a nation that is Catholic, speaks Spanish and follows Hispanic traditions. In this version, *mestizaje* functions as a mechanism for stratification that marks racial differences and extols processes of 'whitening' (Wade 1997: 59).

Then there is the version of the notable local families, enthusiasts of a Riosucio specificity within a regional context. These are the region's learned elites, who use the rhetoric of *mestizaje* in order to mark distinctions between themselves and the people of Manizales and other *paisas*.[8] Theirs is the most salient interpretation of carnival. Far from being limited to the elites, its currency permeates discursive practices, even including those of the protagonists of the festive performance. *Carnavalero* Alberto Ospina, for example, emphasizes the mestizo nature of the town, the Devil, and the carnival:

I have worn many costumes, but I like the Devil's costume very much because to me he is the central part of carnival. To me he has been the central figure of carnival, and to me carnival encompasses all that is *mestizaje*: black, Indigenous and white. As I see it, the Devil is neither European, black or white. No, this Devil of ours is completely full of *mestizaje* . . . (personal interview 2006).

Cuadrilla leader Galletta, on the other hand, attributes the origin of the Devil to the cultural agency of Riosucio elites at the beginning of the twentieth century:

Our Devil is an invention of intellectuals, and he is of such magnitude that in spite of being symbolically bad, those Riosucio intellectuals who created him in 1912 put him up as a good Devil. This is the only town where children can't possibly be afraid of the Devil. Children in Riosucio are never afraid of the Devil—they enjoy him, tease him, they dress up in costume, they put Devil's horns on their heads. It's the only town where the women have a good time putting on horns, and husbands are happy to see their wives in horns, even if they end up being cuckolded 30 or 40 times; here that's not a problem (personal interview 2006).

That 'good Devil', an oxymoron in profoundly Catholic places, reconciles opposites and settles conflicts, be they between generations, sexes or ethnic or political groups. Galleta continues:

Our Devil is so good that we can place him in the priests' atrium and he presides over the duration of the fiesta from there. The church can't accuse him of perversity because everyone . . . you've seen the collective hysteria on Saturday, all revolving around this myth of ours, our great Devil. Our Devil is a figure that provides us with all kinds of inspiration regarding language and thought, and not of submissive thought but of critical and analytical thought . . . (personal interview 2006).

There is also an Indigenous reading of the issue. Although historically stifled and silenced, this point of view has been gaining strength since the 1991 Constitution set in motion a process of re-indigenization. Where carnival is concerned, Torres is among those who most enthusiastically embrace the Indigenous cause. 'Riosucio is comprised of 57 Indigenous *parcialidades indígenas*,[9] he says, 'that make up a pretty significant presence of descendants of the ancient Membes and Turzagas who inhabited this whole region at [one] time' (Torres Pérez 1998: 13). He further writes:

> In the territory where Supía and Riosucio are now located [. . .] the Turzagas once held fertility festivals which consisted of burying a gourd filled with *chicha de maíz* [a beverage made from fermented corn] that would then be dug up in order to celebrate the life cycle of their existence with religious ceremonies: the sowing of the land, the procreation of the species, and the reiteration of their cosmogony. These events were held around an enormous figure that symbolized those acts and that the conquistadors, upon their arrival, 'logically' identified as 'a horrific deity or Devil' (ibid.).

Recent moves to preserve the country's festivals as manifestations of a valuable cultural heritage have led to the exaltation of these types of ethnic identities, albeit purged of all conflictive elements and of all political or economic implications (Vignolo 2011). As Mara Viveros writes:

> Colombian-style multiculturalism has generated a new language, the language of ethnicity, which has given new meaning to differences and transformed them into legitimate attributes of cultural value. It has also made it possible to celebrate diversity and to adopt a positive view of expressions of the Colombian population's plurality. The trouble is that this multiculturalism has praised difference without questioning its link to inequality, as if all groups were socially equal and their differences were simply a matter of culture (2009: 382).

Since the Devil's trickery makes him capable of bringing various social groups into the carnival, thereby renewing the social contract, Riosucio can be understood as metaphor and metonymy of a new Colombian society. In the name of His Majesty Satan, though, conflicts break out, negotiations are entered into, disputes are settled; what is at stake is access to citizenship rights, political control and economic opportunity in the town.

A Fiesta amid the Conflict: The Indian Carnival

Land has been and continues to be at the centre of the armed conflict that plagues the Riosucio region and much of Colombia. Since the nineteenth century, Riosucio's position as an unavoidable crossroads between the departments of Caldas, Antioquia, Cauca and Chocó has made it a place where antagonistic groups converge. Despite the strong presence of Conservatives from Antioquia, since the beginning of the twentieth century, settlers from Cauca and others have been able to consolidate a fragile Liberal Party hegemony. The conflict between two models of settlement with divergent interests was heightened in the 1940s and 50s, a period of intensified inter-party violence throughout much of Colombia. Carnival festivities were not immune from the political confrontations of the time. As Hermán Pasero, privy to carnival planning, notes: 'At that time mayors were handpicked and appointed. So if the mayor was a Liberal, then the carnival committee was Liberal. If he was a Conservative, like-wise. So there was a conflict between the two plazas . . .' (personal interview 2009).

The violence not only established the power of landowners in the region but also became an active element of social mobility for many *campesinos* who would occupy the land of those who had been killed battling political adversaries. The presence of insurgent organizations, such as the Fuerzas Armadas Revolucionarias de Colombia (Revolutionary Armed Forces of Colombia, FARC), the Ejército de Liberación Nacional (National Liberation Army, ELN) and, above all, the Ejército Popular de Liberación (Popular Liberation Army, EPL) became ever more important in the region. These organizations actively sought to achieve political control—carrying out extortionist and politically motivated kidnappings and acts of sabotage—and to establish control over the local drug and weapons corridors. Pasero, who is actively involved in the recovery of regional folklore, shares his own under-standing of the situation:

> [A company called] Cartón Colombia came to Riosucio to plant pine trees. We have Cartón Colombia to thank for the guerrillas in the cooler, high alti-tudes. The company needed to get the people out of there—they needed to buy those lands, but since people weren't willing to sell, they brought in guer-rillas to get them out . . . . The guerrillas got much, much stronger in our region between 1975 and 1979. There was a wave of killing *campesinos* in the most terrifying ways, and those were people who had a lot to offer, culturally, to our research work on the Dances of Ingrumá. So, we formed a *cuadrilla* for carnival, the Cuadrilla el Combate [Combat Cuadrilla], as a protest against those killings, against the deaths of all those *campesinos*. It was *campesino* leaders that they were killing at that time (personal interview 2009).

Social issues intensified as drug trafficking made its way onto the scene in the 1980s. The coffee crisis and the slowly decreasing viability of small farming gave way to the arrival of new caciques with ties to the cocaine trade. The holdings of these new landowners were expanded primarily through the acquisition of productive lands by any means necessary, to be used mainly for raising cattle or for mining.

Of course the 1993 death of Pablo Escobar and the end of the tragic period of the first drug cartels did not end the problem either in Caldas or in the rest of the country. Beginning at the end of the 1990s, there was a rapid expansion of the Autodefensas Unidas de Colombia (United Self-Defence Forces of Colombia, AUC), a unified structure of regional paramilitary groups. Clara García, who works in the Communities-at-Risk Project at Defensoría del Pueblo, one of Colombia's national oversight agencies, explains:

> Certain illegal armed groups use a strategic corridor in the region of Antioquia, Caldas, Risaralda, Chocó and towards the Pacific Coast. This makes this entire territory a strategic zone. These private armies, whose goal is the control of drug-trafficking routes and the purchase or expropriation of lands through the use of terror, carry out selective crimes and massacres targeting both guerrilla collaborators and innocent civilians. This is the politics of terror, in which paramilitary groups can often count on the collusion of state bodies (personal interview 2009).

Molano, for example, reports the following:

> At a place called La Herradura, Gabriel Ángel Cartagena, the Indigenous candidate for mayor of Riosucio, was assassinated in July 2003. Three other members of his political movement were also killed and four more were injured. One survivor recalls that the road between the municipal town centre and Guamal, jurisdiction of the Cañomomo-Lomaprieta Indian Resguardo where the victims lived, was shut down by an unidentified 'authority'. The 'real' authorities gave the usual explanation: it was the guerrillas. But three years later, the attorney general indicted Cartagena's rival in the mayoral race, Arcadio Villada, of the Partido de la U political party, along with Cesar Mejía of the paramilitary group Cacique Pipintá and Captain Jorge Arturo Osorio of the National Army. All of them were convicted and Ferney Tapasco, ex-member of Congress and president of the Liberal Party in Caldas was also implicated in the assassinations (2008: n.p.).

Conflicts over land ownership and the economic crisis of coffee production led to a massive exodus that in the late 1990s and early 2000s took on the dimensions of a true diaspora. Thousands of families left the region, driven out by violence or in search of a better life in other parts of the country or abroad. The number of displaced was staggering.[10] The flow of displaced population was proportional to the intensification of the phenomenon at the national level in the middle of the 1990s.[11]

The endemic armed conflict that has plagued the region for several decades has produced a growing tension between Riosucio's urban centre, inhabited primarily by white or mestizo settlers, and the largely Indigenous districts around it. This tension is expressed in the arena of electoral politics, often marred by political killings.[12] One of the municipality's anomalies is that it has the largest Indigenous population in the entire coffee region.

Apart from some small communities of Emberá-Chamí people with a population of about 1,800 in the northwestern part of the municipality (among the most affected by forced displacement), the majority of the Indigenous *resguardos* were founded after the institution of the 1991 Constitution. They are made up of *campesino* families who have begun a complex process of re-indigenization, teaching younger generations the languages, festivals, rituals and customs once thought to be irretrievably lost. The Indigenous communities' fundamental strategy for political legitimation and access to economic resources is that of cultural empowerment, and cultural identity and belonging critically depend on the possession of territory and the identification with it. Regarding Riosucio, Molano writes:

> They contrast these Devil's carnivals and these Encuentros de la Palabra [Encounters of the Word][13] with the bloodshed and impunity that surrounds us. The old struggles for land and the minerals that underlie it continue. In spite of the killings, judicial persecutions and the burning of their property titles at notary offices, the Emberá-Chamí people of the region have not abandoned their territorial claims. They have lost their language and their [traditional] dress, and they know that only by defending their territory will they survive as a culture (2008a: n.p.).

The defence and championing of Indigenous culture allows for the defence of territory and vice versa—the latter being an indispensable condition for the continued existence of a culture. At stake is the control of the mineral resources and natural riches of the region. As García goes on to say:

> There is displacement and forced recruitment in the Indigenous *resguardos*. There have been massacres, dangerous accusations, threats, [and] deaths . . . . There has been a significant presence of paramilitary groups and of guerrillas . . . . They are very poor and vulnerable communities; there is little work and little economic activity. The new Indigenous territories here in Riosucio have a lot of mining; it is rumoured there is a lot of gold, a lot of coal, and it seems too that there is uranium . . . . So multinationals add an additional threat. The national government gives them permission to come into these communities, conduct studies and begin extracting resources. They say they are concerned not about the environment but supposedly about producing jobs for the community. They produce immense ecological damage, though, and Indigenous culture will also be damaged; their way of life will be changed . . . . Another issue is the constant stigmatization of

the Indigenous community. At every turn they are accused of being guerrillas and of being in collusion with this or that group. So they are targeted by other illegal groups (personal interview 2009).

The process of re-indigenization must engage in the appropriation of festive rituals in order to be recognized as legitimate with regard to cultural rights, and thereby guarantee access to differentiated forms of citizenship (Vignolo 2011). In a brutally unequal society such as Colombia's, where upward socioeconomic mobility is not possible for the vast majority of the population and paths to political demands are often blocked, cultural terrain becomes the main battlefield for exercising forms of active citizenship.

In Caldas, as in large parts of the country over the last two decades, 'many Indigenous and Afro-Colombian communities have looked to ethnic identity itself in order to be able to negotiate with various state authorities over critical issues such as land ownership, the effective administration of justice, control of law and order, access to health and educational services, and to some form of social welfare' (ibid.: 149). César Cuello, an Indigenous resident of one *resguardo*, speaks candidly about this:

> Carnival is a strategy, a mediating strategy in a conflict that isn't over . . . But this carnival strategy has already achieved its objective, and well. I'm not saying that carnival is a matter of social cohesion. No, for Riosucio, it's a mask. Otherwise, the challenges faced by the population would no longer be a normal part of collective life . . . Indigenous expression, though, is yet another strategy, the strategy of cultural assimilation that has been clearly experienced by ethnic minorities, by Afro-Colombians and by Indigenous peoples. It's been legislated for that purpose . . . (personal interview 2009).

Perhaps the most paradigmatic example of what Cuello refers to is the birth of the Indian carnival, an attempt by Indigenous groups to revive old traditions using the model of the urban carnival. Sofía Rueda, a student from another part of the country, finds the different versions she hears a bit confusing:

> The *resguardo* festival is now called the Indian Carnival. They highlight an Indian just as in Riosucio they focus on a devil. They form street music groups, issue decrees and perform on *chirimías* . . . They do the same things with *cuadrillas*; they visit homes . . . They have everything like in the Riosucio carnival, just smaller. That's why it's confusing to us, because we ask ourselves, well, which came first? Because [the organizers] say that the Indian carnival came first, that it used to have a different name, but it came first, that it's been around for many years, and obviously, that people would go to the *resguardos* and get ideas, then they started to do the same things

at the Riosucio carnival, only bigger. It seemed logical, but then it didn't any more, so it's still unclear to us. Some folks tell us one thing, and others say another (personal interview 2009).

Giovanny Bravo, schoolteacher and member of the Consejo Regional Indígena de Caldas (Regional Indigenous Council of Caldas, CRIDEC) says:

> We've gone to the Indian carnival with our dances, we've participated. It's something that really unites us, because every *resguardo* has its own activities, but they invite groups from other *resguardos* . . . Each *resguardo* has its own cultural style, though. In the Cañamomo and Lomaprieta *resguardos*, of course, the *chirimía* and dance are quite valued. In La Montaña, another *resguardo*, it's about music played on stringed instruments, as well as the *chirimía* and the dance groups that are more autochthonous. The idea is to reclaim much of what is related to ceremonial dance. The Riosucio carnival,

FIGURE 2. The Carnival of the Indian in 2007. Photograph by Álvaro Moreno Hoffmann.

on the other hand, has lost many of its traditional elements. It used to be that cultural aspects were much more valued. These days it's much more about partying and other things brought in from outside that have nothing to do with the cultural side of things. Before, all the *resguardo* groups would participate. This year there was little of that, given that for a while now there have been some clashes with the *resguardos* (personal interview 2009).

However, many are sceptical of this process of appropriation and invention of traditional festivals; they see it as opportunistic, motivated by vested interests. Pasero, for example, contends:

That's the little festival they've come up with now, just to do something different from the urban sector ... When the government gives so much power to [the Indigenous *resguardos*] and gives them cash (and you know that poor people lose their minds with cash and don't know what to do with it), our Indigenous peoples supposedly take to reclaiming their former collective, cultural and ancestral memory. The first thing they do is to go to all the Indigenous communities of the country. They go to the Sierra Nevada[14] and see a ritual or something good to bring to our rural communities; they hear something strange, and 'Well, then, let's put this in our language' ... They ought to pay attention to what's in front of them and start looking into their own past, looking back ... But no, they don't take well to suggestions. Fifteen years ago, they began to take this from one culture and that from another, borrowing from cultures all over the country.... They play a game of double identity: they're Indigenous when they'll get some benefit from the government—but at other times, no. 'We're the people.' Indigenous? Are you kidding? When it comes to military service, they're all Indigenous. When it comes to paying taxes, they're Indigenous as well. But when there are things that will benefit people from the urban sector, then they aren't any more. They're the people. 'Indigenous? How could you possibly think we're Indigenous?' They adopt one identity or the other out of convenience. They'll take whatever side is more advantageous to them (personal interview 2009).

This is evidence of a highly conflictive yet complex relationship. The vast majority of the residents in the urban centre are willing to recognize the importance of the Indigenous component in the historical make-up of carnival and in the general construction of the nation, but they refuse to attribute any cultural value to the process of re-indigenization. Pacho Trebol, a friend of Pasero, says:

The Guambiano Indigenous people of Cauca, yes. They preserve their identity from the moment they're born until they marry and until they die.

Why? Because they haven't been acculturated, because they struggle and defend their *mingas*.[15] People have just begun to organize in Caldas, though. Once they saw that the government had to give them some royalties or other support because they were *resguardos* and that they had rights over their territory, then they began to organize. If you went to Sipirra before, the *guarapo* was served in a gourd, and your cup was a calabash. Now you go there and they give you disposable cups ... I think that people working in social organizations for the sake of their communities need to also be concerned with consciousness-raising: 'See, you're Indigenous because of your race, because of your blood, because of your beliefs ...' (personal interview 2009).

Festive rituals are one of the main elements that eventually determine who can claim to belong to an ethnicity, which, since the Constitution of 1991, also grants access to an important political and judicial status—though often only on paper. Those who defend the process of re-indigenization demand that the right of the poorest and most marginalized populations to restore their own culture be respected after 500 years of colonial domination. Those who oppose the process argue that re-indigenization is a matter of a fictitious identity, what Gayatri Chakravorty Spivak (1993) might call a 'strategic essentialism' that allows them to obtain undue advantages. As Molano puts it:

Landowners and other locally powerful individuals argue that there are no Indigenous people in the region, just mestizos, so the *resguardo* is not legal. They argue this on the premise that the inhabitants are of mixed ancestry, being descendants of Spanish colonists and English, French and German entrepreneurs who came to work the gold mines, together with the black slaves who replaced the Indigenous labour force when it was depleted because it was weak and 'lazy'. Therefore, there are no Indigenous people. According to a pamphlet distributed three months ago in Riosucio, those who stake claims to the land are nothing but 'scoundrels'. Between 1985 and the present day, official Indigenous councils in the region have recorded 307 murders, their victims identified by official identity documents (2008b: n.p.).

Behind all of this are the great mining interests that have stoked the flames of the conflict in recent years as a result of the extraction bonanza across the country, a bonanza Al-Jazeera has referred to as 'Colombia's gold fever' (Comité Cívico Prodefensa de Marmato 2011). Molano concludes:

In an open letter to President [Álvaro] Uribe, the 'powerful' people of Riosucio advise the government: 'As things stand here, it is best to speed up the megaproject proposed by the state and multinationals to make

Riosucio, Marmato and Quinchia an important mining district. We know that the riches of the subsoil belong to the state and not to the Indians. And the gold in the subsoil of this land is abundant.' The multinationals pursuing concessions are Kedahda and AngloGold Ashanti. The conclusion couldn't be any more apparent (2008b: n.p.).

A Conflict within the Fiesta: The Carnival of the Diabla

The significance of the Diabla becomes clear in this historical and geographical context—it emerges from the sense of discrimination that sectors of the Riosucio population perceive in the organizing of the carnival. The group at the forefront of this outlandish form of protest against the supposed arbitrariness of the Riosucio carnival organizers is called La Barra de los 30. According to Enrique Jaime, a *carnavalero* and a member of one of the town's traditional families, it is a group that has emerged from sectors on the margins of city life: street artists, artisans, the unemployed, along with sex workers, addicts, petty criminals, etc. 'Well,' Enrique Jaime says, 'with the Diabla, there's something really interesting. The Diabla represents marginality in the Riosucio municipality, its humble people.'

On the other hand, La Barra leader Beto Guerrero, an artisan and self-identified street artist, says:

> La Barra de los 30. Most of us have been around since about the 1960s. This means that La Barra is at least 40 years old, and we've been like that, forward-thinking. The '30' are people from the neighbourhood, lifetime friends.... We opened up a space for those artists who'd been marginalized, and I was among them. A lot of people realized that you can do what you want in a town, in the province (personal interview 2007).

The role of La Barra in the carnival has traditionally been linked to the *corralejas*, or bullfights. Although somewhat neglected in folklore studies, *corralejas* are fundamental to the symbolic and monetary economy of the Riosucio carnival—they are among the oldest events at the carnival; and, given that they are the only ones with an entrance fee, they finance it as well. The town's butchers were the first sponsors of the *corralejas*; their organization handled logistics and provided the money as well as the first *manteros*, or bullfighters.[16]

Alberto Ospina, who worked for many years in the bullfighting business, tells how those events came to be held on the Plaza La Candelaria: 'They used to be called *toreos*—and the entire plaza would be fenced off, letting the bull loose in there. Whoever was in the plaza would enjoy themselves provoking the bull and hiding among the trees in the central area' (personal interview 2006). Later, the event was moved to an area close to the cemetery in a squared-off ring, where it is still held.

Ospina, as mayor of the carnival, changed the ring to an octagon, in order to keep the bull in constant view of the spectators by preventing it from retreating into the corners, thereby livening up the confrontation between bull and bullfighter. The object of the *corralejas* is not to kill the bull but to defy it, as a demonstration of the bullfighter's bravery and manliness. But it is also a space for circus feats and carnival games.[17] A large number of men, generally young and generally drunk, attend the spectacle, where sometimes more than one bull is set loose at a time. Children and, with very rare exceptions, women are prohibited from participating.

In exchange for free admission to the fairgrounds, the members of La Barra—a mostly male group—often face off against the bulls as *manteros*, exhibiting their acrobatics and courage. A few of them proudly show off scars from gorings and other wounds incurred in this game of life and death where man confronts beast. Since the early 1990s, though, La Barra has been characterized by another, even more transgressive form of participation: the construction of a large effigy of a she-devil, the Diabla. Guerrero himself describes the origins of this idea:

> I had painted the Diabla about 23–24 years ago, on the walls of the *galería* [the roofed market plaza]. When I painted it, I had some conflicts with the members of the Junta . . . 'If we can't speak,' we said, 'if the people can't

FIGURE 3. Mural of the Diabla on the walls of the Market Plaza. Photograph by Álvaro Moreno Hoffmann.

speak, man, we're going to do something that they won't like.' And I think we hit the nail on the head. 'Let's build the Diabla,' we said, 'since we already have her painted on the walls!' So we made the Diabla in secret, and the first time we brought her out was on the Friday of carnival week, in the middle of carnival, and the Junta came down on us. Because we like the people and we like the Devil—but the Diabla is a symbol. To us she's a symbol now, but at first it was a kind of rebelliousness (personal interview 2007).

The emergence of an alternative figure to the Devil, the absolute sovereign who opens and closes the festival, at first generated unease in many sectors, especially among the carnival organizers. It is a parody that has destabilizing political effects in terms of 'social trouble', and potentially 'gender trouble' (Butler 1990). The effigy of the Diabla mounted on a hand-pushed carriage is the same height as the Devil, about 10 feet tall with a rather disconcerting face. Her voluptuousness exalts the sensuality

FIGURE 4. Cabeza de la Diabla. Sin fecha. Head of the Diabla. Undated.

of a carnivalesque female body. A group of young prostitutes (called *diablas*) standing outside the workshop where the Diabla is prepared describe her: 'We're making the Diabla—big tits, big butt, big pussy .... This is our Diabla' (personal interview 2007) On the other hand, her face has decidedly masculine traits, accentuated by make-up that gives her an obvious moustache. Highlighting the sexual ambiguity of this festive character and also indirectly mocking her creator, one of the sardonic commentaries around town is that 'The Diabla looks like Beto [Guerrero]!'

Worth noting here is the rise of a queer figure, alien to the traditions of both the *matachines* and the social circles that control the carnival. Nonetheless she is a very powerful figure, faithful to the deep language of carnival, its practices and its imaginaries, and able to insert herself into the ludic and performative celebration, gaining ever-greater credibility and visibility with each passing year. It is an excellent example of the dynamics through which mimicry and masquerade contribute to the subversion of gender identity, of any supposed biological essentialism, even beyond the explicit intent and claims of its creators.

During her first public outing, the police block the path of the Diabla, leading to a confrontation with members of La Barra who try by any means to bring the effigy to the Devil in the upper plaza. Guerrero describes the scene:

> When we brought out the Diabla, a big problem broke out. As we walked in front of the stage in the middle of carnival, the people from the Junta all came at us; I mean wham! But more than anything else, the trouble was with the Junta, because right from the start we saw that other people were defending us. Well, the townspeople, right? When the police came near us, more folks joined in with us. We in the Barra kept moving forward and more people kept joining us (personal interview 2007).

Since then, the same 'game' has been played at every carnival. Those of La Barra try to take the Diabla as close as possible to the Devil up on the plazas and authorities try to prevent this one way or another. On more than one occasion, blows have been exchanged.

The rebellious group never speaks against the Devil. On the contrary, one of its preferred arguments is that the project came about because the Devil felt lonely and needed female companionship. Many people associated with the carnival, however, see the Diabla as an affront to ritual and a threat to tradition. Gurrero explains his position:

> The Junta says that the Devil is the only symbol of the carnival. Well fine, people accept that because the Devil has been around since about 1800. But this is a popular carnival. It belongs to the people, and we, the artists,

want to do things, you see? . . . People love carnival and people love the Devil. I love the Devil, of course . . . But these days, and ever since quite a few years ago now, I love the Diabla more. I would give anything for the Diabla (personal interview 2007).

As the years have gone by, physical confrontation has given way to negotiation. The Diabla has been gaining popularity among the people of Riosucio, who admire her aesthetic quality and are amused by the appearance of a character who departs from tradition, providing a space for mockery, sarcasm and humour, given the sexual innuendo and rebellious demeanour. The police's fear of greater disturbances in the middle of carnival season in a town already characterized by acute social conflicts has led to a loosening of prohibitions. The appearance of the Diabla is allowed, although only in predetermined places at specific times.

Little by little, the Diabla earned the right to enter the lower plaza, and subsequently the upper plaza, but never at the same time as the Devil. The authorities are determined to avoid her unsettling presence alongside the king of the festival. In addition, the guardians of tradition will not tolerate the participation of the transgressive she-devil and her Barra entourage in the official functions of carnival. The mayor, the Junta, the police and the firefighters oblige Guerrero and his collaborators to bring her out clandestinely, to periodically move her to different spots and to remove her late at night so that she is not be present in the morning in plain sight of Riosucio residents.

The path taken by the Diabla seems ever more like a carnivalesque Via Crucis. Her acolytes wheel the heavy carriage along the steep streets, station by station, through the most symbolic parts of town, facing physical barriers and legal prohibitions in an ongoing attempt to achieve the longed-for union with her infernal mate. La Barra men push her up and down the streets like a Virgin or a patron saint in a Holy Week procession, a performative metaphor of a religious but carnivalesque procession with a whiff of sanctity, accompanied by a multitude in an altered state that blends uninhibited partying, ritual drunkenness and mystical exaltation. The group resembles something between a crowd of zealous soccer fans and a congregation of fervent religious devotees. This produces a striking impact, given its ability to capture and represent the essence of an upside-down world.

The Diabla was finally able to celebrate her Passion in 2007. Several factors contributed to the demise of established hierarchies in carnival planning. The negotiations between La Barra and carnival organizers met a crisis at the beginning of festivities because the former was not given the agreed-upon admission tickets to the *corralejas*. Their response was to organize a boycott, as Guerrero describes:

FIGURE 5. Via Crucis of the Diabla in 2007. Photograph by Álvaro Moreno Hoffmann.

The thing is that there had already been an agreement with the Junta for 40 tickets to each *corraleja* . . . . But when we went to pick up the 40 tickets, all of a sudden they told us that there were only 20 . . . . Twenty tickets are nothing to them, but to us they matter . . . . And we're the ones who put on the show down below; they know it . . . . So if we can't get in today then we won't be there tomorrow or Wednesday. And I think our participation in the *corraleja* is indispensable; it's necessary. Without La Barra there's no *corraleja*. Even if the Junta says it isn't so, tomorrow or the next day they'll know that we're the ones who make the *corraleja* happen (personal interview 2007).

The issue isn't limited to negotiating economic relations; at stake is citizen participation in the public arena—in this case, the bullfighting arena. It is there in front of the entire town gathered together that the marginalized become the centre of attention, and society agrees to include the excluded for their ability to establish a relation with the horned beast, the bull-devil king of the festival.[18] Other members of La Barra speak out more vehemently; for example, Julio Martínez:

They did wrong by the people; not by us, but by the people—because who is entertained there? We're not the ones who go there to be entertained. What we do is risk our lives. Anyone can see that what we do is risk our lives. People enjoy seeing that, but they're the ones who make money off it! And look at what they come out with. Shameless! They say that carnival is 'cultural heritage'. The nerve of them, you know? They want people to think it's something it isn't (personal interview 2007).

In this already tense climate, there was an unforeseen tragedy. Ladino, carnival mask maker and a great friend of La Barra, was mauled by a bull during the *corraleja* and died from his injuries. News spread across the plaza like wildfire. Despite an urgent wave of whispers, cries and tears that mixed with the usual festival laughter, the carnival continued as though nothing had happened. News of Ladino's death seemed at first to be heard in the lower plaza, then moved up towards the Church of San Sebastián. It spread in centrifugal waves past the meat market, out to the *corraleja* and the cemetery. Between a *merengue* and a *ranchera*,[19] the news came over the loud-speakers in the voice of a sports announcer: '... for the tragic death of Hugo Ladino.' Grief mixed with rage. The next day, a tearful Guerrero spoke regretfully:

> No, I feel terrible .... Honestly, it was a huge blow for me, as it was for every-one in Riosucio. And especially for us carnival people. Chorizo was a *car-navalero*, a partygoer, a drinker, a terrific guy. A great man, a mask maker .... A true friend. God, if I had been there, I would have got him out, but we weren't there at that *corraleja* and .... If those of us from Los 30 had been there, surely we would have got our brother out. We wouldn't have let him get mauled by a bull (personal interview 2007).

The decision was unanimous among Guerrera and La Barra. Making the most of the solidarity they had been able to inspire for their Diabla and the unpopularity of the Junta that year, they steered the Diabla all the way to the lower plaza next to the Devil, where they set her ablaze. The final celebration was to be all about her. Barra member Martínez cried out: 'We were forced to set our Patroness on fire so the town would listen to us. It's not just four or five rich folks, it's the people united!' Although firefighters arrived to put out the unanticipated blaze, it did not spoil the triumph of the Diabla.

Final Thoughts

Both the Indian carnival and that of the Diabla are examples of 'invented tradition' as defined by Eric Hobsbawm and Terence Ranger: '[A] set of practices, normally governed by overtly or tacitly accepted rules and of a ritual or symbolic nature, which seek to inculcate certain values and norms of behaviour by repetition, which auto-matically implies continuity with the past' (1983: 8). This set of reiterated practices, which Richard Schechner calls 'twice behaved behaviors' (2002), makes for competing representations of tradition in the public sphere (Taylor and Townsend 2008). In Foucauldian terms, these devices are endowed with a certain degree of rationality, which answer to an emergency, to a crisis (Castro Gómez 2011): for example, the growing struggle over land in the case of the Indian carnival and the exclusion of certain urban sectors in the case of the Diabla.

New collective subjectivities are forged out of these practices; not the other way around. It is through the recovery of traditional dances, music and rituals in rural areas that a growing number of *campesinos* begin to identify themselves as Indigenous. Similarly, if it were not for their participation in *corralejas* and the creation of the Diabla, La Barra de los 30 would not have developed beyond its identity as a group of friends and neighbours.

The ritual efficacy of the new proposals and their ability to take root in foundational myths depend greatly on the credibility they may or may not attain within the community. The ad hoc development of new festivities generally imposes foreign models onto local dynamics unless it results from a serious formative process. This graft rarely puts forth new shoots.

The Indian carnival, for example, came about as a 'conflict-mediation strategy', as one interviewee put it. In spite of the good intentions of organizers, its instrumental origin has been all too obvious, making it a not particularly credible project. The almost literal copy of the rhetorical and material apparatus of the Riosucio carnival in a context of re-indigenization was incapable of convincing people either inside or outside the *resguardos*. Instead of providing a festive bridge between the urban and the rural, it seems to have generated nothing more than a useless and dangerous controversy over assumed cultural primacies in the region, worsening the already difficult relationship between city and country.

The process of positioning the Diabla, on the other hand, has already accomplished many of its goals, both implicit and explicit. There is no doubt that the Diabla is now established as a central character of the carnival, even if she has been unable to reach full acceptance in the official narrative. As for La Barra, it has won a fundamental cultural right and can no longer be excluded from carnival planning or access. Its leader Beto Guerrero is acclaimed as one of the most prominent local artists and rumour has it that sooner or later the Junta will offer him an opportunity to design and build the effigy of the Devil. In 2011, he was asked by the Junta to provide his voice to the Devil for the carnival's opening speech, perhaps the most distinguished role of the entire festival.

The playful role of the Diabla has already transcended the festive sphere and been transformed into an exercise in citizen participation. There remains, however, an underlying concern—the provocation that she represents has seriously challenged the dramaturgical mechanisms of carnival, given that, as Girard (1972) points out, the figure of the scapegoat is not only indispensable but also very difficult to replace. The burning of an effigy other than the ritually prescribed one is an evident affront that profoundly endangers the symbolic economy of sacrifice.

How will carnival tradition adjust to the future? With friendly coexistence of a Diablo and a Diabla? With a return to the status quo, where the Devil will recover his place as the central and only figure? With a fusion of two effigies into one androgynous figure? Or with a proliferation of devilish effigies competing among themselves around town? And will festivities in town once again be able to attract people from surrounding rural areas and Indigenous communities?

The politics and poetics of the Riosucio carnival will be defined by how these types of disputes are resolved in coming years. Perhaps not even the Devil himself knows the answer. To ensure that the Devil's energy brings future festivals to life, one need only invoke him with the words spoken by Ladino after providing his voice to the effigy just days before his 2007 death:

> With God's help, the Devil took me on and it went real well for me. When he appeared, I simply asked him, 'You know what, man? . . . Can I ask you to please put your spirit in my body so I'll be able to give something in turn to your people, to my people, as a *matachín*?' So the Devil entered my body through every one of my pores, through every one of my nerves, and as a *matachín* I just gave out what he deserves and what I could give. He takes on the magic provided by Mother Earth or what others might call Pachamama [Mother Earth], and the magic of the spirits of the afterlife, the spirits of art and artists, the spirits of bullfighters who have died but who come and guide our hands and guide our conscience when we invoke them. The thing is that when I'm excited after a few drinks, I often feel the need for the Devil's presence inside me. Then I invoke him with this prayer:
>
> > Oh Devil of carnival
> > Come back and return to life
> > And with your tail ablaze
> > Come light up my mind
> > So I may safely get out of this predicament
> > Out of this dark and difficult trance
> > Into which I'll enter
> >
> > (personal interview 2006).

Notes

This text is the fruit of extensive field work carried out under my direction between 2006 and 2009 by student researchers Laura Sánchez and Diego Ortiz. I want to express my deep gratitude for their commitment to the project, as well to all the people in Riosucio who helped us throughout the whole process. I also thank the members of the Tepoztlán Institute for Transnational History of the Americas and of the research group Play, Fiesta and Power of the Instituto Hemisférico de Performance y Política for their generous comments, critiques and suggestions upon reading a draft of this text in 2010.

1   This and other voices cited in this text are also included in my documentary *Una cita con el diablo* (2009). The interviews I have referenced were carried out under my guidance by a student team made up of Laura Sánchez, Diego Ortíz, Dayana Moreno and Natalia Zamudio over the course of two periods: December–January 2006–07 and January–February 2009. Some names and personal information have been changed when interviewees' statements could be controversial.

2   I use the term 'cultural memory' in reference to the work of authors such as Pierre Nora, Chaim Yerushalmi, Jan Assman, Andreas Huyssen, Elisabeth Jenin and Susan Stewart, among others. In the title, however, I opt for the term 'historical memory', used more commonly in the current political and academic debate in Colombia. For further exploration of this matter, see Center for the Study of Cultural Memory of the School of Advanced Study, University of London, Comisión por la Memoria Histórica (Historical Memory Commission) and Centro por la Memoria, la Paz y la Reconciliación (Center for Memory, Peace and Reconciliation), both of the latter in Colombia.

3   Indigenous territories in Colombia with collective property and recognized structures of governance.

4   Verses by the famous carnival organizer Tatínez, recited by Hugo 'Chory' Ladino.

5   Like the town, the cemetery is divided into two parts, one of them elegant and monumental and the other simple. The two parts of town face each other on either side of the road that leads to Sipirra. The segregation of the dead follows complex criteria including their family ties and more mysterious aspects regarding the promiscuity between the living and the dead. One thing is for certain, though—not everyone has access to the most elegant blocks of the cemetery. The great Tatínez could not be set to rest there, for example, but was buried elsewhere, lost among the graves. It is curious that the procession in homage to the dead *matachines* pays no such homage to the greatest among them, because it is limited to the monumental section of the cemetery. There is an epitaph over Tatínez's grave: 'When I die and I am buried, / I want to be in a coffin made of rough, unpainted wood, / To show the people what we were, what we are / And where we will end up. A cross of the same wood / The tomb will say "Tatínez, who in life was a carnival singer." / [signed] Tatínez.'

6   Official website of Riosucio in Caldas, Colombia: 'Nuestro municipio, información general: historia' (available at: www.riosucio-caldas.gov.co; last accessed on 5 March

2010). The last two sentences have been recently deleted from the web page, perhaps owing to a controversy regarding the absence of documented proof to attest to this foundational date. However, a reference to the date of 7 August 1819 remains.

7   In this context, the mixing of European, Indigenous and African ethnicities, identities and cultural practices.

8   The *paisa* region in northwestern Colombia refers primarily to the department of Antioquia but also to Caldas, Risaralda and Quindío.

9   An Indigenous community that has collective control over its own territory and a traditional leadership structure.

10 The Red de Solidaridad Social (Social Solidarity Network) estimates that there were approximately 40,877 displaced persons in the larger coffee zone between 1999 and 2003. This was a massive increase compared to the period of 1994–99, when two-way displacement (exodus and reception) amounted to only about 790. In 2002 alone, there were nearly 19,781 displaced, the majority from the department of Caldas. At the same time, an average of 7,000 per year entered the region between 2001 and 2003.

11 To a large degree, this was due to attacks by paramilitary forces during the late 1990s and early 2000s, although an increase of counter-attacks by guerrillas worsened the problem as well since the civilian population experienced pressure from both sides. It was only towards the middle of the decade of the 2000s that the situation returned to relative calm, given the suppression of guerrilla forces by the army and the apparent demobilization of paramilitary groups.

12 An Indigenous person became mayor for the first time in 2006. This was after Motato Largo and Maria Fabiola Largo, two Indigenous leaders with political aspirations, had been assassinated during the previous elections. Further intensifying the political environment, the administration was subsequently challenged by urban sectors who questioned its management of resources and ambiguous relationship with guerrillas.

13 A regular series of inclusive cultural events dedicated to creating a space for dialogue and reflection, with a particular focus on the collective and individual contributions of those who are less often heard—Indigenous people, Afro-Colombians, minorities, youth and displaced people, among others.

14 Region in northeastern Colombia, home to very different Indigenous traditions.

15 Collective work tradition of the Guambiano people in the southwestern department of Cauca.

16 Other cartographies of the carnival have emerged in field work. For example, 'the cycle of meat'—within the spaces of meat markets and stockyards, intimate relationships between guilds of butchers, bullfighters and *matachíns* can be seen. However, an analysis of this aspect of the carnival is not within the scope of this essay.

17 One of the main characters of the Riosucio *corraleja*, for example, is the *torero gallina* (bullfighter-hen), who dons an impeccable bullfighting suit but has a hen roosting

on top of his head. His role is to entertain the audience seated farthest from the bull, explaining to them why he methodically flees from the animal while his less elegant peers confront it.

18 The bull and the Devil are closely related in the Riosucio imaginary. The great game of death between man and beast that takes place at the *corralejas* is directly associated with the burning of the Devil and the burial of the gourd used to serve *guarapo*, the events that bring the carnival to a close. Celebrating the Devil, his horns and his tail makes a clear reference to the bull that is sacrificed, be it physically or symbolically. Moreover, there are countless tales in which the bull is associated with stories of demons and apparitions. A nine-year-old girl, for example, tells this story: 'There was once a young man, a nephew of Doña Gloria . . . who lived down there in the Grovillas. He went down there drunk during Holy Week and a golden bull appeared before him. The bull started to chase him and he got so scared that he quickly sobered up. He ran through all the meadows and arrived at the home of Doña Gloria. 'Aunt Gloria,' he said to her, 'give me a cross and some holy water—a bull is chasing me.' She gave him what he asked for, and then he said to the bull, 'Here I am, bull, here I am. Come and get me.' When the bull charged at him, he threw the holy water in its face and held up the cross. The bull left, but the next day a great mound of sulphur appeared on that spot.'

19 Caribbean and Mexican musical styles, respectively, both popular throughout Latin America.

The Virgin of Candelaria and Her Dancing Devils of Puno, Peru

MIGUEL RUBIO ZAPATA

> They danced like birds, like demons and angels on the field, to the delight
> of the sun [...] like a river whose waters come from very different universes,
> the ensembles at the feast marched in (Arguedas 1967: n.p.).

Of all the mask dances, the Puno Devil's Dance, symbol of the Festival of the Virgin
of Candelaria, has attained the greatest fame, although questions and debate remain
regarding its origins. It has existed throughout the Altiplano region that unites Peru
and Bolivia by Lake Titicaca since the pre-Hispanic period, and we can therefore
maintain that it is more ancient than the current territories of both countries.[1]

The Department of Puno, located on the meseta of Qollao, a region known as
the Altiplano, consists of 13 provinces. Since the pre-Inca period, the diverse kingdoms and cultures of the highlands, such as the Collas, Lupacas, Omasuyos, Pucará,
Tiwanaku, Uro and Puquina, developed throughout this region. Inca culture, headed
by the Inca Túpac Yupanqui, was later integrated with these groups, before the advent
of the Spanish conquistadors. Yupanqui, hoping to return to the ancestral roots of
Manco Capac and Mama Occllo, founders of the Inca Empire, came from Cusco to
impose his reign over the kingdoms of the Altiplano, making use of the Inca system
of reciprocity and the force of arms.

In this way, groups belonging to the Chimú, Chanca, Nazca, Huanca, Yarowilca
and Canaris, as well as groups from other areas of ancient Peru, including some from
Quito, Otavalos and beyond the Equator, such as the Lampatos and the Chanas, settled in different areas of the highlands. This allowed for a diversity of ethnic groups,
who preserved their cultural identities throughout the centuries, leading to a vast
diversity of dress, culinary forms and traditions, and of costumes and dances, many
of which are now extinct or in the process of extinction. Currently, Colla consists of
108 districts and more than 3,500 peasant communities. Each district and each community practices its own distinct dance that often differs from those of its neighbours.

The cult of the Virgin of Candelaria is associated with a massive conglomeration
of dancers within which the devils stand out. Its venerated statue is zealously cared
for at the Church of San Juan Bautista, said to be the same one built in 1675 upon a
sacred *huaca* in Pino Park, on a modest and rustic chapel, with a roof made of straw,

meant for the instruction of the Indians and providing shelter for the statue of the Virgin. With the passing of time, by around 1875, its condition had improved and its completion, as we know it now, took place between 1880 and 1895. On 7 February 1988, by a bishopric decree, the temple was granted the status of 'Holy Sanctuary of the Virgin of Candelaria', and was erected as the centre of worship of the holy effigy, placed on the main altar, inaugurated finally in 1901.

The Purifying Fire

Fire is an element that symbolizes life and also the natural habitat of devils. Candela and Candelaria are a cultural symbiosis that is reflected in the ancient traditional ritual of the Entrance of Q'apus in which the highest authorities of each community summon the townspeople to come out and initiate the festive cycle in homage of the Pachamama (Mother Earth). In the present day, they do so before the patron saint.

On the eve of the festival, representatives from different peasant communities arrive at the door of the San Juan Church. The municipal authorities arrive with their livestock (horses, llamas, donkeys, among others) carrying dried branches picked from woody shrubs like the muña or the tola tree, which are used for igniting the great bonfire of Q'apu that will burn in the four corners of Pino Park in order to purify and banish the evil spirits.

The bonfire is an offering to harmonize the atmosphere and to prevent the frost and the hail from ruining the fields of potato and coca crops and other fruits in bloom; it is a means of communicating with the guardian deities so the crops are not damaged. It is also a moment to speak with the Pachamama and god of fertility who lives in the *Uku pacha* (inner world), from which she offers the fruit that gives life to humans and animals. This is why, within the logic of reciprocity of Andean culture, she is rewarded with rituals of gratitude, known as *pagos* (payments) or *despachos* (offerings), with gifts such as wine, seeds, sweets, etc. The coca leaf is the main element of the ceremony, serving as a sacred plant that mediates between the inner world of the Pachamama and the Apus (guardian spirits) and the outer world of men. These rituals, or payments to the land, are carried out religiously during the season of cultivation.

This ancestral agricultural calendar has incorporated the worship of the Mamacha Candelaria, in whose honour, during this time, the greatest patron-saint festival of Peru takes place. It is also one of the biggest festivals of Latin America, comparable to the carnival of Oruro in Bolivia and the Rio de Janeiro carnival in Brazil. The celebrations of the Mamacha Candelaria begin around 24 January and culminate around 18 February, as a prelude to the carnival.

According to the Quechua and Aymara cosmogonies, the Festival of the Virgin of Candelaria, or Mamita Kanticha, is strongly linked to the agricultural cycles of sowing and harvesting and its purpose is to serve as an offering to Pachamama. Through postcolonial cultural juxtaposition, Candelaria is the one who intercedes in the face of natural forces as she is the Christian and mestiza representation of the Virgin and of the Pachamama.

The Festival of the Virgin of Candelaria has two dates: the main, opening day and the eighth/*octava*. The celebrations of the opening day begin on the eve of the first day of the festival, with the ritual of the Entrance of the Q'apus. The following day, the dancers arrive from the countryside to join the procession alongside the *sikus* (panpipe) troupes.

A legend about the festival, originating in Oruro, Bolivia, tells that thousands of years ago, Wari, a deity of the highlands, unleashed giant serpents upon the region inhabited by the Uros. When the reptiles were just about done with the Uros and finished destroying their villages, thrusting onto them their tongues of fire, the Virgin of Candelaria appeared, a dark/black Virgin who turned the ophidians to stone. She has been worshipped since then. The fire-breathing serpents have since transformed into the dancing devils of the present-day festival. They dance around the Virgin until their expulsion by Saint Gabriel, the archangel, and his sword. José María Arguedas interprets the profound motivations of this event:

> In the Altiplano there is a coexistence of Quechua and Aymara traditions, which are quite different from each other, and during the colonial republican period, there emerged in that great region forms of cultural *mestizaje* between these two pre-Hispanic human nuclei and that of the Western world, to degrees of greater diversity than in other areas. As a consequence, there is a greater complexity and diversity of traditions in the Puno population, and each group, strata or ensemble, found in the dancing and singing the freest and broadest form to express its outer world (1967: n.p.).

An Army of Devils

The Puno Devil's Dance has traditionally incorporated into its ancient tradition an army of devils that, nearing midnight, literally bursts into perfect formation in the arms plaza of Puno amid fireworks and bombards. They come after having greeted the Virgin. The devils' troupe, made up of members of the Peruvian Army, consists of 750 dancers, accompanied by five musical bands that play 'militarized' *diabladas*. The parade of worship becomes a devilish military march, resounding through the city, circling 10 kilometres while dancing, the spectators never allowing them to rest.

Letting down their guard is impossible—it is after all the army and it is warmly received on each street.

Roberto Martin Tovar Ortiz, infantry major of the 4th Mountain Brigade in the Department of Instruction of the Peruvian Army in Puno, explains the current circumstances, motives and process of participation of the Peruvian Army in the Festival of the Virgin of Candelaria. Since Puno is a border province and a zone of armed conflict against subversive groups, the main function of the armed forces until the 1990s was limited to one of security. In Tovar's words:

> During that time, neither the National Police nor the army could much associate with the traditional dances of the Festival of the Virgin of Candelaria, because, above everything, our mission was that of 'safety', public safety, protect the tourists, ensure their ability to participate in the festivities, prevent attacks, in order to avoid any kind of sabotage, any subversive action within the festival activities' (personal interviews 2007–09).

However, beginning in 1994, the National Police began participating in the festivities, with the Peruvian Army joining them in 2006. Everyone dances in this troupe. From soldiers to senior officials, colonels, commanding officers, majors, captains, lieutenants, along with three army bands, they travel approximately four hours to arrive at the stage where they will participate in the festival's contest. The people support them:

> [I]t was the first time we performed and it gave us great pleasure because people clapped for us ... they have seen themselves reflected in their army, who has, for the first time, participated in a contest ... on each block we made a commitment to them and rather than resting, we had to dance for them, maintaining discipline and order .... This year the army has danced in its entirety. Officers, petty officers, troops, officers' wives, their daughters, the technicians' families, friends of the Department of Puno .... Whoever wanted to and was able to be a part of the *diablada* was given a costume and permission to rehearse and dance (personal interviews 2007–09).

As Silvia Rivera Cusicanqui points out: 'The space of the festival is a disputed space, insofar as it is a border space where the state seeks to exert its control.'[2] One must not forget that in Bolivia, the Virgin of Candelaria of Copacabana was crowned and declared queen of the nation in 1925. Her appropriation by the Peruvian Army is related to its victory over the Shining Path in 1995 and also with its disputes with Bolivia. There is thus an effort to impose an official dance without variations, in stark contrast with the varied practices of the Aymaras of the Altiplano.

Mythology of the Mascarero, *or the Mask Maker*

Master Edwin Loza Huarachi, a Puno mask maker, deems unsatisfactory the theory that the Devil's Dance is a Catholic mystery play. Instead, Loza suggests the need to delve into the worldview of the Aymara people, opting thus for calling what is now known as the Puno Devil's Dance the 'Dance of the Anchanchu' (personal interview 1987–97).

In the Aymara language, the Alaj papa is the kingdom of light, of good and kindness, located in the higher regions of the world where God resides. On the opposite side lies the Manqha pacha, kingdom of darkness and evil, situated in the lower regions of the world. In-between these two realities live the Aymara, inhabitants of the Aka pacha, which represents 'the reality in which we live'.[3] Whoever lives in the Aka pacha must know how to work out the equilibrium between both forces in order to live well. How is this achieved? It is accomplished by expressing gratitude to the Pachamama with offerings and payments, and by knowing the spirits who inhabit the kingdoms of light and darkness.

Loza explains:

> In the Manqha pacha kingdom reside the *anchanchus*, malevolent and gentile spirits. They are the owners/masters of the mines. This is why whenever a mineral vein is detected, one must first request permission from the Anchanchu. In ancient times, a virgin llama was sacrificed, making with it a payment or offering (in the form of a grease mould above which sheets of the metals found in the mines would be placed), and incinerating it with manure. Around it a dance would take place, accompanied by *zampoñas* (panpipes) and ceramic masks adorned with taruca (North Andean deer) horns (personal interview 1987–97).

Then, the shaman/healer called *layqa* inspected the ashes and read in them the will of the Anchanchu, represented in the dance by the taruca horns. Upon witnessing this, Christians associated it with a demonic dance. Thus, at the beginning of the eighteenth century, colonial power introduces a new character—the Archangel, who leads the dance, and who, sword in hand, directs the choreography.

St Michael the Archangel dons a shirt with puff sleeves, a flared skirt and tall boots, a breastplate, a Roman steel helmet and small wings. His is a ferocious mask. In his right hand he carries a flaming sword, and in his left a shield. Similarly, the Chinas Diablas have become a part of the dance. They are female characters played by men who symbolize the Seven Deadly Sins. Flirting with the men in the audience, they dance with acrobatic leaps, constantly entering and breaking away from the troupe. They wear a blouse, a skirt and calf-length boots; their hair is braided and they carry a handkerchief in each hand. They have bright eyes with long eyelashes and a double-pointed pug nose. Small snakes slither over their foreheads. Two small horns, a dishevelled wig and a small crown complete their costume/image.

The control over the devils by the Archangel is the transposition in the dance of a hierarchy that emerges from a different worldview. However, these changes don't belie the mythical and ritual scope of the original festival and dance, which now appear submerged, camouflaged and blended into a festive Christian structure in honour of the Virgin of Candelaria. Consequently, there is a clear continuity of pre-Hispanic icons, such as the serpent, Andean symbol of wisdom, which appears over the nose of the devil's mask in the pagan atmosphere that takes over Puno during the first two weeks of February.

The task of the colonizers was centred on eradicating that whole worldview, and, while they were able to effectively introduce the Christian religion, its images and definitions, into popular customs and thought, it is clear that a failure to understand and the inability to accurately interpret indigenous beliefs prevented them from fully obliterating them. It is there that the syncretism continues to be the object of research.

The various evangelizing missions were faced with the need to make use of already existing artistic elements in the indigenous communities, such as the dances and the music. They then imbued their performances with elements of Catholicism, illustrated by the European brass wind instruments currently used in the large bands that accompany the dance troupes of the Festival of the Virgin of Candelaria.

The source of the religious syncretism we continue to practise today is thus clear. With the arrival of Catholicism came the separation between good and evil, punishment and rewards, devils and the angels, and power and submission. The mission of eradicating pagan idolatry imposed a new faith, vilifying Andean guardian deities in order to foment fear and encourage the search for refuge in God and in the good He represents.

Paying homage to the gods with music and dance is as ancient as the ritual of the *pago a la tierra*, later fused with the worship of the Virgin in lavish dance celebrations that are an expression of religious and cultural syncretism and of a tradition in flux. We can speak of fusion if we assume the existence of equivalent values, the Mother Earth with the Virgin of Candelaria, for example, or of a religious coexistence between the shaman's table and the Mass officiated by the Catholic priest. It is not accidental that the cathedral of Puno is built facing the sun and the lake, and that coexisting on the facade, to the side of St Peter and St Paul, the Holy Ghost and St Michael the Archangel, are icons native to these lands, such as the flower of *cantuta*, the puma and the two Indian mermaids who play the *charango*. Taking note of these elements of cultural convergence, we can assert that the architects hoped not only to exhibit their material and creative capacity but also to give expression to their spiritual ancestry in their work, like true heirs of those who built Tiwanaku[4] and Sillustani.[5] We are, thus, faced with a blend of Christian and pre-Hispanic elements, a combination of rites of divergent origins. Becoming aware of how this syncretic mechanism functions is essential to our understanding of what occurs during the celebrations in honour of the Virgin of Candelaria.

The Devil's Dance was not always as it is now. A long process of transformations has modified the typical characteristics of the European Devil. We now have a company of devils, headed by the lead, or commanding, devil, the great character of the festival, who wears an immense mask with a Quri Anchanchu (gold crown) or Qullqi Anchanchu (silver crown). His face is covered by multicoloured rattlesnakes and other reptiles that slither about his enormous eyes and mouth. At the centre of the mask, green three-headed lizards ride across his nose.

The lead devil has big, serrated ears; his mouth is outlined by sharp mirrors and endowed with strong fangs. A toad is seated on his cheek or just below his mouth. He has very large, sharp horns and seven small masks that represent the deadly sins. He wears a cape that is embroidered entirely with gold or silver thread and abundant precious stones. It is the most luxurious of the costumes. Long ago, the masks were made entirely of plaster and would sometimes weigh up to 5 kilogrammes; now they are made of brass, hence lighter.

Enrique Cuentas Ormaechea, scholar of Puno culture, notes:

[L]ater, given the influence of Bolivian artisans, the traditional fangs were replaced by decorated glass or crystallized plaster. Likewise, the native reptiles have been replaced by dragons, which emerge from between the horns. The horns, which at the beginning were pointed and sharp, or thick and blunt, were later replaced (approximately half a century ago) with twisted horns that, like the dragons adorning the mask, denote an Asian influence and somewhat resemble Tibetan masks and those of some pre-Hispanic cultures (Sechín, Chavín, Nazca, Mochica) (1986: 42).

The Devil's Mask: Possible Meanings

The meaning of each of the figures within the mask of the Devil's Dance is a magical universe of representation and interpretation. Rafael Girard (1978), French theorist and researcher of the origins of various Latin American cultures, lists each of the elements that make up the mask:

(1) On the mask, the twisted horns represent the body of a headless serpent. Its head is the mask itself. In the Catholic transposition, that ophidiiform body is

interpreted as Lucifer's horns, but the devil's horns are not usually depicted in a twisted shape. Those serpents with twisted tails that seem to emerge from the divine head are headless, because their head is the head of the character itself, which, in turn, references the pan-American motif of the serpent with a human head, which represents the god of fertility.

(2) On top of the mask, one can see a three-headed serpent with its jaws open. This composition signifies the numeral seven, in two series, one of three and another of four, and is fashioned after the cosmic model of the three diurnal positions of the sun (east, zenith and west), combined with the series of four, figured on the legs and corresponding to the suns located on the four cardinal points (summer, autumn, winter and spring). According to the genesis of this sacred number, so explained and illustrated, this constitutes a true expression of Aymara theology.

(3) But on other masks, the top consists of a spider, also an important figure in Andean religion. It also has six small heads entwined by snakes and lizards, amounting to seven with the main head, a number symbolizing the Seven Deadly Sins in the Catholic worldview, and the gods of the heavens in Aymara theology, the sons of the Pachamama, such as Rainbow, Thunder, Lightning, Rain, Hail, and Frost. In the mask are also present feline figures. The mouth has sharp fangs in the shape of an *n*, reminiscent of many sculptures and paintings of the Tiwanaku and other Andean cultures. In short, the accessories that characterize and adorn the devil, such as frogs, toads, lizards and serpents, are, in Andean rituals and beliefs, rain animals that symbolize good omens and wealth.

(4) The devils of this famous dance are a vibrant expression and glorification of indigenous religious sentiment that the annihilators of idolatries were neither able to understand nor wipe out. They failed to see that the Devil's Dance is dedicated to the Virgin, who is the equivalent of the earth mother of the Aymaras. She is the queen of carnival, the same one invoked by the *yatiris*, or healers, during the ceremony for the new potato harvest, itself celebrated during carnival.

The masks of the Devil's Dance are, as Lisandro Luna states, 'Horrific expressions that have reached perfection' because in them 'there is so much superhuman force, such a great sense of monstrosity, that they give an exact impression of the mythical character they represent' (1975).

As José Morales Serruto and Ana Isabel Morales Aguirre explain:

Some researchers affirm that the original meaning of 'La Diablada' is one of pleading and gratitude to the Pachamama for the good harvests and that its origin dates back many years before the arrival of the Spaniards, and for this reason, the presence of El Tío, el Marcari o Huywiri, a protective entity,

(ABOVE) **FIGURE 1.** Devil Mask in performance. Photograph supplied by Miguel Rugio.

(BELOW) **FIGURE 2.** The army participating in the diablada in Puno, Peru. Photograph provided by Miguel Rubio.

god/lord/keeper of the earth's riches in Aymara mythology, is of greater note than that of the devil (2009: 23).

How a Devil Is Made

Certainly, the production of the masks to be worn with *trajes de luces* (luminous/bright costumes) for the Festival of Candelaria is very complex, especially that of the lead devil's mask. Some are true works of sculpted art, in which the iconic precision demanded by tradition and the custom-fitted alterations and comfort for the dancer wearing it must converge, accounting for exact volume and weight. This great mask has traditionally been made of brass—making it similar to the metal masks derived from the pre-Columbian tradition—as well as plaster, cardboard, glued cloth and felt hats, often used in pairs: one for the front part of the mask and one used as a helmet. Small animal heads are also sculpted and casts made from them are then placed over the mask, which is rounded off with embroidery appliqués, pearls, faux gems, sequin, multicoloured feathers, etc.

The making of the horns is quite a laborious task: sewing tocuyo cones to which a liquid plaster is applied with glue; then filled with sand, twisted and mounted on a piece of wood until they are completely dry. At the point in which the cones are stiff enough to be attached to the mask, they are emptied of the sand. This technique has been almost entirely replaced by masks made of brass. However, craftsmen such as the master mask maker Edwin Loza continue to make masks using traditional methods. They meticulously apply rows of *fil-a-fil* (braided thread, intertwining white and coloured strands) on the horns' surface in order to give them a sense of rhythm and volume. On the lead devil's mask, the eyes were traditionally made of burnt light bulbs painted on the inside. Once the mask has all its appliqués and attachments—animal heads, fireflies, toads, serpents, miniature devils, cardboard toad-shaped ears and so on—the painting process begins. Lastly, the illuminating details are completed, such as the teeth, generally made with small triangular mirrors.

Amiel Cayo, actor, dancer and mask artisan, suggests that the changes in the festival are reflected on the masks: 'The current use of embossed brass has become customary and at the same time, production has become accelerated and commodified so that masks have become mass-produced to the point that there is even use of chrome-plated and nickel-plated brass/*latón*. Similarly, the designs have also undergone permanent changes' (personal interview 2007).

Edmundo Torres, Puno artist, mask maker and collector, veers from tradition in order to implement his unique designs and tailoring. Sometimes he creates a cast of the face of the person who will wear the mask, after which he models a clay mask. He then creates a plaster-of-Paris print and a plaster-of-Paris cast, thereby creating a negative model/pattern to which he applies powdered chalk with glue, cotton and gauze, making a mixture that is both hardy and light.

Other Masked Dancers Who Dance with the Devils

Approximately 70 groups wearing *trajes de luces* participate during the festival's *octava*: devil troupes, *kallawayas*, *kullawadas*, *morenadas*, *reyes caporales* (foremen), black kings, *zambo* foremen, *sikuris*, *tuntunas*, *wifalas*, *sayas*, *tinkus*, *tobas*, *waka wakas* and panpipe players, among others.[6]

Traditional celebrations and the relationships they entail and represent are in constant flux, and dances undergo significant changes from one year to the other. This is due to the fact that the principal driving force of the dance is the contest, which encourages and rewards what is novel in the dance—innovations in form, mixing of characters, the disappearance of some and the birth of others. Tradition thus shows signs of life and this is how it is registered in collective memory.

The Puno Devil's Dance has also tended to incorporate human characters called *figuras*, such as the skeleton and the viceroy depicted as an elderly man. The latter, according to Cuentas, 'symbolizes the owner or master of the mine in which the devil resides' (1986: 41). He wears a gold-and-silver-embroidered jacket, with faux appliqués, a white wig with a hat and a mask that reveals his golden teeth.

There are also characters derived from film and television, such as 'the red-skin', 'the Mexican', 'the vampires' and 'Superman', among others. As for animals repre-sented in the dance, the gorilla stands out—a large character covered in immense plush overalls made of sheep or llama skin. The presence of these characters corre-sponds with a prior script that referenced the sequential passages of Christian mystery plays—hence the Creation-story animals, those of life and death, and of the battle between God (represented by St Michael the Archangel) and Evil (represented by Lucifer and the Seven Deadly Sins). Finally, it is the Virgin of Candelaria who deter-mines the triumph of the Archangel.

Masked Body: Memory and Meaning

When the dancer performs, tradition is made current and interpolated for the con-temporary world. There are codes received from the masters by way of the body, which the dancer retains and makes his/her own. The life of the character emerges once the dancer transforms the energy that seeps through the mask's rigidity.

Wearing a mask creates a distance for it allows one to observe without being observed, as if looking through a window. The spectator tends to look and to fix his/her gaze on the mask's eyes, creating an interactive relationship. In those small movements, a crossing of gazes occurs, a playfulness provoked by the dancer peeking through those 'windows', knowing he/she is not seen. This is an attribute, a power granted by the mask. The master artisans tend to take great care in the production and the painting of the mask's eyes because they know that its life is concentrated there.

The mask could simply be a character's face; but masking involves the whole body of the person who wears it. The attire, which functions as performer's skin, is supplemented with handkerchiefs, wigs, hats and canes. The purpose is to create a new body, with a memory that flows through the alphabet of a dance, where the staged act of the dancer becomes a particular code of representation.

It is often said that the mask hides one body in order to reveal another, different body. On the contrary, the mask is an invitation to transform the body of the one who wears it. To inhabit a mask is, indeed, to put oneself at its service, to receive it and to be transformed.

Notes

1   This is a reference to the clash between the two countries regarding the origin of the Devil's Dance. With respect to this, Pastor Landivar writes:

> Bolivia and Peru's relations are already strained due to the tension between Presidents Evo Morales and Alan García, but now the Devil has stepped in. Bolivia has threatened to sue Peru in the International Court of Justice to defend its cultural rights to the traditional Diablada, or Devil's Dance, performed at the Oruro Carnival, which Peru also claims as its own. The controversy arose at the Miss Universe pageant on 23 August [2009] where, according to *Opinión*, Peruvian contestant Karen Schwarz wore the traditional devil's outfit (*Dialogo*, 27 August 2009).

Jesuit anthropologist Xavier Albó concludes:

> The only hindrance now in all of these celebrations shared by Oruro, Puno and Iquique are those borders which make us feel that we're different from one another and even each other's enemies, because of different economic and political interests which have created the polarities Chile vs Bolivia and Peru and, now, Bolivia vs Peru, with the presidents of both countries screaming epithets at each other. This polarity has proven more devilish than the dancing devils, who are rather seductive and endearing. Were it not for such tensions, what would make most sense is for all of us to be happy to share this common cultural and religious heritage that could do so much for bringing together western Bolivia with southern Peru and northern Chile (*Lamalapalabra*, 26 August 2009. Available at: http://revistalamalapalabra.blogspot.com/2009/08/fronteras-endia-bladas.html; last accessed on 26 August 2014).

2 Comments made during a festive devils editorial retreat in San Cristobal de las Casas, Chiapas, Mexico, August 2010.

3 Incan mythology considers three levels: Ukhu Pacha which is down and inside; Hanan Pacha or Jana Pacha which is outer and above; and the Kay Pacha which is here and now. Silvia Rivera Cusicanqui (2009) argues there are actually four levels, including an unknown world. This fourth virtual level generates a permanent imbalance, to be corrected through ritual.

4 'The city of Tiwanaku, capital of a powerful pre-Hispanic empire that dominated a large area of the southern Andes and beyond, reached its apogee between 500 and 900 CE. Its monumental remains testify to the cultural and political significance of this civilisation, which is distinct from any of the other pre-Hispanic empires of the Americas' (UNESCO, 'Tiwanaku: Spiritual and Political Centre of the Tiwanaku Culture'. Available at: http://whc.unesco.org/en/list/567; last accessed on 2 September 2014).

5 'Set on a peninsula in Lake Umayo, 34 km from Puno, is Sillustani, a burial site where one can see a number of striking tombs belonging to the Colla people (1200–1450) whose culture developed in the northern region of the lake in an area called Hatuncolla' ('Sillustani', *Wikipedia*. Available at: http://es.wikipedia.org/-wiki/Sillustanil; last accessed on 2 September 2014).

6 According to the Puno Regional Federation of Folklore and Culture, in February of 2008, approximately 156 autochthonous dance and costume troupes participated in the festival.

Masks

A Photographic Essay

AMIEL CAYO

Amiel Cayo's masks are faces that represent the otherness and the self
   behind our ego.

Our real personality, in spite of the obvious desire to be somebody else.

Glances filled with questions coming beyond time.

Shapes of weird faces, whose anxiety splits the evening in two.

Gusts of frozen light by a nimble, invisible paintbrush.

Smiles that look more like jaws caught in the fragments of a broken mirror.

His masks mean more than what they really represent.

Inner disguises of some abolished person.

Owls living in the imagination of an uprooted poet.

Resemblances of devils exiled for not having stopped the course of the
   centuries.

Jose Luis Ayala

PUNO

Bear

These characters, also known as *ukumari*, dance in small groups within larger parades. They are the favourite attraction because of the funny ways in which they dance. They represent the spectacled bear, a typical animal of the tropical forests of our country. In recent years, other animal figures are being incorporated—for instance, monkeys, gorillas and orangutans. This, and all subsequent photographs by José Luis Macedo. All masks created by Amiel Cayo.

PUNO

Kusillo

Kusillo is a tireless jester. *Kusillo* in Aymara means 'funny'. This character can be found in the *waca-waca* parades and in other pastoral dance groups. Nevertheless, they come out in big numbers in the village of Juli during the celebration of the Señor de Exaltación (Master of Exaltation) and the Virgen de la Natividad (Virgin of Nativity) every year on 8 September.

CUSCO

Saqra

You will see these characters during the celebration of the Virgen del Carmen in Paucartamba in Cusco region, climbing rooftops and hiding their faces so the Virgin doesn't see their eyes. *Saqra* in Quechua means 'feline', but today the word is connected to the devil, or with the evil forces of darkness that have nothing to do with the Devil of Christianity.

LAMBAYEQUE

Diablico

The dance of the Diablicos is from the town of Mochumi and other towns on the northern coast of Peru. The mask is inspired by an anthropomorphic character of the Mochica culture that flourished between 100 to 800 CE. The devil as a character is common in all celebrations. For many people, he represents Lucifer or the Catholic Devil. There is a convincing explanation that refers to the arrival of the Spanish, when any type of non-Catholic worship became worship of the Devil. Nevertheless, Peruvians who kept on practising their own rituals and worshipping their own gods in clandestine ways, in many cases, moulded their gods as devils. In many traditions, a pact with the Devil in reality represents a pact with the gods repressed by Western culture.

LAMBAYEQUE

Sacerdotisa Moche (Priestess Moche)

Many depictions in the iconography of the Mochica culture refer to this important character. She is a woman crowned with a headdress made of serpents. In her hand she holds a cup with which she supposedly offers blood from a human sacrifice to the Lord of Sipán.

LIMA

El Son de Los Diablos

The only references to these characters are found in the watercolours of the traditionalist painter Pancho Fierro, who left behind a variety of illustrations where these characters appear masked, accompanied by a harp and a *cajita* (a box-shaped percussion instrument). The Diablo Mayor leads the group, easily distinguished by his gorgeous outfit and his massive mask decorated with feathers. He carries a whip to punish the devils that do not behave. The Diablo Mayor is followed by many devils that dance in a line, jumping and every now and then leaving the line to scare onlookers. The mask is a representation of the black slaves brought as labourers in colonial times.

The Devil, Temptation and Penitence in Oruro's Carnival Pageant

THOMAS ABERCROMBIE

Introduction

Every year during carnival time in Oruro, Bolivia, the city's elites temporarily put aside their usual disdain for the customs, superstitions and dress of the country's dominated Indigenous peoples and '*clase* popular', in order to dance through the streets in 'Indian' clothes, performing 'Indian' dramas, in a complex, mixed-genre spectacle.[1] On the one hand, their dancing is part of a folkloric pageant with strong patriotic overtones, celebrating as local and national heritage both 'Indians' (I refer here to a cultural construction, which urban elites[2] sometimes identify with rural Indigenous people),[3] and the presumptively pre-Columbian chthonic earth deities—themselves intertwined with the devil—that they associate with the 'Indian past'. On the other hand, elites also describe their participation in these masked dance dramas as a form of penitential homage to the Virgin of the Mineshaft, patroness of the city. She is a locally celebrated incarnation of the Christian powers whose mission is to conquer diabolical pre-Columbian deities in order to civilize and thereby save Indian souls. That these two contradictorily valued discursive avatars of an Indian other can coexist within a single narrative form poses the paradox that is the subject of this essay.

While Oruro's carnival is a massive event with over 5,000 dancers and a very large audience, it is today but one, and not the largest, of such performances.[4] Similar events take place in other Bolivian locales (such as Copacabana, La Paz, Quillacollo), at different moments in the religious calendar. Religious/folkloric processions dedicated to miracle-working saints are waxing in popularity in Bolivia.[5] Everywhere, it seems, newly refurbished elaborations upon what are some very old missionary plays, along with some newer and more 'ethnographic' representations of the country's Indigenous heritage, are now celebrated by the county's elites and their aspiring imitators.[6]

A wide variety of dance types are to be seen in these pageants; and since the nature of the Indian's role in the national future remains unsettled, debates rage over the dances' respective degrees of authenticity and religiosity. As a result, some dances are waxing in popularity while others are on the wane. Some dances (like the Incas, the Diablada and the Morenada) derive from sixteenth-century Spanish *autos sacramentales*, in which dramatized narratives re-enact the conquest and conversion of the heathens and the subordination of devils to the Christian faith. The newest dances on the scene, which conform to what we might call 'ethnographic realist' canons, strive to capture the 'true essence' of contemporary Indigenous cultures, seeking authenticity in costume and choreography by relying on living 'informants'. Individual dancers, of course, participate for widely varying motives and interpret that participation in a variety of ways (to 'revindicate indigenous Bolivia', to celebrate the country's heritage, to enjoy collective solidarity—including repeated social events, parties, etc.—with peers, to demonstrate cultural resistance to Church, State or Yankee imperialist homogenizing pressures and so on).[7] But all dances, missionary or not, participate in a conquest-and-conversion macronarrative that structures the larger processional frame—all the pageants, the carnival included, begin with presumptive pacts with the devil/underworld forces in hopes of lucre, and a promise of penance to the Virgin or Christ in exchange for grace. Dancing while embodying the temptations of the flesh is carried out as a penitential act and bodily offering, in fulfilment of a vow to a particular devotion and image of Christ or the Virgin, before which dancers pray at the procession's end, which returns participants to routine life.

It appears, indeed, that the sin for which such penitence pays is that of letting out the participant's 'inner Indian'. Devotees routinely engage in a variety of magical practices—coded as 'Indian'—in the context of Bolivia's miracle-saint shrines. Members of the 'popular classes' as well as elites hire 'Indian' shamans to burn incense bundles and empower business-enhancing amulets and seek out the dark forces of earth deities (with presumed pre-Columbian origins) to which Indians are held to have special access. Yet these forces—and practices—are intelligible only through their articulation with the Christian powers, and more canonically Christian practices, which domesticate them in a cosmological struggle much akin to the conquest and conversion topoi of folkloric dance. It is this dual nature of pilgrimage pageantry that makes it a favoured arena for working on the vexed issue of national identity.

Yet, until the 1940s, such spectacles were assiduously avoided by the country's elite, the self-styled *gente decente* (read 'whites') who condemned these dances for their plebeian and Indian excesses and their superstitious and unrefined content. Today, however, elites dominate most of these performances, having almost everywhere supplanted the urban cholo labour associations that since independence have kept them going against a strong current of elite censure. The 1940s onward, these festivals have been imbued with patriotic values and are much trumpeted by journalists and politicians as emblems of regional and national pride. For its carnival, Oruro claims the title of 'National Folklore Capital',[8] and the city's elected officials do not miss the opportunity to lead the procession and applaud from the review stand. How can one account for this upsurge in apparent sympathy for Indian heritage, in a country characterized over most of its history by a rigid structure of social inequality in which Indian or mixed-race-and-culture status excludes one from privilege? What does masquing and dancing mean for those who participate? What messages are conveyed in the representations and narratives they perform? What are the implications for those whose cultural forms have been thus appropriated and those who are represented?

Scrutiny of the actual content of Oruro's pageant performances show that they dramatize a story about the ideal Bolivian citizen's struggle for being. Oruro's carnival pageant frames liturgical drama about Indian wildness within a saint's-day celebration ending in an unmasked repentance and Mass, a day that in Oruro coincides with the classic Lenten denouement of Carnival. This morality play stipulates that the fully civilized citizen can realize himself only through redemption from a sinfulness towards which he is drawn by dangerous temptations located in the bodies of Indian women.[9] Via this almost Manichaean (or perhaps Albigensian)[10] message, such pageants assimilate enlightened nationalists' pastoral romance with Indian nature to the story of the Fall. Through such an internal contradiction, this tragic romance calls for renunciation of the beloved along with consummation. To a cynical critic's ear, the romance that calls for elites to consummate their desire for the Indian siren before renouncing it (and her) rings like a too-familiar justification for rape. Such are the sometimes-dark ironies of the mixed-genre infatuations of folklore. As drama critics, we might bemusedly appreciate these ironies as clever semiotic effects. But the stories of pageantry are also about very real struggles between the powerful and the powerless that contribute, through the colonization of minds, to the maintenance of political, economic and cultural domination.

While I focus here upon the history of pageant dance dramas, and their significance to urban nationalist schemes, I also seek to cast light on the relationship among the elite's depictions of their Indian other, an urban mestizo-cholo popular-culture tradition that is the most immediate source of dance-dramatic forms and (without describing them here) the actual rural cultural orders that pageantry claims to represent. We may begin with the dichotomy between elite European urban and subordinate Indian rural orders as posited in much of Bolivian postcolonial discourse. But their relationship can only be fully appreciated by focusing as well on a third term that mediates it—the mestizo-cholo or mixed-culture sphere whose locus is in rural elites and mining or urban working classes.[11]

Historical Views of Race, Ethnicity and Class in Bolivia

To the tourist, the dances of Bolivian pageantry might suggest that the Indians and Spaniards of the conquest period continue to be the country's only kinds of social actors. The very premise of the Death of Atawallpa drama performed by Oruro's Incas troupes, for example, takes participants back to a colonial ontogenesis. Other dances, too, portray an essentially dichotomous polity, whether composed of Spaniards and Indians, angels and devils, slave drivers and slaves or saints and sinners. Through sustained homology, all seem to collapse into an overarching opposition between the civilized Christian Spaniard and the savage diabolical Indian. To the degree to which in Bolivian society high social status is pegged to an absence of indices of Indianness, the tourist observer would be correct to conclude that Bolivians all, in most people's eyes at least, belong to one or the other category.

Although they continue to be important as stereotypes and stage roles, however, Spaniards (now *criollos* or *blancos*) and Indians (now *campesinos* or 'Indigenous peoples') are not the country's most populated social categories. Instead, that distinction is reserved for a dual frontier between the two, inhabited by people who call themselves, or are called, 'mestizos' and 'cholos'. Regarded by creoles as closer to Indians, and classed by Indians as nearer to creoles, what I call the mestizo-cholo sphere is both large and complex, with a deep cultural past and a home in the *vecino* elites of rural towns[12] and artisan/labourer popular sectors of urban *rancherías*.

Not perhaps since the late seventeenth century have the urban dances such as those of Oruro's carnival been performed by rural Indians. Instead, this was the identity-producing prerogative of urban Indians, which is to say, of the mestizo-cholo sphere. Artisan guilds monopolized the dances of Oruro's carnival until the mid-1940s. Enacting the Inca's death at Pizarro's hands was one means by which urban labourers strove to mark their membership in guilds, and to break out of an 'Indian' status in which elites tried to keep them. The irony that concerns us here, that is, resides in the fact that these dance dramas, insisting on such an absolute ethnic/racial dichotomy, have been the means by which members of an internally stratified middle sector have defined themselves as non-Indians, while through their very participation in such activities they marked themselves as non-Spaniards, which is to say, in the terms applied to them by elites since the late eighteenth century, as an Indian-identified *vulgo* or plebe.

Colonial Cultural Stratification and a Bolivian Fashion System

Key to carnival in Oruro, and to all the similar saints' pageants of Bolivia's cities, is costumed dancing. A wide variety of dances portray several forms of alterity, in which male roles involve the costumed embodiment of devils or archangels, Hollywood-style wild Indians, African slaves in blackface or in Baroque costume, Incas or Spaniards, or 'ethnographically realistic' portrayals of rural peoples' indigenous dress. Notable, however, is that most female costumes conform to a single dress style, that of the urban chola, with flared pleated skirts, frilly blouse, jacket and bowler hat. Women's roles, that is, reflect the costume of the urban figure of the interstitial chola as market vendor or domestic servant, while male costume tends towards the exotic. Both kinds of costumes and roles partake of a certain 'world upside-down' intransigence: male roles portray violent, wild and subversive types (or their domesticators) while female roles tend towards the chola, yes, but the chola as temptress. To understand why the dances of urban artisans and proletarians should divide in this way, we must attend to the larger Bolivian fashion system and its historical development.[13]

It is perhaps not too ironic that when elites put on 'Indian' clothes in their pageants, to become more authentically—natively—Bolivian, and rural people go upscale and civilize themselves[14] by switching to urban dress styles (and even into the 'Indian' costumes of urban pageants), they both do so to affirm their respective visions of and membership in national culture. Yet a greater irony is that both rural assimilationist and urban folklorizing moves draw heavily—but usually without acknowledgement—upon the traditions and costume proper to the mestizo-cholo stratum that is otherwise reviled by both rural Indians and urban creoles.[15]

Spanish colonial policies divided Spanish from Indian 'republics' (towns) and aimed to keep Indians out of Spanish towns, Spaniards out of Indian ones. Yet colonial Spaniards, who acquired many of the privileges of Spanish aristocracy (freedom from tributes, etc.) merely by being in the Indies, had also to avoid the stain of manual labour that had in Spain served to stigmatize the plebeian *pechero* (tributary).[16] This meant that every Spanish town and city was soon full to bursting with Indians and Africans, needed not only in mines but in every would-be Spanish (and creole Spanish) kitchen. Rural-to-urban migrants in the sixteenth century, as today, underwent a transformation, joining interstitial, non-Spanish/non-Indian mestizos born of mixed unions. The ideal of separate republics quickly fell by the wayside, in spite of the creation in every city of separate parishes for Indians, and efforts to relegate to them Africans and mestizos too. Ever since the first few generations of mestizaje, phenotype had been an unreliable indicator of category.[17] Instead, dress and the performance of exclusively honourable occupations sealed the social position that in the Indies[18] came with Spanishness.

In elite Spanish houses, the principle of *patria potestas* made the master of the house the guarantor not only of his kinswomen's behaviour but also of his servants'.[19] Given that Indians, like women generally—especially plebeians—were ascribed a propensity towards a weakness of will in sexual matters that could besmirch the master's honour, vigilance was necessary.[20] In the colonial context, application of the honour and shame patriarchal principal led to the sort of sexual domination that made concubinage seem to be a natural thing and produced large numbers of illegitimate mixed-blood offspring.[21]

By the eighteenth century, Spanish, mestizo, city Indian (who were called *indios criollos* for having lost their ties to their original rural 'nations') and rural Indian statuses were well demarcated only as positions in the colonial division of labour. This made room for massive levels of social climbing and passing (of Indians for mestizos, mestizos for Spaniards, etc.) that threatened to undercut the very categorical schema on which colonial rule was based. In recognition of this crisis, the crown produced the Royal Pragmatic of 1776, extended to the colonies in 1778, which gave Spanish elites an additional tool for preserving their privileges (Lavrin 1989: 18–20; Seed 1988: 205–26).

Station was marked, however, not only by occupation but also by dress. Edmond Temple's 1830 engraving of the social classes of Potosí illustrates the dress styles of its social classes at a moment just after Bolivian independence (1830: I, plate between pp. 292 and 293). 'Spaniards' per se (those born in the Iberian peninsula) are absent,

FIGURE 1. 'Inhabitants of Potosí, In Front of the Cathedral'. From Edmond Temple, *Travels in Various Parts of Perú, including a Year's Residence in Potosí* (1830), VOL. 1. Photograph by author.

having been displaced by creole-Spaniards (those born in the Indies, and thus of suspect 'nation'), who are in this illustration (the three rightmost figures) labelled as creole ladies and gentlemen. On the far left, Temple shows a 'peasant Indian' couple, while on either side of the Franciscan friar are a cholo artisan and a chola.[22] The woman in the foreground (with the little girl and the fancy shoes about which Temple has much to say) is a type he calls 'an Indian inhabitant of the city', wearing a costume distinct from both 'peasant Indian' and 'chola'. She belongs, in an earlier terminology, to the 'creole Indian' niche, but the term 'creole' had by Temple's day been reserved exclusively for Españoles Americanos.[23] Note also that the couple Temple calls cholo and chola would have been labelled, only a few years before, as mestizo. The disappearance of the term *indio criollo* and the displacement of 'mestizo' by 'cholo' mark, I believe, a moment of transition in which the distinction was in process of disappearing. In the twentieth century, there is only one basic (female) mestiza/chola dress; differences in style now correspond to regional affiliation, not intra-region stratification. Absent from Temple's illustration is the male 'city-Indian', as distinct from the 'cholo artisan'. It is likely that the collapse of a distinction between culturally and racially, nationally or ethnically intermediate men was already complete. Note also that the male mestizo-cholo's clothing, with the exception of his patterned cape, is scarcely distinguishable from that of the creole gentleman—today's gender gap in costume was already present in 1830.

Corpus Christi and the Carnivalization of la Plebe: Fusion and Fission of the Body Social

Concern about the destabilizing effect on colonial hierarchy of the emergent socially mobile middle stratum led to moves to regulate ceremonial life. From early on, Spaniards had introduced the elaborate civic processional rituals of the Renaissance court in which subjects demonstrated their fealty to the two sovereigns (see the studies in Jacquot 1975). Most characteristic, perhaps, was the militantly ordered and ordering procession of Corpus Christi (Very 1962). Through it, the rigidly separated parts of the urban body social were symbolically reintegrated as the body of Christ (and king). Thus in the cities of the Indies, social classes that were ethnically marked—including the guild confraternities of all the trades—danced in procession according to their positions in the overarching social hierarchy as defined by Spanish elites who led the way accompanied by the royal standard and the Host in its solar monstrance.[24]

Early colonial accounts paint a picture of Indians marching according to their nations, from outskirts of town to the plaza and matrix church. It was in the context of such totalizing processions that authorities introduced the theatre of evangelization, the well-known *autos sacramentales* from which derives Spanish Golden Age theatre and Oruro's carnival dance. Documentation of their performance from the sixteenth century is conclusive but sketchy and without the details that we might like. Fray Alonso Ramos Gavilán (1976[1621]: 221) describes a military parade of 'Incas' (some of whom may indeed have been Incas) during celebrations honouring the opening of a new temple for the Virgin of Copacabana in her namesake pilgrimage town, in 1614; Arzáns de Orzua y Vela describes an Easter procession of 'Incas' in 1555, including the production of eight comedies, four of which represented the Inca history from its origins to its 'ruin' (1965[1702–35]: I, 95–9).[25] Elsewhere in his massive history he notes other 'Incas' plays between 1590 and 1642. One was authored by a Potosí poet in 1641 (ibid.: II, 86). The wide distribution of these dances in, especially, mining centres suggests that they probably have a long history in Oruro as well. Whenever they arrived, these allegories of conversion and submission to the rule of God were translated into colonial idioms. Such processional dramas—which were sometimes mounted on moving vehicles, or played on elaborate temporary stages, and sometimes necessitated the memorization of complex playbooks—would have stretched the resources of levied rural Indian workers beyond credibility. Instead they were organized, financed and played by artisan guilds, as was true in Europe.

As in Spain, the craft guilds of the Indies were organized as confraternities, with patron saints and religious duties apart from their roles in more totalizing productions. Although we can imagine that such organizational forms were encouraged in the first century of the colony, by the mid-eighteenth century, they had clearly become worrisome to the forces of order, in part because of their raucous performances, and in part for being made up largely of non-white, non-Indian *castas*, ancestors of today's mestizo-cholo urban majority. In the Lima of 1750, one such processional dance—most likely a Seven Deadly Sins or Moors and Christians drama, as it was to take place on the feast of St Michael—was to be the Trojan horse through which (probably guild-organized) Indians and mestizos sought to introduce an insurrectional army into the centre of town (Spalding 1984: 273–4). The following year, panicky officials in Potosí called for reinforcements from the Audiencia capital when a carnival procession of a guild of Indian and mestizo 'unofficial miners' (that is, mineral thieves, on which see Tandeter 1981), which also involved the use of arms in a dramatized battle, looked like rebellion to the city's elites.[26] The late-eighteenth century saw crown measures to ban public performances such as these, and indeed Corpus Christi and Holy Week festivals, along with patron saint processions, were progressively tamed and turned into sombre penitential affairs.

But it was too late for such hygienic measures, especially in the context of pre-Lenten carnival. Efforts at suppression only served to send mestizo-cholo ritual activities further underground, into the mineshafts, and out to the periphery of town and the sometimes prohibited rituals of rebellion-like carnival. Even the efforts of Oruro's creoles to ally themselves with rebelling Indians in 1781, in order to claim independence from a Spanish crown that had treated them with disdain, backfired in these circumstances. Disaffected by their exclusion from administrative offices, which were preferentially given under Bourbon policies to Spaniards born in Iberia, the creoles of Oruro called upon rebellious Indians of the provinces to join them in an alliance of all Americans (meaning all those born in Peru), asking them to invade the city and kill the Spaniards. These events took place on 10 February, as it happened, in carnival season. The creole heroes of this ill-fated revolt have given their names—as revolutionary patriots—to the city's streets, and the date of their plot to its main plaza, but they gave their lives to Indians (who did not make overly fine distinctions between peninsular and creole Spaniards). Some managed to escape (only to fall into the hands of the king's men) by donning the clothes of their Indian servants to slip away from the carnage. Not recalled in Oruro's patriotic programmes, this may have been the first dance of carnival Indians through the city's streets.[27] The second had to wait until the 1940s.

Conditioned by the repressive surveillance of elite authority, the urban plebe, whose Christian practices as well as persons were marked 'Indian' by their peripheralized occupations and residences, were in a position to develop the conversion allegories of their dramas in quest of their own destinies and identities, in the space between God and the Devil into which they had been cast. In Potosí, miners still celebrate miraculous crucifixes, which they call Tata Q'aqchas and which play a role analogous to the Virgin of the Mineshaft in Oruro—they counterbalance devotions in the mines and on the outskirts of town to diabolized incarnations of Indian mountain deities, such as the Tios (also called Supays, on which see Taylor 1980), to whom miners in both Potosí and Oruro make offerings. Until it was revalued by 1940s indigenism, such practices flourished as a popular culture, deemed vulgar and 'Indian' by elites and incompatible with now more refined displays of horsemanship and bull fights, balls and 'high-culture' theatre.[28]

Elite persecution of plebeian processional theatre did not come to an end until the mid-twentieth century. From the late eighteenth century until then, there were two carnival processions in Oruro: one belonged to the elite, who on carnival Saturday carried out a short procession, dressed in a variety of orientalist visions (like sheikh and harem-girl outfits), ending up in gala balls; and the other pertaining to the vulgar Indian masses, who in carnival Sunday's procession (which successive municipal ordinances sought to prohibit) replayed the old themes of colonial theatre.[29]

Only in the twentieth-century republic, with the rise of *indigenista* thinking—almost always tied to socialist visions—have living Indians, and their supposed primitive communism, been extolled as models for the nation. Achieving its first great rise in the 1930s and 40s, during a period of increasing preoccupation with labour movements and a strong anti-oligarchical bias among a formerly abhorred mestizo-cholo element (which had become indispensable and influential in the lower bureaucratic and industrial administrative strata, especially after the massive mobilizations of the Chaco War, fought between Bolivia and Paraguay from 1929 to 1933), indigenism found its political strength in the Movimiento Revolucionario Nacional which came to power in 1952.

Bound up with unionism and comunitarian ideals and often with idealized visions of primitive communism, *indigenista* interest in things 'Indian' was still focused on the most ancient and authentic—which is to say, the least colonial—aspects of rural culture and was tied to a paradoxical demeaning of mestizo-cholo culture per se (see Arguedas 1967; Tamayo 1910). But by eliding cultural differences between rural 'Indian' and urban mestizo-cholo cultures, by re-labelling mestizo-cholo belief systems (such as those involving the Mother Earth / Pachamama and the evil masculine deities of the mines) as authentically ancient and 'Indian' ones, and by Indianizing both the provenience of urban dance dramas and their representational content, the predominantly mestizo-cholo dance drama and religious complex could be made to stand in for that of the Indian. If the most auspicious forms of indigenous culture for the purposes of indigenist creole nationalism were those with pre-Columbian pedigrees, these could by such sleights of sign be found in the barroom, the marketplace and perhaps even in the kitchen.

The characteristic displacements in the *indigenista* romance with the Indian past are well exemplified in the narrative line of the much-read 1947 Bolivian novel *La Chaskañawi*, published by the teacher-publisher-writer Carlos Medinaceli. Forsaking the possibilities of university education, Adolfo—a promising young member of the creole elite (of presumptively Spanish and non-Indian heritage)—is drawn to his doom by his attraction to Claudina, an alluring chola barmaid (of mestizo and therefore part-Indian extraction) who is known by the Quechua epithet of 'La Chaskañawi', 'starry eyes' or 'long eyelashes'.[30] The book is an often-reprinted standard in Bolivian schools and universities. The novel illustrates how easily—and compellingly—the language of politics and domination underwrites that of desire. As Doris Sommer (1991) has argued of other such canonical texts, its place in the national canon results from the degree to which it predicates patriotic zeal upon a cross-class romance signalling the emergence of the nation's required homogenous citizenry. The novel offers in the vivacious Claudina an appealing alternative to the vituperative denunciations of the *cholada* presented by his predecessors Alcides Arguedas (*Raza de Bronze,* 1919) or Enrique Finot (*El Cholo Portales,* 1926). But the book is also read as a cautionary tale, one that offers its elite audience a moral lesson against the dangers of allowing patriotic class-crossing rhetoric to give way to a betrayal of creole class values. The story, that is, brings to life the profound postcolonial conundrum faced by the project of Bolivia.

Although the novel is set in the 1920s, its theme of creole infatuation with the indigenous, set amid a subplot of oligarchical intrigue against a liberal government, reflects the concerns of the 1940s when it was written and published. In that complex period, which I can only summarize here, a new stratum of the urban bourgeoisie and state bureaucracy, developed from among the mestizo-cholo junior officers mobilized in the disastrous Chaco War, found a voice in national politics. Their position strengthened by a rise in unionism in the mines and the influx of socialist ideas, they had achieved national power in the government of President Gualberto Villarroel in 1943. Although he was subsequently killed in a coup led by an alliance of Stalinists and Falangists, the repression of *rosca* (conservative oligarchical) governments from 1946 to 1952 led only to the victory of the *indigenista*-filled Nationalist Revolutionary Movement party in the revolution of 1952. With their victory came an enormous wave of unionization and nationalization, and also a new vision of patriotism and national progress which mobilizes Bolivia's native strengths against the forces of imperialism.

It has been only in this context that the nationalist romance with the indigenous blossomed in Bolivia. But as one might expect, the romance has been with heroic visions of a state-endowed pre-Columbian past, projected onto domesticated Claudinas, not so much with the Indian present: nationalization might have been justified by some as a return to 'Inca socialism' (as glorified in Baudin 1928, and debunked in Murra 1978[1956]), but the revolution's agrarian reform act aimed again—like nineteenth-century liberalism—at privatizing Indian landholding. Likewise, elite solidarity with the oppressed proletariat has been ambivalent, at best, as is made clear in the history of carnival since the 'postcolonial situation' finally arrived in Bolivia in the 1940s.

A Post- (or Neo-) colonial Carnival

In *La Chaskañawi*, Adolfo is lured into his first public acknowledgement of his submission to Claudina when, unable to resist her seductive dancing during carnival, he leaves the scornful creole audience and joins in with the dancing *cholada*. This 1947 novel here recaptures a turning point in Oruro's carnival—in 1940, a few elite indigenists first expressed their solidarity with the 'Indian' working class by joining the

Diablada dance organized each year by the butchers' union. But this sort of direct challenge to ethnic/class barriers did not last long. In 1944, elite dancers withdrew from the butchers' group to found their own dance group, with their own miniature image of the Virgin of the Mineshaft, weekly prayer sessions and charter.[31] In that same year, the ill-fated reformist president Villarroel invited the butchers' group to give a command performance in La Paz (Montes Camacho 1986), marking the beginnings of an explicitly politicized promotion of folklore. Since Villarroel's time, it has, however, been the elite group that has moved to the centre of the national stage. With a high concentration of Oruro's doctors and lawyers—whose wives would not be caught dead, outside of their carnival dances, in the cholita outfits worn by their maids and butchers' wives—even this group's weekly practice and prayer meetings, which may include lessons in folklore, receive attention. They have sometimes been honoured by the presence of the mayor and the high clergy. They do, however, strive to remain true to traditions learnt from the butchers, chewing coca leaves during their prayer meetings and performing the Quechua language *relato* about St Michael and the Devil-Sins in their dance. Notwithstanding that the butchers changed their name to 'Gran Tradicional y Auténtica Diablada' on the birth of the elite group, members of the upper crust consider the elite group's dance more precise, and their costumes— even practice uniforms—more polished than the butchers'. It has been elite 'Indian Devils' and 'cholitas' who have travelled most widely abroad to represent Bolivia's national heritage, and who have become most fully emblematic not only of Oruro but also of the nation as a quintessential representative of 'Indian' Bolivianness.[32]

They are not alone in striving to become so. Today, with a population greater than 100,000,[33] Oruro's carnival fields over 40 dance groups—and perhaps 5,000 dancers—every year.[34] Every year, up to six Diablada groups take to the streets, including, apart from the above group and the butchers, one organized by a railway workers' union in 1957 and others formed by neighbourhood associations. Likewise, the Morenada has blossomed from its original base in a single group formed in 1913 (in the working-class *ranchería* neighbourhood, the old Indian parish), to a total of more than a dozen today, including the derivative Negritos, Reyes Morenos and Caporales groups. Here, participation includes middle-class (meaning non-cholo) neighbourhood associations, several unions (workers of a foundry, pasta company, state mining trust) and a few school-organized groups.

The larger of these groups field hundreds of dancers each; but not all the dance forms typical of mestizo-cholo organizations have achieved such popularity. The Incas dance, for instance, which features a play (in Quechua and Spanish) about Pizarro's defeat of Atawallpa, has received considerable scholarly attention but is today represented by only two, much diminished groups.[35] Failing similarly are the

Cullaguadas and Llameradas, dance types in costumes amounting to the everyday dress of the mestizo-cholos who perform them. Neither straightforward representations of Spaniards and Incas nor transparent mestizo-cholo self-representation is suitable for the development of a nationalist vision of Indian heritage, which prefers devils, wild Indians and wanton maidens in the company of their virginal and angelic tamers.

More appealing to the tastes of progressive youth are the derivatives of a dance type that was called, in the early years of the twentieth century, Chunchos. Two of these groups are on record in the 1910s. Falling on lean years, they were reinvigorated in the 1970s by an influx of youths and have since inspired the formation of new groups organized by university students and a ballet school. Although renamed Suris (from an Altiplano dance) and Tobas (after a Chaco region culture), and reworked following a Hollywood 'red-skin' pattern, they derive from indigenous dances representing the 'wild Indians' of the pre-Christian past (and the 'untamed' jungles).

Given that what makes these dances essentially Bolivian is their presumed portrayal of Bolivian Indian essences, representational authenticity is increasingly an issue of debate among participants. Moved by dissatisfaction with the colonial features of some dances, recent, pro-Indian reformers have gone back to the countryside in search of what they claim to be purer Indian sources for their carnival images. The new and progressive dance genre of the 1980s might be termed 'ethnographic realism'. If an earlier generation of indigenists were satisfied with the 'Indians' they could find in the marketplace, mines and kitchens of the city (that is, with mestizo-cholo constructs of selfhood through the combat of Indian and Christian forces), the younger generation looks to ethnography for its images.[36]

Above all, however, youthful dance-group organizers call on their own experience as ex-*vecinos* and traders in the countryside for their inspiration, in order to capture the real (if fast disappearing) Indian in his authentic homespun and rituals. This means, of course, homespun clothing, panpipes and *tinku* (ritualistic combat). The result is 'ethnographic', perhaps. But with ethnographic realism comes ethnographic exoticism and the romance of the pastoral, which aims at capturing the Indian in his least civilized moment. In the countryside, the ritual battles known as *tinkus* take place in the context of patron-saint festivals; blood thus spilled ties in to the festivals' complex ritual synthesis of llama sacrifices and Christian Eucharist. Oruro's carnival *tinkus* are silent on such connections. Instead, they foreground only exotic indices of violent Indian wildness.

Since indigenist elites first joined in the dances of mestizo-cholo *tinku* guilds in the 1940s, their vision of carnival dancing as a unifying tradition within which a

FIGURE 2. Modified cholita costume of Morenada *predilecta*. Photograph by author.

national identity might be staged has become generalized. It has received the blessing of political leaders, and drawn increasing numbers of the assimilating middle and lower middle classes into the procession, if generally in groups segregated according to the niches of social stratification. Nonetheless, at the same time that mestizo-cholo traditions about the relationship between Indian heritage and the civilized life have been adopted for nationalist purposes, and even as the pageant cholita becomes a key figure in carnival narratives, cholos and cholitas themselves have been increasingly marginalized from the patriotic and devotional core of the spectacle.[37] Oruro's Adolfos may have been drawn into the dance by its original Claudinas but the cholita roles in the dances in which they participate are, today, played mainly by decidedly *de vestido* women who employ *de pollera* cholitas as their maids.

Even among the dance groups with humbler membership (excluding the butchers' union Diablada and part of the Cullaguada and Llamerada groups), cholita roles are played largely by women who are themselves *de vestido*, even if their mothers were *de pollera* cholitas. The narrative topos embedded within, especially, the Diablada dance, must encourage cholitas to abandon their polleras.

In the Devil Dance, faux cholitas flaunt their sexuality. The *predilectas*, beauty queens elected to lead the cholitas sections in many dance groups, parade in scooped blouses and shortened polleras.[38] Especially salacious are the masked china *supays*, 'female devils', consorts of the devil who would tempt men away from the path of righteousness.[39] But they only do so until they approach the end of the route. There, before the largest crowds, they and their devils are humbled into submission to St Michael and the Virgin as, one by one, the Seven Deadly Sins fall to their knees before the seven counteracting virtues. Even china *supay* cholitas—carnival's Mary Magdalens—can be redeemed by heeding the sexuality-renouncing example of the Virgin.

Although most of the 20 or so different kinds of dance groups lack their own playscripts, all dances participate in the narrative insofar as the processional route itself becomes an allegory of the road towards the redemption of the nation's citizens. If in pre-*indigenista* days, elites sought to keep the 'vulgar' carnival procession out of the civilized city centre, the parade route today is increasingly pegged to the milestones of national pride. Beginning in a peripheral neighbourhood near the old Indian *ranchería*, dancers file up Pagador Street, named after the hero of the would-be 1781 Indian–creole alliance. They then progress to Bolivar Street, proceed through the central square, the 10th of February Plaza (named for the date of that much-heralded alliance), up Junin Street (honouring the site of a decisive independence battle), onto Civic Avenue, where political officials wave from the review stands. The procession ends in the Plaza of Folklore, in front of the Temple of the Virgin of the Mineshaft. Here, all masks are removed and all dancers renounce their devilish Indianness (and the personal sins so marked) and promise future piety before receiving a special Mass in honour of the Virgin.

The message of carnival dancing, in which temptress passions are externalized by creole women dressed as cholita wantons, is that this kind of sexuality—the 'degenerative' danger of which is assigned to the 'Indian' plebe—must be resisted and repressed for God and country. It is conquered and tamed by the Virgin of the Mineshaft to whom the dancing is dedicated. As we have seen, dance-group members offer their dancing in penitential self-sacrifice to the Virgin who is also carried during the procession in miniature at the head of each group. Through such penance, dancers may learn to obey God's law and thus 'free themselves from that infernal dragon'.[40]

Virgin, Pachamama, Cholita: Sexual Peril in the Indian 'America'

A Bolivian version of France's Marianne—beautiful and heroic symbol of the republic—is now difficult for elites to create and sustain. But when the New World was finally recognized as new, it was often portrayed as the personified America, an exotically savage seductress, inescapably attractive to her European suitors, who cast themselves as her protectors. In the early Bolivian republic, she was transformed into an Inca princess. Edmond Temple portrays the Incan 'America' in his gravure of the feathered chola dancers of a provincial town pageant (1830: II, plate between 48–9), about whom he describes an elaborate erotic fantasy (ibid.: 46–51).[41]

FIGURE 3. Frontispiece to Don Juan de Larrinaga Salazar, *Memorial Discursivo sobre el oficio de protector general de los Indios del Peru.* Courtesy of the John Carter Brown Library.

FIGURE 4. 'Night Scene in the Curate's House'. From *Travels in Various Parts of Perú, including a Year's Residence in Potosí* (1830), VOL. 2. Photograph by author.

Such figures can still be seen in carnival dance, but 'America' is no longer an Inca princess danced by cholas but a cholita performed by an elite woman. This figure clothes the dark side of allure—which is temptation towards sinful Indian wildness—in the already-suspect moral body of the cholita. Elite men in this postcolonial context might often construe Indian women (as the cholita maidens) as sexual objects to be rescued from dark Indian sacrificial suitors, as in the plot of *La Chaskañawi*, but the dramatic and processional narratives of carnival remind them at every step that in doing so they would deny their heavenly mother, the renouncing and pure Virgin who is patroness of the city and the nation. Oruro's citizens have thus sought to endow the Virgin with pre-Columbian roots, reconciling her to the native earth.

In one of the most widely diffused accounts of the Virgin's appearance in Oruro, illustrated in a comic-book/pamphlet (*Supay: leyenda de Wari* 1981) circulated by folklorists before carnival, the Virgin of the Mineshaft first appears in the days before the Spanish conquest. She comes in the form of a beautiful *ñusta* (an Inca princess) in order to save the potentially law-abiding pre-Columbian Uru people from monsters sent by their angry and evil underworld god Wari, whom they have offended with their goodness.[42] In another version of the story (Beltrán Heredia 1956), Wari has enchanted the Urus by the glitter of gold and silver. When the *ñusta* arrives, Wari seeks to possess her. The Urus mend their ways and come to her aid when she refuses to submit to Wari's advances, so he sends the monsters against them in vengeance. In the images of the Virgin carried by the faithful she may appear meek and mild, obeyer of laws, but in this story she comes armed and dangerous.[43]

The story's theme echoes that—portrayed in the Diablada dance—of the Archangel's banishment from Heaven of Lucifer and his minions, who have been recast as the evil inspirers of Indians' original pagan religion. Rather than destroying and banishing the Urus (as does the solar-Christ in the well-known Aymara story in which they are termed Supay-Chullpas), the *ñusta*-Virgin comes to save Urus threatened by pre-Columbian Wari, himself a form of Supay (devil, in missionary Aymara/Quechua). She banishes Wari and his minions from the pre-Columbian past to the contemporary underworld, entombing him within the bowels of the earth and turning the monsters to stone. At one and the same moment, the story rescues Oruro's presumed pre-Columbian Indian ancestors from an ignominious past by turning them into the heroic bearers of a classical civilization, and preserves, in the entombed Wari and the remnants of the monsters, a potential source of telluric power and mineral wealth.

FIGURE 5. The Virgin/Ñusta defeats Wari. Frame from pamphlet *La Leyenda de Wari y la Virgen* (Oruro, n.a., n.d.). Photograph by author.

The story also clearly conveys a moral message about the value of renouncing not only luxury and greed but also sexuality, especially sexual contact between a lascivious and evil male Indian demiurge and a virginal ñusta. The story thus inverts the gender relationship between Spanish conquerors and the feminized native American landscape, making the newcomer Virgin into sort of anti-cholita, whose renunciatory actions are a model for the redemption of cholita temptresses tarnished by their association with the 'infernal dragon'.

The masculinized telluric powers of this story—turned now into the diminutive but still potent devil images called Tios (Spanish for 'uncles')—are revered yet by miners seeking new ore deposits. On the first Friday of every month, especially the Friday before the carnival, the Tios, in the form of small devil images within the mines (sometimes depicted with outsized erect penises), receive libations of alcohol, offerings of coca and the blood of llamas. The petrified remains of Wari's monsters—especially the serpent, toad and lizard found on the outskirts of town—also receive offerings on these days.[44] Attended especially by struggling members of the urban petty bourgeoisie (small merchants, mine owners, truck drivers, smugglers), 'the toads' (as they are collectively called) can provide devotees access to the silver, money and commodities they covet, so long as the offerings made to them are properly subordinated to the Virgin. Devotees may 'become Indians' in dance and by propitiating 'indigenous devils', so as to tap into pre-Columbian sources of wealth production, but they do so within a wider framework in which they are subsequently obliged to become happy slaves of the renouncing Virgin, as both devils and morenos acknowledge in song.

In this broader narrative-topographic context, even those Indian dances without their own playscripts—including the pro-Indian ethnographic representations—are framed so as to play out their roles in full. This is also true for the market-vendor cholitas who have been progressively excluded from the 'civilized' core of the carnival procession. They still play themselves, however, on the outskirts of town, in the space where Wari's monsters predominate and where the carnival both begins and ends.

The last act of the carnival season comes after Ash Wednesday, on the Sunday following the carnival, known as Temptation Sunday, in reference to the temptations of Christ in the desert on his pilgrimage to Calvary. On this day, hundreds of marketeering cholitas dance down a street famous for its open-air chicherías, from an extramural marketplace to the precinct of Wari's petrified serpent. Accompanied by their husbands, they dance in their own polleras, in the comparsa style of rural towns. Masses of middle-class Orureños flock to the area to watch and eat picnics in on the hillsides, and to drink chicha in stands set up by Cochalas, the chicha-vending cholitas of Cochabamba lampooned in anti-carnival.[45]

In this context, after both the serpent and the Virgin have received their respective devotions, and after Indian-like vices have been subordinated to civic and Christian virtues, one 'Indian' divinity still receives cult. In the context of Temptation Sunday, the centre of attention is again the cholita, dancing in her own clothes, but also the Pachamama, the feminine incarnation of the Indigenous past and the one divine being vouchsafed by indigenists and cholas alike. Pachamama is at once the clearest and most opaque of all the Indian gods. Her position among the gods is complex and matched in ambiguity only by that, among humans, of the cholita. Indeed, when the Pachamama is represented in human form, she is cast as a stout and resolute cholita.

Conclusion: *The Return of the Repressed*

In this connection, certain implicit asymmetries deriving from the colonial order are thrown into bolder relief. Such is the case with the notable gender disjunction in the cultural criteria of ethnicity and class that is clearly visible in *La Chaskañawi*. In it the (ambivalently) valued but alluring strengths of native culture, linked through maternal bonds to the national soil, are projected onto dominated women, cholas like Claudina, while native cultural debits are attached to the threatening and brutish masculinity of dominated men. In both cases, of course, elite recensions of the Indigenous stem from the process of 'ostensive self-identification through negation' (White 1978: 121), in which Indigenous men and women are conceived in terms of what they lack from the elite repertoire of values rather than what they possess on their own. In this, Indian men, brought into urban workshops as the elite's impure mestizo-cholo hands, and Indian women, cholitas ensconced in market-stalls and elite households, inherited the lacks imputed to the vulgar estates and lower classes of Spain—an absence of ennobling honour and shame. But they also inherited by their Indianness a tie to the homeland coveted by elites, and in this the supposed wanton accessibility of the cholita/Pachamama as mistress/adoptive mother is revalued as a vehicle to patriotism. Thus the narratives of elites are able to recast the colonial asymmetry of power into the tragic romance of their particular *amor patria*.

In their twentieth-century passage to the post- and neocolonial situation, nationalist elites have found it necessary to romance the precolonial past of the ex-colonized. But they do so in the chariest of ways, revalourizing 'the Indigenous' in terms of class and gender such that nothing is ever what it seems. The complex semiotic manoeuvres of pageants like Oruro's carnival make it possible for participants to simultaneously celebrate and vituperate Indian heritage, and to assimilate the dominated into sexual fantasies of the upper-class cultural descendants of Spanish conquerors even while projecting blame for the initiation and consequences of this 'romance' onto their 'temptress' victims. While this seems a truly difficult semiotic achievement, it has been greatly facilitated by the nature of their source material. Elements of the rural culture of conversion and self-civilization have been adapted to the ends of the anti-Indian urban mestizo-cholo working-class culture, which struggles to become non-Indian with the same determination that elites employ to peg it as such. In their recensions of this topos, self-civilization has become self-hatred and contradictions of gender and ethnicity have become the torments of the prison house of class. These have then been taken up with a vengeance by elites.

The conversion narrative in all its guises embodies a cultural synthesis that is about the coming-into-being of a social whole, in which conversion can never be completed and where the 'whole' is always envisioned as an ongoing antagonistic relationship between mutually unassimilable parts. In a way, the cultural insularity of Spanish and Indian that these narratives presuppose and propose to transcend is recreated in the very enactment of such narratives in their various contexts and versions. In the more isolated of rural towns, members of fiesta-cargo systems continue to sacrifice and play out *tinkus* in colony-derived but counter-hegemonic festival rituals. But it is the theatre of nationalist elites that continues to provide a hegemonic canon to which rural Indians and the mestizo-cholo popular classes must respond, whether by emulating, revising or rejecting it. Whatever option they choose, there is little room for manoeuvre now that colonialism has given way to nationalism. Whether launching programmes of resistance in isolated hamlets or on the stage of national politics, these are constrained by the conceptual schemas, market forces, armies and lending consortia of the postcolonial world.

Notes

1   The present essay is a foreshortened version of an article published two decades ago (Abercrombie 1992). I have not updated the analysis or cited the abundant work published since then on carnival, devils, cholas or pageant politics, nor have I tried to account for shifts in pageant practice and the nationalist embedding of dance since the 2006 election of Evo Morales (who has made a show of joining in carnival dance since election to office, like many prior presidents). The biggest shift in folkloric pageantry since Morales (starting a decade before his election) is the increase in parallel performances, usually prior to the 'main event' of rural peoples, performing 'customs' in their own clothes, as part of a contestatory 'Anata Andina' that aims to call urban folklore into question. Devils, temptresses and penitence, however, play little part in these new events. Although I do not cite them in the text (completed prior to its initial 1992 publication), many works have since explored its themes, including my own work on colonial/postcolonial intercultural production (Abercrombie 1996; 1998), and another essay on Oruro's carnival,

expanding on the postcolonial predicament/nationalist angles (Abercrombie 2003). Max Harris (2002; 2003) has called my analysis into question in his own work on Oruro's carnival, finding that my attention to the conversion and conquest framing narrative and the work of penitence leaves too little room for considering costumed dancing as a form of resistance. For further work on the history of costumed festivals and processional dance, see Margot Beyersdorff (1997), Juan Carlos Estenssoro (1991), Antoinette Molinié (1995) and Juan Pedro Viquiera Albán (2004). The history of elite projects involving Indians in Oruro has been explored by Fernando Cajías de la Vega (2004), Oscar Cornblit (1995) and Ann Zulawski (1995). Just how *indigenismo* applauded Incas while decrying contemporary Indians is explained in Cecilia G. Mendez (1991). On the roles of folkloric festivals and the image of the chola in indigenista and contemporary political imagination, see Robert Albro (1998, 2000), Rossana Barragan (1997), Andrew Canessa (2005), Marisol de la Cadena (2000), Leslie Gill (1994), Daniel M. Goldstein (2004), Laura Gotkowitz (2007), Zoila S. Mendoza (1999), Silvia Rivera Cusicanqui (1996), Josefa Salmón (1997), Julie Skurski (1994) and Mary Weismantel (2001). The rise of the Indianist movement is treated by Xavier Albó (1991), Charles Hale (1997)and Sarah Radcliffe and Sallie Westwood (1996). The arrival of regional folkloric competitions and the performance of tradition is treated by Stuart Alexander Rockefeller (1998). On the tios of the mines, see Pascale Absi (2005) and Enrique Tandeter (1993). In a model ethnography of folkloric dance in Quillacollo, Tobias Reu (2009) finds sociality, of a sort akin to the 'civil society' voluntary associations which formed the backbone of the 'sectores sociales' that brought Morales to power, to be in itself a major goal of participation. Field and archival work in and on K'ulta, Condo, Oruro and Potosí was supported by the Joint Committee on Latin American Studies of the American Council of Learned Societies and Social Science Research Council, Fulbright and the Wenner-Gren Foundation for Anthropological Research. An early draft of this paper was written while a Rockefeller Foundation Resident Fellow at the Institute for Advanced Study, School of Social Sciences, Princeton, NJ. Bolivians too numerous to list deserve special thanks (see acknowledgements in the original essay). Responsibility for errors remains, however, entirely mine.

2   By 'elites', I here refer to relatively comfortable bourgeois professionals and those whose participation in the festival accompanies upwardly mobile aspirations.

3   In Bolivia, the category 'Indian' is a construct largely of elites and anthropologists. I use the term (with or without scare quotes) in reference to these categorical constructs. Since the 1952 revolution, the core of persons designated as 'Indian'—rural subsistence producers living 'traditional' lives—have been termed *campesinos*, 'peasants', although this term, too, has become stigmatized, as euphemisms often are. While 'Indian' has been re-appropriated by the mostly urban *indianista* (as opposed to *indigenista*) movement led by Aymara- and Quechua-speaking intellectuals (see Albó 1987), it remains for most rural people an insult. I label rural cultural formations 'rural peoples' or 'rural groups', which must be understood through their forms of self-identification and in relation to the larger sociocultural wholes in which they

are enmeshed. See Thomas Abercrombie (1991) on the problem of ethnic, racial and language labels in the Andes.

4 On Oruro's carnival, see Augusto Beltrán Heredia (1956), Julia Elena Fortún (1961), Alberto Guerra Gutierrez (1970; 1984), Niver Montes Camacho (1986) and June Nash (1979).

5 The procession of Gran Poder in La Paz has been studied by Xavier Albó and Matías Preiswerk (1986). The pilgrimage-pageants of Copacabana and Quillacollo have had little attention.

6 As we shall see, 'play' is the operative word here. The very fact that Indian roles are play-acted lets dancers enjoy both being Indian and renouncing the Indian. Theatrics help to insulate elite pageant participants from fully understanding the contradiction; they certainly need not experience the pain to which such ambivalence leads in the lives of those portrayed in dance.

7 Dance groups are organized as confraternities tied to neighbourhood, trade or class.

8 And, since 2001, a UNESCO Masterpiece of the Intangible or Oral Patrimony of Humanity.

9 Doris Sommer has noted that this struggle engenders a special form of allegorical relationship between nationalist politics and novelized romance in nineteenth-century Latin American novels (and in twentieth-century indigenista novels like La Chaskañawi [1947] by Carlos Medinaceli). She argues that liberalism's need for homogenous citizenries produced a plethora of stories about cross-class romance, in which conservative neocolonial outlooks provided obstacles along the path to consummation (1991: 109–10). Sommer finds 'a metonymic association between romantic love that needs the state's blessing and political legitimacy that needs to be founded on love' (ibid.:121).

10 Manichaeanism, named for a third-century Persian, progagated the idea that humanity was created as a result of a cosmological struggle between the independent principles of good (purely spiritual, embodied in light) and evil (material, embodied in darkness), which continue to war. It resembles the orthodox Christian dichotomy between light and dark, good and evil. The Albigensian sect was an ascetic form of Manichaeanism that flourished in Europe between the eleventh and thirteenth centuries, persecuted by the Inquisition for their heretical refusal to accept the divinity of Christ while embodied and hence the Eucharist. By extension, the terms—especially Manichaean—are often applied to those who believe in absolute, opposing principles of good and evil without reference to the specific cosmology that produced the Manichaean beliefs. Perhaps qualifying as Manichaean are Orureño appeals to the devil/Indigenous deities for material prosperity alongside penitential bodily offerings to the Virgin for spiritual well-being.

11 See Linda J. Seligmann (1989) for a recent analysis of the chola in Peruvian society, and a useful review of the literature on 'cultural brokers.' The shamanic complex discussed by Michael Taussig (1987), with analogues in Bolivia's pilgrimage centres, also seems to occupy this cultural space.

12 In rural indigenous towns, *vecinos* are those who, affiliating themselves with 'national culture' and living rather through commerce than from subsistence farming, define themselves as non-Indigenous. The term derives from colonial usage—in Spanish-dominated cities, *vecinos* were those with private property and full rights in municipal affairs as opposed to those who were merely resident (with a fixed abode) or present (without one). In the nineteenth-century rural context, the term came to label those—now called mestizos rather than *indios*—who hoped for full citizenship status through their participation in capitalist property and economic regimes.

13 For an illustrated history of La Paz cholita dress, see M. Lissette Canavesi de Sahonero, who traces the dress and the label 'chola' to provincial lower-class types of Madrid (1987: 23). On the semiotics of cloth and clothing in the Andes, see Verónica Cereceda (1986), Teresa Gisbert et al. (1987), Mary Ann Medlin (1983) and Lynn Ann Meisch (1986). On bodily decoration as a signifying social skin, see Terence S. Turner (1980). There are as yet no region-level Andean studies of the clothing system as a whole. On Guatemala, see Carol Hendrickson (1990).

14 In the rural context, store-bought clothes are called *ropa de civil*, a usage perhaps learnt by those conscripted to the Bolivian military.

15 The ethnographic literature has also been ambivalent about the mestizo-cholo—works sympathetic to 'rural indigenous cultures' execrate the mestizo-cholo as an anti-Indian exploiter; works on the urban and mining 'proletariat' sympathize with them as an exploited class. For background, see the bibliography in Seligmann (1989).

16 Commercial activity was formally habilitated in a royal pragmatic of 1682, which decreed that 'to maintain [. . .] manufactures [. . .] is not contrary to the quality, immunities and prerogatives of the nobility [. . .] so long as those who [. . .] maintain manufactures do not labor with their own persons but through their servants and officials' (Kamen 1983: 263, quoted in Bakewell 1988: 176). On the 'crisis of the aristocracy', see José Antonio Maravall (1979; 1984) for whom resulting efforts to discipline *el vulgo* typify the Baroque.

17 'Over time Spaniards and Indians mix in a way that transforms the offspring completely into whites with coloring, in the second generation, that cannot be distinguished from that of Spaniards, yet they are not called Spaniards until the fourth generation' (Juan and Ulloa 1978b: 291).

18 In the imperial and colonial era, Spain's New World possessions were called Las Indias, a usage dating from Columbus' famous mis-identification of the Americas with the land of the Grand Khan (India). And from there, the identification of the inhabitants of Spain's new lands as 'Indians'.

19 Women of the Indian and *casta* lower orders were in Mexico thought especially capable in the application of love magic (Behar 1989), like Spain's Celestina.

20 On the policing of the excesses of, especially, plebeian women in early modern Seville, see Mary Elizabeth Perry (1980, especially Chapter 10). Recent studies of colonial efforts to control women's sexuality, and the relationship between gender,

class, race and ethnicity include Silvia Marina Arrom (1985); Patricia Seed (1988); and Asunción Lavrin (1989). For the Peruvian case from Inca to colonial times, see Irene Silverblatt (1987).

21 Even the late colonial paintings illustrating complex racial terminology portray racial types engaged in work activities by which they were, perhaps, determined. For examples, see Angel Rosenblat (1954: plates between pp. 168–9) and Silvia Marina Arrom (1985: 102–3).

22 Note that the chola's dress style, quite similar to contemporary chola costume, is significantly different from, if modelled on, the creole lady's dress (see Canavesi de Sahonero 1987). It is strikingly similar to both mestizo and Spanish creole or 'white' costumes of the mid-eighteenth century, which Jorge Juan and Antonio de Ulloa saw as differing primarily in the quality of cloth, not in design (1978a: I, 368–70; and plate 13, between pp. 378–9). Note that *blanco* (white) became a frequently used descriptor only in the 1780s, just as *criollo* was becoming problematic for the numbers of Indians and Africans who were also called that.

  Note that Temple's male cholo is fully distinguishable from the creole only by his (removable) patterned cape.

23 While 'creole' in the Spanish Indies came to mean 'white of Spanish origin' (once *indios criollos* had been reduced to cholos and *negros criollos* to *negros*), in the British West Indies, by contrast, the term 'creole' came to be taken as a term of admixture.

24 On the transfer of such spectacles to the Indies, see José Juan Arrom (1967), Constantino Bayle (1951) and Richard C. Trexler (1984).

25 Arzáns' description of the fiestas of 1608 is analysed by Lewis Hanke (1956–57).

26 'Potosí 1751. Testimonio de la causa contra varios yndios por querer seguir la costumbre del robo de metales' (Testimony of Charges against Various Indians for Intending to Continue the Custom of Theft of Metals) (Archivo General de Indias [General Archive of the Indies], no. 807, Lima). At this time, Bolivia—which became an independent republic and named after Simon Bolivar in 1825—was known as Alto Peru (Upper Peru). See Miguel Rubio Zapata's essay in this volume for more discussion of Peruvian devil dance and for masks that signify the seven deadly sins. —Eds.

27 These well-documented events are analysed in Cajías de la Vega (1983; 1987).

28 See Peter Burke (1978) on the sixteenth- to eighteenth-century European creation of a 'high public culture' distinguished from plebeian practice. King Charles III officially forbade the public performance of *autos sacramentales* during Corpus Christi in 1780 (ibid.: 242).

29 Oruro newspapers of the late nineteenth century to about 1940 describe elite carnival balls in great detail, along with histories of carnival going back to Roman and Greek sources, but bypass colonial Spanish ones. A 1924 notice typifies references to 'Indian' carnival: 'As usual the workers' groups of Diablos; Incas; Sicos; Tundikis; Llameros; etc. etc. will continue dancing through all the streets of the city. These uncultured customs persist again this year, but we shelter the hope that by next year

they will have been abolished' (Manuel J. Rodriguez, *La Palestra*, 28 February 1924. My translation).

30 Claudina localizes her powers: 'Estas tetas arrastran más que cuatro carretas' (These tits pull more than four carts) (Medinaceli 1978: 136). Here the author limits to the cholita the powers assigned to women generally in the Spanish saying: Pueden mas dos tetas que cien carretas (Two tits can do more than a hundred carts) (Brandes 1981: 220).

31 Celebrated in Oruro during the carnival, the Virgen del Socavón is, like the Virgin of Copacabana from whom she descends, an advocation of Candelaria. Her feast honours the 'Purification of the Virgin' on Candlemas (2 February), established as a confluence of Mary's purification, following Judaic law, eight days after Jesus' birth, and a Roman procession of candles. Arzáns' baroque literary history of Potosí (1965[1702–35]) attributes many miracles to Copacabana and Candelaria, usually in connection with Indians' mine accidents.

32 On the Diablada, see Julia Elena Fortún (1961).

33 Oruro's population has doubled to over 200,000 since the author's original 1988 fieldwork there.

34 Founded as a silver-mining town in 1606, Oruro achieved rapid growth when it became a station on Bolivia's first rail line. With mining in decline, Oruro has lately prospered as the hub of the country's smuggling trade. On Oruro history, see Alberto Crespo (1967), José de Mesa and Teresa Gisbert (1970) and Ann Zulawski (1985).

35 Nathan Wachtel (1977) treats the Incas dance of Oruro. Luis Millones (1988) and Manuel Burga (1988) provide ethnographic and historical studies of this dance in Peru.

36 Some of the organizers and members of two groups, the Tinkus Tollkas, 'sons-in-law/wife-taker Tinkus', and its spin-off, Tinkus Huakchas, 'orphaned Tinkus', are former *vecinos* of a provincial town, to which some still return to bulk their Indian godchildren's produce, photograph 'real' *tinku* battles and purchase 'costumes'.

37 This has also happened in the Virgin of Urqupiña celebration in Quillacollo, from which former *campesino* groups have been purged. As Xavier Albó and Matías Preiswerk (1984) note, this has not happened in the Gran Poder festival of La Paz, perhaps because of the greater social distance between the elite of the capital and the dancing resident clubs.

38 Each group's *predilecta*, who wears a beauty-queen sash, is elected in intra-group pageants from among each group's *walipoleras*, cheerleaders who wear especially short polleras, knee-length high-heeled boots, etc. The *walipoleras* head each section of the larger dance troupes. More women dance the 'ordinary' cholita role, wearing something closer to 'real' cholita dress, if always more risqué.

39 Until the 1970s, the china supay role was danced exclusively by men in drag, adding yet a further layer of sinfulness to the temptations they offered.

40 So wrote the seventeenth-century chronicler Ramos Gavilán (1976[1621]: 251; my translation) of the liberating powers of devotion to the Virgin of Copacabana.

41 The dance was part of the celebration of the Exaltation of the Cross in Caracollo, a way-station on the highway between Oruro and La Paz.

42 In Fig. 5, the title page of Larrinaga Salazar's 1626 manual on the office of the 'protector general of the Indians of Perú', the Indian 'America' huddles in chains under the protective wing of the Hapsburg eagle. She says: 'Sub umbra alarum tuarum protege me' (Protect me under the shadow of the wings), to which 'the crown' replies: 'Corona Inclyta Proteget te' (The glorious crown will protect you). This request and reply literally, though without acknowledgement, quote two separate biblical passages: Psalm 16:8 and Proverbs 4:9. In the latter, wisdom (*sapienta*) is the presumed protector, who will protect 'Corona Inclyta', that is, with a glorious crown.

43 She is, according to Ramos Gavilan (writing of Copacabana), '[. . .] Empress of Heaven [. . .] before whom demons tremble [. . .] a warrior [so] strong, that no enemy remains whose head has not felt the force of [her] feet.' (1976[1621]: 254. My translation).

44 On the Tios, see Taussig (1980), drawing on Nash (1979). The latter draws on Guerra Gutierrez (1970). On Taussig (1980), see Tristan Platt (1983) and Peter Gose (1987).

45 These events go nearly unnoticed by Oruro's newspapers and politicians. Carnival dance groups compete on Temptation Saturday for prizes in a folklore festival in Oruro's stadium but do not dance on Temptation Sunday. Elites do come on Sunday to watch and have picnics, in which libations to the Pachamama are frequently heard.

The Diablada of Oruro
A Photographic Essay

MIGUEL GANDERT

Flying into El Alto, the Bolivian Indian city at 4,000 metres on the Altiplano above La Paz, I am struck by the contrast of the two neighbouring cities—La Paz, its old colonial roots, with its intrusion of modernity, and El Alto, its urban sprawl, unfinished brick buildings spreading as far as the eye can see. El Alto is the twenty-first-century migrant city: in 1952, its population was 11,000; it is estimated now to be over 850,000, surpassing the population of its older neighbour.

Thinking of the words from the late Mexican anthropologist Guillermo Bonfil Batalla's book *México Profundo* (1996), I try to make sense of the tension I see with my camera. Bonfil Batalla describes the conflict as between the imaginary linear time of Europe and profound circular time of precolonial America. According to Bonfil Batalla, this clash is reflected in heart of the mestizo, descendent of both worlds yet never fully accepted by the dominant society. The idea of Indio is still considered lower class and an insult when spoken. It is hard to find fidelity with the imaginary when the face in the mirror reflects the profound.

In conversations with Bolivian anthropologist Javier Romero, we discuss good metaphors for the Andean world—agriculture representing the indigenous past and circular time, contrasted with mining as linear time and the symbol of European oppression. Although there was mining prior to Spanish conquest of the Americas, gold and silver were the driving force for the earliest conquerors. If one-third of the minerals had stayed in Bolivia, instead of bankrolling Europe for three hundred years, Bolivia would have been Switzerland.

In February 2002, I was in Bolivia for Carnaval. It was a historic year for the festival and I was excited to be there. The proclamation of Carnaval de Oruro in May 2001 as Masterpiece of the Oral and Intangible Heritage of Humanity by UNESCO reinforced the significance of ritual to the identity of Bolivia.

Waiting in La Paz, I didn't know if I would make it to Carnaval. The rural people of Bolivia had blocked the road between La Paz and Oruro with enormous boulders, stopping commerce and tourist travel in order to get the attention of the national government. These blockades or *bloqueos* are a non-violent form of civil disobedience practised by the peoples as a key strategy, used to change laws as well as overthrow central governments. The *bloqueo* was one of the tactics that helped the indigenous people assert their political will, resulting in the 2006 election of Evo Morales, a *cocalero* (coca grower), as Bolivia's first Indian president.

Negotiations between the government and the rural people continued; tourists, dancers and musicians did not know if they would be able to make the pilgrimage to Oruro. But as luck would have it, the day before the Entrada, the most dramatic part of the ten-day celebration, the *bloqueo* was removed and I was able to join thousands of pilgrims to Oruro's Santuario de La Virgen del Socavón, the Virgin of mine disasters, a chapel which had been constructed on top of one the region's richest silver mines.

The pilgrimage, in which over 40,000 dancers and musicians participate, traditionally begins with the Diablada. The ritual of the Dance of the Devil is thought to go back to the Uru people of the region and, according to dance leaders, is believed to been performed for 2,000 years or more. In addition to the Diablos, condors and bears are also represented in the dance and are thought to date back to its earliest period.

With the coming of Spanish colonial Catholicism, the devils took on a new symbolic meaning. The dancers pride themselves on being descendants of miners and, like family, the devil is referred to as El Tío (uncle). Like the Diablos, the miners are sentenced to work in hell, the underground mines. It is ironic that as many as 400 devils were led by only one pale-skinned, blue-eyed, caped Archangel San Miguel. The cacique, when asked about the symbolism of this inverted power structure, looked at me as if the answer was obvious, 'It was all the *españoles* ever needed.'

For the Indian and the mestizo, there is still a need to create a fidelity to the profound. Thus, when a community feast is celebrated, they sacrifice, pray and dance to both the past and the present. The Diablada of the Carnival de Oruro celebrates the multilayered cultural heritage of Bolivia. The stories expressed in these dances negotiate and mediate indigeneity and Christianity whose conflicts remain unresolved to this day.

FIGURE 1. Gathering of the Diablada, Oruro, 2002.

FIGURE 2. El Tío with trident, Oruro, 2005.

(ABOVE) **FIGURE 3**. Santuario de Nuestra Señora del Socavón with silverware and plates, Oruro, 2005. (BELOW) **FIGURE 4**. Diablo with condor and soldier, Oruro, 2002.

(ABOVE) **FIGURE 5.** El Tío with horns, Oruro, 2005. (BELOW) **FIGURE 6.** Las Diablas, Oruro, 2005.

FIGURE 7. El Tío with reptiles and condor, Oruro, 2005.

(ABOVE) **FIGURE 8.** Andean bears, Oruro, 2005. (BELOW) **FIGURE 9.** Dance of the Diablos, Oruro, 2005.

(LEFT) **FIGURE 10**. Condor with Diablos and San Miguel, Oruro, 2005. (RIGHT) **FIGURE 11**. Diabla with large horns, Oruro, 2005.

FIGURE 12. Archangel San Miguel, Oruro, 2005.

Resignified Devils
Performing Imaginations of Peruvian Blackness

MONICA ROJAS

Twenty-seventh February 1988 was a sweltering day in Lima. I arrived at one of our leaders' three-storey house around 11 a.m. and was immediately directed to the rooftop terrace. On my way up I greeted people already in costume going the opposite way on the steep and narrow stairs. On the roof I found people getting ready in the small space enclosed by four unfinished brick walls, narrowly avoiding getting entangled in clotheslines as they changed. I looked out over rooftops of worn-out colonial and modern buildings. In the distance, facing east, I could see houses recently built out of mats, cardboard and sometimes bricks at the bottom of hills on the outskirts of the city. Someone's request for a safety pin interrupted my viewing. I proceeded to begin getting dressed. Participants helped one another put on our black bandanas and costumes over a background of non-stop jokes and laughter. We were happy and excited about what was about to happen.

It was noon and the sun was close to the highest point in the sky when the dancers and musicians lined up near *plaza las cabezas* (the heads). We were getting ready to dance around the streets of el Rimac neighbourhood as it used to be home to a large number of Peruvians of African descent. In all there were around 25 of us, people of all ages and colours. There were members of the newly formed Movimiento Negro Francisco Congo (MNFC or Francisco Congo Black Movement), their family members and friends, Grupo Cultural Yuyachkani members, professional dancers and feminist activists. We had been invited by Juan Carlos 'Juanchi' Vasquez (president of the MNFC and an accomplished dancer) specifically to participate in this event. What I remember most from the overall experience is the spirit we brought to the practices and, of course, the day of the parade. Oh yeahhh! We all shared a strong interest in learning about and spreading our ancestral traditions and identities as Peruvians, and, most importantly, giving voice to the cultural contribution of the people of African descent in Peru. And although this art form had traditionally been a male dance, men and women (the majority, in fact) alike wanted to be part of this revival. It was fun. We, leaders and dancers, were finally there. It was the day, our day. The drumming began and very quickly the crowd around us tripled. We formed two columns and, at the call of the bell, we began our parade.

That day we danced the limeño Son de los Diablos (Devil's dance from Lima), a street masquerade parade dance whose origins date back to thirteenth-century Corpus Christi celebrations in Europe, which arrived in the Americas with European colonization (Santa Cruz 1974; Tompkins 1981; Durand 1988; Romero 1988; Rivas 2002).

These Corpus Christi festivities organized their procession in an order that mirrored the social hierarchy. As captive enemies in ancient Roman traditions or as evil forces in the Apocalypse, people and institutions of lowest social rank initiated the processions representing the grotesque figures: '[I]n Lima, [these] dancers were only blacks' (Rivas 2002: 43). Since Lima was the city with the highest concentration of black people in the western hemisphere during the seventeenth century (Bowser 1974), it is no surprise that the city's Corpus Christi celebration was characterized by the participation of African descendants. At these processions, all the brotherhoods or *cofradías* opened the parade divided into male and female groups. Within the male group, some paraded as birds, animals, devils or monsters with horns (Rivas 2002; Tompkins 1981).[1]

Since its origin, this dance evolved and reached me, 700 years later, as a staged dance. However, I didn't fully appreciate it until I was recruited to help return the Devil's dance to the streets on that hot summer day in February 1988.

In this essay I recount the history of the Son de los Diablos to show how the colonial and postcolonial performative contexts in which this dance emerged and re-emerged helped shape this art form throughout history. Recognizing the colonial imposition of this dance upon the Afro-descendant population in Lima as the first stage, I identify four more important moments in the history of the Son de los Diablos: the resignification of this dance by Afro-Peruvians and its transference to the carnival context; the staging of the dance and other dances in the effort to construct an Afro-Peruvian repertoire and identity; the revival of the dance and its return to the streets; and the adoption of this dance by theatre groups who identified it as a rich source of theatrical techniques and artistic expression.

This dance, with its history, is significant in that it shows how Afro-Peruvian artists and activists resist misinterpretations by resignifying symbols as part of their unique culture and tradition. Elizabeth Alexander's work (1994) inspired me to think of how the space between the stage and the daily experiences of Afro-Peruvians opens an avenue to think about what images or memories—primarily racially determined but also marked by region, class, gender and experience, and viewed differently by different subgroups (i.e. Afro-Peruvians and non-Afro-Peruvians)—are triggered at the moment of collective spectatorship. Moreover, how do Afro-Peruvians imagine themselves and are imagined through a current version of the Son de los Diablos whose interpreters are mostly mestizo and criollo?[2] My discussion, framed within these questions, will explore efforts, contradictions, concerns and successes within the Afro-Peruvian artist and activist community. I will sometimes weave a personal narrative reflecting upon my close involvement in and practice of this dance during its revival in the late 1980s, its direction in the 1990s, my fieldwork in 2004 and, later on, when I, a diasporic Peruvian, introduced the US Northwest to the Son de los Diablos.

Staging

I was born into a limeño middle-class family two months before General Juan Velasco took over power in the military coup of October 1968. I remember the economic stress towards the end of his dictatorship (1968–75). Everything was scarce. I see myself holding my mother's hand waiting in endless queues to purchase sacks of rice and sugar. One of my earliest musical memories of the time is a TV show called 'Danzas y Canciones del Peru' (Dances and Songs from Peru). This was also the time when patriotic songs such as 'Y se llama Perú' (It's Called Peru) became popular. My father told me that Velasco requested Peruvian composer Augusto Polo Campos to write this song, and, he added, 'that's also when we limeños started hearing Andean music on the radio for the first time.'

In a historical study of the musical production in Peru, both Zoila S. Mendoza (2000) and Thomas Turino (1991) describe how Andean music was promoted to represent Peru as a nation in different periods of time: after the Peruvian–Chilean War of the Pacific (1879–83), during the Republican era and during the government of Augusto B. Leguía (term 1919–30). The next important period was during Velasco's government when his strong nationalist agenda led to the proliferation of cultural institutions, this time, at the national level.

One very important umbrella organization founded in the 1960s was the Casa de la Cultura (Culture House), which in 1972 became the Instituto Nacional de Cultura (INC or National Institute of Culture) (Turino 1991; Mendoza 2000). Velasco sought to incorporate folkloric music and dance from different regions into the construction of a 'truly integrated national culture that fully assumes the multiplicity of cultures of the Peruvian reality' (Mendoza 2000: 71). One strategy was the creation of a national dance group: El Conjunto Nacional de Folklore, whose first elected director was the artist Victoria Santa Cruz. This nationalist trend and the selection of Santa Cruz as the director of the national dance group were the result of previous national and international events.

The 1950s and 60s saw the civil rights movement in the US and the independence of African and Caribbean countries. Social movements around the world at this time provoked changes that marked a period in history some theorists see as the break between the modern and the postmodern eras. There were new questions about differences and excluded voices, and new social concerns that influenced those intellectuals who began rethinking the sociocultural and political situation of Africans and African diasporic groups—as was the case in Peru. These events paralleled a wave of Afro-Peruvians, among them mostly indigenous peoples, migrating from the rural areas as part of a migration spurt in the 1950s and 60s. Heidi Feldman (2000) notes that both Afro-Peruvian migration and a threat of the Andeanization of Lima may have spurred the capital city's elite to defensively reaffirm their criollo culture by looking at Afro-Peruvian art and including it as part of the criollo repertoire.

It was then that a group of intellectuals took certain musical and dance genres with heavier African influence to the stage for the first time. The pioneer of this group was white upper-class Peruvian intellectual José Durand. With the aid of multifaceted Afro-Peruvian artist Porfirio Vasquez, Durand reunited a group of Afro-Peruvian and non-Afro-Peruvian artists and presented them at the prestigious stage of the Teatro Municipal de Lima (Municipal Theatre of Lima) for the first time in 1956 under the name of Compañía Pancho Fierro (Pancho Fierro Company, named after the early–nineteenth-century popular watercolour painter usually considered 'mulatto'). Durand accomplished this 'in spite of the disgust of many exquisite idiots' (Campos 1987: n.p.) and 'the strong prejudice and racism of the time' as Durand himself told me during several conversations between 1987 and 1988.

Durand had a particular relationship with the Son de los Diablos. 'My aunts, who were already old then—and I'm talking 1925 or 1926!—taught me how to walk with a Son de los Diablos song,'[3] he told me. Durand's Pancho Fierro Company revived this song and staged this dance for the first time in 1956.

Within the next two years, a few members of Pancho Fierro left the company mainly for monetary concerns (Durand, personal communication, 2004). One of these members was Nicomedes Santa Cruz, considered Peru's most famous Afro-Peruvian poet, intellectual and activist known mainly for his *décimas*, who decided to start a new project with another key character in the creation of a new Afro-Peruvian repertoire—his sister Victoria. In 1958, Victoria and Nicomedes created their own company called Cumanana with new artists and a few former members of Pancho Fierro. Artists and researchers see this moment as the turning point of a new era. Victoria and Nicomedes isolated certain music and dance genres, which until then had been part of a larger coastal criollo repertoire, helping create both an Afro-Peruvian repertoire and identity (Romero 1994; Durand, personal communication

2003). This unique repertoire included the *festejo* and the *landó* as the two most important umbrella names for other subgenres. One of the *festejo* subgenres is the Son de los Diablos, a dance featured by Cumanana and subsequent projects led by Victoria Santa Cruz.

Coincidently, parallel to the birth of Compañía Pancho Fierro and Cumanana, the Son de los Diablos as a street carnival dance began to fade away from Lima. There are several explanations for this phenomenon. The most common—and most probable—explanation is the prohibition of carnival celebrations in the late 1950s under Manuel Prado's government. An article in *Música Peruana* explains that since the 1930s, Peruvians, from both upper and lower classes, unhappy with the political, social and economic situation in the country, found in carnival the best opportunity to protest in a subtle way. Then violence reached its peak in 1958; Manuel Prado prohibited carnival celebrations around 1959 by supreme decree N. 348 and the Son de los Diablos vanished from the streets. The disappearance of this dance at this time helped highlight the importance of 'rescuing' it for the stage.

Through their compilations, recordings and theatrical works, Victoria and Nicomedes Santa Cruz not only tried to tell the history and the contribution of Afro-Peruvians but also attempted to raise awareness among them about their past and present. However, the success of the Santa Cruzes' work helped their pupils find monetary alternatives. Many of them left Cumanana to teach or to form their own groups, as happened with members of Victoria's 1960s Teatro y Danzas Negras del Peru. The best example is the famous Afro-Peruvian dance group Peru Negro (Black Peru), formed in 1970 and born out of the company members' realization that their artistic skills could generate a steady income. According to Feldman (2000), both Peru Negro and Victoria Santa Cruz (as the director of the Conjunto Nacional de Folklore) received strong support from Velasco's government. This support made an impact on the creation of an Afro-Peruvian repertoire and identity.

People in charge of 'rescuing' and promoting these art forms are usually members of urban, cosmopolitan, intellectual, middle-class groups (Dalhaus 1980; Turino 1991, 2000; Rice 1994; Scruggs 1999; Mendoza 2000; Guss 1980). They influence the staging of traditions by utilizing folklorization as a tool to shape the idea of an anonymous 'authentic' identity. In Peru, folklorization became essential to state efforts for national-identity construction (Mendoza 2000) in which the Conjunto Nacional de Folklore embodied the multiplicity of cultures in an integrated one- or two-hour show. The final product, however, presented a wide variety of problems and contradictions. Time limitations on stage meant showing those features that would be considered 'most representative', 'most traditional' or 'characteristic' of the people represented (for example, a costume, a song). This system of symbols informs the larger population of what is 'representative' of those minorities depicted on stage.

In the case of the Afro-Peruvian tradition, the Santa Cruzes' work sought to educate Afro-Peruvians and the larger population about their past and to raise consciousness about their present. To achieve this, many of the songs and dances that were staged used colonial times as a context. Javier Leon (2003) points out that around this time, the iconography of US minstrelsy also influenced the imagination about black Peruvians, contributing to the construction of a Peruvian blackness with similar stereotypical physical features. This is seen in characters such as Doña Pepa (a Peruvian version of Aunt Jemima) who wears a bandana, polka-dot dress and apron and is usually an icon of Afro-Peruvian cuisine.

While in the US 'civil rights movement and anti-discriminatory laws have, if anything, heightened the sensitivity of the nation's population about racial discrimination' (Oboler 2005: 75), Peru has not experienced such a process. Therefore, symbols such as Doña Pepa, and everyday commentary related to stereotypical phenotype (for example, thick lips, bulgy eyes, wide noses), although similar to stereotypes in the US, are embedded in different discourses that, on one hand, hide or disguise racist attitudes in Peruvian society and, on the other, resignify these symbols as icons of Afro-Peruvian culture.

FIGURE 1. Rustica banner.

Throughout history, artists and activists who promote Afro-Peruvian art use these same symbols and the traits of their cultural subgroup they have learnt to be 'characteristic' or 'traditional' in order to construct a unified identity that simultaneously empowers them, distinguishes them from the rest of the population and is recognizable by the larger audience as 'theirs'. While some artists have found in this mutual relationship a source for a stable income, others (especially in the popular-theatre arena) have resignified these symbols to empower Afro-Peruvian identity. They see them as 'tradition' but through a resignification of that which makes them traditional—that is, the contribution of artists such as Victoria Santa Cruz as opposed to a tradition informed by a colonial past.

State promotion and consequent commercialization of these art forms' choreographies, costumes, symbols and songs helped create a standard repertoire and a model for subsequent dance companies. The Conjunto Nacional de Folklore's and Peru Negro's Son de los Diablos are the staged versions of this dance that I encountered in the 1970s. In the 1980s the Son de los Diablos experienced another transformation.

Revival

By the late 1960s and early 70s, Nicomedes Santa Cruz, inspired by the US civil rights movement, the Black Power movement and the independence of African and Caribbean countries, began to speak, in his poetry and his newspaper articles, about social justice and discrimination. A young generation of Afro-Peruvian intellectuals felt the need to become active in the Afro-Peruvian community and saw in Nicomedes the leader they were lacking. One of these young activists was Jose 'Cheche' Campos, an educator and now a professor at the Enrique Guzman y Valle University in Lima (better known as La Cantuta).

The first attempt at organizing the collective was Cheche Campos' Instituto de Investigaciones Afro-Peruano (INAPE or the Afro-Peruvian Research Institute) in early 1980s. Among the people who joined Campos' efforts was Andrés Mandros. A younger member of the Afro-Peruvian community, the accomplished artist Juan Carlos 'Juanchi' Vasquez, met and developed close ties with Mandros as they shared similar political interests. Through this friendship Juanchi envisioned the creation of the MNFC[4] (also referred to as the movimiento), which seemed, and still seems, for many the greatest hope for Afro-Peruvians thus far.

On the first page of their 1987 manifesto, the presidential committee of the MNFC and the rest of the executive board state:

Hacemos un llamado a todas las personas identificadas con la causa del negro en el Perú para juntos impulsar este movimiento, autónomo, pluralista y democrático; orientado hacia la construcción de una patria libre, donde convivamos todos los grupos étnico-raciales con nuestras diferencias pero sin prejuicios ni discriminaciones raciales.

[We make a call to all peoples identified with the black Peruvian cause to unite and propel this autonomous, pluralist and democratic movement; oriented towards the construction of a free nation, where all ethnic groups live together in harmony with our differences but without prejudices or racial discriminations].

And the movimiento hit like a tidal wave.

In early 1987, the MNFC board conducted a ceremony to bless the movimiento at Juanchi's house in Condevilla, a neighbourhood in northern Lima. It was at this gathering that Juanchi invited me to help start an MNFC dance company. I had recently become a marinera limeña national dance champion, and Juanchi's father, Abelardo Vasquez, had taken me under his wing. While taking a break from dancing, sitting on the edge of the pavement outside Juanchi's house, Juanchi explained over the clicking sound of glasses, bottles, conversations, '¡salud!' and loud salsa music: 'The first thing we are going to do is learn how to dance the Son de los Diablos for a carnival parade next year.'

In the documentary *El Son de los Diablos*, produced by TV Cultura in collaboration with the MNFC, Juanchi explains: 'We as members of Francisco Congo pursue the revaluation of the sociocultural contributions made by our presence in the last 400 or more years. We took as our initial step the Son de los Diablos festivity that we practised decades ago in the streets of Lima' (Romero 1988). MNFC members believed that the return of the Son de los Diablos to the streets served best their activist efforts. It is widely believed that this dance that was first imposed upon the Afro-descendant population was later adopted and used by Afro-Peruvians as a symbol of cultural resistance within carnival celebrations.

Resignification

William Tompkins writes that from 1817 onwards, the Catholic Church began to severely criticize the use of devils, giants and other grotesque figures in the processions and prohibited their use during religious celebrations (1981). Perhaps because of decreasing clerical domination, or gradual changes since Peruvian independence from Spain in 1821 and the later abolition of slavery in 1854, the Devil's dance began to be practised during other festive celebrations such as local patron-saint festivities and carnivals. Nicomedes Santa Cruz writes that by the end of nineteenth century, the Devil's dance was well established in several cities throughout Peru, and that by the time of the abolition of slavery, Afro-Peruvians had appropriated this dance as a symbol of cultural resistance (1974). The Son de los Diablos 'found its place within the secular context of Carnival, which already employed much masquerading and theatricals' (Tompkins 1981: 258) and it is believed that this dance was used as a 'rebellion' within this secular celebration.

In the carnival, structural transformation and social protest is sometimes communicated by turning an idiom 'upside down'—the idea of 'symbolic inversion'. Barbara Babcock defines 'symbolic inversion' as 'any act of expressive behavior which inverts, contradicts, abrogates, or in some fashion presents an alternative to commonly held cultural codes, values and norms' (cited in Alonso 1990: 73). The use of spurs and spades by the Afro-Peruvian devils depicted in early nineteenth-century watercolour paintings suggests that Afro-Peruvians utilized the image of the devil to symbolize the dominant white European elite. While these paintings date back to 1821 and 1830, it is difficult to assert whether Pancho Fierro illustrated a Corpus Christi or carnival celebration (see Figures 2 and 3). Regardless, these images have been used to defend the idea of symbolic inversion supporting Nicomedes Santa Cruz's argument about the use of the Son de los Diablos as a form of cultural resistance during carnival celebrations.

Apart from Fierro's watercolours, some of the earliest visual testimonies of this dance in Peru are found in the eighteenth-century painting collections of Martínez de Compañón under the title of 'diablicos'. These depictions show one dancer in particular, which scholars recognize as a 'head' devil (Durand 1988; Romero 1988), wearing a large, grotesque mask, and the 'appearance of a goat or large-nosed man, with long pointed ears and horns' (Tompkins 1981: 262). The mask covers most of the head and long feathers decorate some type of hat or crown. This devil wears a colourful outfit with a short-sleeve shirt, usually a red sash tied around the waist with a bow and knee-long black pants decorated with white frills. He wears white tights and spurs on his shoes, holds a spade or sometimes a whip, and is followed or surrounded by musicians. Musical instruments displayed in these paintings are the *cajita* or small box, the *quijada* or donkey jaw, the harp carried over the shoulder and a string instrument that resembles the guitar or vihuela (see Figure 2).

Today, with increasing difficulty, we can still find limeños who remember the Son de los Diablos in the context of carnival. My deceased grandmother, for example, coming from a lower-income criollo household, grew up in La Victoria barrio, a neighbourhood known for being traditionally 'black' and one of the last ones to see the Devil's dance before it disappeared from the streets. She remembered seeing the Son de los Diablos when she was very young. The clearest memory she had, however, was of the popular head devil nicknamed Ño Bisté. Francisco Andrade, better known as don Churrasco or Ño Bisté (Sir Beefsteak) received his nickname and popularity from his 'thick lips'. A subconscious collective memory about Ño Bisté, maintained

(LEFT) **FIGURE 2.** 'El son de los diablos'. (RIGHT) **FIGURE 3.** 'Sigue el son de los diablos'. Watercolour paintings by Pancho Fierro.

through storytelling in the criollo community and supported by a Son de los Diablos song whose lyrics include Ño Bisté's 'voice' calling attention to his own lips,[5] helps construct a legend that points to aesthetic ideals in the Peruvian national discourse of blackness. Without having witnessed Ño Bisté, this storytelling tradition becomes the evidence of things not seen but the thing one 'remembers' the most, as in my grandmother's case. 'And it's true!' My grandmother said. 'His lips were remarkably big!' This comment is an example of how physical characteristics, although they represent conscious or unconscious racism, go unmarked in the Peruvian context. The legend of Ño Bisté, like Doña Pepa, has become part of the national imagination about blackness.

Other testimonies describe the Son de los Diablos as a step-dance competition among devils who took turns to compete on street corners. A head devil and several minor devils or demons composed the ensemble. The devils advanced in lines and sometimes made choreographic figures like the cross (if viewed from above). The devils would stop at barrio-corner convenience stores or in front of a house to dance in exchange for liquor or money. Some testimonies recall the head devil as a strong dancer, almost an athlete who would combine this audience–performer interaction with acrobatics while carrying a big book and a quill, dancing and pointing at individuals whose name he pretended to write on his 'candidates for hell' list.

As mentioned earlier, all this disappeared from the Lima streets in the mid-twentieth century.

The Revival Continues

Son de los Diablos rehearsals for the Carnaval Negro 1988 began on 30 January of that year in the patio of a car mechanic's shop where one of the MNFC officers worked. We soon moved rehearsals to Yuyachkani Cultural Group theatre space. Juanchi trained us fiercely. He opened each rehearsal with an hour-long intense warm-up followed by another hour of Son de los Diablos instruction. Alongside, we participated in a mask-making workshop. Each of us made our masks and shaped our clay moulds based on stereotypical ideas of black features, as informed by Ño Bisté among others: thick lips, wide noses, bulgy eyes. No one questioned this trend. On the contrary, it made sense. In our collective minds, we were not only representing devils; in reviving this dance we were representing black men representing devils—hence the masks and their features were 'shortcut' to the multilayered representation of a new Afro-Peruvian Son de los Diablos.

On the day of the parade, Juanchi insisted we not take off our masks in any circumstances. We were supposed to be anonymous until we arrived at the destination. And so we didn't. It was difficult—remember it was February, the hottest month of the year in Lima. We had our masks on, black bandanas covering our heads, shirt and pants, knee-high socks and shoes; we were jumping, running, playing with the audience, counting, making mistakes, sweating. As I tried to see the path, I could also see surprised passers-by; looking up I saw people gathered in their windows like bundles of flowers; looking further up, children on the roofs of tall buildings trying to hide from people's view after pouring a bucket of water on the dancers or anyone who happened to be on the way. Tears mixed with sweat rolled down my cheeks when I saw my sister crying. I cried again when I saw my two-year-old niece on my dad's shoulders, with a scared but amazed expression. Turn around this corner; cars honk; 'that dog keeps barking.' Kids running, scared and defiant. Old and dirty colonial buildings; my past and my present; fellow Peruvians at their doors or windows, having their first encounter with this dance; new generations who had no idea of its history. 'Have they been informed? What are they thinking? What are they learning? Where are we in the routine? We are almost there . . . we are almost there—no, one more block . . .' And we made it! 'Can I take it off now?' I took off my mask and I almost fell over another dancer who had already collapsed in the greens of the Jardín Recreo Villacampa Park, the end point of the parade dance. We hugged, said 'good job!' and reunited with family and friends who congratulated us for the excellent performance while children stared at our faces surprised to see what had been behind those terrifying masks. We had just done something historic. We had returned the Son de los Diablos to the streets of Lima.

At the end of point of the parade dance, there was a stage and powerful sound system set up for an upcoming criollo show. Before the show began, my father called me energetically and pulled me to the side. He was upset because the MNFC members had been handing out pamphlets with political content. My father wanted to make sure that I was involved in the Son de los Diablos only for the cultural aspect of it and not for political reasons without realizing that this might not be possible. I was 19 years old and mostly oblivious of such possibilities. I had a difficult time understanding what my dad meant, especially because he made sure that such pamphlets never made it into my hands. I remember my father with a big frown talking to Juanchi near the stage. Juanchi just nodded.

This was the time of Alan García's first government (1985–90)—difficult, dangerous and unstable times in Peru when social and economic crises reached their peak, as did political violence. It was 1988, the year Sendero Luminoso (Shining Path), the Communist Party of Peru, a Maoist guerilla insurgency, had began expanding and started attacking urban zones to weaken the central government. Of course, my parents were very (and constantly) afraid that my involvement with groups that had an obvious agenda might lead to an attempt on my life, either from a bomb in the street or from the government's hand; young civilians had by then began to disappear. At some point my parents pleaded for me not to socialize with certain people so frequently. But I ignored my parents' request and continued with my regular activities, with no heed to possible consequences.

The following year I was back in the streets dancing the Son de los Diablos. The carnival in 1989 took place around La Victoria, and in 1990 around San Miguel, a district near Callao, the main Peruvian port and the entryway of slaves for centuries. But after the 1990 parade, there was a marked decline in interest among everyone, mainly because MNFC began to have internal conflicts. Members split to form a new organization and this was the beginning of a subsequent proliferation of Afro-Peruvian organizations that continue to form as I write this history.

Adoption

Among the dancers in the MNFC's Son de los Diablos revival were members of Yuyachkani Cultural Group,[6] whose involvement in the 1980s revival has contributed to the historical continuity of this art form. Yuyachkani members found the Son de los Diablos particularly interesting because it involved the impersonation of a character (a devil), demanded intense body training, the use of a mask, rhythm, interaction with the audience and, most importantly, because it was rooted in tradition. In Yuyachkani member Ana Correa's words, they found in the devil's dance 'a gold mine for acting training'. 'The Son de los Diablos introduced us to a new type of resistance: the fiesta, the tease, the mockery of the oppressor, and the recognition of blacks' contribution to the cultural expressions of Peru as a nation' (*Memorias* 1987).

Yuyachkani members saw the Son de los Diablos for the first time in the 1970s in a theatre production by Victoria Santa Cruz's Conjunto Nacional de Folklore. The opportunity to learn about the dance with Juanchi in the 1980s became for Yuyachkani the achievement of one of many goals they had set for themselves. Once they learnt it, they began to use the Son de los Diablos as part of their teaching curricula. This phenomenon influenced this dance in several ways.

In 1993, Yuyachkani started a theatre school in their theatre house and hired me the following year, under Correa's supervision, to teach a Son de los Diablos workshop to their theatre students. I had learned this dance from Juanchi and I felt that through this workshop I was passing on his teachings. I was giving back what I had received. I taught this dance to the best of my capacity and tried to be true to Juanchi's teachings. In doing so, I felt I was aligning with the initial intentions of the MNFC to return this dance to the streets of Lima, yet the process and result were strikingly different.

My theatre students at Yuyachkani were mostly middle-class mestizo and some criollo young men and women. They had paid a fee to receive acting training at Yuyachkani. The Son de los Diablos classes were part of a larger curriculum and the prominent motivation for learning the Son de los Diablos was to learn theatrical techniques. Correa made interesting innovations to the 1993 version of this dance. One of these, which apparently had not been part of the Son de los Diablos before 1993, was the use of stilts. The head devil of the group I trained in Yuyachkani used stilts; this incorporation has persisted and proliferated among Son de los Diablos groups, as I witnessed during my fieldwork in 2003–04. Correa conducted a very solemn ceremony to initiate these theatre students as the new carriers of this tradition.

Soon after, I left Lima to pursue higher studies in the US and, after eight years of short and irregular visits, I returned to the city in 2003 for an extended stay to conduct my fieldwork. One of the first surprises early in my research was to find extensive Afro-Peruvian activism that had spurted through the years since MNFC. Coincidentally, at the moment I arrived in Lima, some of these Afro-Peruvian organizations were in the planning stages for a yearlong commemoration of 150 years of the abolition of slavery in Peru.

Upon my arrival Correa called me with the idea of organizing a big carnival parade with the Son de los Diablos as part of this commemoration. Given my experience with this dance as a dancer, choreographer, and now researcher, I accepted the invitation and joined her and Luis Sandoval (director of the Afro-Peruvian theatre group Teatro del Milenio) to form the organizing committee. The increased Afro-

FIGURE 4. The author with her Son de los Diablos students at Grupo Cultural Yuyachkani house.

Peruvian activism I had just learnt about suggested a potentially far-reaching event that could make an impact on the larger Afro-Peruvian community. We began planning the 2004 carnival.

Correa explained that there were about six different Son de los Diablos groups that emerged from workshops Yuyachkani members and Yuyachkani theatre graduates had conducted around the country. There were children and youth theatre groups based in the outskirts of Lima, a group from Cusco, the students from the Escuela Nacional Superior de Arte Dramático (ENSAD or National School of Drama), Teatro del Milenio and, of course, Yuyachkani theatre students whom I had trained. In addition, we encouraged the participation of professional dance groups like Centro de Música y Danza de la Universidad Católica (CEMDUC or Center of Music and Dance of the Catholic University), the Escuela Nacional Superior de Folklore Jose Maria Arguedas (ENSFJMA or José María Arguedas Advanced National School of Folklore) and X siempre Peru (Forever Peru), a professional dance group led by Juanchi's nephew Pierr Padilla. Most of these groups, however, were comprised of non-Afro-Peruvians.

The parade took place on 29 February 2004. This year's black carnival had a few innovations. There was a wide use of stilts and new instrumentation that included

Brazilian drums, a Mexican *guitarrón* and pentagonal *batajones*. This event also included characters that helped frame this Afro-Peruvian event in colonial times. The parade included women representing house slaves wearing the standard colonial dresses popularized by Peru Negro and other groups. There was also a colonial town crier we all referred to as the *pregonero*. Playing a 'black' character, he walked along the parade announcing the commemoration of the abolition of slavery. Using the stereotypical black accent, he sometimes recited Nicomedes Santa Cruz's popular *décimas* while greeting and mingling with the audience. He wore a dark brown half-mask that was bug-eyed, with wide nose and thick moustache, a straw hat, white shirt with prominent frills on the chest, a black waistcoat (opened to let the frills show), orange pants decorated with white frills, white socks and black shoes in the colonial fashion as depicted in Fierro's nineteenth-century watercolours. A character that paraded with the Luna Sol children troop identified as 'Doña Tomasa', also displayed similar features. In addition to her mask, her breasts and buttocks were padded and exaggerated to represent the female version of an imagined "blackness" (see Figure 5). Some practices remained unaltered. The devils' masks showed the same facial features introduced in the 1980s revival. As before, the circulation of these stereotypical images seemed acceptable in the context of this carnival that was seen as the extension and expression of activism.

FIGURE 5. 'Doña Tomasa' with Luna Sol group performing at Carnaval Negro, 2004.

Through detailed analysis of video recordings, surveys, interviews and long discussions among the organizing-committee members and some participants, my research showed that five out of eight Son de los Diablos troops were theatre groups, and three were professional dance companies. There were approximately 200 participants in the 2004 black carnival among dancers and musicians. Approximately 10 per cent were of African descent while the rest included mestizos, criollos, a white minority and some native Peruvians, almost mirroring the ethnic breakdown of Peru.

Only a very small minority knew about this dance as part of a family tradition. A slightly larger minority had taken it upon themselves to investigate and learn more about this dance before the carnival. The majority did not know much about the history of this dance or only knew that it is part of the Afro-Peruvian repertoire. In addition, 9 per cent danced to continue their ancestor's tradition, 30 per cent to help promote the contributions of Afro-descendant people to the Peruvian national culture and 60 per cent to improve either their dance or theatrical skills. New motivation, new artistic elements and new membership marked a new era for the Son de los Diablos.

Since the 2004 carnival, Correa and Yuyachkani have taken it upon themselves to keep the Son de los Diablos parade dance alive in the streets of Lima during carnival and other times of the year. However, the participation of Afro-Peruvians continues to decrease. Extensive conversations with Afro-Peruvian leaders and artists who gradually withdrew from their active participation in this project reveal a sense of appropriation by theatre groups and a belief that it is no longer attached to an Afro-Peruvian cause. Others see this appropriation in more racial terms and describe the Son de los Diablos as a new mestizo form of dance with an Afro-Peruvian vestige. 'It would have been important to continue this dance as a source of integration for Afro-Peruvians but this event has been opened to include other people and artistic expressions, which is not bad, but we Afro-Peruvians need something with which we can identify. The Son de los Diablos had the potential' (combined anonymous interviews, 2005, 2010).

Since the first draft of this essay, a newly formed Afro-Peruvian organization called Únete Afro (Unite Afro) facilitated a weeklong event to, among other goals, 'rescue' the Son de los Diablos. 'This dance is currently being practised. It is alive and in the streets every carnival. What do you mean by *rescatar*—rescue?' I asked one of this organization's leaders and historians. His concern, he explained, is that although one can find the dance on a stage or the street, its significance and history have been lost. This concern thus marks a recurring phase in the history of the Son de los Diablos, which reveals a push and pull in terms of how the dance is viewed and utilized; what's been projected and by who; what's been perceived and how it is interpreted; who is using the dance and for what purposes. This tension reveals perhaps two poles of a spectrum, one that is artistic and one that is activistic. My close ties to the Son de los Diablos and my continued research help me understand this tension, which mirrors my own internal conflicts. My involvement in the Movimiento Negro Francisco Congo promted me to examine my role as an artist and activist.

Closing Remarks

Since my arrival in the Pacific Northwest, I have been devoted to educating others academically and artistically about the presence of Afro-descendant people in Peru and their contribution to Peru as a nation. Building upon my experience from the 1980s and 2004, I introduced this dance to Seattle in the summer of 2005. I taught a workshop and directed a Son de los Diablos music-and-dance troupe for a street parade through the Fremont Arts Council. During the process of organizing this performance, it became clear to me that this context was drastically different from that of Peru with which I was more familiar. The challenge was to educate the participants about the history and importance of the dance they were to perform. While the art form was mobilizing, it wasn't necessarily in the spirit of Afro-Peruvian activism.

We were unable to acquire 'authentic' costumes because of lack of time and interest in generating resources. Most importantly, however, participants were more concerned about heat and dehydration than in-depth connection to a history that involved slavery and the empowerment of a people through the dance they were about to perform. At the first words of complaints about heat, sweat and suggestions of tank tops and skirts for costumes, I remembered that hot summer day in February 1988 in Lima and the asphyxiating heat behind those masks made worse by black bandanas and knee-high socks, which did not make us flinch for one moment from being true to the tradition. This for me was the stark realization that my teachings needed a different approach. Later on one of my Son de los Diablos students from this workshop, Rose Cano, invited me to contribute to her own projects and asked me to choreograph the Son de los Diablos for a couple of parades. She also recruited me to work with Sandoval, with whom I had collaborated in 2004, to help stage the Son de los Diablos among other dances within the context of an adaptation of Sandoval's Teatro del Milenio play *Callejon* (The Alley).

This brief introduction of the Son de los Diablos then catalysed a series of events that would set the stage for an in-depth exploration of Afro-Peruvian cultural traditions. Over the long term young dancers and local musicians, diasporic Peruvians and community members began to question and reflect on their relationship to Afro-Peruvians and became instrumental in the development of my arts organization called DE CAJON Project. As a diasporic Peruvian intellectual bearing an African diasporic tradition, I strive to serve as a balanced extension of artistic and activist efforts in Peru; my primary goal is to provide education about the contributions of the African descendents to Peruvian culture. Thus, while my artistic introduction of the Son de los Diablos to Seattle seemed activistically ineffective, it eventually led to the elevation of awareness among Northwest audiences of Afro-Peruvian traditions. Hence I am bridging Juanchi's and many other artists' and activists' efforts.

The contextual challenges are not lost on me, however, with regard to perceptions of race and projection of culture. At a performance, the crowd of spectators, the display of bodies on stage and the different symbolisms displayed through their art give the performance the flavour of a museum-like exhibit: picture-like and legible (for consumption). These technologies create the appearance of 'objectness' by separating an object-world from its observer. Understanding representation as 'everything collected and arranged to stand for something [. . .] everything set up, and the whole set-up always evoking somehow some larger truth' (Mitchell 1988: 6), the dance, the costume, masks, all contribute to an imagination of black Peruvians as well as their history, everyday experiences, presence and absence. The absence of African descendants in the performance of the Son de los Diablos today suggests a representation of Afro-Peruvians as imagined largely by a majority of mestizo and criollo dancers. This is not unique and is the case in many dances from other regions of Peru such as *la morenada* in Puno, Los Negritos de Huanuco in Huanuco, or the Qapac Negro in Cusco. Because of this cycle, there arises yet again the need to rescue the Son de los Diablos in the Afro-Peruvian community to speak of their presence and cultural contributions. But the Son de los Diablos has never stopped being practised. As a testimony to the presence and contribution of Afro-Peruvians, the dance has proved effective in that it is not only alive but also ever changing and continues to generate alternative modes of mobilization and integration among artists and activists both Peruvian (Afro and non-Afro) as well as non-Peruvian.

Thus, the colonial and postcolonial performative contexts in which the Son de los Diablos emerged and re-emerged speaks to the position of Afro-Peruvians in Peruvian imagination, national identity and social history. Within the frame of religious, governmental institutional control or grassroots organizations, the Son de los Diablos continues to serve as a source of art, resistance and social mobilization.

Notes

1   Frederic Bowser (1974) writes that one way in which authorities tried to restrict the freedom for blacks to assemble was through the creation of *cofradías*, Catholic-sponsored brotherhoods. The first *cofradía* for blacks in Lima was established in the 1540s; others came about as the number of Africans grew—by 1619, there were

15 sodalities for blacks and mulattos in the capital. Run by Dominicans and Jesuits, *cofradías* were the most effective vehicles to convert Afro-Peruvians to Catholicism. These *cofradías* fulfilled a broader social function in helping blacks reconstruct their identity: they offered spiritual and material support and became an important site of socialization and source of solidarity for both slaves and freed slaves to maintain and reinforce their cultural practices. Each *cofradía* was headed by a caporal, a type of president of the assemblies. If there was a slave within a *cofradía* who had been of royal lineage in Africa, then he or she became king or queen of the brotherhood and was treated with special respect by the members (Bowser 1974; Tompkins 1981; Rivas 2002). *Cofradías*, however, eventually became spaces for conflict and divisions, developing hierarchies that differentiated darker-skinned blacks from lighter-skinned individuals, poor from rich and free blacks from slaves (Hünefeldt 1994: 98). In other words, *cofradías* accommodated the master–slave relation. Despite this, *cofradías* helped give slaves and freed slaves a sense of community, 'and as the slaves' identification with former ethnic groups waned with succeeding New World generations, these old divisions gave way to the creation of a new Afro-Peruvian community and culture' (Tompkins 1981: 23).

2   The word criollo in Peru has long since deviated from its original meaning, which was used to refer to the children of Africans born into slavery in the New World. Later the term also described children of Spanish settlers born in Peru to set them apart from 'real' Europeans. Criollismo, the expression of being criollo, was reappropriated by lower- and middle-class white and black Peruvians as a means of defining their own Peruvian culture that was neither European or Indian (Feldman 2000: 32). Being criollo today involves certain practices and lifestyles that differentiate a dwindling minority in a vast and increasingly complex Lima and the larger urban coastal culture. In Peru, race and class are closely tied. The term criollo as a coastal culture (more than racially defined), shaped by the historical coexistence of whites and Afro-descendant people along the coast, is an unmarked categorical name that includes people across class. Class is identified when the term criollo is marked by racial categories such as 'white criollo' and 'black criollo'. A 'middle-class criollo' implies different degrees of racial mixture.

3   See William Tompkins (1981) and Monica Rojas (2007) for a transcription, translation and comparison of this song as collected by them from Durand.

4   Francisco Congo or 'Chavelilla' is known to have been a slave during colonial times who organized a group of runaways gathered at a *palenque* (a hideaway spot for runaway slaves) during the second decade of eighteenth century. This group, composed of both men and women, demanded the formal authorities to let them live in peace in the mountains of Huachipa and asked to be given the abandoned lands of the area in order to develop and live on them. The answer Francisco Congo received was prison and death.

5   During the first half of the twentieth century (exact date is unknown), Fernando Soria composed a popular *festejo* that describes the Son de los Diablos dance. One of the strophes says: 'Yo soy el diablo mayor y me llaman Ño Bisté, por esta bemba

que tengo tan grande mírela usté'!' (I am the head devil and they call me Ño Bisté, because of the thick lips I have—look at them!).

6 Yuyachkani is a Quechua word that means 'I am thinking, I am remembering'. By exploring this idea, Yuyachkani Cultural Group has been creating theatre since 1971 through collective creation inspired by the members' social and political commitment expressed in the content of their work and in their pedagogy. This group was cofounded by Miguel Rubio Zapata, who is a contributor to this volume.—Eds.

Caribbean and Afro-Atlantic Devils

Diabolic Suffering, Whips and the Burning of Judas
Holy Week in Cabral, Dominican Republic

MAX HARRIS

Elías Piña is a small town in the western Dominican Republic on the border with Haiti. Its festive devils wear corrugated-cardboard masks decorated with chicken feathers, vegetation and other natural materials. They dress in skirts made of dried plantain leaves and carry whips. Traditionally, they appear between Thursday and

FIGURE 1. Diablos of Elías Piña.

Saturday of Holy Week. According to Dagoberto Tejeda Ortiz, the Diablos of Elías Piña 'are really angels; they are guardians who purify the town, liberating and eluding the presence of negative energy in the community. Their mission is not destruction but protection' (Tejeda Ortiz 2008: 510–12).[1] The *diablicos sucios* (dirty devils) of La Villa de Los Santos, on Panama's Azuera Peninsula, wear grotesquely fanged masks and carry inflated bladders (see Fig. 2). Led by a priest, they leave the church after Mass on the feast of Corpus Christi to spin and dance their way through the town.

FIGURE 2. *Diablicos sucios* of La Villa de Los Santos, Panama.

'According to myth,' Alejandro Balaguer reports, 'the *diablicos* are dancers who once followed Lucifer but have now been forgiven their sins and have joined others on the path of righteousness. Redeemed from their past evil, they are dancing tirelessly through the streets of town' (2010: 22).[2]

Neither of these descriptions fully explains the ambiguous character of masked devils who take part in religious festivals in Mexico, the Caribbean and Central and South America, but both suggest that any simple identification with the irredeemably evil demons of traditional Christian theology badly misunderstands the role of festive devils in the Americas. 'The festive connotation of devils is not always demonic' (Harris 2003: 8); it is often also devout. It is this double nature of festive devils that I explore in this essay. I begin by briefly recalling, for comparative purposes, what I have written elsewhere about the role of festive devils in the Fiestas de Santiago Apóstol in Loíza, Puerto Rico (ibid.: 33–47).[3] I then examine at greater length the very different mix of devotion and devilry to be seen in the Cachúas (horned ones) of Cabral, in the southwest corner of the Dominican Republic. Like their counterparts in Elías Piña, the Cachúas take to the streets during Holy Week.

The area around Loíza is one of the deepest pockets of Afro-Caribbean culture in Puerto Rico. Its history, like that of Cabral, is deeply rooted in the cultivation of sugarcane and the accompanying institution of slavery. Each year, on the three days following the feast day of Santiago Apóstol (St James the Apostle) (25 July), the people of Loíza honour three images of the saint with a series of processions from Loíza along the coastal road to Medianía, three miles away. Loíza is the seat of local government and boasts the oldest parish church on the island, dedicated since 1645 to San Patricio (St Patrick). Medianía, whose church is dedicated to Santiago Apóstol, is 'where the poorer people live'. The smallest of the processional images of Santiago, whose original is said to have miraculously appeared in a cork tree in Medianía, is known as Santiago de los Niños (St James of the Children). It is believed to work miracles on behalf of the powerless.

The images of Santiago are escorted from Loíza to Medianía by a multitude of festive marchers in everyday clothes, generic Carnival costumes and traditional disguises. The four traditional groups of maskers are known as *locas* (crazy women), *viejos* (old men or ancestral spirits), *caballeros* (gentry) and *vejigantes* (those armed with bladders) or *diablitos* (little devils). The *locas* are cross-dressed men. The *viejos* wear ragged clothes and unpainted cardboard masks. The *caballeros* wear wire-mesh masks that caricature aristocratic Spanish features. The devils, by far the most numerous of the traditional masqueraders, wear loose-fitting, multicoloured body suits that reveal, when the wearer raises his arms, an arc of translucent material that connects sleeve to side like bat wings. Their faces are hidden behind elaborate horned masks, most of which are carved from coconut shells and given exaggeratedly African features. Others,

FIGURE 3. *Vejigantes* of Loíza, Puerto Rico.

borrowed from the *vejigantes* of the island's largest Carnival at Ponce, are shaped from papier-mâché and give form to fantastic monsters. Whereas the *vejigantes* in Ponce still carry inflated animal bladders on sticks, those in Loíza do not; some instead carry inflated paper bags or balloons. The *vejigantes* have a long and continuous history on the island. They were first recorded in its capital city, San Juan, in 1747 (Juan and Ulloa 1978b[1748]: 178). Later, one nineteenth-century observer remembered, among the maskers who filled the streets of the city every Sunday in June, 'an infinite number of blacks dressed as demons to whom they give the name of *vejigante*' (López Cantos 1990: 204).

Various explanations have been offered for the processions and their accompanying masqueraders. To my mind, the most compelling sees the festivities as a joyous annual exodus from the seat of local civil and ecclesiastical power to the place where the smallest of the Santiagos miraculously appeared to bless the powerless. The patron saint of Medianía, to whom the marchers express their devotion, is one who embraces and protects the poor, the women, the children, the dead, the crazy, the cross-dressed, the little devils and, if they abandon their claim to higher rank, even the *caballeros*. The *diablitos* are the ultimate symbol of marginalization, representing all who have been demonized by traditional theology and by the secular powers to which the church has too often allied itself. They are horned devils, enslaved Africans, free black men and women, welfare recipients (of whom there are many in Medianía) and others misrepresented and misused by those in power. At no point do the little devils resist the progress of Santiago. They are not his enemies. On the contrary, they act as his escort.

Cabral is a small town some eight miles inland from Barahona. Although Cabral shares with Loíza a history of sugarcane cultivation, its festive devils are not accompanied by other maskers representing *caballeros* or European plantation owners. This absence of a dramatic foil complicates the devils' own identity. The seasonal setting of Holy Week further confuses matters. Whereas the Fiestas de Santiago Apóstol in Loíza celebrate a patron saint's gracious friendship, Holy Week in Cabral provides an underlying narrative of exemplary suffering and betrayal. The dramatic role of the festive devils in Cabral is not merely double but conflicted and, to my mind, much more troubling.

Whips are the dominant motif of Cabral's Holy Week festivities. When I arrived late on the afternoon of Good Friday (2 April) 2010, the stations of the cross were being enacted in the atrium of the parish church. A black teenager, wearing only baggy shorts and a crown of leaves (not thorns), was roped to a makeshift cross (see Fig. 4). Two 'soldiers', in jeans and T-shirts, stood to one side. One carried a whip, the other a hammer, weapons already used to enact Christ's scourging and nailing to

(LEFT) **FIGURE 4**. Representing the Crucifixion. (RIGHT) **FIGURE 5**. Effigy of the Júa (Judas).

the cross. Two girls, wrapped in thin cloaks to represent the mother of Christ and a second Mary, stood a little further off. A little later, Christ was taken down from the cross, carried into the church, and 'buried' beneath a table in the sanctuary. The actors, like the members of the watching congregation, were all Afro-Caribbean.

Afterwards, I made my way back to the small triangular Parque Municipal (town park) in the centre of Cabral. On top of the obelisk at one corner of the park was a life-size effigy known as the Júa (Judas). The effigy was dressed in the traditional costume of a Cachúa: a thin, multicoloured body suit that, like that of Loíza's *vejigantes*, displayed translucent bat wings beneath his raised arms.[4] His mask was a traditional papier-mâché animal mask, having two horns, a crocodile's long snout and sharp white teeth. It was painted in the national colours of red, white and blue. Like the 'soldier' who scourged Christ, Judas carried a long whip. Judas would be burnt on Easter Monday.

My next stop was at a temporary tin-roofed open shelter, about a hundred yards away, where Dr Temístocles Féliz Suarez was enthroned in a large rocking chair, making whips from braided sisal and carved wooden handles.[5] Temo, as everyone calls him, is Cabral's well-respected physician and the *jefe* (chief) of its Cachúas. As well as whips, he makes masks for the Cachúas.[6] Completed masks and whips were

(LEFT) **FIGURE 6**. Dr Temístocles Féliz Suarez and an assistant make whips. (RIGHT) **FIGURE 7**. Cachúa whips, masks and costumes on sale.

on display beneath the shelter. As he worked, Temo talked to me about the town's festivities, drawing a careful distinction between the activities of the Cachúas, who have been part of Cabral's Holy Week celebrations 'since the nineteenth century', and the newer Carnival *desfile* (parade) that takes place late on Saturday afternoon. Despite the tendency of national folklorists to include both under the single rubric of 'Carnival' (Tejeda Ortiz 2008: 514–16; Pérez 2008: 25), Temo insisted that the Cachúas take part in a *juego* (game or play) unique to Cabral and that only the parade, first held in Cabral in 1974, was a 'Carnaval'.[7] It is the game of the Cachúas that concerns me here. In the street beside the shelter, young boys—not yet in costume— were cracking their whips. The whips sounded like exploding fireworks.

Whips are an intrinsic part of the Easter narrative: Christ was scourged (John 19:1). Flagellation, as an expression of identification with the suffering of Christ and as a mode of self-mortification, has long formed a part of Holy Week festivities in Spain and its former empire (see, for example, Webster 1998: 25–9; Trexler 2003: 21–41; Weigle 2007[1976]; Sánchez 1991: 48–51). Whipping, in the Caribbean, has another, more recent referent: enslaved Africans were whipped by both white owners and black overseers (see Figure 8).[8] A visitor to a Cuban sugar plantation in the 1840s reported 'the incessant sound of the whip', not so much as a form of punishment (although it was certainly used to flay captured runaways and the insubordinate) but as a means of keeping the exhausted awake and working. 'Four hours' sleep was considered sufficient for a slave, and [...] twenty hours a day for five to seven months out of the year was the normal working day' (Hall 1971: 17–18). Sugarcane is still one of the main commercial crops of the Dominican Republic.[9]

FIGURE 8. Working in sugarcane fields, nineteenth-century illustration.

Whips are widely used in folk performances elsewhere. Since a complete catalogue would be tiresome, I will limit myself to personal experience. I have seen whips
used in Mexico and New Mexico by 'clown' figures responsible for keeping dancers
in order.[10] Such festive authority figures, often called *viejos* or *abuelos*, may crack their
whips but they rarely strike their fellow dancers. I have sidestepped more aggressive
Carnival maskers in Galicia as they lashed the backs of a hungry crowd (*peliqueiros*
of Laza's Carnival; *cigarrones* of Verín's Carnival; see Harris 2003: 144–56). During
Carnival in Trinidad, I have been threatened with a whipping by a friendly Jab Jab

FIGURE 9. *Peliqueiros* in Laza, Galicia.

(Devil Devil) and spoken to a Pierrot Grenade who told me that, in the old days, his predecessors would duel not only with words but also with whips (ibid.: 188, 196–7; see also Crowley 1988: 73–5; Carr 1988; Riggio and Gibbons in this volume, pp. 189–220).

Even closer in kind to Cabral's Cachúas were the *gracejos* (clowns) from Mexico's Sierra de Puebla whom I saw take part in a *danza de los negritos* ('dance of the little blacks'). Dressed in old jackets, animal-skin chaps and masks made of animal skin, the *gracejos* carried 30-foot rope whips over their shoulders. After each round of the dance, a pair of *gracejos* would uncoil their whips and fight each other, taking turns to unleash a cracking shot while the other leaped to avoid the stinging blow (Harris 2003: 58–9). Similar, too, are the Qolla dancers of the Peruvian Andes, who engage in whipping battles as a form of penitential devotion to their patron saint. Such mutual flagellation 'proves their physical strength and courageous virility' while also 'cleansing their sins' (Mendoza 2000: 195–202; see also Harris 2003: 121–3, 125).[11]

Some uses of whipping in folk performance, especially in the Caribbean, recall the days of slavery. Others, such as that in Galicia, refer to more local forms of historical abuse. Yet others are penitential, a game of *machismo* or simply a way of making noise. These purposes are not mutually exclusive. All may be true of Cabral's Holy Week festivities.[12]

Cabral's Cachúas, Temo said, are allowed to prepare and even to practise *fuetazos* (cracks of the whip) on Good Friday, but they are not permitted to disguise themselves or to engage in battles before midnight on Saturday morning. To do so would be a *pecado* (sin). This schedule has changed over the years. Previously, the Cachúas 'took an indirect part in the rites of the church', appearing after the Easter Vigil ended on Saturday morning. In 1956, after the Vatican's Renewed Order for Holy Week restored the Easter Vigil to Saturday night,[13] the Cachúas' festivities were postponed until midnight following the Vigil. In the same year, in Santo Domingo, the dictator Rafael Trujillo declared Easter Monday a national holiday and staged a massive parade in honour of his daughter Angelina. The Cachúas took advantage of the holiday to extend their festivities in Cabral. Since 1960, they have been allowed to appear after the church bells ring at midnight on Saturday morning and to continue through Monday evening. Their link with the Easter rites of the church, however, has been lost: '[R]ecent years have produced a rupture between piety (*religiosidad*) and the festivities of the Cachúas' (Féliz 2003: 11).

I saw the Cachúas in action for the first time on Saturday morning. Some were in full disguise. Other men in the streets, known as *civiles* (civilians), carried whips but went undisguised. Many of the masqueraders were youngsters in partial or simplified costumes. One group of boys performed for anyone who would watch, showing off their skill with whips and—an even greater source of pride—their ability to take the lash without flinching. The victim stood motionless and expressionless as the whip struck his legs. The boys never spoke, remaining silent even as they

FIGURE 10. Boys fight with whips.

extended a hand for a small donation. This capacity to absorb pain in stoic silence was a central motif of the Cachúas' performance.

The Cachúas' *disfraz* (disguise) has been modified over the years. The traditional disguise consisted of a mask and a colourful body suit. The mask was made of papier mâché, layered with coloured *papel vejiga* (crepe paper) and then glazed. Topped with two horns, the front of the mask resembled 'the beak of a parrot, the face of a dog, a deformed human face, the snout of a pig, a crocodile, a bull or some other bird or animal (ibid.: 6; see also Tejeda Ortiz and Rosado 2010: 125). The body suit, traditionally red, yellow and green, extended from hood to knees. The lower legs were protected with thick stockings. On the back was sewn a large black cross.[14] Small 'wings' unfolded as the wearer's arms were raised, transforming the Cachúa into a bat or a malignant 'bird of the night' (Tujibikile 1993: 48–9). Nowadays, the wings are larger, the suits reach the ankles, the colours vary widely, and only about half the Cachúas bear the cross. Many wear traditional masks but others sport store-bought or simpler hand-made alternatives (Tejeda Ortiz and Rosado 2010: 147–8, 161–2; Féliz 2003: 6–7).

More than 20 years ago I realized that signs visible only in performance, especially those that run counter to official scripts or first explanations, can point to ambiguities or otherwise unacknowledged layers of meaning in folk performance. Naive questions about such signs, just because they seem less intrusive than the probing

FIGURE 11. Young Cachúas wear the cross.

inquiries of a professional anthropologist, can yield helpful insights (see e.g. Harris 1993: 116–19; Harris 2000: 21–3; Harris 2003: 59–61).

I approached the young woman in charge of an exhibition of photographic images of Cabral's Carnival. I asked, 'Why do some Cachúas wear a cross on the back of their costumes?'

She said, 'It's a symbol of the crucifixion.'

'Because it's Holy Week?'

'Yes.'

'So the Cachúas are Christians?'

'Yes.'

'Not devils?'

'No. Devils are in La Vega.'

La Vega hosts the country's largest Carnival. Its Diablos wear elaborate, fanged devil masks of considerable ferocity (Tejeda Ortiz 2008: 367–400; Tejeda Ortiz and Rosado 2010: 88–94; Valdez 1995; Pérez 2008: 31).

When I reported this conversation to a middle-aged friend, himself a Cachúa, he demurred. 'Some wear crosses,' he said. 'Some don't.' He did not. 'The Cachúas,' he insisted, 'are *diablos cojuelos*.' *Diablo cojuelo* (lame devil) is the generic name given

FIGURE 12. *Diablos cojuelos* of La Vega.

to many of the Dominican Republic's festive devils, including those of Cabral, La Vega and Santo Domingo.

The *diablo cojuelo* has a long literary history. Some find his first appearance in Part Two of Cervantes' *Don Quijote de la Mancha* (1615), when Quijote and Sancho Panza meet a troupe of actors travelling in costume from one performance to another on the octave of the Feast of Corpus Christi. An 'ugly demon' drives the players' wagon. Another follows on foot, 'dressed in motley [*bogiganga*] and many bells, and carrying three inflated cow-bladders [*vejigas de vaca*] on the end of a stick' (Cervantes de Saavedra 2004: 2.11). Because of his resemblance to the bladder-wielding devils of La Vega and Santo Domingo, some folklorists in the Dominican Republic reckon this second devil to be a *diablo cojuelo* (Lizardo 1974: 153; Valdez 1995: 28; Tejeda Ortiz 2003: 108), but Cervantes identifies him only as a 'dancing devil of the bladders [*demonio bailador de las vejigas*]' (Cervantes de Saavedra 2004: 2.11). He is an ancestor of Puerto Rico's *vejigantes* and their kin in the Dominican Republic but he is not a *diablo cojuelo* as such.

A generation later, Luis Vélez de Guevara wrote *El diablo cojuelo* (1641), a picaresque novel in which the lame devil of the title introduces himself as a minor demon, a maker of mischief, and the inventor—among other things—of the saraband, the chaconne, puppets, tightrope walkers and mountebanks. 'I am so named,' he says, 'because I was the first of those who rose up in heavenly rebellion, and of those who fell [...]; and because the rest fell on top of me, they crippled me, and I am left most marked by the hand of God and by the feet of all the devils' (Vélez de Guevara 1968: 116–17).[15] Over the course of the novel, he leads a human companion across the rooftops of Madrid, revealing and commenting on the evils and hypocrisies below. In 1869, José Martí borrowed the title *El diablo cojuelo* for the short-lived journal in which he published his first writings advocating Cuban independence. 'This devil,' Martí wrote, 'is not a devil, and this *cojo* is not lame' (1991: 1.31).

The festive *diablos cojuelos* of the Dominican Republic are neither satirical nor overtly political. Nor are they visibly lame. Perhaps, Pedro Muamba Tujibikile suggests, the use of the name in Cabral recalls a time when enslaved Africans were not only whipped but also shackled, able to walk only with a limping, shuffling gait (1993: 40–1).

Tujibikile also proposes a way of understanding the double nature of the Cachúas. The Cachúas, he writes, are the embodiment of 'the tension between freedom and slavery'. For every referent there is an 'anti-' or opposite referent. As devils, armed with whips, they represent 'the enslaver, the colonizer'. As *cojos*, they represent those abused by slavery. At the same time, as festive maskers, they are free to burlesque the oppressor.

The whip is a means of exploitative torture and a sign of 'the submission, the suffering resistance [. . .] of the enslaved', but in the hands of the Cachúas it is also a sign of resistance and freedom. The horned animal masks point to the demonic behaviour of the oppressor and the treatment of the enslaved as animals. Enslaved Africans were hunted with dogs, trapped in pits, housed in sheds like pigs and used as beasts of burden like oxen. On the other hand, Tujibikile suggests, the masks point to the bull-like strength of the enslaved, their endurance under suffering and their struggle for freedom.[16] The bat wings signify that slave hunters, like evil spirits, operated under cover of darkness, but also that 'night was the time of insurrection, of the war of liberation' (ibid.: 39–50).

Tujibikile, a missionary priest of the Congregation of the Immaculate Heart of Mary, served in Cabral in the 1990s (Tejeda Ortiz 2008: 516). He found in the Cachúas a reflection of his own liberation theology. I wish I could endorse his analysis —it would be consistent with my reading of the Fiestas de Santiago Apóstol in Loíza. But what I saw in Cabral did not strike me as a festive celebration of God's 'preferential option for the poor' (Gutiérrez 1988: xxv). Cabral's *diablos cojuelos* are not devoted to a saint who freely embraces the poor, the oppressed and the demonized. Insofar as the Cachúas identify with religious images, it is with the whip of scourging and the cross of crucifixion. Insofar as they have a patron saint, it is the Christ of Good Friday.

The Cachúas' cross spoke to me not of liberation but of the 'degraded form of Christianity' purveyed by slave masters, 'offering everlasting rewards in the hereafter in return for submission to slavery on earth' (Hall 1971: 34). As an example of such plantation Christianity, consider this typical Spanish argument in favour of the religious education of enslaved people in nineteenth-century Cuba:

> Without religion to control them, they will never carry out well the tasks which are assigned to them, nor be loyal to their masters. Without religion which teaches and directs them, containing them with the thought that beyond this world, [this] place of trials, there is another of ineffable and eternal glory, for those who suffer here with resignation their misfortunes and fulfill with exactness their duties, and of endless torment for the bad, it is materially impossible for them to serve well nor attempt to conserve a life which is for them an insupportable weight [. . .]. The consolation which our Divine Religion offers to the unfortunate makes them endure not only with resignation, but even contentment the privations and labours consequent to servitude (Archivo Histórico Nacional, National Historical Archives, Madrid; testimonies of the proceedings established to examine the causes that occasion frequency of suicide among the enslaved, Opinion of Attorney Olañeta, cited in ibid.: 45).

Christianity on plantations was too often little more than a means of social control and an antidote to suicide among the enslaved.

Such attitudes have too often been an ugly subtext of Christianity wherever subordinate suffering has benefited those in power. This encouragement of voluntary resignation has been particularly evident during Holy Week, when preaching and ritual designed to enforce the stability of social strata has focused more on the example of Christ's patient suffering on Good Friday than on his startling resurrection on Easter Sunday. Since the days of the early church in Rome, Christ's agony on the cross has been offered as an example to the enslaved:

> Slaves, accept the authority of your masters with all deference, not only those who are kind and gentle but also those who are harsh. For it is a credit to you if, being aware of God, you endure pain while suffering unjustly. If you endure when you are beaten for doing wrong, what credit is that? But if you endure when you do right and suffer for it, you have God's approval. For to this you have been called, because Christ also suffered for you, leaving you an example, so that you should follow in his steps (1 Peter 2:18–21).

FIGURE 13. Holy Week flagellants in the Philippines.

The message of patient suffering has also been internalized not only by the enslaved but also by generations of free men and women. It is still ritualized in popular Holy Week performances: bloody annual reenactments of the Passion abound throughout the Hispanic world; public flagellation is still practised on Good Friday.

I suspect that the Cachúas' game testifies, at least in part, to this longstanding internalization of Christian suffering. Insofar as the Cachúas are devils armed with whips, they represent unjust slave masters, brutal overseers and all who profit from the sufferings of others. Insofar as they are *diablos cojuelos*, they are suffering devils, themselves injured by the falling weight of other devils. And, insofar as they are Christians, marked by the cross, they are those who follow Christ's example, enduring without flinching the pain heaped on them. They remain silent because Christ, too, 'was oppressed, and he was afflicted, yet he did not open his mouth' (Isaiah 53:7; see also 1 Peter 2:23). Their fortitude is an expression of both *machismo* and residual piety.

This may be true despite widely varying degrees of awareness of these layers of meaning among individual Cachúas. Conflicted scars left by the historical traumas of conquest and slavery often find expression in dances, plays and games of whose meanings the performers are not fully conscious and which they could not otherwise adequately articulate.[17] Such scars may testify not only to pain inflicted but to pain caused. Afro-Caribbeans, whatever their personal ancestry, live in the shadow of slavery. This shadow carries with it not only the memory of colonial Christianity's insistence on the enslaved's unflinching submission to unjust suffering but an even more troubling cultural memory of black complicity. This, too, if I am not mistaken, finds expression in the Cachúas' game.

In Loíza, a distinction is drawn between European *cabelleros* and demonized black men. No such distinction is drawn in Cabral. Those who whip wear the same disguise as those who are whipped. While the Cachúas may at times pick on unmasked *civiles*, this is, I think, a practical matter of controlling the playing area rather than a means of shaping the narrative. Cachúas whip one another. Whipped, they remain silent, refusing to flinch at the lashing given by their fellow Cachúas. At its deepest level, this is not a dramatization of violence inflicted by others but of violence inflicted by those like themselves.

Slavery fed not only on the abuse of enslaved black men and women by white owners but also at times on the complicity of black overseers. 'Our grandparents tell us,' Tujibikile writes, that 'the white man' hunted Africans for the slave trade 'with the complicity of black traitors [*negros traidores*] who were appointed overseers [*capataces*]' (1993: 47–8). In the Americas, too, the whipping of enslaved black men and women was frequently carried out by black officials. Tujibikile juxtaposes the image of a black prisoner being whipped by an equally black 'executioner' in early nineteenth-

FIGURE 14. Public whipping of an enslaved man, Brazil, 1816–31.

century Brazil to a recent photograph of a Cachúa and his unmasked black helper tying their victim to a pole in preparation for a whipping in Cabral (ibid.: 44) (see Figure 14).[18] In St Domingue (now Haiti), 'free blacks were conscripted into military service in 1724 and organized into the Compagnie de Nègres-Libres. [...] The main duty of this company was to pursue fugitive slaves' (Hall 1971: 116). 'Those who were "loyal" could also gain their freedom by capturing "troublesome leaders of maroon bands" of runaways' (ibid.: 76). Tujibikile claims that the mutual whipping of the Cachúas 'mocks' (*burla*) this history of black-on-black violence, but I suspect that it also enacts, whether consciously or otherwise, a measure of unresolved guilt and hostility.

It is in this context that the burning of Judas makes most sense. Setting fire to an effigy is a common practice of folk rituals throughout the world. Burning an effigy of Judas is peculiar to communities familiar with his betrayal of Christ. In Cabral, it has an additional resonance. For much of the twentieth century, a life-size *muñeco* (doll) representing Judas was hung on a tree in a neighbourhood of Cabral known as El Hoyo de Los Perros. People threw stones at it. Taken down on Easter Saturday morning, the doll was led through the town on a donkey. Finally, after the Easter Vigil, it was burnt outside the church. The punishment of Judas was the responsibility of the whole town. The Cachúas were 'passive participants in this activity' (Féliz 2003: 8–9).

In 1956, after the Easter Vigil was restored to Saturday night, the burning of Judas, too, was delayed until the church bells had rung at midnight. Moved from its

FIGURE 15. Cabral cemetery, Friday evening.

familiar time slot, the custom fell into neglect. When the Cachúas took charge of the popular activities of Holy Week, they revived the practice. It is they who now dress, pillory and burn the Júa. Dressed like a Cachúa, he is one of them. His conflagration, no longer linked to the Easter Vigil, takes place at the close of festivities on Monday evening in the cemetery a few hundred yards from the church (ibid.).

FIGURE 16. Burning Judas, Monday evening.

I had explored the cemetery with a Cabraleño friend on Friday evening. He reminded me that only Cachúas were allowed among the tombs on Monday evening. For all others it would be a place of danger. My friend described the scene: hundreds of Cachúas standing on top of the tombs, all cracking their whips at once, making a noise like war while the Judas went up in flames. 'If one of the *civiles* were to be found in the cemetery with the Cachúas,' my friend said, 'he would be killed [*matado*].' He showed me a long scar caused some years ago by whips striking his face.

By late Monday afternoon, the Júa had been removed from his place atop the obelisk in the town park. A few Cachúas engaged in whipping battles nearby, but gradually the park quietened. The remaining Cachúas wandered east along the main road out of town. The quietness was only temporary. An hour later, a roiling mass of several hundred Cachúas returned, cracking their whips, bearing the effigy of Judas, and forcing traffic to detour along side streets. The mob of Cachúas was a maelstrom of noise, heat and dust, sweeping through the square on its way to the cemetery. A crowd gathered outside the gates to watch in safety.

The burning of Judas is a rite of considerable emotional intensity. Xiomarita Pérez calls the Júa 'a political symbol of power' (2008: 25), but this is misleading. Of all the villains of the Holy Week narrative who reappear in folk performances in the Americas, Judas is the only historical figure who lacked political power. Pontius Pilate, the Pharisees and the Roman soldiers, all of whom appear in various roles in American folk dance and ritual,[19] exercised a measure of real political power during the days leading to Christ's execution. But Judas was a disciple, able to wield brief power only as the one who handed Christ over to the Jewish authorities. He was complicit in Christ's suffering not as an external enemy but as an internal traitor. Much as Tujibikile might like to see in the effigy of Judas an image of 'the white colonizer' who perpetuated the system of slavery, he has to admit that Judas 'also represents the black or mulatto accomplices [. . .] and traitors to the cause of freedom' (1993: 53–4). It is as a symbol of internal betrayal that the Júa is burnt in Cabral. His immolation is, at best, a means of purifying the community of the scars of such betrayal and, at worst, a displacement of conflicted feelings of anger and guilt onto a convenient scapegoat.

Discreetly but unmistakably, the Júa also has a more recent referent. While Judas is abused, a refrain is sung:

Jua, Jua, Jua, e,
lo mataron por calié.

[Judas, Judas, Judas, eh,
They killed him as a *calié*.]

(Tejeda Ortiz 2008: 515; 1998: 1.184, 188–9)

Caliés were informers in the service of the Servicio de Inteligencia Militar (SIM or Military Intelligence Service), commanded by Johnny Abbes García during the last years of the dictatorship of Rafael Trujillo (1930–61). Recruited from all levels of society, from shoe-shine boys to dignitaries, *caliés*—like Judas—spied on friends, neighbours, employers and colleagues. 'They often took advantage of their position as "informers" to avenge an insult, to settle an account, or simply to harm a neighbour' (Peña Rivera 1977: 231–2; see also Crassweller 1966: 328–34). Later, the term *calié* was used to refer to all those who, as officers, thugs or spies, had worked for the SIM. It is in this broader sense that *caliés* play so prominent a part in Mario Vargas Llosa's novel *The Feast of the Goat* (2000), but even in this fictional account of the Trujillo regime their role as informers remains important. One character recalls 'the infinite nets of espionage that Johnny Abbes García and his vast army of *caliés* spread into every corner of Dominican society' (ibid.: 36). As a *calié*, Cabral's Júa recalls not only the treachery of the biblical Judas and the complicity of black 'traitors' in the time of slavery, but also the more recent trauma of espionage and betrayal during the Trujillo regime.[20]

The Cachúas' game may contain other allusions to the era of Trujillo. Rereading *The Feast of the Goat* less than a month after returning from Cabral, I was struck by the frequent references to treachery, betrayal, 'Judases', scapegoats, devils, endurance under torture, complicity and even 'slavish loyalty' to Trujillo. One of Trujillo's assassins thinks bitterly of the 'perverse system Trujillo created, one in which all Dominicans sooner or later took part as accomplices' (ibid.: 143). Consider, too, this passage from Rober Crassweller's biography of Trujillo. A political prisoner

> was told he would be killed if he did not confess. An iron whip, the *cantaclar* so familiar on these occasions, was used to force him to walk to a nearby slope overlooking the cliffs[. . .]. There the terrible instrument was aimed at his head. He raised an arm in defense, and an Army cadet, infuriated, rushed at him and showered blows on his back [. . .]. More than fifty blows of the whip fell on him. His flesh was torn open (1966: 111).[21]

I find it hard to believe that the whips wielded by Cabral's Cachúas and other festive devils in the Dominican Republic reach back to the trauma of slavery while somehow managing to bypass the more recent trauma of systematic torture of real or suspected dissidents under Trujillo.

Trujillo was assassinated in 1961 but his legacy endured. Only in 1996 did the Dominican Republic finally hold recognizably fair elections. The scars of political repression run deep. Another of Vargas Llosa's characters, returning to the country after 35 years of exile, remarks, 'Something from those times is still in the air' (Vargas

Llosa 2000: 401). If I am correct, the identification of Cabral's Júa with a *calié* from Trujillo's regime is testimony to the power of unresolved trauma to linger in the air even during communal festivities.

The reader may wonder, though, if I am reading too much into the actions of the Cachúas. After all, their only overt reference to the crimes of the Trujillo era occurs in the refrain of a song barely audible above the cracking of hundreds of whips. Perhaps, but I would point out that contemporary Spanish fiestas address the trauma of the Spanish Civil War (1936–39) and the subsequent dictatorship of Francisco Franco (1939–75) no more directly and no less powerfully. The popularity of festive devils in Catalonia, for example, has multiplied exponentially since the death of Franco. Although their historical origins can be traced to the great fifteenth-century Corpus Christi processions in Barcelona and elsewhere (Very 1962), festive Catalan *diables* now serve as markers of autonomous regional culture. They are popularly thought to have their roots in pagan ritual. Without naming Franco, their growing numbers enact a festive rejection of the dictator's centralized Catholic triumphalism.[22]

Spain's fiestas and *danzas de moros y cristianos* (festivals and dances of Moors and Christians) also engage in a festive renegotiation of the Franco legacy (see Harris 2000). Ostensibly referring to the long struggle between Moors and Christians for control of the Iberian peninsula between 711 and 1492 CE, these performances now end in an enactment of reconciliation between former enemies. They embody a longing for *convivencia*, the ability of distinct ethnic, religious and political groups to live alongside one another in peace. Individual members of the towns and villages in which such fiestas and *danzas* take place remember the Franco era with widely varying emotions, depending on their own personal histories and political affiliations. The significance of the longing for *convivencia* in such communities is obvious. The fiestas do not need to state it directly.[23]

There is, however, an important difference between these Spanish fiestas and Holy Week in Cabral. The transformation to democracy in Spain since Franco's death in 1975 has been comparatively smooth. Under such conditions, it is now psychologically possible for those who mask as festive devils, Moors and Christians, to enact (albeit without naming Franco) the end of repressive triumphalism and a hope for *convivencia*. In the Dominican Republic, the restoration of democracy has been much slower. The long aftermath of the Trujillo regime is still a recent memory. The much longer cultural memory of slavery and the Holy Week narrative of guilt, atonement and voluntary suffering also weigh (consciously or otherwise) on the minds of those who mask as Cachúas. Under the circumstances, it is perhaps not surprising that the Cachúas' mutual whippings and their final immolation of the *calié* Judas seemed to me to bear witness less to festive freedom than to unresolved trauma.

As horned devils, then, the Cachúas represent abusive power, whether it be that of Roman and Jewish authorities at the time of Christ, white plantation owners in the days of slavery or Trujillo and his collaborators during the dictatorship. As those who bear the cross, they represent all who follow Christ's example of silent suffering without flinching, whether under slavery or more recent forms of oppression and torture. With even greater dramatic power, they both mask and expose deep cultural scars of betrayal and complicity. The Cachúas whip one another and finally burn the consummate symbol of their own treachery. If I am correct, the festive devils of Cabral are not comic messengers of inclusive divine grace, such as I saw in Loíza, but troubling witnesses to the still-unresolved scars of slavery and a brutal dictatorship.

Notes

1 All translations from Spanish in this essay are by me unless otherwise noted. For more on the Diablos of Elías Piña, see Dagoberto Tejeda Ortiz (1998: 1.199–202); Dagoberto Tejeda Ortiz and Odalis Rosado (2010: 114, 150, 160, 163); Xiomarita Pérez (2008: 28).

2 For more on the *diablicos sucios* of La Villa de los Santos, see Julio Arosemena Moreno (1984: 95–107).

3 For more recent studies of the Fiestas de Santiago Apóstol en Loíza, see Lowell Fiet (2007), the several essays in Fiet (2006–07) and also his contribution in this volume (pp. 168–88).

4 Noting the similarity, Werner Féliz suggests that elements of the Cachúas' costume may have been brought to Cabral from Puerto Rico 'at the beginning of the twentieth century' (2003: 1–2).

5 An almost identical whip, used in the days of slavery, can be seen on the cover of both volumes of Carlos Esteban Deive (1980).

6 For one of Temo's masks, see Tejeda Ortiz and Rosado (2010: 147).

7 Féliz makes the same point, adding that the Cachúas are now being 'carnivalized' (2003: 10, 12). Pedro Muamba Tujibikile, too, complains about the negative effect of commercialized Carnival on the Cachúas (1993: 65–7).

8 For a chilling set of images of whips and whippings from the history of the slave trade and life under enslavement in the Americas, see Jerome S. Handler and Michael L. Tuite, Jr (2008), For official legislation allowing the whipping of enslaved Africans in colonial Hispaniola (now Haiti and the Dominican Republic), see Deive (1989: 237–40).

9 The province of Barahona is a notable exception to the general rule that most of the Dominican Republic's sugarcane is cultivated in the eastern half of the country.

10 *Viejos* of the *danza de los matachines* in Zacatecas, Mexico; *abuelos* of the Pecos Bull Dance in Jemez Pueblo, New Mexico; *abuelos* of the *danza de los matachines* in Bernalillo, New Mexico); *negritos* of the *danza de la pluma* in Teotitlan del Valle, Oaxaca, Mexico (Harris 2000: 10–11, 168, 240–1, 246–9).

11 For the more brutal sling and whip battles at Ch'iaraje, Peru, in which prisoners are taken, beaten and sometimes killed, see Benjamin Orlove (1994: 135–7). E. F. Im Thurn reports whipping battles among the Arawak Indians of Guyana (1901: 141–50).

12 The same may be true of other festive devils who carry whips in the Dominican Republic, such as those from Elias Piña, Guerra, Monte Cristi and Santiago de los Caballeros (see Pérez 2008: 28–9, 33, 39; Tejeda Ortiz and Rosado 2010: 144–6).

13 For the changes in the Easter Vigil, see, for example, Adolf Adam (1981: 63–4, 75–82).

14 In a photograph of a Cachúa from Barahona (Lizardo 1974: 149), there is a cross on the forehead of his mask and a skull and crossbones on each of his wings.

15 Another version of the *diablo cojuelo*'s origins, popular in the Dominican Republic, has him so exhausting the patience of Satan with his mischief that he is thrown to earth, thereby injuring his leg (Pérez 2008: 40; Erickson 2014).

16 The festive devils of Monte Cristi, on the northwest coast of the Dominican Republic, are called *toros* (bulls) (Tejeda Ortiz 2008: 476–7; Pérez 2008: 33).

17 See, for example, my discussion of 'unconscious hidden transcripts' in Harris (2000: 25–7).

18 The Brazilian image, one of a series of drawings made by Jean-Baptiste Debret between 1816 and 1831, was first published in Debret (1834–39: 2.139–40, pl. 45). (Note, too the image of the burning of an effigy of Judas in Rio de Janeiro on Easter Saturday morning, in ibid.: 3.163–4, pl. 21.) For this and other images of black men administering whippings, see Handler and Tuite (2008).

19 See Max Harris (2000: 21–7) and Guy Stresser-Péan (2009: 327–30) for the dance of the *santiagos* and *pilatos* in Mexico's Sierra de Puebla; Bernard Fontana (1979: 128–52) for the role of *fariseos* (and an effigy of Judas) in the Holy Week celebrations of the Rarámuri (or Tarahumara) of northern Mexico; and Richard C. Trexler (2003) for the role of Roman soldiers in the Passion Play of Iztapalapa, Mexico City.

20 Féliz also cites the refrain but insists that it is nothing more than a playful improvisation guided by rhyme and meter. The Júa, he says, represents neither the black overseer of enslaved Africans nor the more recent *calié*. He is 'the traitor who sold Christ'. Nothing more (2003: 9). Werner Féliz, a native of Cabral and a Cachúa, may be right, but I have my doubts. In conversation, Dr Temístocles Féliz Suarez agreed that the Júa represents both Judas and the *caliés*.

21 Vargas Llosa also refers to whips as a means of torture in the era of Trujillo (2000: 328, 336).

22 See my discussion of the festive devils of Manresa, Berga and Vilafranca del Penedès in Harris (2003: 3–18).

23 See, for example, Harris (2003: 29–32). As the memory of Franco fades and North African immigration increases, the Spanish fiestas and *danzas de moros y cristianos* are beginning to address a more immediate need for *convivencia* between immigrant Muslims and native Spanish Catholics.

Our Everyday Devil
The Brazilian Embodiment of European Catholic Tradition

ZECA LIGIÉRO

Perhaps it was Father Manuel da Nóbrega who first introduced the concept of Devil in Brazil. In his reports from Brazilian lands on Native customs written in 1549 in Bahia, he describes a shaman named Caraíba (Caribbean), a prophet who was able to communicate with the spirits through trance, which would turn him into a messenger between humans and the divine.[1] He used a musical instrument called maraca (a rattle made from dried fruit of a gourd) and spent time with indigenous women in a cabin set apart from others, called 'dark house' or 'ritual cabin'. Nóbrega considered this shaman Caraíba an agent of the Devil and his female devotees as possessed ones.

Nóbrega was a pioneer in introducing the indigenous culture to the notion of Hell as it was conceived by the Holy Mother Church, comparing the rituals of shamanism of our indigenous peoples with those practices fiercely fought against by the Inquisition in Europe a few decades earlier. He thus contributed to the invention of a new tradition: tropical hell with feathers, which began to populate the European imagination. An anonymous Portuguese canvas from the sixteenth century depicts Satan, the king of demons, sitting on his throne, wearing a headdress of feathers in the shape of a crown; he is not only a king but also an Indian 'page'. From that time on, the evil power of the European devil became associated with the savages of the Americas; the new image of Satan dominated the environment, subjecting innocent settlers and the Jesuits to temptation and untold suffering, the fantasy obviously reversing the reality of millions of Native Americans devastated by a relatively small group of European invaders carrying diseases of the body and mind.

Father José de Anchieta, Nóbrega's partner and another member of the Compania de Jesus, was the progenitor of the Devil's invasion in Brazil through more than a dozen plays—known as *autos*—written in mediaeval style about the martyrdom of Christians and saints.[2] Colonists, sailors and domesticated Indians staged them in open-air performances as a way of converting the new villages founded by the Portuguese to Catholicism. Anchieta kept the entire production under his control: the writing and the staging as well as the costumes and songs. He was one of the first missionaries to learn to write in Tupi, the native language spoken in the region

FIGURE 1. The Devil with Brazilian headdress. Drawing by Zeca Ligiéro, after a seventeenth-century Portuguese anonymous canvas.

where he lived. He used this knowledge to reinforce his didactic condemnation of the local habits of drinking alcohol, smoking psychotropic herbs and worshipping nature deities. In fact, he considered all Amerindian habits harmful and thus associated them with that dangerous entity with horns and tail.

Nóbrega and Anchieta's perception of Catholicism contrasts significantly with the view of previous invaders, as recorded by the scribe Pero Vaz de Caminha who, along with Pedro Alvares Cabral, arrived in Brazil in 1500. Caminha described the Amerindians as innocent, almost angelic figures. He wrote directly to the king of Portugal, reporting the success of the trip and the first sight of Brazilian lands as a sort of tropical paradise populated by innocuous, beautiful and harmless beings.

Without malice or eroticism, but as an interesting curiosity, he drew attention to the properly shaved genitalia of the woman, who liked walking naked and showering several times a day, putting emphasis on the tropical native habits as an exotic tradition of a people very different from the European ways. Some years later, however, when the Catholic Church's tentacles spread into America, such a sense of primitive virtue was lost and innocent habits, now considered to be sexualized nakedness, became an impure source of sin. Thus, European colonists brought the concept and formulae of the Devil and his court of fallen angels and followers to the New World and settled them in a paradise among tropical foliage, under coconut palms and banana trees. Furthermore, the Portuguese crown contributed to the hellish new reality, for besides randomly chosen sailors (whose origin and training are well known) and mercenaries, unwanted people in Lisbon, such as criminals, thieves and murderers, were given opportunities to populate the New World. In the new land, those who did not cooperate with the Portuguese colonization process were considered infidels, suspected of witchcraft or of having made a deal with the devil. Amerindians had to be baptized and wear European clothes, as well as learn to work with tools that they did not know of and for purposes that they could not imagine.[3]

Once the black population had become more visible in the streets of major Brazilian cities, the Devil was re-imaged in various forms, colours and shades. No more feathers and plumes: he instead began appearing in different ways within various rituals and celebrations, either Africanized or urbanized—sometimes wearing a mask, made of leather or other natural materials, with exaggerated expression or sometimes as a slick 'dude' wearing a Panama hat, a white linen suit and two-toned loafer shoes, as the so-called Brazilian *malandros* resembling the Cab Calloway style of 1920s Harlem. They were almost always in the company of sexy women in red and black dresses who, in turn, soon became associated with witches and black magic.

The cultural battle between Catholic and African traditions has left three main analogues to festive devils: the *palhaço* (clown) of Folia de Reis (Festivals of Kings that fall between Christmas and Three Kings Day, i.e. 6 January); the Eshu (or Exú) of the Candomblé religion; and the Eshu of the Umbanda religion. These three represent a cultural legacy present in different contexts throughout Brazil. If in the very beginning of the process of colonization, the Catholic Church, together with the Portuguese Crown, was severe and repressive, a later policy allowed the proliferation of diverse manifestations inside Catholic fiestas in order to encourage conversion to Christianity.[4] As a result, a formidable range of African and Amerindian representations became part of everyday life for many people.

By the beginning of the eighteenth century, the Catholic Church allowed African dances and the use of the drums to accompany Catholic processions, as long as they took place outside the churches. That assimilative practice, as well as the continuation of African worship, produced the festive forms that we may take as analogues to the festive devils that appear in other cultures.

The Three Devil Characterizations

The clowns of Folia de Reis—a parade of musicians and clowns that ends the Christmas cycle of celebrations—are typically diabolical figures. The other two devil analogues marked by excessive bodily and sexual play are the Eshus who appear in the Candomblé and Umbanda. Because they do not adhere to Catholic dogmas and are typically from African cultures, they are viewed by the majority of Brazilians (the almost 90 per cent of the population who are Catholics and Evangelicals) as the *real* devils, although many important people including even some of the permanent staff of these Christian religions, pay some homage to these entities in significant moments of their lives.

Among the Catholic representations, the *palhaço* or clown appears in the Festival of Kings, which happens often in the southeastern region (the states of Sao Paulo, Minas, Rio de Janeiro and Espirito Santo) and only rarely in other areas of Brazil. Using animal masks with grotesque and exaggerated expressions, they are often performed by people of African descent for this Catholic celebration. Although the African elements of such performances are obvious, folklorists who have studied them as strictly Catholic rituals have not focused on them. One can see how deep-rooted African rituals are in Catholic festivities in many other areas in Brazil where similar celebrations takes place, such as the Seahorse, the Epiphany, the Marujada and so on.

Although the clown in a way represents the Devil in integrative manifestations performed in a circular arrangement or in processions, and sometimes on stage, it has been so well adapted to Catholic rituals that people believe the Devil to be the most entertaining part of the celebrations, albeit embodying an unholy aspect of the celebrations. Such an unholy aspect is complementary, in its own way, to the worship of Catholic saints. In this case, there is no suggestion of Devil worship or even of any African divinity itself, though the attitude towards the body, the costume, and the nature of the dancing and singing leaves no doubt about the origin in a tradition that had its own life in Africa before migrating to Brazil.

The Eshus of Candomblé and Umbanda religions, although showing parallels with icons of African ethnicity in Brazil, are commonly associated with the figure of the Devil. In Candomblé, Eshu is central to the African resistance in Brazil, while in

Umbanda this same figure has absorbed most of the characteristics traditionally attributed to the Catholic Devil. In fact, Umbanda religion has also incorporated Catholic saints and the ideas of Christian charity.

None of the three performances overtly represents the figure of the Devil, but all have some aspects of the Devil's unchained and ambiguous behaviour: his well-known irreverence, sense of humour, tendency towards free play and disrespect of hierarchy. Although all three celebrations have their own wit, there is no blasphemy involved in the portrayals. Thus, these figures are not associated with the traditional figure of the Devil as portrayed by the mediaeval Catholic Holy Mother Church. These three include tender, loving, sensual and sometimes lush figures, whose goal is to bring out the inner life by spreading joy and blessing to the needy and the suffering.

Though analogous to the Devil, they remind people of a remote past, evoking their ancestral lands with traditions of respect, freedom and love between brothers and sisters. The cultural atmosphere, deriving from community celebration, creates its own dynamics centred in the powerful trio of singing, dancing and drumming, which provides the nerve centre for African performance traditions rooted in the sacred.

Using Richard Schechner's definition of 'restored behavior' (1985) as well as his studies of the relationship between play and ritual, this essay will describe these three Afro-Brazilian performances that integrate ritual and play, blending into the tone and rhythm of popular traditions that are often generically identified as 'Brazilian'.

The Clown of the Festival of Kings: A Play of Body and Words

Usually it is on Christmas night that the Folia de Reis[5] appears for the first time in the small villages deep inside Brazil. A member of the group carries a banner with the image of a protector saint, begging money for the journey, invariably bringing at least a couple of clowns called *palhaço de Folia de Reis*. The performance of these masked mavericks—commonly called clowns because of their playful nature and behaviour—breaks the solemn religious chant that announces the birth of the sacred child. The relationship between play and ritual, involving the clown, which, in its capacity to unsettle through wit, is linked with the Devil, establishes an ambiguity that was negotiated early on as the Catholic Church in Brazil attempted to convert both the indigenous population and those brought in for enslavement.

In an interview with Aressa Egly Rios da Silveira, Father Medoro—an intellectual priest—identified the term 'acculturated' as common in theological language: 'faith acculturation' is how a person appropriates the Christian faith, so it can reflect her or his personal, familial or group experience. According to Medoro:

Today, the Catholic church is concerned with pluralistic faces of the religion; the rituals are no longer based solely on a Eurocentric model. We believe we must and can develop our own expression. God transcends all cultures. [...] God has no religion. We produce what is religion in order to appropriate something that belongs to God. In this sense, creativity, diversity become as rich as possible (cited in Rios da Silveira 2009: 159–60).

Father Medoro's speech explains the evolving practice of the Catholic Church as it adapted to (or was 'acculturated in') the cultural context of Brazil. From the early nineteenth century, Christians in several Brazilian states gradually began to tolerate the use of drumming and other African styles of celebration in demonstrations, such as the Congadas and Reisados, as a way of popularizing Catholicism. The Count of Arcos, the governor of Bahia between 1810 and 1817, signed a decree allowing African celebration with drums in order to ease tensions between slaves and masters, followed by authorities of other states (Ligiéro 2014: 26). However, there are written records of black brotherhoods created by slaves and free blacks in the eighteenth century, using African performative elements in their celebrations. These brotherhoods were responsible for the churches of St Efigenia, St Benedict and Our Lady of the Rosary among others. Although Christians, they held secret African rituals in their temples, which included the powerful African performative trio of singing, dancing and drumming (Ligiéro 2011: 131). The etchings of nineteenth-century European artists, such as Johan Moritz Rubendas and Jean Baptiste Debret, who had visited Brazil on scientific and artistic missions, provide extensive testimony to the use of drumming and dancing in Catholic celebrations during that time.

In spite of radical changes that the African customs brought to the performative aspects of Christian celebrations, researchers have generally affirmed only the Iberian characteristics of the Folia de Reis, ignoring their African or Amerindian associations. Though most Folia de Reis, and associations and religious society called Congo and Mozambique, are constituted of those of African descent, it is in the *palhaço* that one may find clearly the dynamics that I call cultural matrices, found notably in the figure's dance, with its multidimensional movements, and in his struggles to express itself in vulgar language.

Typically, the *palhaço* represents Herod, who hunted children to kill the newborn Christ, intruding into a revelry that narrates the journey of the Magi to find Jesus. The clown embodies an internal contrast between his festive, comic aspect (*burlador*) and the negative figure of Herod that he represents,[6] thus carrying within himself the dichotomy between good and evil that is one of the hallmarks of the festive devil throughout the Americas. Representing the forces of evil, the masked performer never comes close to the flag emblazoned with the image of the venerated saints until the end of the day, when he fulfils his ritual before the flag, usually near the ground, by kneeling or even placing his forehead on the floor as a way to salute the object, in a classic pose called Candomblé *dobalê*, used to greet African deities and important religious authorities.

Despite his nominal link with the Christian tradition (through Herod) and his appearance in a Christian festive context, the Folia de Reis clown looks more like a figure borrowed from African ritual, though his terrible appearance, in a goat mask,

FIGURE 2. *Palhaço* (clown) de Folia de Reis of Cruzeirinho, Laje do Muriaé, Rio de Janeiro, 2012. Photograph by Zeca Ligiéro.

does suggest a character who might have made an infernal pact. Indeed, he does sometimes have horns, although never a tail. His behaviour, mocking, ironic and fast-paced, breaks the monotonous music that tells the story of the persecution of the baby Jesus and the long journey of the three Magi to Bethlehem. The *palhaço* thus represents much more than the Christian evil. Along with his dance, he uses 'foul' language to sing, recite and narrate stories satirizing the community, criticizing social ills as high prices, referencing political issues both national, such as former prime minister Luiz Inácio Lula da Silva's policies, and international, such as the American invasion of Iraq.

In her seminal work, Ausonia Bernardes (2004) points to a lexicon of movements and dance steps of Afro-Brazilian culture that are transmitted orally by masters to young clowns so they can create their own styles, developing mechanisms to interpret the tradition in the face of contemporary moves in which his own community is steeped. Ausonia records the ongoing dialogues first in the rural traditions, where many of the groups are founded, and then in their migration to big cities, where the tradition is rebuilt, while adding other 'urban' bodily movements. Not coincidentally, some of these newly assimilated movements belong to traditions associated with Afro-North America, such as break dance, rap and funk.

One could superficially assume that these break-dancing or rapping clowns are 'killing' the tradition. However, to the contrary, in the cities the tradition is enlivened and renewed through dialogue with performative, Afro-derived body language without losing its main characteristics. The matrix of singing-dancing-drumming identified with African ancestors is preserved, but in this context associated with Catholic saints.

Rios da Silveira, researching groups of Folia de Reis in the Paraiba Valley, sees a crisis of values in many groups and realizes that the lack of a cultural policy at a municipal level generates problems and mistaken views with regard to these groups. Regarding the importance of the role of the clown, she notes that for the community member, a performance of the clown gives prestige and visibility, a legitimate social role which the performer does not always find in everyday life. He becomes 'special' during the ritual. Rios da Silveira also sees a strong connection with culture funk (especially in the city of Valencia Folias), where one may find a large number of clowns (not just two or three as tradition dictates), as well as the entry of women dressing as clowns in these processions (2009: 180).

Despite the informality that characterizes the performance of these clowns, one can perceive how they maintain the exceptional scenic virtuosity, always so charged by the master guardian of the traditions. The mask itself, originally made of leather, is now in many cases being made of foam, carpet, rubber and plastic (which can also be purchased ready made) in order to make the most spectacular performance. Thus, masks formerly hand-crafted now have an increasingly industrialized character, sometimes even including lamps or flashing lights. While the traditional African matrices are being reconfigured and partly even lost, the essence of the central matrix has been preserved.

The Folia de Reis *palhaço* is undoubtedly in part a descendant of mediaeval European clowns, as most Brazilian scholars assume.[7] However, the attribution of this to only Iberian traditions is clearly incorrect. The dynamic, gestural movement (as defined by Rudolf Laban's body-movement theory) does not resemble European dances.[8] The representations and movements of the clown's body, as well as his language, more obviously derives from the world of samba or, in contemporary terms, from hip hop and capoeira. Furthermore, his wardrobe, which is in no sense European, is closer to deities who were masked in the African tropical forests of Angola and Congo or in Nigeria's Geledé festivals. Thus, in this figure, we perceive and experience a Catholic tradition transfused with African elements.

The Transformations of Eshu:
From Yoruba Lands in Nigeria to the Candomblé Houses in São Salvador, Bahia

Although Candomblé is not a mass religion the way Catholicism and Evangelic Christianity are, it has gained huge popularity in Brazil because it is centred on the worship of Yoruba deities called Orishas. The beauty of Candomblé dances, their rich and complex clothing, all the mystery involved in their rituals, and their profound ethical sense, as well as their strong connection with nature have drawn the attention of artists, anthropologists and others worldwide.

Eshu (or Exú) is an Orisha from the Yoruba pantheon imported from Nigeria. Special and different from others, though equally important, Eshu is the only Orisha who likes to play, tease, eat in excess and to openly embrace such a lifestyle; he is also a messenger between humans and all the Orishas. One may identify elements of the Greek god Hermes in Eshu in his role as messenger, and in his magical prowess and capacity for divination. Like Hermes, Eshu's myth has also been greatly expanded over the centuries because of his role as the gods' messenger—and therefore the god of communication. He is regarded as the patron of thieves and the helpless, as well as of ambassadors and all those who cross borders. In ancient Rome, Hermes became Mercury, the god ruling the market, sales, profit and trade. Similarly, Eshu is the lord of the crossroads, the master of time and space, the master of communication. He embodies all of human life in its Eshu aspects, for he not only governs the genitals but, in relationship to economic concerns, he is also the patron of those who want to accumulate energy in the form of money.

The connection between the European Devil and the Yoruba Eshu leads back to the early encounters recorded by priests who, along with colonists, participated in the invasion of Africa and who baptized the indigenous peoples' character as the Devil. In my research on Eshu in Africa and Brazil, I noted differences in his representation:

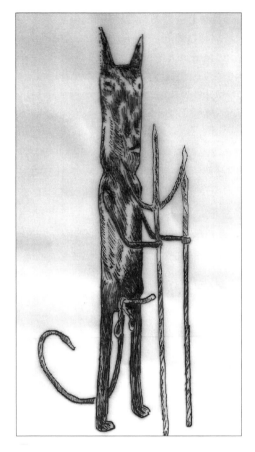

FIGURE 3. Eshu or Exú. Zeca Ligiéro's drawing after a statuette from Bahian popular market

Eshu, whose clay statues have eyes and the mouth of cowrie shells (used in divination), and whose wooden statues show him with an enormous phallus, frightened the early priests into associating this Orisha with their Catholic Devil. But it was more than his libertine features, or *ebó* (offering) with the goats and roosters anointed with alcoholic beverages, which begets uncontrolled, amoral, and chaotic life.

If, for the Catholics, the Devil was the mysterious and immoral force of uncontrolled instinct, this identification was not passively accepted by the Afro-Brazilians; rather they affirmed it as form of rebelliousness. Eshu's independence and internal consistency as an Orisha were neglected, while his vindictive countenance—in harmony with the problems of the oppressed—was emphasized. Instead of a phallic spear extending from the center of the head, a pair of 'devilish' horns sprout from his forehead signifying rupture and savage anarchy against white Christian Portuguese dominances. Thus, although the African beliefs concerning Eshu have not been discarded, representation of this Orisha is concentrated in an image borrowed from Christianity. One consequence of the syncretism is that Eshu continues to be poorly understood as the most human of all the Orisha, the messenger and playful fellow, truly outside the realm of good and evil (1993: 107–8).

The main difference between Brazilian and African Eshus and the Catholic Devil is that, in a mythological sense, Eshu is sometimes an insatiable, playful and irascible infant and sometimes remarkably respected by his adherents for his deep sense of ethics in relation to human destiny; an example of both flexibility and consistency, when upset he can become the opposite. Although considered ambiguous, his ethical principles are well known and he has enough noble attributes not to be concerned with forcing or luring people into bad behaviour—unlike the Devil whose sole function is to do so.

Candomblé public ceremonies usually take place at night. At six in the evening, practitioners perform a ritual called *padê* (meeting), in which they offer white flour, yellow meal (with palm oil) and water, praying and asking for protection from Eshu. This tribute is intended to please him and to forestall any trouble that he might make, for once he is satiated he does not disturb the evening ritual. However, when there is an *iyaô* (son of the saint) in the Candomblé house who is willing to manifest Eshu through trance, he appears, but only in the *iyaô's* head. Once the deity emerges, he can manifest in both male and female mediums.

In the public celebration known as *xirê*, he dances vigorously, twisting and moving in opposite directions. Sometimes he seems to play himself, by pretending he wants to fight other deities (who are also manifested) or even the priests who conduct the ritual, but everything ends with a friendly embrace.[9] In this dancing ritual, Eshu inserts a little play into one of the imaginary fights, in which he pretends to drink from a bottle of *cachaça* (his favourite alcoholic beverage) as if he were drunk—a kind of meta-theatre that reflexively illustrates a thorough knowledge of the playful ambiguities of his own behaviour.

As defined by Schechner in his study of similar processes in other contexts (1988), the performance of Eshu balances behaviour in terms of the scenic elements of play and ritual. His lively and joyous dance contrasts with the dark and threatening aspect of his altars set up at the usually narrow entrances of Candomblé houses. Such altars are called *peji*, in which clay statues and sharp iron tools are carefully arranged and covered with clotted blood of sacrificed animals; large amounts alcoholic beverages are poured over the statues and the tools, whose odour is strong and unmistakable.[10]

The Transformations of Eshu:
From Candomblé in Bahia to Umbanda in the Whole Country

In Umbanda, a religion created in Brazil and popularized by the beginning of the twentieth century that congregated African traditions (Kongo/Angola, Yoruba and Ewe/Fon with Amerindian practices and Christian and spiritualist traditions), Eshu is not exactly a mythological or archetypal figure, although the term is used to name a legion of the spirits of dead people who led a life of crime and disgrace. After having passed through a portal from life on earth to the world of the dead, they cannot get rid themselves of suffering, much less of their earthly vices, especially drinking and smoking, which seem to be their only compensation for eternity.

These entities are simply called 'People of the Street' or Eshus (devils). Their leaders are depicted with horns and tails, like demons. The most popular are Eshu Tranca Rua, Eshu Marabô, Eshu Tirirí, Eshu King of the Seven Crossroads, Eshu Mangueira, Eshu Velvet and Eshu of Rivers (Alva 1987). To create this typically Brazilian pantheon, Umbanda adherents borrowed not only pictures of the Catholic Devil but also a whole collection of Catholic saints whose attributes are interwoven with those of the Orishas; to these were added the teachings of the French leader Allan Kardec,[11] the founder of spiritism, as well as indigenous traditions and the traditions from the Congo–Angola. In fact, one can say that Umbanda recreates the Devil in its backyard, though its 'little devils' are slaves to their addictions and attached to the pleasures of life. Sometimes described as monstrous criminal minds, they do not seem to have the capacity for free will to change human destiny.

During rituals, Umbanda Eshus come down to earth to drink, eat, smoke, advise and heal people and give blessings in their own way. They are charitable: their great mission is to help the faithful to free themselves from suffering, diseases of body and soul, afflictions, black magic, evil eye and all sorts of psychological and financial problems. They come down to earth also to be indoctrinated by the masters of Umbanda, who teach them the path of devotion, so that they may spiritually evolve within the doctrine's principles. By means of healing people, an Eshu might evolve to the point that one day he will not need to come back to earth any more (see Ligiéro and Dandara 1998).

The Eshus are also associated with a typical Brazilian figure, the so-called *malandros*, the best known of whom is Zé Pelintra, from Lapa district in Rio de Janeiro, a sort of symbol of the bohemian behaviour of men who, in the early twentieth century, dwelt between the hills and the city, where radio and theatre artists would frequent the casinos and dancing houses playing the tango and the samba.

FIGURE 4. Zé Pelintra. Photomontage by Zeca Ligiéro.

The image of Zé Pelintra became so popular after he died that it is said that any *malandro* called himself Pelintra, turning into a sort of Eshu (see Ligiéro 2004). The female counterpart of Eshu in Umbanda is the 'Pomba-Gira', a name that comes from the Kikongo word *bombozila,* which means crossroads (see Ligiéro and Dandara 1998), represented as a voluptuous woman, sometimes with bare breasts, sometimes totally naked, though usually wearing red with details in silver or gold. A half-breed, brunette or blonde, usually with long and bulky hair, she has a constant smile and seems to squander happiness, her big breasts exposed or semi-exposed under a sensual low-cut dress.

There are few images of this deity as a black woman. In the ritual of the People of the Street, Eshu and Pomba-Gira recreate a ballroom in the yard, where they dance together, entwined, and change partners according to their temperaments and musical tastes, which range from samba, bolero and tango rhythms to other lesser-known musical styles. A remarkable feature of the Afro-Brazilian performances in general is this interconnection between play and ritual. Aspects that usually clash in the so-called Western religions have found in the traditional Afro-Amerindian celebrations a fertile ground to relax and meet with the forces of nature—these, as Eshu deities, are at the same time coherent and chaotic.

In religions in which humour is not understood as sacred, play can be fatal to a believer. Not so here. Black African traditions do not encourage blasphemy or disrespect towards other religions and their gods; on the contrary, within those traditions, deities and ancestors are very tolerant and have a great sense of humour and some, especially Eshus, are masters of the playful.

Adapted to the life of the People of the Street, playful scenes achieve this balance perfectly—the celebration space is decorated with flowers, food spiced with seasonal flavours, and cocktails, *cachaça* being the preferred beverage along with a good supply of iced beer. During the ritual (or party), all entities (Eshus and Pomba-giras) dance, play, talk, gossip about one another's behaviour and interact with the audience, giving people advice on love, money and sex.

However, even the contemporary story does not stop with this healthy playfulness in the representations of Eshu. Even now in the teachings of Evangelical Christian churches, African traditions that permeate any Afro-Brazilian religion, such as Candomblé and Umbanda, have become synonymous in a darker and more dangerous way with the demonic—as alliances with the Devil, they are seen as 'primitive cults' concentrating evil and terrible power, tied to sin for ever and to the darker, noncomic aspects of the Christian Devil. In recent years, police have reported several incidents of burglary in Candomblé and Umbanda houses by supposed church affiliates who destroyed statues and other ritual items, often using physical violence against members of these communities, thus promoting a sadly increasing crusade against practices they see as witchcraft and satanic rituals:

> The *yaloriyá* Gilda died of massive heart attack in 1999 after members of a Pentecostal church raided her house and hit her on the head with a copy of the Bible. This is the crudest image of religious intolerance that is increasing in Brazil, which has just been denounced at the United Nations. This sectarianism is aimed especially against the religions of African origin, as in the case of the Gilda, the priestess of Candomblé, according to the report delivered this week by the Commission on Combating Religious Intolerance (CCIR) to Uhomoibai Martin, chairman of the UN Human Rights Commission. It extends against other religious beliefs including the Jewish, Catholic, Muslim and the spiritualist.
>
> The document submitted by a multi-sectorial committee of different faiths reporting 15 cases treated by the CCIR in four Brazilian states accuses the Charismatic Churches, especially the Universal Church of the Kingdom

of God of assault, harassment and of spreading religious intolerance. It is found in speeches delivered to convince people to join such churches, which is mostly based on the 'demonization' of African-Brazilian religions, 'Jews have become the "Christ killers", Catholics "demon worshipers", Protestants are accused of being "false Christians" and Muslims "evil" for following Muhammad instead of Jesus,' the document says.[12]

Nevertheless, despite the distorted portrayal of the playful performances of the Eshus and of Afro-based religious practices as scenes of satanic worship or uncontrolled orgies, 'evil things' do not go on in such gatherings. What really takes place is a celebration of fellowship. Insofar as the Eshus resemble festive devils, they embody the cathartic, healing energies of these creatures.

Final Considerations

I have attempted to find analogues to and show some faces of the festive devil in the tropical soils of Brazil. Of course, instead of sulphur our devils prefer perfume with lavender, orange flower water. No true lovers of the fire, they like hot beverages, rejuvenating spirits. Obviously, they generally favour love, sex and sometimes the slutty. Strong also is the passion for money, which represents the fullness of earth's energy. The *palhaço de Folia de Reis* is delighted when someone throws coins on the floor for him to snatch. For believers of Candomblé, one wishing to ask a favour of Eshu must place seven coins at the intersection and shout the name right. We also have demon hybrid forms, not prone to do evil but to promote earthly happiness for the devout; they bring blessings, sparing no efforts since the supplicant does not transform their lives into a hell of stupid requests.

These three figures, in different ways, remind people of their often distant ancestral lands, where respect for human life is sacred. Thus, they stand as guardians who, having survived the violence and destruction of their Afro-Brazilian history, have kept alive their ability to play, dance, sing and enjoy a sense of humour. They embody the continuity of traditions and wisdom of Africans and their descendants in the Americas.

Notes

This essay, originally written in Portuguese, was translated into English by the author.

1   Manuel da Nóbrega (1517–70) was appointed in 1549 by the Provincial of the Jesuits from Portugal following Tomé de Sousa, the first governor of Brazil. He developed intense missionary work which resulted, in 1554, in the founding of the college's Piratininga Plateau, the nucleus from which grew the city of São Paulo. In

collaboration with José de Anchieta (1534–97), he managed to pacify the Tamoios in 1563.

2   Anchieta wrote of 'St Ursula Auto' and 'Auto of St Lawrence', among others, in which the Native Brazilians embodied the Devil figure by singing and dancing their own rituals restored from their own traditions.

3   The connection between the King of Portugal, colonists and the Catholic Church has been celebrated in art for centuries. In 1861 it was immortalized by a Victor Meirelles painting called *The First Mass in Brazil*, in which both conquerors and priests share a space where a cross is being planted under the curious eyes of an audience of natives. This image appeared on Brazilian banknotes from 1932 to 1975.

4   A legacy of Portuguese colonization, Catholicism was the state religion in Brazil until the Republican constitution of 1891, which established the secular state. The census conducted in 2000 by Instituto Brasileiro de Geografia e Estatística (IBGE or Brazilian Institute of Geography and Statistics) pointed out that 73.8 per cent of Brazilians (about 125 million) identify as Catholic, while 15.4 per cent (about 26.2 million) state they are Evangelical (conservative Evangelicals, Pentecostals and neo-Pentecostal) and only 0.3 per cent say they are followers of African traditional religions such as Candomble, Tambor-of-mine and Umbanda.

5   This is a group (a band and the clown and someone with the flag of the saint, who in Arazil are called *folioes* or merrymakers), but the event is not a festival. It is a group of pilgrims who, during day and night, go from place to place begging for money in exchange for divine songs. The songs are about Christ's birthday and the persecution by Herod of all children, Jesus in particular.

6   This opposition is in itself characteristic of King Herod's appearances in European mediaeval drama as well, where he is a blustering, overly dramatic bombast and, thus, comic as well as viciously tyrannical.

7   Folia de Reis is described on the Internet as 'Festival of Portuguese origin and a Brazilian tradition' (available at: http://culturaseafectoslusofonos.blogspot.com/-2011/12/-folia-dos-reis-festa-religiosa-de.html; last accessed on 9 December 2014), although all the participating members are Afro-descendants. In the website of the Portuguese Consulate in Brazil, it is described as such: 'Festival of the Kings, a religious Portuguese celebration that became tradition' (available at: http://-embaixada-portugal-brasil.blogspot.com/2011/12/folia-de-reis-festa-religiosa-de-origem.html; last accessed on 9 December 2014). Again, all the pictures captured show solely Afro-Brazilian members.

8   Laban (1879–1958), a Hungarian-born German, developed a system of analysing movement in relation to the dynamic use of the body in space.

9   *Xirê* is a generic name given to all the public ceremonies in houses of Candomblé, where all the Orishas of the house are present.

10 Usually each Orisha has its own *peji*, in some cases, collective *peji* of family-related Orishas.

11 Hippolyte Léon Denizard Rivail (1804–69) was an educator, writer and French translator. Under the pseudonym of Allan Kardec, he became famous as the encoder

of spiritualism (neologism created by him), also called spiritism (Ligiéro and Dandara 1998: 61).

12 Inter Press Service, 'RELIGIÃO-BRASIL: Intolerância é denunciada nas Nações Unidas' (Religion—Brazil: Intolerance is denounced at the United Nations), 2 July 2009 (available at: http://www.ipsnoticias.net/portuguese/2009/07/america-latina/religiao-brasil-intolerancia-e-denunciada-nas-nacoes-unidas/; last accessed on 1 April 2015). The CCIR was created over a year and is composed of 18 religious institutions that defend human rights, such as the Israelite Federation of Rio de Janeiro, the Umbanda Spiritist Congregation of Brazil and others associated to Protestant, Catholic, Muslim, Candomblé and Buddhist religions as well as to Indigenous and Gypsy groups. The CCIR has emerged from the 'increasingly urgent need for the defence of those adherents to religions of African origin, faced to the destruction and demonization of their religious practices,' says the above report delivered to the UN.

'The *Vejigante* Is Painted / Green, Yellow, and Red . . .'

LOWELL FIET

Prucutá, prucutá y bueno que está
Toco, toco, toco, toco
El vejigante come coco
El vejigante comió mangó
Hasta las uñas se las lambió
Vamos muchachos pa'la marina
Para comer pan y sardina

[and in another variation]
Adiós papá, adiós mamá que me voy
con la comparsa . . . a gozar
El vejigante está pintao
Verde, amarillo y colorao . . .[1]
(Popular verses)

If the action of the processions of Santiago Apóstol (St James) functions as perform-ance, as a symbolic and aesthetic act designed and 'restored' to communicate specific meanings, even though ambiguous, multifaceted and masked, then that performative takes shape and lives within the imaginary of the attending public—those that wait by Highway 187 in Loíza, Puerto Rico, on the afternoons of 26–28 July to watch, as well as those, whether or not in costumes and masks, who 'march [with] the saint' on the same route. As was supposedly the case of the religious/secular plays of European mediaeval theatre, in some versions, precursors of the local processions, the devils (mischievous, sensual and, at times, aggressive and rude harassers) continue to be the most attractive characters of the festivities. Within African traditions of carnival, the disguised devil-trickster holds a central dramatic position which is also evident in the festivals and popular ceremonies throughout the Caribbean and circum-Atlantic region. The particular Loízan version of the *vejigante* (trickster/diablo), in conjunction with the fancy-dressed *caballero* (gentleman or knight), the manic but playful teasing of the *loca* (wild or crazy woman) and the *viejo* (old man, sometimes *loco*), usually delights the spectators/participants. The audience has arrived in the name of Santiago Apóstol, but they wait for, observe and react to the energy, clownishness, selfish pleas-ure and visual lustre of the masks and costumes associated with the liminal character of the *vejigante* and its carnivalesque companions.

FIGURE 1. A *comparsa* or mas of *vejigantes* in the processions of Santiago Apóstol. This and all other photographs in this chapter are by and courtesy of the author.

Within the context of the Caribbean carnival sketched by Antonio Benítez Rojo (1989), it seems appropriate to affirm that 'there are no fiestas without diablos' and, in the context of Puerto Rico, that diablo is generically described as the *vejigante*. However, this also means there are different ways of defining a *vejigante* and identifying its functions within a variety of festival and carnival activities. Annual celebrations in Loíza, Ponce, Ponce Playa, Arroyo, Dorado, etc., include the presence and mischievousness of *vejigantes*.[2] In some cases, there is a noticeable difference between the 'simulated' *vejigantes* (who wait passively, disguised in traditional masks or in Hollywood-inspired rubber-monster masks, for the events of the municipal government's programme) and the 'subterranean' *vejigantes*. The latter seem to almost magically appear on the margins of the events, defying authorized purposes by, first, mocking the spectators if they do not receive the attention, drinks, money or other favours requested and, second, representing generalized physical-sensual pleasure in contrast to religious Catholic veneration or institutional order. Nevertheless, the Loíza *vejigante* is usually neither simulated nor subterranean. It represents a corporeal and spiritual presence inseparable from the complex nature of the processions of the saint.

FIGURE 2. The 19-horned and bearded Sol Boricua or Puerto Rican Sun is a mask designed by master mask maker Raúl Ayala.

In Ponce, the *vejigantes* carry inflated bladders or inflated toys, such as oversized baseball bats or hammers, to fight among themselves and scare children and other spectators. Many children are also dressed up as *vejigantes* during the carnival activities; but almost never will a respectable and somewhat rebellious adolescent wear a traditional costume with a papier mâché *vejigante* mask. The Hollywood- and Halloween-inspired masks (*Star Wars*, *Planet of the Apes*, *Friday the 13th*, etc.) dominate the streets during the carnival parade. The adolescent crowd appears to feel more irreverent and non-conformist in the 'foreign' masks than they do by wearing the traditional ones. For them, the papier mâché or *cartón piedra* mask, regardless how elaborate its artistry, seems best suited for children, tourists and museums, rather than for use in the streets. Nevertheless, the other *vejigante*, the subterranean version, continues to show up on the last night for the funeral of the Sardine, Ponce Carnival's closing event. This traditionally dressed *vejigante*, with its imaginary beast-like face, horns, a mouth full of teeth, and wild eyes, insistently demands coins and other favours, dances and drinks all night and, at times, proves a nuisance to the official organization of the event.

The Ponce *vejigante* masks vary from simple styles, without horns, to multi-horned and crested masks that are visually very complex and captivating. The masks demonstrate such elaboration and dimension in their combinations of colour, crests, pikes, horns and teeth that many of them lose their functionality in street perform-ance and are destined for galleries and art-and-craft stores. For example, the masks created by the deceased artist Alberto González represent the Ponce mask as a work of art that demands exhibition as sculpture, removed from its effectiveness as festival art. Some styles of the coconut mask of the Loíza *vejigante* run the same risk. The more elaborate masks are frequently created for collectors, galleries and museums. Their size makes them unmanageable in a long, hot street march and their horns can be dangerous during rapid movements in the processions. Over a decade ago, 'foreign' and fantastical rubber masks also proliferated in the processions of Santiago Apóstol in Loíza, especially among adolescents and young adults. The municipal legislature reacted by restricting the use of such 'non-traditional' masks and costumes during the fiestas. Rubber masks have since been almost totally excluded and, since 2008, a profusion of traditional and innovative styles of locally crafted *vejigante* masks has been observed.

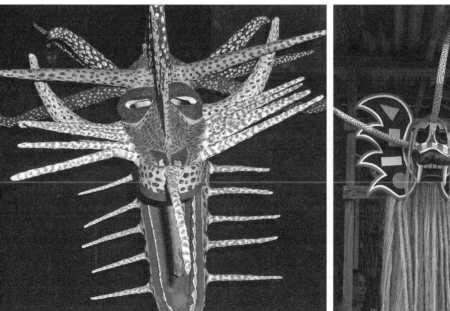

(LEFT) **FIGURE 3**. This elaborate papier mâché *vejigante* from Ponce was crafted in the early 1990s by Alberto González. (RIGHT) **FIGURE 4**. This large 'geometric' *vejigante* from Loíza, made from two coconut husks, is the work of master mask maker Pedro Laviera.

Occasionally, a mask from Ponce surfaces in a Loíza procession; outside Loíza a generalized confusion exists in terms of the differences between the two masks. The cover of the 1992 edition of Francisco Arriví's well-known play *Vejigantes* (1957) ironically portrayed a papier mâché Ponce mask rather than the traditional coconut mask from Loíza, where the play's first act takes place.[3] The difficulty in distiguishing the two *vejigantes* arises from the fact that contemporary advertising trends tend to combine the elements of traditional festivals and reinforce the focus of local anthropology on the Iberian elements within the two traditions. In contrast, this essay intends to distinguish them based on the fact that not only are they different celebrations but they also arise from different traditions, at times with shared meanings but derived from and developed under disparate conditions: the more Iberian *vejigante* of Ponce's Pre-Lenten Carnival and the more African *vejigante* of the Fiestas of Santiago Apóstol of Loíza.

An exploration of these differences helps to better understand the nature of the drama and spectacle that erupts on Highway 187 in Loíza during the fiestas. When seen as 'performance' (regardless of whether the term is used as Melville J. Herskovits [1940], Victor Turner [1982], Richard Schechner [1990] or Jon McKenzie [2001] have used it), the *vejigante* takes on the most dynamic and aesthetic part in the development of *egungun* or ancestral elements in the sacred/profane Afro-Creole carnival of Loíza. The *vejigante*, the most complex and yet relatively undefined character that walks through the political-cultural portal opened by the *caballero* (knight) within the restrictive Catholic, colonial, slave-holding plantation society of nineteenth-century Puerto Rico, represents a collage of overlapping elements: cooked and raw, secular and religious meanings, sensual and comic appetites, threatening and simultaneously affectionate behaviour, and phantasmagoric features contrasted with everyday human pleasures. The specific and local Hispanic-Afro-Creole mythology also projects general and universal themes of the relationship of the dead to the living, rebirth and renovation, liminal spaces that allow for the rehearsal of physical, geographical and social transformations, and pasts and presents that fuse the gaps of the unresolved 'social drama' (Turner 1982) that accompanies the African experience in Puerto Rico and the Americas in general. Although all the elements of its syncretic origins cannot be specifically identified, the sensual and astute Diablo-trickster-clown-*vejigante* of Loíza is the only performer or carnival character without whom it would be impossible to conceive of the Fiestas of Santiago Apóstol as they have existed throughout the previous two centuries and into the present one.

What or who does the *vejigante* represent inside Loízan specificities? The answers vary considerably. No specific theory or genealogy exists that can clarify with certainty if the *vejigante* directly mirrors African origins (such as Julie Taymor's diablos in *The Lion King*), European origins (such as the *bojiganga* that appears in the pages of Cervantes)[4], a mixture, fusion or coincidence of the two 'origins', or a new and hybrid expression that relates exclusively to the Afro-Puerto Rican context. Or perhaps, in the twenty-first century, it represents a tradition too contaminated by anthropologists, playwrights, global consumer products and municipal and state intentions to stimulate the international tourist market to make reasonable distinctions any longer. If we look at the processions of Santiago Apóstol as the expression of a 'social drama', then traditional characters such as the *vejigante* should also play a role (as they possibly did in the past) in finding ways to approach new social ruptures that impact the adolescent population of Loíza and the rest of Puerto Rico: increasing school-dropout rates, adolescent pregnancies, limited economic options, idleness, underemployment, substance abuse, the violence of drug trafficking as well as the violence at home and in schools.

In the version presented by Arriví in V*ejigantes*, the *vejigante* who dances in Loíza is Benedicto, a Galician who 'seduces' Toña, the young Loízan dancer. It seems important to note that Arriví captures an essential but often overlooked feature of the *vejigante*: the sensuality within an unsupervised and unregulated environment that permits visceral pleasures of drinking, eating, dancing and singing as well as sexual encounters and deviations. Every manifestation, parade, procession and celebration also disguises the rite of fertility and the process of finding a lover/partner. The

FIGURE 5. A brilliantly coloured *vejigante* approaches a young woman.

carnival transformations that Mikhail Bakhtin[5] proposes are, in many ways, based on the temporary suspension of the norms of usual sexual conduct. This can result in 'inappropriate' couples or, as projected in Arriví's play, a way for an unequal couple to attain, even in an ambivalent way, what it desires: for him, to taste the *animalidad* (youthful sensuality) of the dark-complexioned Creole and keep her as his consensual lover, and for her, to change her social status and give birth to a daughter with a complexion lighter than her own.[6] Nevertheless, as in the sensual mulatto poetry of Luis Palés Matos or Puerto Rican intellectual Tomás Blanco's attempt in the 1930s to differentiate the music and lyrics of the plena from the 'barbarous' African-influenced bomba, the example of Arriví's *vejigantes* loses part of its pertinence by being suspended in the context of antiquated sexual attitudes and racial politics.

Unlike the *caballero*, the *loca* and the *viejo*, the *vejigante* does not seem to have a direct referent within the plantation system or colonial society. The name seems to derive from *vejiga* (bladder)[7] because of the inflated goat, pig or cow bladders that were (purportedly) used, in one version, by the *vejigantes* (representing the Moors) to fight with the *caballeros* (representing the Spaniards) and, in another version, by them to castigate with blows the spectators who refuse to give them money, drink or other favours. In general, the *vejigantes* from Loíza no longer carry *vejigas* while, as previously mentioned, those in Ponce still use pig or cow bladders or inflated plastic toys to menace passers-by and one another. The perception of the *vejiga* is further complicated by comparison with the practices by other kinds of Caribbean tricksters/diablos of simulating fights or competitions in which weapons such as bladders, sticks or whips punish more through humiliation than through pain. A bladder or *vejiga* is but one of several possible weapons but it does not necessarily define the *vejigante*.

The painter Samuel Lind writes that 'a *vejigante* without a *vejiga* is like a warrior without his sword' (2005). His intent seems to be to rescue memories, real or imagined, of *vejigantes* with *vejigas* in the streets of Loíza. However, there are very few *vejigas* in Ricardo E. Alegría's 1949 film *La Fiesta de Santiago Apóstol de Loíza Aldea* and the ones that do appear are not the large, inflated bladders of Ponce's *vejigantes*. Rather, they seem to be small goat bladders attached to thin sticks and resemble the padded paper bags on sticks (dowels) that a small minority of *vejigantes* now carry during the processions in an obvious attempt (like Lind's essay) to rescue the *vejiga* from relative obscurity.[8] The situation proves ironic: in Loíza, the Spanish conquerors (*caballeros*) neither ride horses nor carry swords, and the Moors (presumably, the *vejigantes*) do not have *vejigas* or other weapons. As a matter of fact, if there were indeed swords, *vejigas* and fights at one time, their functions and motives now seem almost entirely lost.

FIGURE 6. A small minority of *vejigantes* in Loíza carry simulated *vejigas* such as the one seen here.

A whip fight between the winner and loser constitutes the most popular element of the competition of reciting verses from Shakespeare's *Julius Caesar* in Creole English during the carnival on the Grenadine Island of Carriacou. The game is playful yet very serious: the whips are made of a strong electrical cable, while cardboard hoods and special headgear underneath the embellished costumes protect the 'actors'. Similar play-fights characterize almost all Afro-Caribbean celebrations and carnivals. In Santiago de los Caballeros in the Dominican Republic, for example, *vejigantes* of different barrios, using masks of varied colours and styles, can still be found 'fighting' in the streets. In Loíza, recent municipal codes explicitly prohibit the carrying of sticks, bats or any other instruments that could cause physical harm during the fiestas. But that measure appears unrelated to the use of inflated bladders or the symbolic fighting between Moors and Spanish knights.

It seems reasonable to assume that the word *vejigante* relates to the word *bojiganga*, which describes the mediaeval carnival process in which jugglers and buffoons utilized instruments (perhaps *vejigas*, as described by Cervantes) to punish their spectators. Nonetheless, rather than having a possible etymological root, the origin of the *vejigante* from Loíza could as easily have resulted from the attempt by

Spanish colonizers to name African-influenced expressions in terms of their own understanding and vocabulary. In this way, the European *bojiganga* converts into the Caribbean *vejigante*, but only within the confines of the colonial language. There is another, perhaps more interesting, possibility. It is altogether conceivable that what emerges in *Don Quijote* as *bojiganga* already has its roots in Africa. This would mean that the European–Spanish carnival dates at least as far back as the arrival of Ladino[9] African slaves in the late fifteenth century or, earlier still, to the Crusades or the occupation of the Iberian peninsula by Moors (see Benítez Rojo 1989: 183). It could even date back to the Roman Empire and its importation and assimilation of a multiplicity of foreign cultural practices. African 'transculturation' could have influenced the perception of the *vejigante* from two directions: one through Europe and its multicultural development; the other through the enslaved African workers who began to arrive in Puerto Rico at the beginning of the sixteenth century. Although speculative, this hypothesis[10] reflects as firm a historical base as previous ones that concentrate strictly on the syncretic development of Catholic-African cultural and artistic forms. In fact, it would be a great irony if the Spaniards named the *vejigante* because the word they knew and adapted (i.e. *bojiganga* or *begigante*) already had African roots—yet another case of the material, linguistic and cultural appropriations by Europe of India, China, the Middle East, Africa and the Americas from at least the thirteenth century onwards.

But today's *vejigante*, like the African carnival mummers or devils of *The Lion King*, is not the Christian Devil, nor does it represent Satan, unconditional evil or

FIGURE 7. In spite of objections by evangelical Christian groups, it is difficult to interpret the *vejigante* as being evil or devil-like in any but the festive sense. This star-eyed design is a case in point.

eternal Hell (and it probably never has). The celebrations of Corpus Christi in Los Santos, Panama, use a non-mischievous and frightening papier mâché mask with very sharp teeth and two upright horns that emerge out and away from the skull. In contrast, the *vejigantes* of Loíza and Ponce are not diabolic in the Christian sense. They can be frightening because of their bestial shape, horns and teeth, but their purposes are not malevolent, for they are more interested in pleasure than in evil or sin. In another example, St Lucian poet Derek Walcott remembers the Franco-Catholic carnival character of 'the Devil in red underwear, with a hemp beard, a pitchfork and a monstrously packed crotch, backed by a molasses-smeared chorus of imps [that] would perform an elaborate black mass of resurrection at the street corners' (1970: 22). It was not an evil or infernal devil but, rather, a pathetic one—most likely with a cowbell tied to his tar-stained rear that would represent the African population's vision of the elite white devil. The *vejigante* from Loíza shares some but not all the characteristics of the ferocious devil from Panama and the buffoon from Saint Lucia. Its principal function differs when understood outside a Christian context. Even the apparent selfishness revealed in its (part acted and part real) pursuit of sensual pleasures serves the purpose of calling dead ancestors to return and enjoy life.

The coconut mask reinforces the impression of sensuality, the enjoyment of the physical pleasures as well as mischievous and transgressive joy. It is made of the dry and smooth exterior shell or husk of the coconut. The material is porous, light, resistant and durable and, with few tools (a machete, handsaw and knives), a skilled artisan readily carves the features of the eyes, the mouth and the nose, adding teeth and horns made from other parts of the coconut tree. The teeth, however, are frequently made from bamboo splints. Sometimes a long tongue is added and, for exhibitions, a cigar—although these features do not always appear in the masks used in the street processions. Since around 2005, new styles have emerged that emphasize a particularly thick and sensuous tongue. The colours added begin with the white gesso used to seal the pores of the carved features, after which oil or acrylic paint is applied: black and white to emphasize the features, while red, yellow and green (the presumed colours of Santiago and San Patricio) as well as royal blue and orange for special effects, although other colours and tones are also used. Some masks are even painted to resemble the Puerto Rican flag.

The brilliant colours of the masks are relatively new, said to be added in the 1950s by Greek artisans brought to the island by the Puerto Rico Industrial Development Company and the Institute of Puerto Rican Culture to work with local mask makers to develop the masks as marketable products for export. Earlier, the coconut shell would have been left in its natural colour and only the human features would be added along with small dots of colour.[11] Although Don Castor Ayala was

FIGURE 8. This *camparsa* of *vejigantes* displays a wide range of colors and styles, including the Puerto Rico flag to the right.

the Loízan artist who most influenced the painting of the entire smooth outer surface of the coconut shell, it remains important to recognize that many other artists from Loíza also carve and paint *vejigante* masks. Don Castor's son, Raúl Ayala, is currently the most prominent (see Figures 2 and 9). Along with the traditional mask with three horns made famous by his father, Raúl has extended the tradition with more elaborate styles, with some masks with 20 or more horns, hemp beards, teeth carved in the same coconut shell and more brilliant colour combinations. These masks have names, such as Sol Boricua, Cumbé de Cocales, Monalisa, Obiguaiza, Tristeza Encantada. Perhaps his most fascinating design presents a yin-yang mirroring effect in green and yellow. It is named Yagrumo, after a local tree with large leaves that are brown on one side and silver on the other.

Another artist whose masks have gained prominence in Loíza and the US is Pedro Laviera. Working in styles different from those of Raúl Ayala, Laviera seems to make formal experiments that explore how far the artist can go by working with the coconut mask as a medium. Carlos Ayala, another innovative mask carver who worked with coconut and wood and also attempted to rescue a style of the mask once made from tin, was accidentally killed in a drive-by shooting in February 2011. At 42, he was the youngest and most innovative of Loíza's most important mask makers (see Figure 11).

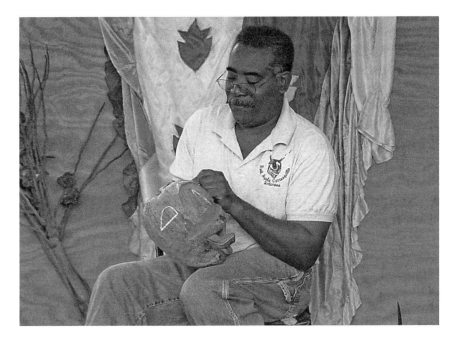

(ABOVE) **FIGURE 9.** Raúl Ayala carves a mask in his workshop. (BELOW) **FIGURE 10.** Pedro Laviera displays one of his geometric masks.

FIGURE 11. The design, colouration and beard of this mask, worn here by the artist, shows some of the innovative work of Carlos Ayala Calcaño.

The *vejigante*'s one-piece cover-all costume with hood usually mirrors the colours of the mask. The fabric is ample enough to permit the *vejigante* to run with arms extended and catch the wind like a sail or a kite. This flying aspect has motivated the idea that the *vejigante* with its horns and teeth might represent a bat with its vampire associations of blood thirst, evil and the Devil. Although this is attractive as a theory, the *vejigante* seems too popular and enjoys his irreverence too much for it to represent a vampire.

Along human facial features, many African masks, along with those of North American Indigenous groups, frequently represent animal heads. These heads, in some cases large skulls like that of a bison, can be realistic or mythical and phantasmagoric. The *vejigante* mask, whether from Ponce or Loíza, suggests imaginary animal characteristics and dream-like anthropomorphic faces, much like animal masks, such as the Jaguar from Panama, the Horsehead from Jonkonnu in Jamaica and papier mâché mule and zebra heads from Barranquilla in Colombia, which also integrate animal and human features. Perhaps the mask most similar to the Loíza *vejigante* is the Cowhead from Jamaica, which has cow's horns attached to a base of calabash or coconut and a wire-screen face mask. In the Afro-Jamaican context, the horns represent prestige and superior strength. Fernando Ortiz has documented images of the 'diablito' Ñáñigo and the Kokorioko from Cuba, which also serve as visual referents for the design and materials of the costumes as much as for the aesthetics and efficacy of the *vejigante*'s performance (1981[1951]: 480).

The Pitchy-Patchy, another character of the Jamaican Jonkonnu celebration, shares several qualities with the Loíza *vejigante*. Being the most popular character in the festivities, it runs, threatens, growls and plays with the spectators. Its brilliant costume consists of hundreds of multicolour fabric swatches or 'patches' made of shrubs and leaves that supposedly substitute for the Jamaican Maroons' war camouflage. Although the Pitchy-Patchy does not wear a mask similar to that of the *vejigante*, the Maroon metaphor clearly frames both characters. In Jamaica, the camouflaged warriors sought refuge in the treacherous terrain of the Cockpit Country, whereas in Loíza the rebellious slaves and, equally importantly, the free blacks and mulattos resisted white Spanish authority by expressing their relative freedom and cultural lineage through the *vejigante*'s sensuality, jocose fierceness and ironic irreverence. Although no distinct relationship results from these comparisons, acting, playing or performing the *vejigante* in the fiestas signifies freedom—both the liberty to enter into the liminal and libertine open space of festivity and the more palpable freedom of the Maroon who escapes from the plantation or municipal authority, even if only for a day.

FIGURE 12. This thick-tongued *vejigante* seems to represent a thirst for tasting pleasure.

The refrain 'El vejigante comió mango / Hasta las uñas se las lambió' centres on the body in terms of the pleasures denied by enslavement and poverty on the one hand and on death on the other. This is the basis of 'cultural resistance' and dictates the need to continue dancing, singing, enjoying and loving, 'even if they kill me'. It also means continuing to give life to the ancestors who cannot enjoy these pleasures except, in Joseph Roach's vocabulary, through their living substitutes or 'surrogates' (1996). Thus acting or playing the *vejigante* is also a symbolic form of spirit possession, sometimes individual and at other times collective, through which the ancestors can return to the living state through the *vejigante*'s body. The informal and formal acts and plays (*comparsas*) by *vejigantes*, in groups or as individuals, coincide and combine with ludic actions and antics in a polysemous parade of diverse rhythms, meanings, colours, movements, sounds and gestures that accompany and complement the processions of three separate saints.[12] Of these, Santiago of the Children, known as Santiaguito, is the saint whose hand-carved statue was originally found under a cork tree and taken to the town's church. It miraculously returned to the tree, a process that recurred three times. As a result, the saints 'live' in the community and not in the church, and every year they make their journeys of renovation. All

FIGURE 13. The image of child-like Santiago de los Niños or Santia-guito includes the head of a Moor beneath the horse's hooves as well as religious amulets and favours.

three processions proceed on foot from Loíza's central plaza to the Las Carreras neighbourhood, a distance of approximately 5 kilometres, where legend says that Santiaguito was found 200 years ago, if not much earlier. Ironically, perhaps, the small wooden saint revered by the Afro–Puerto Rican community of Loíza also represents Spain's patron saint, Santiago *matamoros,* St James, the Moor Killer. The speculative, but once widely accepted, claim that this *santo de palo* reflected features of Yoruban sculpture has been discredited in more recent scholarship.[13]

In a recent interview, the New Zealand–born Puerto Rican mask maker and per-formance artist Deborah Hunt commented that the visual-plastic impact of the *veji-gante*'s colours do not permit the mask to function effectively in a formal theatrical context. The expressions do not change, and hence, according to Hunt, its place remains out of doors as a 'street performer . . . a sacred clown' (see Tabares 2004–05). However, it is essential to add that the Loíza *vejigante* is never just its mask. It is also its costume and body. Furthermore, it never acts alone. The street fills with *veji-gantes,* each varied in colour, form and expression, as well as with *caballeros, locas, viejos,* the followers of the saints and other participants. This display constitutes the 'dialogic' form that Bakhtin attributes to the carnival with its polyphony of voices

FIGURE 14. This grouping of *vejigantes* includes a woman at the centre.

(1984b: 101). Moreover, according to Michael Hardt and Antonio Negri, the plural and interactive composition of the carnival also 'puts in motion an enormous capacity for the innovation, innovation that can transform the reality' (2004: 210). Thus, the *vejigante* assumes multiple meanings in the web of characters, voices and colours in the street performance of the procession.

According to this analysis, the *vejigante* also assumes the position of the most sacred character of the fiestas in relation to its role within a generalized African cosmology. Funso Aiyejina and Rawle Gibbons explain this relationship:

> The establishment of affectionate filial relationships between the living and their ancestors in Africa is effected through the sacred masquerade festivals, overseen by members of the cult of ancestors, which comprise ritual sacrifices and the manipulation of reality to simulate the ritual return, on an annual basis and in times of crisis, of ancestors. During these festivals, the returning ancestors fraternize with the living, entertaining with songs/chants, graceful dance steps, magical feats, and generously bestowing their blessings on them.
>
> Conceived as returnees from heaven, African masquerades are dressed in special outfits made from cloths of different colours. They are usually covered from head to toe, wearing improvised shoes and wooden masks or netting over their faces to facilitate vision and conceal the identity of the maskers (2000: 6–7).

Thus, it is entirely possible that the Africans and their descendents are immediately recognized in the European clown-buffoon-joker-*bojiganga* elements common to the practice of the masquerade art in African rituals, ceremonies and mummings, and the political need to conceal their sacred forms within these similar European traditions is also clearly noted. Since the plantation system did not allow the enslaved open communication with their ancestors, 'the intensity with which Africans entered into the carnival tradition derived from a perception of carnival as the only legitimate public means of maintaining their tradition of ritual masking' (ibid.: 7). Evidently, many of the subterranean African religious elements remain undocumented, and it may be too late to document them because they have either been erased or even further submerged through public exposure during the last 50 years. However, it is not difficult to imagine a process in which, 'being forced to emphasize the cultic dimension of their religion, the African also manipulated the religion of the slave master into becoming the unwitting carriers and preservers of his religion' (ibid.: 9). That may mean that the Afro-Puerto Rican community's selection of St James the Moor Killer was fully intentional (as opposed to ironic). More importantly, this choice allowed the community to also preserve the aesthetics of the African carnival and masks as they adapted them to their changing social conditions, creating new plastic, visual and rhythmic forms of performance still evident in the streets of Loíza.

In the Loíza processions, if the *caballero* imitates the saint and the colonial Spanish master to show loyalty to and acceptance of their European traditions, he also functions as the doorman who admits the entry of the ancestors and the sacred African elements in the shape of the *vejigante*. That the *vejigante* hides its identity behind actions and images semi-acceptable to the church, the Spanish or American colonial authority or today's globalized consumer society should come as no surprise. Regardless, it is impossible to doubt its African roots, at least in terms of the function of a cultural performer who embodies submerged secular and sacred meanings still vital to the Afro-Puerto Rican population.

In Arriví's play *Vejigantes*, the third act should be the moment for Clarita, the granddaughter of Toña and Benedicto (the Galician who disguises himself as a *vejigante* to seduce Toña, the dark-skinned mulatta) to reclaim her African heritage through the Afro-Creole image of 'negritude' represented by the Loíza *vejigante*. Curiously, she can only see 'disguises' that turn the country into a 'nightmare of masks', and she wants to 'overcome' the 'evil spell [*embrujo*] of *vejigantes*' (1970[1957]: 106). Eventually, Clarita desires 'to free [her] heart from the *vejigante*'s disguise and love [her] people as they are' (ibid.: 116). 'As they are,' however, does not include the *vejigante* as a positive, transgressive agent that seeks balance for survival. The negative references to the 'nightmare of masks' and the '*vejigante*'s spell' should, perhaps, be directed towards the 'simulated' *vejigante*-white-satyr-grandfather. However, Clarita's words create a projection of the *vejigante* as something malevolent and diabolical, a curse instead of the sacred-profane presence that keeps alive, no matter how distant, the African roots as well as the *loiceñidad* (Loízan-ness) of the people of Loíza, their ancestors and, by extension, Puerto Rican culture as a whole. If there is something diabolic in the *vejigante*, it is the mischievous irreverence, both sensual and ironic, that confronts adversity, it is *lo bailao* (the 'dance') that can never be taken away.

Even if the identity, function and significance of the *vejigante* cannot be defined with perfect precision, it continues to serve as a metaphor of the encounter of conditions that coincide and interconnect in the search for possible transformations within the inequalities of the Afro–Puerto Rican experience: the past and the present, the ancestors and the living, Africa and the diaspora, slavery and freedom, the sacred and the secular and the 'foreign' and the 'traditional' that 'interact' like 'a ray of light with a prism' (Benítez Rojo 1989: *xxvii*). I propose that the *vejigante* 'performs' like

FIGURE 15. During the past decade, the sound system of the Carretón Alegre (on the left) play-ing pan-Caribbean music has become a permanent feature of the fiestas. The *vejigante* to the right of the Carretón is Carlos Ayala Calcaño during the fiestas of 2010—his last.

that light—reflected, distorted, and recomposed—a light that always refracts into others to create a rainbow of colours and possibilities, a kaleidoscope in which change, even when based on repeated structure and dramatic elements, always remains possible. This begins with the living, real and corporeal body of the street performer with his mask and costume, which transforms through the performance into another, more mysterious and ethereal body encircled by myths. The *vejigante* has a genealogy as extensive as Pan (half-man, half-goat) and Dionysus-Bacchus (god of festivity, dithyrambs, pleasure, fertility and renovation) that extends beyond Greece and the West towards the Middle East and Africa.

Perhaps this merely represents desire, an exaggerated, romantic and overly opti-mistic version of necessary intransigence and cultural affirmation. Perhaps the con-temporary *vejigante* ('simulated', passive and institutionalized) already succumbs to commercialized nostalgia and a folkloric role frozen in time, promoted by popular anthropology, the media, tourism and state and municipal governments. The *vejigante* is not a shaman, healer, priest or griot. However, it continues to embody, even when partially dormant, cogent impulses essential to the health and well-being of the com-munity: irreverence, rebelliousness, pleasure, transgression and sensuality on the one hand; ingenuity, irony, physical resilience and prestige on the other. ¡*Viva Santiago*! ¡*Viva el vejigante de Loíza*!

Notes

An earlier version of this essay (*'El vejigante está pintao / Verde, amarillo y colorao...'*) appears as Lowell Fiet (2006–07). It adapts materials from Chapter 5 of Lowell Fiet (2007) but includes materials not previously published there.

1   Prucutá, Prucutá (onomatopoetic) and how good it is / Toco, Toco, Toco, Toco (tap tap, tap tap, tap tap, tap—rap rap, rap rap, rap rap, rap rap)/ The *vejigante* [trick-ster/diablo] eats coconut / The *vejigante* ate mango / Licking his fingers right down to the nails / Hey guys, let's go to the marina / To eat bread and sardines / [and in another variation] Farewell father, farewell mother, I am leaving / to join the mas [masquerade] to celebrate / The *vejigante* is painted / Green, yellow and red . . .

2   The masked *caballero* on the Día de los Inocentes in late December in Hatillo, Puerto Rico, acts a role that resembles more the character of the *vejigante* than it does the *caballero* of Loíza.

3   This happened without the knowledge of the playwright and was corrected in the subsequent edition in 2000. See Francisco Arriví (1970[1957]).

4   See Miguel Cervantes de Saavedra (2004: 627). The translation of *bojiganga* in English is 'mummer' or 'dressed in a mummer's costume' (Cervantes de Saavedra 1949: 576). This seems to be the same mummer, morris or Moorish dancer that Shakespeare alludes in the description of a 'wild Morisco, / Shaking [...] his bells' in *King Henry VI, Part II* (*c.*1591) (1999: 3.1.364–6). This Morisco character prob-ably arrived in England at some point during the fifteenth century, if not before, and there is no doubt that one of his homologues—the *bojiganga*?—also arrived in Spain around the same time. Stephen Greenblatt refers to the British mediaeval tra-dition of '[l]eaping morris dancers—from their supposed Moorish origin—with bells around their knees and ankles, cavorting with dancers wearing the wickerwork contraption known as the Hobbyhorse. Bagpipers, drummers, and fools dressed in motley carrying baubles and *pigs' bladders'* (2004: 39; my emphasis).

5   Here, besides the comments about carnival in Mikhail Bakhtin (1984a: 101) and Michael Hardt and Antonio Negri (2004: 209–11), the analysis of Antonio Benítez Rojo (1989: 183) and Fernando Ortiz (2002) (that also refers to Bakhtin—'the dialogic form', 'the polyphonic music', 'the plurality of carnivalesque voices'—and to the fourteenth-century *Libro de buen amor*, with its interwoven Islamic and Christian sources) must also be noted.

6   The play seems to reflect the same misogyny of Frantz Fanon (2008: 41–62). In more modern vocabulary, the action of 'seduction' and 'surrender' seem more like sexual harassment and date rape.

7   The word *begigante* appears in the Puerto Rican lexicon in 1747 (*Boletín Histórico de Puerto Rico* 1925: 178).

8   During the 2006 and 2007 processions, the already minimal use of imitation blad-ders on sticks had all but disappeared.

9 Ladino in this case means Spanish-speaking or acculturated. It applies principally
   to Jews and Africans in Spain both before and after 1492. A rather large group of
   Africans, both free and enslaved, lived in Spain in the mid to late fifteenth century.
   The Africans who sailed with Columbus were already acculturated or Spanish-
   speaking for they lived in Spain. Africans transported directly to the Caribbean and
   who did not speak Spanish or spoke in pidgin were referred to as *bozales*.

10 Mervyn Alleyne explains:

   > It is often said that black Africans were brought to the Caribbean to
   > replace the Indians as slave labour. However, the fact is that Africans
   > began to arrive with the conquering armies of Spain. Slavery had been an
   > old tradition in the Old World. In the fifteenth century (at the end of
   > which Spain had begun its colonization of the Americas), Jews, Moors,
   > Berbers, Arabs, and Eastern Europeans were still part of the slave labour
   > force of the Mediterranean world. From 1440, the Portuguese began
   > bringing sub-Saharan African slaves to Europe via direct Atlantic sea
   > routes (rather than overland as had been done before). By the 1650s, only
   > the Iberians still actively practiced slavery in Western Europe, and only
   > non-Christians were being enslaved.
   >
   > By the second half of the fifteenth century, sub-Saharan Africans
   > became the predominant group in the western Mediterranean slave
   > labour force. Between 1450 and 1505, 140,000 slaves from Africa were
   > brought to Europe [. . .]. Some of these African slaves made up half or
   > more of the armies conquering the New World (2002: 115).

11 Samples of these antique masks donated by Ricardo Alegría form part of the 'The
   African Heritage' collection in the Museum of the Americas (Ballajá) in Old San
   Juan. (Economic conditions in Loíza in the pre–Second World War era could also
   help explain why earlier masks were not elaborately painted.) The speckled style
   has been rescued, in part, in some of the painted masks of Raúl Ayala and in masks
   without any paint by the younger artist Carlos Ayala.

12 There are three variants of Santiago (St James): Santiago of the Men, Santiago of
   the Women and Santiago of the Children.

13 See Ricardo E. Alegría (1956). Max Harris (2001) contests the Yoruba hypothesis
   presented by Alegría. Also see Fiet (2006–07).

Pay the Devil, Jab Jab
Festive Devils in Trinidad Carnival

MILLA COZART RIGGIO AND RAWLE GIBBONS
WITH RAVIJI

> The outlaw is the only hero, the devil is the only ally in a world in which both justice and God are on the enemy's side.
>
> Ana Maria Alonso, 1990

Grounded in Emancipation, both of the body and the spirit, Trinidad Carnival imbeds its African origins in the heart of a festival that is entirely Caribbean and transformative. As we consider the plethora of festive devils that have emerged from this carnival, it is important to note the distinctive role of Trinidad itself, as an oil-, gas- and methanol-producing modern nation.[1] Without question, the festive devils of Trinidad reflect this history and are, in Paolo Vignolo's terms, 'an expression of resistance, resilience and adaptation vis-à-vis the imposition of a capitalist mode of production' (see p. 339 in this volume).

However, Trinidad has a crucial and complex relationship to its own modernity that helps to define the rhythm of a culture in which the seasons are still measured by the festivals that mark them. Following closely behind its energy exports in the economy of Trinidad is its exportation of Carnival around the world. This festival is often credited with defining the character of this island republic in which the claim that 'We are Carnival people' is reiterated. As a centre of energies both spawned by and resistant to emergent modernity, Carnival not only has a production industry of its own but its ethos also provides a powerful counter-balance to those who would measure the productivity of the culture only by its modernizing efficiencies. In its capacity both to stabilize and to create cultural meaning and value beyond the celebration itself, Carnival has a kind of transforming magic.

In this sense, Carnival is obeah—not as the dark arts but, as Afro-Trinidadian artist Leroy Clark uses the concept, as the power to magically bring things into effect. Carnival has the capacity to transform perception, consciousness and, therefore, being—how you place yourself in the world. And willy-nilly, whether you will or not, Carnival invokes the ancestors, encoding kinaesthetic memory in a way that is often unconscious. Trinis play their mas[2] or do their Carnival thing, without even needing to know why.

Levels of Signification: Social, Mythic and Cosmic

One of the problems of disentangling the many layers of significance in Trinidad Carnival is coming to terms historically and symbolically with the essential Afro-Caribbean base of the late-nineteenth-century festival and its hybridity as it developed. Without getting into the complex philosophical, historical and sociological debate about the concept of 'blackness' and its many racial and social constructions,[3] we have created a nomenclature that allows us to separate the *social* history of Carnival as an event evolving in a particular set of plantation-economy circumstances from *mythic* associations that the colour black had accreted, both in relationship to the demonic itself and to a variety of ancestral histories.

On the *social* level, blackness implies 'race', with all the evaluative gradations of skin colour invented and applied by colonizers to maintain ethnic hegemony. In the Americas, the term carries with it the history of a people whose enslavement was justified on the grounds of their colour, who still found a way to create and affirm new collective identities. In Trinidad, the Afro-Trinidadian takeover of the Catholic pre-Lenten Carnival, which evolved as a vehicle for the celebration of Emancipation throughout the second half of the nineteenth century, belongs to this history. But it extends beyond the Afro- to include also a variety of 'darker' groups, most notably the population that arrived from India as indentured workers.

Myth—a mechanism that simultaneously empowers and disables—serves as the imaginative medium for the construction or, as we argue, de-construction of blackness or darkness as a cultural signifier. Blackness in the European imaginary is associated with the demonization of those sometimes known only as 'darkies'. Very early on in Christian art, the 'fallen angels', kicked out of Heaven because they followed Satan in his uprising against God, visibly turned from white to black as they fell from Heaven to Hell, the place newly invented for their habitation. Black became the colour of the Devil, particularly in association with red, the colour of fire, passion and blood. This myth of demonic blackness was heightened in the Americas by the demonization of Indigenous peoples, as well as descriptions of the enslaved Africans and other non-white, non-Christian people whose labour fuelled the plantation system.[4] A description of Christmas revels in 1847 Trinidad depicts 'a multitude of drunken people [. . .] dancing, screaming, and clapping their hands like so many demons' (Charles Day, quoted in Cowley 1996: 41). Co-opted by those whom it stigmatized, however, the mythic notion of blackness became a potent source both of power and festive danger, embodied in the often forbidden practices of music, drumming and collective festivity—and in the emergence of a variety of devil characters. John Cowley refers to this as 'the Dionysian aesthetic' of the 'jamette' (those beyond the boundary of social respectability) Carnival of post-Emancipation Trinidad, which he links to the 'assumed association' between 'African magic' and 'devil power': 'The jamettes were expressing "solidarity without authority". They represented revolt, obscenity (the flouting of taboos), fearlessness, and rejection (both a focus for defiance and its introspective opposite). Underlying these is an unstated but assumed association with African magic, the devil and devil power and "blackness."' (ibid.: 124).

Mythic blackness in the Americas thus suggests the ritual transformation of social blackness (race, ostracism, social servitude and invisibility) into sources of power, pride, mystery and dread. Moreover, if social blackness applies fixed markers to create its multiple perceptions of reality, its festive manifestation is far more elusive —it can be independent of the colour black. That mythic blackness can be masked (disguised, hidden or subversively celebrated) or harnessed in many forms is itself a factor of its power.

If the *social* and *mythic* notions of blackness are both cultural constructs, black-ness and darkness also connote *cosmic* mystery and balance: the darkness that in many cosmologies is presumed to have given birth to light and order; the night that follows day, often metaphorically identified with death in the cyclical turning of the sun and moon. The metaphorical identification of darkness, night and even winter as a darker time of year with death and destruction have a long history not related to race or identity. Carnival, however, brings these associations together. As a springtime festival that in Trinidad is also an Afro-based Emancipation celebration, Carnival, in its regen-erative powers, incorporates all of these significations. Mas, as Carnival performance, is where such meanings meet, are processed and played out. Mas is the creative process that allowed the 'demonized' to answer those who imposed such definitions on them by:

1. Appropriating the very power for which they had been condemned;

2. Portraying their detractors in the same or even worse light;

3. Creating alternative narratives.

Festive devils are creatures of these courses of action.

Throughout the Caribbean, festive devil figures appear particularly in Christmas masquerades such as Jonkonnu (Jamaica, Belize, Bahamas), Papa Diable or Toes (St Lucia) and the St Kitts masquerade. In Trinidad, the folklore of the island is rich with demonic incarnations, both female (*la diablesse, soucouyant*) and male (the *lagahoo*). But as a character, the festive devil appears primarily in pre-Lenten Carnival. The season that extends from Christmas to Easter, as marked on the Christian calendar, is the darkest season of the year, leading to the rejuvenation of springtime. Although, in a culture as close to the equator as Trinidad, seasonal variation is relatively slight, Carnival nevertheless encodes, among its many significations, the notion of seasonal and personal rebirth, sometimes mediated by the creatures of the dark.

In the entwining histories from which modern Trinidad Carnival evolved, African practices—including portrayals of festive majesty and royalty as well as embodiments of jumbies (spirits) and the appearance of ancestral masquerades— merged not only with Catholic customs and Carnival masking but also with the festive practices of Indo-Trinidadians, Chinese and the many others who make up this kaleidoscopic island nation to establish multilayered festive devil embodiments. Because of its pervasively liberating energies, Trinidad Carnival powerfully attracts unto itself, absorbs and makes room for virtually any celebratory practice that lies in its path. It is the most inclusive of Caribbean festivals, even absorbing and blending other festive traditions, giving them potent, renewed life in new forms in a transformed space.

Among the earliest of its expressions are its devils. Trinidad Carnival 'demons' are noted as early as the 1840s, only a few years after Emancipation. In 1847, according to Charles Day, 'negroes, bedaubed with a black varnish, [. . . one of which] had a long chain with a padlock attached to it' had appeared in Trinidad carnival (quoted in Cowley 1996: 39). The *Port of Spain Gazette* in 1856 complained of 'devils' in the streets; in 1858, of 'semi-savages' creating 'hellish scenes' and 'demoniacal representations' of earlier slavery days (quoted in Hill 1972: 25). Specific records for the ensuing decades are scarce. However, the African appropriation of Carnival between Emancipation (completed in 1838) and the late nineteenth century climaxed in the battle between stick fighters and the police in what would be known as the Canboulay Riots of 1881. Though the energy of resistance and defiance—of praying to the devil when the gods are not on your side—would be discouraged as the festival gained social acceptability, it could not be exorcized. Contestation between this 'Canboulay energy' and the social power of the sanctioning elite virtually describes the evolution of Trinidad Carnival.

By 1888, figures painted black, sporting whips, with demonic body shapes and dancing postures, wearing black Pierrot-style caps with pointed, hornlike appendages appear in the forefront of an engraving by British illustrator Melton Prior of a Carnival parade in downtown Port-of-Spain, Trinidad's capital city. Into and across the turn of the twentieth century, as *lavways*,[5] *kaisos* (calypsos) and chants morphed from French patois into English, the appearances of mud maskers, demonic characters painted black, with whips and sticks, or what would become the jab jab fancy devil seem to have remained a persistent, though not yet catalogued or differentiated, aspect of Carnival. In 1908, two years after Patrick Jones brought the first dragon or devil band, Khaki and Slate, to Port-of-Spain, a 'teacher' in the *Port of Spain Gazette* described the 'devil' as 'the heroic copy' for boys in Carnival:

> The devil also has his share in the all-absorbing pageant, for he is the heroic copy for numberless boys who are never more pleased and happy than when rigged out in a close-fitting, to their mind, infernal garb, wildly running through the streets, long-pronged wooden forks in their hand and lustily whacking their vertebral appendages, to the huge delight of themselves and their admirers (*Port of Spain Gazette* 1908: n.p.).[6]

Features of this description—such as the 'long-pronged wooden forks'—are the standard emblems of devil mas. However, more centrally, the description of boys running 'wildly' through the streets 'lustily' whacking themselves testifies to the liberating joy of playing devil. The festive devil transgresses, subverts and reverses order and respectability with his intoxicating sense of freedom. The celebratory subversion and compelling affirmation that characterize devil performances throughout the Americas, where the devil figure has long been entwined with European colonialism and its aftermath, are central to Trinidad festive devil performances.

Among its many traditional, culture-bearing characters, three categories of festive devils emerge in Trinidad Carnival:

1. Fighting devils: warriors known as jab jabs or 'pretty devils', in association with their Carnival cousins, the boismen or stick fighters;

2. Polluting devils: embodied primarily in jab molassi, blue devils and related figures;

3. Parading devils: courtly characters from the dragon bands, including imps, beasts and a variety of 'gownmen', ranging from Lucifer to the Bookman of Hell. These characters perform danger and threat as acts of ritualized spectacle.

1. *Jab Jabs and Stick Fighters*

> It have people does do Christmas and Ramayana; we does do jab jab.
>
> Ronald Alfred, The Original Jab Jabs

Warriorhood—finding the warrior in you—is basic to the act of cultural resistance. In circumstances of bondage or subjugation of the individual and his culture to the will of others (such as enslavement or indentureship), the capacity to survive may depend on establishing an identity that separates the interior, unchained self from the shackles that limit physical freedom. Thus it is that, both historically and metaphorically, Carnival, as it evolved throughout the nineteenth century in Trinidad, inevitably incorporated the African warrior mentality. Embodied initially in 'bands' of stick-wielding, whip-cracking, flambeaux-carrying boismen (defined in the French Creole of the time by the wood they wielded), the Carnival warriors asserted an identity separate from that which had been assigned to them by those who brought them over the dark waters to the plantation world that had become their home.

The first boismen and whip-cracking revellers were Afro-Trinidadians who carried either sticks or whips or perhaps both, claiming primarily urban turf as their own.[7] By the middle of the twentieth century, however, they had evolved from their common roots into stick fighters (the original 'boismen') and the more rurally based jab jabs (the whip-cracking devils), distinguished not only by their sticks and whips but also by their cultural ancestry: the Afro-based boismen and the Indo-defined jab jabs who played what had, by the 1950s, become known as 'coolie mas'.[8]

Though both groups manifest the elemental resistant energy associated with devil masquerades, stick fighters are not devils, whereas the jab jabs (devil devils) are nominally so represented. Both have their origins in the nineteenth century; both initially wore the 'pretty' clothes that jab jabs still wear and that some stick fighters (notably in the borough of Talparo in the centre of the island) still ceremonially don, though seldom when they are actually fighting (see Figure 1).[9] Both stick fighters and jab jabs use chants, some of which involve the notion of the devil. One interesting example from the nineteenth century cited in Andrew Pearse's interview with Mitto Sampson (1988[1956]) goes:

Djab se yo neg
Me Die se nom-la bla
(The Devil is a black man
But God is white)
Hannibal (Norman le Blanc), Trinidad chantwell (singer)

According to Sampson, when stick fighters sang that song, they felt themselves infused with the spirit of the devil himself and were completely anaesthetized against their opponent's blows.

In this instance, the 'devil' is not a horned, pitch-forked infernal, but a process of becoming, the outward climax to an inner drama—a manifestation. This process is by no means unique to the stick fighter alone. King Jab Jab Ronald Alfred speaks of the East Indian involvement in jab jab as perhaps linked to their Kali worship[10] and the flagellation to which the manifested body is subjected in some Indian portrayals, a quite likely thesis.[11] Furthermore, both types of mas follow similar preparation routines for bodies, minds and weapons. This involves physical training and

FIGURE 1. Ainsley Mohammed (left) from Couva, and Evon Ralph (right) from Talparo, competitors at the stick-fighting finals, Point Fortin, 2006. Photograph by and courtesy of Pablo Delano.

dexterity, sexual abstinence, spiritual guidance and protection (oils, herbal baths, dreams and charms). Whips, like the boismen sticks, can also be 'mounted', that is, spiritually prepared in order to render them toxic and thus insure victory over opponents.[12] This practice, as in stick fight, is regarded as unfair and 'doing bad', of bringing bad obeah into a festive arena that is defined, as Alfred's evidence makes clear, by the celebrative spirituality of the mas: 'You might say that in Carnival longtime, everything is devil; this is a pretty devil . . . . My thing is not to be evil . . . . You might see the devil there in the ring, but it is not evil . . . a good spirit, a Carnival spirit: we call it a jumbie' (interview with Tony Hall, Florence Blizzard and students at Trinity House, Curepe, 2011).

Traditional Carnival, whatever the mas, has spiritual connotations that lie outside the Christian dichotomy of God and Devil, even when those concepts are nominally invoked.

Apart from external similarities in traditional costumes, boismen and jabmen often band together where they belong to the same community. They share a musical repertoire. Alfred's challenge song is a stick-fight *lavway* suitably adapted for jabmen, with emphasis on their function as invaders of 'the town':

Send a message
Send a message on the ground
Send a message
Jabmen come in the town.

Unlike boismen, however, jab jabs are not only warriors, physically and spiritually, but also mischief makers. Donald Fernandez of Belmont had begun playing the mas during the second decade of the twentieth century. Initially, he recalls the ferocity of the mas:

What led me to choose, in the early days, playing with Devil Bands, I don't know, perhaps it was the snapping whips. Throwing out the whip that curl(s) around your opponent's waist and dragging him onto you, re-reeling it out at a safe distance, following up with slashes, or exchange of slashes if he is your equal, call for dexterity on both sides. Meanwhile, the enthusiastic spectators shouting, gesticulating, backing up their favourites, as by this time, both bands are entwined into a melee. Torn costumes, bruises, cuts, swollen joints are the aftermath (n.d.: n.p.).

But the jab jab—like the jab molassi—also carried a long fork that had other, more mischievous purposes as Fernandez graphically illustrates:

There are other queer aspects that go in as fun, such as the raiding of fruit vendors. The long Devil fork is a thieving weapon, for on each side of a vendor there would approach a Devil menacing her. While doing as she must give her attention to one, her tray falls prey to the other. With his prize he would [fill] each tooth; if the prong is full, he raises his fork aloft for spectators to view: Satan has won his ill-gotten goods. I once witnessed a pathetic sight: a distraught, old vendor, having lost her produce that way, went down on her knees in prayer, calling vengeance on her marauders. A sympathetic onlooker comforted her by putting a dollar bill in her hands.

This incident may have touched me. The following year I was leading my band of Bats (ibid.).

Socially, in terms of the history of Carnival, the stick fighters and jabmen evolved from nineteenth-century Carnival, where collectively they embodied the assertive energy of Carnival itself, in its most powerful warrior form. Like other warrior mas, jab jabs established reputations in their own communities, then pursued island-wide fame, not as individuals, like the boismen, but as communal bands identified with specific geographical areas. These bands did not just display their prowess; by also invading 'town', they caused havoc wherever they chose to roam. It is not unlikely that this disruptive narrative may also describe their own view of their relationship as subjects to a marauding colonial authority.

Like both the jab molassi and dragon bands, jab jabs have a King Jab, who leads the group, takes the first challenge, gives and receives the 'biggest licks'. Whipping was the regular form of punishment passed down from slave plantation to indentured estates to prisons, schools and, indeed, homes. The whip—in any of its forms—was thus a powerful symbol of authority and an instrument of fear. The courage to confront the whip and 'take licks' is as esteemed as the art of wielding it in this social context.[13]

Though, like all traditional Carnival characters, boismen have suffered attrition to their ranks over the years, the art has proven itself remarkably resilient. Fights are held across the island in what are known as 'action gayelles' (or fighting circles) outside rum shops in such boroughs as Sangre Grande, Talparo, California and areas in and around San Fernando, Trinidad's second city. However, the jab jab groups have greatly diminished since the 1950s, with only two or possibly three groups remaining on the island today.

Ronald Alfred of Couva is the King Jab of the largest of these groups known as The Original Jab Jabs. Started by his grandfather, whom he never met, and continued by his father Winston, until a stroke cut short his activity some years ago, this jab jab band is grounded in the Alfred family (Figure 3). Ronald's brother, wife and both his son and daughter regularly play jab jab; his mother cooks, assists with costumes and offers Hindu pujas (prayers) for their protection before they leave the house. The Alfreds charge neither for the costumes nor the whip lessons. They make the whips of strong hemp rope at their home. They use individually painted wire-mesh masks and the usual jab jab costume in colours designed for different functions, though, unlike other Carnival mas groups, they do not make new costumes every year. They invite anyone who will to join the now expanding group, which fielded a band of more than 70 jab jabs in 2011 and again in 2012, keeping alive both the ancestral memory and the present reality of this mas.

(ABOVE) **FIGURE 2.** Ronald Alfred, 'The Whip Master', of the Original Jab Jabs, Carapichaima, Trinidad. 2003. (BELOW) **FIGURE 3.** Ronald Alfred with his daughter Renelia and son Renaldo, and, on the far right, his father Winston Alfred, founder of the Original Jab Jabs, at home Couva, Trinidad, January 2004. Photographs by and courtesy of Pablo Delano.

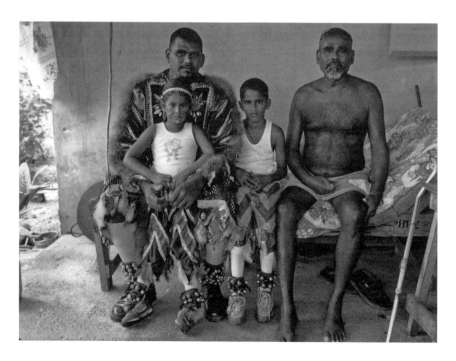

Mythically, in terms of ancestral links and origins, jab jab seems to have offered an early form of inculturation to some members of the Indo-Trinidadian population—behind the mask, everyone could be anyone. Obvious attractions for the Indians include the craft of the costume itself: the mirrors worn on the breastplate (or *fol*) that, according to Alfred, help the fighting jab jabs to defeat their enemies by reflecting sunlight into their eyes, are, for instance, typical of Indian clothing. According to Raviji: 'The colours—meaning the colours and designs of the fabric— and the drama, the way they moved and danced and all those things. It was compelling—the attraction to something you also feared. The other thing about it is the glass work and the ghungaru (the dancing bells) that were all part of the costume were so Indian' (personal interview, October 2011).

Overall, the jab jab is identified by three elements that echo the Indo-Trinidadian ancestry: the ghungaru, which, worn on the ankles, provide the jab jab music, the whips and the fancy clothing with the horned headpieces. Raviji identifies these features with the cane fields, with which Indo-Trinidadians were associated not only through their initial status as indentured workers but, after indentureship, with their continuing work in the fields:

> Three things: the sound of the whips, the bells and the horns. Almost like an amorphed figure of a driver and the animal, the cow that carries the bells and has horns and the whip that meets the animal. It's almost like something out of the cane industry, morphed into a creature called jab jab. When you look at it, jab jab in central Trinidad, all around where they are playing this mas, surrounded by sugarcane fields. The horned animals carrying the burden, the load, almost like the master and the slave have morphed into one figure. Whipping each other. And when they whip, sometimes the whip encircles the character—whipping themselves in a theatrical way. The way it is done is to create fear and to give the impression that they are beating themselves—theatrically and not hurting themselves, but that is irrelevant, for the intention was to be beating others and seem to be beating themselves. And in a way more serious [than theatrical] (personal interview, October 2011).

This inculturation, however, not only defines that which is specifically 'Indian'[14] in this mas, but also touches the commonality with others in the shared space—a shared ancestral cosmology. This is evident in Alfred's insistence that his devil is not evil, his connection of whipping to manifestations in Kali puja, his spiritual preparation—all belong to a view of the universe common to many religions. His use of aarti (a Hindu religious ritual) as part of his departure ceremony shows there is no incongruity in his consciousness between what, in a Christian tradition, might be regarded as sacred action and festive performance. This is a cosmic reality of which traditional pre-Christian religions and non-Christian—including those of Africa, India and Europe—are aware. The all-embracing deity of the season, the Carnival 'jumbie', is as powerful and present as any other, as the quotation opening this section aptly proclaims. The contestation and gaining of reputation through warriorhood is typical of mainly masculine arts.[15] However, while in stick fight, it is the individual fighter who earns fame, jab jabs, masked as they are, represent not themselves but their community and the tradition itself. Their success or failure is owned by their community. Like all mas, jab jabs are makers of their own myth.

At the *cosmic* level, jab jabs demonstrate the potential for disruption or chaos. They are fearsome beings, as their *lavways* declare, coming from the nether regions of the universe. In this sense, they are the Carnival analogue to the Yoruba deity Eshu. In Yoruba cosmology, Eshu, the deity of disruption and chaos, is often spoken of as a prankster, a kind of divine trickster. This perception sometimes masks the fundamental contradiction he embodies—the potency of anomaly and disorder within the very structure of the universe.[16] Eshu reminds us that in life there are no certainties, that nature remains dynamic and disruption may well be the order of the day. His is a power that can only be placated, not predicted, and it is with this awareness that the Yoruba guide their steps from moment to moment, event to event, decision to decision.

Whether through consternation or contestation (the festive *agon*), Carnival devils eliminate both the weak and the over-secure. With their whips, jab jabs symbolically cleanse the community, simulating the skill and strength needed for success and protection along life's journeys. Consciously or not, they connect with elements of the universe to elicit meanings beyond themselves.

2. Jab Molassi and Blue Devils

If you bad, don't die
Walk about and cry
De devil down dey
You will have to pay!

Shadow (Calypsonian Winston Bailey)

Jab molassi are the original, molasses-smeared devils that emerged on the streets right after Emancipation and were famously described in 1847 by Day as 'negroes, bedaubed in a black varnish' (quoted in Cowley 1996: 39). Melton Prior's 1888 etching shows characters who look like jab molassi, though with whips. Pitchfork-carrying 'devils' in 'infernal' costuming are referenced in the *Port of Spain Gazette* in 1908. One early representation of Patrick Jones' 1909 dragon band shows chained characters, some wearing wings, apparently with blackened bodies, dancing the jab molassi dance (see Procope 1988[1956]). Blackness—their badge both of shame and honour—is emblematically heralded in their glistening, painted bodies.

In West Africa, the masquerade tradition generally uses a full costume that completely masks the performer's body. This is evident in Carnival in mas like the Beast, King Pierrot, Pierrot Grenade, Midnight Robber, Moko Jumbie, etc. In jab molassi, the costume essentially is 'black varnish': molasses, paint, charcoal, soot. Picture a post-Emancipation society with a marginalized majority, newly freed from the most unjust and dehumanizing system of economic exploitation, denied land tenure, political status and social recognition and all rationalized on the basis of one single factor—black skin.

Further, for centuries, this injustice was perpetrated on Africans not only physically but also psychologically by demonizing the very colour of their skin: black was evil; white salvation—a dichotomy that still accounts for the self-rejection of many blacks today. The choice to 'bedaub in black varnish' must be seen in this context of assault on the bodies and minds of African people in a situation of their ongoing struggle for survival, justice, recognition and reparation. Jab molassi confronted a society that rendered them socially invisible. Their mas was also a response to those who were in denial of their own 'blackness'. Their narrative of creatures from hell perfectly fit the performers, as a whole theology seemed to have created this space especially for them. Loose on the street, they could scare the hell out of their inventors, create havoc, 'blackmail' people with what they most feared—blackness—and gain some cash.

Jab molassi, a foundation mas of the Carnival, still appears and its most fearsome form is still black.[17] Akin to jab molassi and sometimes identified simply as 'jabs', blue devils paint their clothes and skin blue, often by using azulillo, an ordinary bluing laundry tablet.[18] Currently, blue devil bands appear throughout Trinidad, in places like Point Fortin and Arima. However, they are associated with the lush mountain district of Paramin, north of Port-of-Spain, where they often refer to themselves in their chants as 'jab jab', a designation that Carnival purists feel is a confusion of name, if not identity. In Paramin, blue devils come out in force on Carnival Monday evening, when bands appear in random sequences from various directions in the village square known as Fatima Trace.[19] This competition began spontaneously but, for some years, has been partly organized, or at least recognized, by the National Carnival Commission (NCC), which now offers prizes for those judged to be winners.

Among the devils there is a King Devil, who leads the threatening demands for 'titi' (Trinidad dollars). The King Devil is usually on a leash controlled by another jab, sometimes called an imp, who restrains the king, whether to symbolize enslavement or as a way of restraining the wildness in the festive context, or both. Though the role of King Devil is an honorific usually held for some time by one band member, and might be passed to his son, other devils can exchange roles. The usual move is from percussion to performance, so that a person who this year provides the

FIGURE 4. Paramin blue devils, imp with King Blue Devil on chain, biscuit-tin percussion, devil blowing whistle. Photograph by and courtesy of Jeffrey Chock.

all-important percussive rhythm next year might become a bulging-eyed, drooling monster moving and writhing with dexterity as he pleads for and plays with the dollars thrown or dangled in front of him. Despite the fact that, for the most part, they keep within their own boundaries, the ferocity of their demeanour and their elemental, transgressive threats are often frightening.

According to Ashton Fournillier, a Paramin King Devil, you identify the blue devil by the coloured paint, the pitchfork and the 'blood guts' on the tongue (personal interview February 2011).[20] In addition to the popular blue, they sometimes paint themselves red, green, black or white. Their typical dance involves hooking the feet together, while moving their heads and shoulders, thrusting their pitchforks forward and screaming to the beat of the biscuit tin. Blue devils sometimes also carry painted replicas of cutlasses (machetes). Sometimes they dress only in cut-off shorts, without masks. However, from early on, they carried pitchforks and sported wings (see *Port of Spain Gazette* 1908), which, in recent times, might be decorated with emblems such as Nazi swastikas. Blue devils also wear other kinds of clothes, increasingly use animal masks and, until they were recently outlawed (and occasionally even after),

FIGURE 5. Paramin blue devils on Carnival Monday night. Photograph by and courtesy of Jeffrey Chock.

at times carried live snakes. They sometimes uproot small trees, have been seen to eat small raw sharks snatched from fish vendors or dismember live chickens.

Like some other mischievous traditional characters, they scamper up hills, climb poles and occasionally buildings. One of their most popular antics is to blow large gusts of fire, either on the ground or in the air, by spitting kerosene into the flames of their flambeaux (torches made out of bottles of kerosene). Though blue devils have no formal training, they do often pass the mas down to their children who participate in the bands from an early age.

Thus, blue devil bands are, on the one hand, intrusive—drooling fake blood, sometimes carrying baby dolls skewered on their pitchforks, miming overtly sexual acts, often on one another, and pushing into the faces of the crowd with their demands for dollars; whether they actually carry through, their threat to muddy up those they pass creates genuine fear and sometimes resistance. On the other hand, the threat to pollute does not tell the entire blue devil story. Their touch also establishes a kind of bond with those they encounter, particularly since many of the blue devils—even in the midst of their most ferocious playing—have an inbuilt sense of decorum and a natural desire to protect as well as to sully those for whom they play. This was made evident when in 1995, after warning me (co-author Milla Riggio) that 'as a white woman on that mountain among those devils, you will die', Morilla Montano, 16-times Jouvay Queen who, though she lived at the foot of Paramin Mountain, had never been there on Carnival Monday night, accompanied me to protect me. Arriving in Fatima Trace in a jeep, we were met by bands of blue devils that I had got to know elsewhere in the city. Embracing—and thus covering me in blue mud—the first of these devils, called Kootoo (Andrew Sanoir), assured me that he and his band would 'take care of' me. While I was in Paramin, I was under the protection of the blue devils, one of whom lifted me up and spun me around triumphantly above his head, while my friend Morilla was discovering for herself the fun as well as the power of the Paramin blue devils!

With increasing numbers of children and women included in their bands, blue devils are not only protective of one another but generally contain their own festive violence. They do sometimes appropriate bottles of beer or snatch bread, ice cream or other pieces of food from bystanders or vendors. They play eagerly with willing watchers. Unlike the traditional Carnival character masquerades restored and revived throughout Trinidad in special training camps set up for children under the guidance of NCC cultural specialist John Cupid, the blue devils thrive largely on their own, reinforced by the high demand for their performances throughout the island beyond the Carnival season.

Trinidad has a variety of mud-masking forms. Jouvay, historically one of the earliest and still most popular Carnival celebrations, is a welcome-the-dawn mas, its name derived from French *j'ouvert* (the beginning of the day), which takes place in the very early hours of Carnival Monday, when Jouvay bands cover themselves with mud or paint themselves in the colours of the blue devils. These bands roam the streets from the early hours of the day (formerly from 2 a.m., now usually 4 a.m.) till the full rising of the sun, chipping and wining[21] to steel band or electronic soca music, sometimes competing, sometimes clashing with other bands, but always revelling in

FIGURE 6. Paramin blue devil Andrew Sanoir (Kootoo).Photograph by and courtesy of Jeffrey Chock.

the transition from night to day. Rarely, mud bands will appear even on Carnival Tuesday. Generically associated with these forms of mud mas but having an identity of their own, bands of blue devils, and their forebears the jab molassi, have sustained their traditions and expanded their numbers in periods when other traditional masquerades have tended to fade away or die out. They remain one of the strongest mas traditions in an island in which 'to play your mas' has become for many a metaphor for how you live your life.

Socially, jab molassi and blue devils hark back to the plantation system, when revelling Africans could use molasses and mud or even Trinidad's plentiful tar as weapons, attaining power by threatening to pollute. It is in this in-your-face spirit that they display their most subversive emblems, invoking the power of pollution both literally and metaphorically. As Mary Douglas long ago reminded us, a society partially defines itself by what it calls dirt or regards as polluting (1966). In situations of oppression—of which enslavement is among the worst—those whose humanity is called into question by the very law of the land can, by reversing the clean and the dirty, use the polluting elements as emblems of inversive power. This is what the jab molassi and the blue devils achieve in their drooling revelry.

Though perhaps more than other festive devils, jab molassi and blue devils lose themselves at times in the power of their embodied roles, doing things they would never do outside the circumstance of the mas, they clearly distinguish their normal lives from their character manifestations. In Paramin, a heavily Catholic community, they do not see their embodiment as, in any darker sense, Satanic. In fact, one of the intriguing questions to be asked is how playing Devil Mas is reconciled so easily with the devout Catholic worship of virtually the entire Paramin community. King Devil Ashton Fournillier affirmed that he would not allow his daughter to play jab until she had taken her first communion. Having been thus blessed by the Catholic Church, she could then begin to play devil. In the assimilated world of Paramin, the Catholic Church sanctions and, thus, protects those who play devil. For Fournillier (and others), Christian worship embraces the freedom to play. Exploring that link may help us understand the tension between resistance and assimilation.

Mythically, they are linked to Africa, but they marry their natural blackness gleefully to the blackened images of the Christian Devil, wearing his horns and tail—carrying pitchforks and, formerly, boa constrictors and other snakes. Taking that which has been stigmatized as demonic as their herald, they assume power by loudly assimilating and proudly displaying the demeaning images foisted upon them. The hellish fire, the pitchforks and the snakes echo the appropriation of infernal Christian emblems transformed into ecstatic glee. They revel in the power of the devil to snatch that which is forbidden—and are paid for their efforts. In their demand for money and even in their snatching thievery, they implicitly re-enact the process of extortion that historically was visited on their ancestors. But there is more at stake. In the larger mythic sense, the polluting devil exacts the human soul, as a promise of chaos, which will surely follow if the ancestors are not fully honoured and propitiated: 'Pay the devil, jab, jab.' Mythically, the flames of hell beckon. As Calypsonian Shadow's devil challenges all who think they can do evil and escape: 'If you bad, don't die.'

The ancestral is, in this sense, affirmed not only by the African or Afro-Trinidadian origin of the mas, and the continued affirmation of blackness, but also by the festive appropriation of enslavement: the chains with which an imp will restrain the king or other blue devil may not consciously symbolize enslavement but without question they evoke that aura in their performance. The joyfulness with which they celebrate aspects of their own degradation, the bestiality or subjection implied in their crawling movements, and the sheer glee of their effrontery establish them as resistant, subversive characters. They literally throw in the faces of those they accost their own ancestral sense both of freedom and of the power that comes from simultaneously appropriating the emblems of humiliation and outrageously adopting the props of wickedness.

Cosmically, of all the festive devils of Trinidad, they are the most elemental, their blackness linked to the primal, eternally renewable energies of the universe. Associated with Jouvay, they remind us of our own origins as creatures of dust, crawling out of the mud of evolution and creation, emerging powerfully into the dawn with the staccato rhythm of their biscuit tins celebrating the most basic forms of cosmic energy. Their polluting power is the other side of the mystery they represent—that they also 'contain' the negative, indiscriminate energies of the cosmos, which, if unleashed, create chaos. In embodying these energies and reflecting them on the surface of their skins, blue devils are not dissimilar to the portrayal of the Hindu lord Shiva, whose intake of the poison of the great serpent that lived in and polluted a lake is symbolized by his skin becoming blue. Shiva, who drank the poison to protect all existence on earth from its venomous fumes, was protected by a snake that coiled around his neck to prevent the poison from reaching his entrails and killing him. Thus, the Hindu figure also stands as an emblematic reminder that even the serpent who poisons has his counterpart in the protective serpent: good finally absorbs evil in the mythic cycle of life. It is also interesting in this regard that Carnival in Trinidad often coincides with Shiv Ratri, the festival in honour of Shiva.

In this way, therefore, Carnival enacts and dramatizes cosmic intuitions in a context of festive performance. The energies suppressed or ritually dismissed in one form or another throughout the year return to confront us in the continuous cycle of life, death and rebirth. We pay the jabs for carrying our own negative energies away; if we don't, we deny ourselves opportunities of transformation. Their sexual play—both hetero- and homosexual—reverberates with a sense of primal procreation and the untamed power of sexuality itself. They embody the power of darkness and the potency of the dawn with all its implications of fertility and rebirth.

Jab molassi invoke cosmically primal and elemental as well as ancestral powers, while consistently retaining their own notion of their roles as embodied play, into which they enter and from which they can as easily retreat once the period of play has ended.

3. Dragon Bands: Performing Threat and Danger

I cannot serve two masters at the same time. When I done with that [devil business], then I turn to Church.

Benedict Morgan, Bookman from Hell

Of the three forms of devil mas in Trinidad, the dragon bands are the most spectacular —not only in the literal sense that their performance is largely designed for spectacle but also in the elaborateness of their costumes. Since its apparent origins in 1906, the dragon band differs from other festive devil bands in that it is composed of a more delineated, although evolving, set of traditional characters, usually identified as imps, gownmen and dragons or beasts. The imps generally sport wings and lead beasts or dragons on chains, reminiscent of imps in Blue Devil bands (who may well be modelled on the dragon band imp), accompanied by varieties of gownmen. The gownmen wear long capes or cloaks (hence the name), sometimes wear wings smaller than the imps, often have demonic masks made of papier mâché, and carry various props, representing a varied set of infernal characters ranging from Lucifer and Satan to the Bookman from Hell and a Satanic dandy known as Gentleman Jim. The dragons or beasts—currently the most popular of these characters and the one around which recent bands have been organized—wear full-body costumes in the shape of the beast, ordinarily a dragon, scaled, with the head and tail of the beast and with short front 'legs' (see Figure 9).

Unlike the jab jabs and the jab molassi / blue devils, the imps, gownmen and beasts of the dragon bands do not, as a rule, interact with the crowd around them. Even the character called the Bookman from Hell, whose job is to enter the names of carnivalgoers into his book (and so enrol them in hell), ordinarily only mimics this action. His book is ordinarily a large papier mâché construction, on which he cannot write, certainly not with the fake pen that he carries. The beasts—largely dragons— perform their dance or parade through the streets, playing around with one another, sometimes clashing or competitively performing against another dragon band, or performing for bystanders. They usually neither accost their audience nor play for the titi that blue devils entice from the crowd. In recent decades, dragons and gownmen have performed as individuals, outside the context of an organized group. Whatever form it takes, the basis of this mas is ritualized, stylized performance, which might involve an intricate dance (usually associated with the dragon or imp) or might only involve a sternly authoritative stance, a graceful shuffle and a stare that wordlessly promises to condemn the bystander to hell.

This is not to say, however, that dragon bands do not have links or origins in common with other Trinidad Carnival performances. Bruce Procope describes what is usually thought to be the first of what would become known as the dragon or devil band, brought by Patrick Jones, sometimes known as Chinee Patrick because he was half-Chinese, assisted by Gilbert Scaramoni, in 1906. This Khaki and Slate band

[...] comprised 60 to 70 men and women most of whom wore a jab jab costume, an overall type close fitting merino suit with scalloped collar and a hood fitted with cow horns, rope tails and long socks. To this costume were attached flexible wings worn in the middle of the back and so

constructed as to make a flapping motion when the person wearing the costume moved. The men carried long forks in their hands (1988[1956]: 186).

What this description affirms—illustrated also in Prior's 1888 etching and the
1908 'teacher' description—is that, in their origins, the various devil bands were not
categorically distinctive. The men in Jones' 1906 band wore what in 1956 Procope
would call 'jab jab' costumes of either merino (a cheap white fabric once known as
Chinee banlon) or, for those designated as 'presidents', satin fabric (ibid.). Like the
'devil' of 1908, they wore wings and carried pitchforks. This merger of styles and
forms seems to have characterized the early devil performances of all kinds.

Jones' first band also included women, dressed in satin, and was headed by a
more elaborately costumed figure of Lucifer. Procope says that Jones' inspiration for
the dragon band came first from seeing a picture of a devil being exorcised. Others
report that it was actually a picture of St George and the Dragon, possibly on the
walls of a rum shop, which first inspired Jones (Jeffrey Chock, personal interview
2011). His subsequent reading of Dante's *Inferno* in 1909 further influenced the development of the dragon band, which grew from its khaki-clad origins in 1906 to a fuller
band, including imps holding more elaborately clad beasts on chains and a variety of
gownmen by 1911 (Procope 1988[1956]: 187–8). Unlike the jab molassi and jab
jabs, the dragon bands 'authenticate' their characters with reference to literature (primarily Dante) or images in books.[22] According to Procope, 'many people claim to
have seen books in which were recorded the characters to be portrayed in a dragon
band' (ibid.: 189).[23]

However it evolved or whatever the models for the individual characters (the
beasts themselves sometimes associated with the biblical Book of Revelations), what
is clear is that, in its heyday between the 1910s and the 50s, when its popularity began
to fall off, dragon bands were relatively numerous groups. Now, however, while the
dragons still appear in bands as well as individuals, the gownmen—a dying breed—
play almost entirely as individuals in traditional character competitions, particularly
on the Wednesday before Carnival, Carnival Sunday and Carnival Monday.

Benedict Morgan of Belmont, Trinidad, who, in 2014, at age 88, is probably the
oldest and clearly one of the most decorated living Bookman from Hell, illustrates
the evolution of this tradition. Morgan has played mas continuously for more than
80 years, since he was 6 or 7 years old. He has played in bands organized by
Trinidadian masmen George Bailey and Peter Minshall (with whom he played most
recently in 1987 in Rat Race). He has portrayed a Fancy Sailor in bands brought by
Jason Griffith of Belmont. But fairly early in his career, he settled primarily on the
dragon band. When he began playing, there were 100 or more members in the bands,

(ABOVE) **FIGURE 7.** Benedict Morgan, iconic Bookman from Hell, Viey le Coup performance, Port-of-Spain, Trinidad. (BELOW) **FIGURE 8.** Benedict Morgan, Bookman from Hell, costume with cape and wings. Photographs by and courtesy of Mark Lyndersay.

in which initially, as a youth, he portrayed various characters, until he became the exemplary Bookman from Hell. Morgan has won many prizes over the decades.[24]

Morgan recalls the days when the dragons in his band were divided into 'straight' dragons, those in cages and those held on chains by imps (all of which he refers to as dragon; others distinguish the generic 'beast'—often chained—from the dragon). Now, however, the traditional dragon 'bands are already all mashed up, so I play an individual by myself',[25] continuing, as he explains, at the urging of the NCC, from which in 2011 he expected to win $10,000 titi in prizes in competitions 'down-town' (i.e. Independence Square in lower Port-of-Spain), in Victoria Square on Carnival Sunday, and on Carnival Monday, where he still annually plays the Bookman from Hell.

A former police officer, who used to 'lock people up', as well as a tailor fully capa-ble of sewing his own costumes (as is customary), Morgan has no rituals of prepara-tion for his role other than making his costume, which consists of a long cape, a devil mask, small wings, a breastplate and, of course, the book and pen. His preparation: 'I go, I shave and put on the costume. There are things you must not do in a preten-tious way.' Morgan does not particularly 'like' the character he continues to play: 'I have no history behind my mas,' he says. On the other hand, he is not bothered by the implications of playing for or, in his terms, 'serving' the devil in his mas. The Bookman, as he sees it, 'note all the bad souls in his diary and he pass on to Lucifer to be destroyed in the furnace.'

Despite the lack of ritual preparation for the mas, Morgan takes seriously what he calls the 'devil business'. Though he continues to 'pray in his heart', he feels that he 'cannot serve two masters at the same time. When I done with that [devil busi-ness], then I turn to Church.' Thus, though Catholic, while he is playing devil, he is not 'mixing up costume and Church together'. Just as when he was a policeman, it was his role and his calling until he quit, so now, while he is the Bookman, he serves that master alone. When he leaves the Bookman behind, he will not look back. And he will turn from his service to the devil back to the Catholic Church. Lamenting with many others what he regards as the imminent death of carnival—'all bikinis and panties'—Morgan planned to retire after his 2011 performances.[26] Virtually, his entire family—children and grandchildren—now live in the United States and he looks forward to joining them.

While the gownmen have been reduced to a small number of individual players, the dragons continue to form bands, which in the last two to three years appear to have increased, as well as to play as individuals in the various competitions. On Carnival Tuesday, a single lonely dragon might follow a fancy mas band of 5,000 or more players across the stage at any of the four or five different judging venues in Port-of-Spain. If you can imagine the movement from 5,000 to the single figure of one individual, alone on that same stage, then you begin to perceive the nature of Trinidad Carnival: high and low—there is room in the mas for all.

Trinidad is a multi-ethnic society, a fact highlighted by recent Chinese infusions into a dragon band clash (competition) that takes place on Carnival Friday at the corner of Prince and George Streets, within a block of the historic origin of Chinee Patrick's dragon band at 65 Queen Street. For at least two years (2008–09), this dragon clash included bands organized by recent Chinese immigrants, purportedly sponsored by Excellent Stores, a Chinese-owned retail establishment. Reportedly invited to participate by John Cupid, the Chinese brought Chinese dragons and

FIGURE 9. Individual dragon, Port of Spain, Trinidad. Photograph by and courtesy of Pablo Delano.

FIGURE 10. Chinese dragon in Port-of-Spain Trinidad Carnival, dragon clash, 2008. Photograph by and courtesy of Jeffrey Chock.

(under the appellation of beasts) Chinese lions. The Chinese dragons required multiple handlers to move through the streets, creating a dance step with a ripple effect. The lions—a symbol of good luck for the Chinese—were either one- or two-man creatures; they danced intricate steps, performed by trained Chinese dancers, giving a particular resonance to the concept of beast.[27] The Chinese first entered Trinidad as indentured workers in 1808. Though small, the community has always been powerful in Trinidad. Indeed, through Chinee Patrick, Chinese influence was present in the dragon band from the beginning, though his dragons were not in style Chinese.[28] Chinese dragon bands have existed before in Trinidad but have generally been different from the devil dragon bands. However, in the morning hours of at least two years (2008 and 2009),[29] recent Chinese immigrants brought their traditions into this complex of devil performances. In a moment lifted out of time, the dragons and the extraordinary lions in their street-corner clash once more enriched the ever-unfolding story of Trinidad's multi-ethnic culture.

Socially, the bands have in common with other forms of devil mas their origin in the nineteenth-century evolution of Carnival from its pre-Lenten European origins into an Afro-Trinidadian Emancipation festival. The individual gownmen, like the Bookman from Hell, in some ways resemble the contemporary Midnight Robber, a talking, cape-wearing character who in the wide-reaching 'robber talk' that chronicles

FIGURE 11. Dragon dance, during dragon clash, Port-of-Spain, Trinidad, 2008. Photograph by and courtesy of Jeffrey Chock.

his histories of epic slaughters (10,000 men killed before he was one, for instance) and cosmic powers (such as commanding the sun and moon to stand still) is frequently avenging a wrong done to his 'grandfather'. Both the devil's gownmen and the Midnight Robber hark back to the period of enslavement. When Carnival resumed after the Second World War, particularly in the 1950s, the dragon band with its varied characters, including the gownmen, declined in number. When one looked at the horrors of the war, the notion of hell that might have been valid in 1906 would hardly have created the same primal sense of fear. In any case, the gownmen have become living emblems of a past that is increasingly remote from the experiences of young celebrants.

Though, as Morgan puts it, the bands have now 'mash up'—they live in other ways. Dragons and beasts, for instance, continue to mass in bands together, partly because the energy of the beast, like the polluting wildness of the blue devils or the warrior energy of the jab jabs and stick fighters, recalls the history of resistance in a form that continues to resonate. They transform poverty and degradation into a badge of triumph, even when—in the characterization of novelist Earl Lovelace—the dragon can no longer dance.

Mythically, the dragon band's ancestral history, grounded in the myth of blackness and its African antecedents, resembles that of his fellow devils. What sets it apart is its link not so much to the notion of the Christian Devil, which it shares with the blue devils, but more specifically to biblical and literary representations of that Devil. At the same time, the beast masks continuities that are clearly ancestral—Yoruba Egungun masquerade or Kalabari secret societies. There is some evidence of this in the complete body costuming for this character, as well as the restraining chain, features of Yoruba Egungun masquerades. The dance of the dragon also resembles what co-author Rawle Gibbons has observed of Cuban Ireme masquerade performance, originally from the Calabar region of Nigeria.

Morgan gives an eloquent testimony to the complexity not only of this myth of origins but also to the inevitably assimilative quality of such myths when they are reconfigured over more than two centuries of habitation in a new homeland. Morgan is a Catholic. And though he does not feel that the European religion conflicts with his own ancestral identity, he has, as noted earlier, suspended his normal Catholic worship during the entire time of his playing Bookman—not only during the Carnival season but for all the years he plays the Bookman from Hell. In his service to the 'Devil', Morgan is paying homage to more than even he realizes. Despite the fact that he continues to 'pray in his heart', his active Catholicism gives way to his engagement with the infernal powers of darkness which, though also cast in the Christian mould (as servants of Lucifer), implicitly affirm the power to resist and, in resistance, the authority to oppose.

Cosmically, the dragons and imps are the most obviously archetypal characters in the dragon band, playing into (or out of) a set of cosmic energies that encompass elemental oppositions between water and fire. One of the beast's traditional dances, the 'ballet of crossing the water', is said to mimic the Dantesque crossing of the waters to the underworld but, in a more universal sense, reflects the fire-breather's fear of and antagonism to the element of water itself. As Procope describes, this dance, held by an imp, 'the beast is goaded and provoked but finally allowed to cross the drain, which he does with much fuss feigning fear . . .' (1988[1956]: 189).

Whether feigned or not, the beast's fear of the water reflects a primal, eternal and elemental opposition. Apparently, in the earlier bands, the beast's crossing of the drain was the herald that allowed all members of the dragon band to follow suit, thus engaging them all in the crossing into the underworld that is the devil's proper abode. Now that the gownmen play individually, their cosmic significance lies more directly in the opposition symbolized by the devil mask and angel wings. They are graceful; they assume poses that authoritatively command attention, as they enrol one in the

Book of Hell. They are avenging angels but they serve the agents of hell. Their rule of sway, accomplished without any interaction with bystanders, finally recalls and modifies the opposition between light and dark, between the forces of good and evil, which seem on the surface so easy to distinguish.

In this elemental world, where, in Morgan's terms, one cannot serve two masters at once, the differentiation between the infernal and the divine is not categorically moralized. One is reminded, again, that darkness and night, destruction itself and its accompanying fire, are a part of the cycle of life that, at its base, Carnival itself replicates. And in their mediation between these forces, the gownmen affirm what for Trinidadians is perpetually the third choice—the dialectical assimilation of the light and dark, the reconfigured good and evil into a newly synthesized path.

Conclusion: *The Third Path*

Trinidad Carnival devils ply their various trades and hold their places even now, enacting a pre-Christian cosmology in which the African and Indian converge to manifest a sense of the all-embracing universal rhythm in which all manifestations of being are present and equally powerful until proven otherwise in contest. Such a state predates distinctions based on morality, ethnicity, class, colour. Festive devils take to the streets to mount a ludic challenge to order, orthodoxy and an imposed history. As they cavort, play, threaten, fight, parade and pollute, the power of the mas simultaneously challenges the authority that would marginalize them and affirms an alternative source of equalizing, communal, festive authority with its own values and internal structure. Sometimes pretty, sometimes horrid, often emerging from slime and mud, powerful, engaging through the poles of attraction and fear, at times gracefully dignified, Trinidad festive devils claim their spaces and negotiate their festive rights in a dialectic of play that generates the multiple and simultaneous meanings of mas.

Each form, by definition, plays out its *myth*, one which the performer meets on entering the mas: devils were cast away from a place called Heaven to a place called Hell. Form functions through recognizable and accepted rules of appearance and behaviour. In performance, however, myth becomes play, opening possibilities to actualize, personalize, subvert or obeah the text: Hell becomes the condition under which the performer is/was enslaved but now, as its denizen, he eagerly awaits the arrival there of his oppressors.

At the *social* level, the mas encodes a complex politics of place and time, their known historical and social narratives. Beyond the boundaries of history, however, they enact timeless, ritual functions (*cosmic*) which require not conscious choice, but its opposite—the suspension of will, even consciousness itself, in an immersed participation that leads to the state Victor Turner (1982) calls 'communitas': the collective illumination of a common humanity. Carnival is itself a third space, wherever it is celebrated, that enacts the reconciling of irreconcilables. Here past and present converge, bipolar beliefs are bridged, oppressed and oppressor can be equally transgressed. It is an Eshu space, where the improbable happens and paths of transformation open.

The constant in all the character representations is fear, with the underlying threat of violence, made all the more powerful in the colonial and neocolonial situations of the Americas by the violence on which these nations were founded. The fear invoked in Carnival, however, is festive—isn't it? Violence contained within the festive world sublimates and symbolically controls the violence latent in nature and active in society, the violence without which life does not sustain itself or even survive. Both fear and threat are nuanced by the playful sense of mischief of all the festive devils, even though what they are playing out has a potency beyond the festival itself.

Festive devils share with other Carnival culture-bearers the power of the mas, which while not specific to the devil is his also. He—and increasingly she—has a licence to become, whatever that becoming may be. In a nation of communities, devil mas, along with other types of mas, is handed down by descent or adopted by personal choice. However unexamined that process of transmission might consciously be, festive devils become a key component in the building of community through the enacted and efficacious action of ritual that is part of the obeah magic of Carnival itself.

Notes

1 In 1913, Trinidad was the world's largest exporter of ammonia and the second-largest exporter of methanol. It provides more of the liquified natural gas used in the United States than any other nation. The first working oil well outside Azerbaijan was dug in Trinidad in 1857.

2 The origin of the term 'mas' may be 'masquerade' or 'mask', but mas expresses its own distinct Trini meanings as an art of Carnival performance for self-release through embodied costume, character and music. This definition, provided by co-author Rawle Gibbons, owes a debt to the work of performance-artist-academic Adeola Dewis.

3 See, for instance, Paul Gilroy (1993), Charles W. Mills (1998), Susan Pennybacker (2009) and George Yancy (2012).

4 Of course, the interactive histories of peoples in the Americas is complex, following migratory patterns that lead in many directions, for instance, of the Garifuna, whose efforts to resist British imperialism led to their exile in 1797 from St Vincent to Honduras, whence they migrated to Guatemala, Belize and Nicaragua in the ninetheeth century and to the US in the twentieth century. One of the important studies still to be undertaken is to track the patterns of performance of such groups as the Garifuna, who illustrate that the 'differentiation between the concepts "Black",

"Indian", and "indigenous" is [. . .] complicated and that multiple forms of self-representation exist with regard to these categories,' as Mark Anderson argues for the Honduran case (2009: 7).

5 'Lavway is French patois for "the voice" or "the truth". In origin it was the call-and-response chants of the stickfight. Its rhythm was assimilated into calypso.' Definition from NALIS (National Library and Information System) of Trinidad and Tobago. (available at: http://www2.nalis.gov.tt/Research/SubjectGuide/Carnival/tabid/-105/Default.aspx?PageContentID=90; last accessed on 1 April 2015).

6 We wish to thank our research assistants Lindsay Walker and Kevin Rich for calling this 1908 entry to our attention, and to Florence Blizzard for assisting them in their research, as well as Kathleen Helenese, then librarian in charge of the West Indian Section of the University of the West Indies Library, for facilitating this research.

7 Their common ancestor may well be the nineteenth-century King Pierrot mas that was played by stick men during daytime. John Cowley describes this character thus:

> Gorgeously dressed in gown and cap (padded for protection), each pierrot cleared the way before him by cracking his long whip. He was accompanied by a 'page boy' (sometimes his paramour) carrying a stick. His stickband followed in formation. Proclaiming himself as he sought out a rival, a pierrot's confrontation began with bombastic speeches, then whip lashings [. . .] and finally stickfighting. Stickmen supporters [. . .] joined in at this point. In each instance the object of conflict was to dismantle an opponent's costume. The most elaborate costumes were worn on Shrove Tuesday (1996: 81).

8 In Trinidad, those from India were known consistently as 'coolies'.

9 Stick fighters now tend to wear headbands with more varied, less ceremonial clothing, often cut-off jeans, sneakers and so on.

10 Kali is invoked because she is the 'dark' Hindu female deity, sometimes associated with violence yet also identified as gentle and caring (Ronald Alfred, interviewed by Tony Hall, Florence Blizzard and students at Trinity House class presentation, Curepe, Trinidad, 17 February 2011).

11 Though he has not witnessed it, Hindu community worker and former president of the Hindu Prachar Kendra, Raviji (Ravindranath Maharaj), a partner in this essay, affirms the credibility of such a link.

12 The process of mounting involves rubbing the stick or whip with frog guts and other such substances and burying or leaving it in a cemetery beside a significant grave (such as that of a deceased jab jab).

13 For another perspective on festive whips, see Max Harris' essay in this volume (pp. 129–50).

14 Please note that in this essay 'Indian' refers only to those whose ancestors came from India. In other essays, as in that by David Guss, which follows this essay, and especially those in the Andean section, 'Indian' refers largely to the Indigenous population of the region, as in older North American terminology.

15 There have always been a few women stickfighters, known as 'matadors', and Ronald Alfred's wife and daughter both play jab jab.

16 This is a reality—often defined mathematically—that is scientifically recognized as 'chaos theory'. See, for instance, Stephen H. Kellert (1993).

17 Old-time jab molassi use molasses or motor oil (black). They often have a bobbing tail. Some come out from Erthig Road, Belmont (the corner of Erthig and Norfolk). In a telling reversal, the band Pine Toppers, in the Carnival of 1970, the year of the Black Power movement in Trinidad, brought out '1001 White Devils'. See Guss' essay in this volume (pp. 221–33) for a festive devil in Cumaná, Venezuela, that is directly indebted to the jab molassi of Trinidad, which is only a few miles off the coast of Venezuela.

18 They now use body paint. It is easier to remove.

19 A trace is a place—somewhere between a settlement along one street and a village. It perhaps takes its name from the meaning of 'trace' as the place where a line or a plane intersects another plane. There are seven traces, or neighbourhoods, in Paramin.

20 We are indebted to Florence Blizzard, assisted by Lindsay Walker and Kevin Rich, for this interview.

21 Chipping is a Carnival dance that involves a simple shuffle movement of the feet. It is relaxing and easy to sustain for hours. Wining is a dance that involves pelvic gyrations with strongly sexual overtones, which may be performed by oneself or back to front with others, or in different combinations. Revellers at times 'wine' on the backs of truck beds.

22 This need to use pictured images from other traditions, in this case from Christian illustrations, to 'authenticate' a Carnival character, is characteristic also of a mas known as Authentic Indian, in which costumes are 'authenticated' by their embodied likeness to pictures of Southwest Plains Indians from the United States.

23 Procope could not verify this claim but pointed to illustrated 'religious books' like Frank Loris Peterson (1934[?]). Procope misidentified 'Peterson' as 'Patterson' (1988[1956]: 189).

24 For instance, in 1993 he was honoured for his 'skills' in a portrayal called 'Satan goes to Battle'.

25 This and the following quotes are from Benedict Morgan, interviewed by Florence Blizzard, Kevin Rich and Lindsay Walker, Belmont, Trinidad, 16 February 2011.

26 In fact, he did play mas again in 2012, deferring his plans.

27 We are indebted to the late photographer Jeffrey Chock, himself of half-Chinese ancestry, for information on and images of this event in 2008–09. Chock did not see the clash in 2010 and health problems in 2011 prevented him from photographing this dragon-band clash.

28 Patrick Jones, in 1908, just a hundred years earlier than this recent clash, called his band the Red Dragon Band, because of their red costumes. For the first two years, 1906 and 1907, Jones' bands are reported to have carried effigies on sticks rather

than embody them in characters (Chock, personal interview 2011). And, as photographed by George Duruty, some characters in the early Jones bands resemble contemporary jab molassi, held on chains by their imps.

29 These performances were licenced by the NCC. As noted by Chock, they did not appear in 2010 because of a conflict with the NCC. It is unclear whether this new tradition has resumed.

The Devil in Cumaná
A Photographic Essay

TEXT BY DAVID M. GUSS

PHOTOGRAPHS BY RAFAEL SALVATORE

> And I escaped from hell and live here in Cumaná, where I was
> born in my country, here in Sucre state.[1]

When he was young, he would hang out on the old wooden bridge across the
Manzanares, waiting for tourists to hurl coins into the water below. He would beat
his chest and howl like his favourite film character before diving in to retrieve them.
That's how he became known as Tarzan, a figure he loved so much that he had it tat-
tooed on his arm. His real name was Luis del Valle Hurtado, born in Cumaná,
Venezuela, the first Spanish settlement in South America. Although he had no training, he liked to entertain, and as a teenager was already inventing Indian dances which
he would perform at random in different parts of the city. He even acted in a film,
Lujuria Tropical (1962), an Argentine production in which he had to climb coconut
palms just like his namesake. But it was the figure of the devil that would change his
life forever and be the role he would play for more than 60 years.

The idea for his devil came from a Trinidadian named Ernesto. Tarzan was hyp-
notized by Ernesto and followed him everywhere. 'I was even his drummer,' he said.
'During carnival we went to the military club where I played the marimba. And he
asked "Look, do you want to be the devil for me? The same as me?" And I said, "If
you teach me how to make the horns, I'll make them." '

Ernesto, who was known as 'the sailor', was probably a blue devil or jab molassi
from Trinidad's Carnival tradition (see Milla Riggio and Rawle Gibbons' essay in this
volume, pp. 189–220). He used an empty biscuit tin for a drum, covered his body
with dye, wore horns and probably hid a blood-coloured substance in his mouth that
he could spit out to terrify the public. All these were elements that Tarzan too would
use. But Tarzan's main inspiration was the image of the Archangel Michael, that great
Satan-slayer with huge wings and a sword in one hand and the scales of justice in the
other (see Figure 1). 'I was always using this as my model,' he said. 'I wanted to create
a tradition using this.' And yet, in Tarzan's interpretation, the narrative has been
reversed. It isn't St Michael who stands above a devil he is about to kill; it is the devil

with a trident and wings outstretched who now vanquishes a young Indian boy. Has this image of the 'savage' become the new symbol of evil, and the devil, in some perverse way, part of the Lord's army?

By 1950, at the age of 19, all these ingredients had come together and Tarzan was ready to transform himself into the Diablo de Cumaná. With a combination of wood, cardboard and the inner tubes from a bike, he made wings. He found horns at a nearby slaughterhouse and inserted them into a hat. Then he bought plastic fangs and a ring for his nose, and with rope and wire created a tail. He used soot and ash to paint himself black and annatto seeds to make his tongue and mouth bright red. As part of his preparation, he lit candles to an altar for St Michael and even placed a card with the angel's image in his socks for protection. It didn't matter that he invoked the magic arts of Lucifer. This was his creation and no one else's. And it seemed to work. 'When I transform and make up as the black devil,' he claimed, 'my shadow changes. From up here, people seem tiny when I look at them. I appear tall and strong. How could that be? I don't know, friend. That happens to me through magic. And people ask, "Sir, how do you seem so small and large, so tall?" I think I have a pact with the devil.'

Unlike the blue devils of Trinidad, the Diablo de Cumaná didn't just dance during Carnival.[2] He also appeared during Easter as well as on the feast days for Santa Inés, Cumaná's patron saint, and San Francisco, the namesake of the city's oldest barrio, or simply when he had the urge to transform himself and take over the streets. There was no particular route and certainly no stage. The streets provided that along with the audience which quickly gathered, summoned by the sound of the tin drum. He was a one-man festival, a Pied Piper with horns and wings who both attracted and terrified children and adults alike. And every so often as he raced along teasing and threatening bystanders, he would stop to re-enact the central drama that had inspired his creation. A young boy, made up as an Indian with face and body paint and a simple headdress, would lie down on the pavement. The diablo would then begin to dance around him, singing and rolling his eyes up into the back of his head, and then very ceremoniously raise his trident and slowly pretend to impale the child with it.

While the ritual death of a young Indian was the key event in every diablo performance, it was his humour and improvisation that endeared the devil to generations of Cumaneses. Eventually, his fame began to spread and he was invited to dance in cities throughout the country. He even performed in Caracas at the Palace of Industry, an event he called 'my baptism as the Diablo de Cumaná.' Other forms of recognition came as well, including the National Prize for Folkloric Dance and, in 1994, a declaration as Living Cultural Patrimony of the State of Sucre. By then, years of using soot and other make-up had affected his health. But even with his eyesight nearly destroyed, he continued to dance. There were other, younger diablos now, imitators often driven by a desire to make money. Although flattered, he paid them little mind. In 2013, at the age of 82, he appeared at carnival where he proudly proclaimed: 'I'm the first and only real devil, the grandfather of all the little devils, the one who's danced down every street of my beloved Cumaná, of my beloved Carúpano, of all of Sucre. I'm the devil of the century.'[3]

FIGURE 1. Image of the Archangel Michael which provided the inspiration for the Diablo de Cumaná. All photographs by and courtesy of Rafael Salvatore.

FIGURE 2. The transformation.

FIGURE 3. The transformation.

FIGURE 4. The transformation.

FIGURE 5. The transformation.

(ABOVE) **FIGURE 6.** (BELOW) **FIGURE 7.** In the streets of Cumaná.

FIGURE 8. In the streets of Cumaná.

FIGURE 9 (ABOVE), and **FIGURES 10–11** (FACING PAGE, ABOVE AND BELOW). The ritual drama.

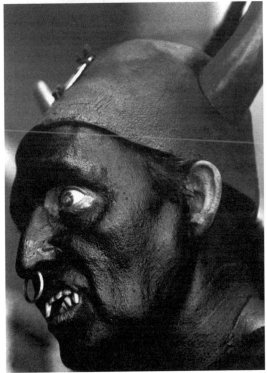

FIGURE 12. Mural honouring Tarzan, the Diablo de Cumaná.

Notes

1   Unless otherwise noted, all quotations in this article are from John Dickinson's film *El Diablo de Cumaná* (Cinematográfica Nueva Andalucia, 1984).

2   Though initially creatures of carnival, Trinidad Blue Devils now perform at events throughout the year. Unlike Hurtado's devil, however, blue devils appear in groups, seldom if ever alone. Like the Diablo de Cumaná, Trinidad Blue Devils do not follow an official route.—Eds.

3   'El Diablo "Luis" catalogado como "El Diablo del Siglo"' (available at: www.carupano.com; last accessed on 20 February 2013).

Venezuela's Corpus Christi Dancing Devils
An Intangible Cultural Heritage
A Photographic Essay

TEXT BY BENITO IRADY

PHOTOGRAPHS BY RAFAEL SALVATORE

The image of a tall and burly character holding a maraca and handkerchief in his right hand, and a sceptre in his left is among the most recent photos by Rafael Salvatore, who has travelled throughout Venezuela to document the importance of the Dancing Devils of Corpus Christi, recently declared by UNESCO as an Intangible Cultural Heritage of Humanity. This image reveals a participant in the ritual donning stockings stretched to his knees, espadrilles covering his feet, as well as a sheer embroidered costume, rounded off by a cape, bearded mask and two horns on his head. In this image, the stocky man stands before the priest, who carries the image of Christ crucified. The man evokes the Devil defeated. It is the oft-dramatized devotee's encounter with the struggle between good and evil.

The ritual's practitioner belongs to one of the *cofradías* or guilds of Dancing Devils of Corpus Christi in Afro-descendent communities, in this case specifically the old and renowned Chuao *hacienda* in the state of Aragua, a geographic region that is home to similar guilds, primarily in Cata, Cuyagua, Ocumare de la Costa and in the capital Maracay, whose barrios include groups evicted from Turiamo. But these are not the only important organizations that observe Corpus Christi, which is celebrated on the liturgical calendar each year on the ninth Thursday after Holy Week. Other *cofradías* in various states also participate in this Catholic festivity: Tinaquillo in Cojedes, San Rafael de Orituco in Guárico, Naiguatá in Vargas, San Millán and Patanemo in Carabobo and Yare in the Bolivarian state of Miranda. The oldest of these originated in the final years of the seventeenth century, and the most recent was handed down from generation to generation during different periods in the nineteenth century.

This selection of photographs by Salvatore depicts an array of the more characteristic styles marking both the differences and similarities among the many followers from each community, which are highlighted by the symbolism of masks representative of various animal species, or of a fantastical demonic zoology; by the hierarchical levels which distinguish the Diablos Mayores or the Capitanes or Capataces or Perreros or Arrieros; by the great variety of costumes in each of the *milicias* whose inspiration is drawn from different places; by the ritual adornments, which, according to ancient lore, serve as critical tools to ward off evil; by the way in which the Almighty is revered; by the combined elements of dance and musical instruments wherein, in some cases, drums and *redoblantes* (snare drums) give meaning to the practice, and in others, the *cuatro* guides the procession enshrined in community and ecclesiastic ties.

Through a broad, global view of this ritual, whether viewed historically or in the current moment, in each case we will see the constant presence of the maraca in the right hand, not as a simple ornament, nor as merely one more object used to stimulate spectators with its rhythm but as a magical link to the ancestors, strengthening the dancer's faith and splendour as he traces the shape of a cross with his footwork.

Based on a document carefully crafted among the numerous aforementioned communities and the Fundación Centro de la Diversidad Cultural (Central Foundation of Cultural Diversity, Caracas), UNESCO put together a collection of the distinctive elements which outlined the actions to be set forth in the Bolivarian Republic of Venezuela for the preservation of the knowledge, norms and secrets of this rich demonstration of popular knowledge. These elements were greatly debated in each region in 2010–11, during which the processes of dialogue and consensus-building were encouraged and a document drafted, containing state policies and outlining specific procedural measures for safeguarding these centuries-old expressions, to be carried out by local communities and communal representatives, in order to counteract the impact generated by market interests and globalizing trends.

This document, drafted by a qualified professional team, which was charged with determining the admission of the Dancing Devils into the Representative List of Intangible Cultural Heritage of Humanity, underscores that the Dancing Devils are a solidifying element in the communities where they are present, thus constituting a vehicle for the transfer of historical memory and ancestral traditions, as well as a space for the development of creativity, aesthetics and formal innovation. Among the Dancing Devils, oral tradition and imitation of the elders are the key vehicles for the transfer of intergenerational knowledge. In this way, when the decision to grant them world recognition was announced in 2012, it was possible to make evident to the countries that make up this branch of the United Nations the richness of a cultural occurrence that gives meaning to the very destiny of these communities, which were previously bound to the *haciendas* for the exploitation of cacao and other crops, such as sugarcane, coffee and indigo, giving way in these spaces to a diversity of popular expressions over time, a product of the combined interactions of three cultures: the American Indian, the European and the African. Among the most deeply rooted of these expressions, the practice that has as its central motif, the Devil's defeat before the Blessed Sacrament stands out.

This represents another victory for the ancestral traditions of the peoples of the Americas whose marvels and revelations show us, amid the continent's landscape, part of the path of our cultural diversity, of our values, of the uniqueness and boldness of communities who continue to affirm their liberty and their sense of belonging to a homeland, profoundly elevating their own elements of creation.

FIGURE 1. Devils of Cata, Aragua State, Venezuela, 2011. All photographs in this chapter by and courtesy of Rafael Salvatore.

FIGURE 2. Devils of Chuao, Aragua State, Venezuela, 2013.

(ABOVE) **FIGURE 3.** Devils of Ocumare de la Costa, Aragua State, Venezuela, 2011. (BELOW) **FIGURE 4.** Devils of Cuyagua, Aragua State, Venezuela, 2008.

(ABOVE) **FIGURE 5**. Devils of Tinaquillo, Cojedes State, Venezuela, 2012. (BELOW) **FIGURE 6**. Devil of Naiguata, Vargas State, Venezuela, 2008.

FIGURE 7. Devils of Patanemo, Carabobo State, Venezuela, 2013.

FIGURE 8. Devil of Turiamo, Carabobo State, Venezuela, 2012.

(ABOVE) **FIGURE 9.** Devils of San Millan, Venezuela, 2013. (BELOW) **FIGURE 10.** Devils of Yare, Miranda State, Venezuela, 2012.

(ABOVE) **FIGURE 11**. Devils of San Rafael de Orituco, Guarico State, Venezuela, 2012. (BELOW) **FIGURE 12**. *Cofradías* of Dancing Devils of Corpus Christi, Venezuela, 2013.

The Devil's Turn

ANGELA MARINO

Long considered one of the grandest and most 'global' fiestas of the Catholic Church, Corpus Christi (also named Corpus Domini) celebrates the Eucharist as the transubstantiated body of Christ and of the social body centred on Christ.[1] Corpus Christi also involves the exorcism of what the Church deems as 'evil' from this social body—the devils.[2] In Venezuela, however, devils have turned things upside down. The Dancing Devils of Corpus Christi, a religious manifestation that takes place annually over Corpus in eleven communities of Venezuela, transforms this dancing devil figure from that which was symbolically purged from the social body to what amounts to a force of protection and cultural determination. The devil's turn is about this process of reversal that takes place through a devotional practice and a broad intergenerational network of production.

While many forces contribute to these performances, as the recent inscription of Venezuela's Dancing Devils of Corpus Christi as a UNESCO Intangible Cultural Heritage of Humanity has brought to focus, the perhaps less-visible agents of this change are the hundreds of people who help produce these dances both inside and outside the organizing bodies of the cofradias. They are the neighbourhood altar makers, the mask makers, guardians of the saints and volunteers. They are family members, oral historians, costume makers, musicians, cooks, flower arrangers and more who see to the elaborate production that takes place year after year—all amounting to a veritable army of social mobilization (Alemán 1997). From this perspective, several questions as to the aesthetic and organizational strategies of these performances arise: What happens to this broader network of mobilization in various modes of participation and spectatorship? What ways do dancers themselves refer to and maintain the transformative power of the social body? How do networks of production influence or dispel the boundaries of good and evil? This essay explores some of these questions in both the physical and social enactment of a turn.

First, the devils of Corpus Christi, indeed, turn. They crisscross in diagonals, switch places, perform spirals and spins, and in some cases the procession turns backwards en masse.[3] Building from Leda Martin's idea of the spiral time, I suggest that the corporeal movement of the dance interacts with and responds to the broader social and political systems of its production in ways that reference this double dimension of a physical and social-political 'turn'. While the devil dances have long been narrated as a battle of forces between good and evil, this long-held practice also opens a space to defuse and heal a history of demonization.

Of course, the history of Corpus Christi has taken its own turns. As promoted in various media today as the legend of Corpus Christi, the story begins in thirteenth-century Belgium with Sister Juliana of Mont-Cornillon who, fearing the decline of religious faith in Christ, envisioned a full moon soiled by a black stain and thus began a campaign for a 'joyful fiesta' to honour the Holy Sacrament. Several years later, a small-town priest, Pedro de Praga in Bohemia sought proof of the mystery of transubstantiation—the actual presence of Christ in the Eucharist—and one day apparently found it. During Mass in the crypt of Santa Cristina in Bolsena, he witnessed the Holy Sacrament soak the altar cloth with what appeared before his eyes as the blood of Christ. News of the event reached Pope Urban IV who, just before his death in 1264, officially established the fiesta of Corpus Christi to celebrate the miracle of transubstantiation.[4]

Responding to the crisis of declining popularity, the Church sought a means to reinvent itself—in part through Corpus Christi. Between 1305 and 1325, Corpus Christi festivities were adopted throughout Europe in an effort to promote the power of the Church and extend its reach into new lands as a global enterprise. Pressure from the Reformation—which raised debates in the Church precisely on the issue of transubstantiation—resulted in enormous investments to bolster the popular manifestation of Corpus Christi as a joyous festive occasion, one connected to civic and municipal alliances.

During the fifteenth and sixteenth centuries, as Corpus Christi spread throughout the Spanish colonies of the Americas, it became one of Spain's most revered celebrations. From its inception in the Americas (and also prior in Spain), Corpus appropriated what Church officials called 'native' rituals—including the devil dances—in its own orchestration of plays, processions and pageantry (Dean 1999). The increased popularity of these dances, as crowds and extended networks of production gained power through them, however, threatened the Church and its ability to control the outcomes of these performances. Where Corpus Christi was designed to rehearse the triumph of the Catholic Church, other meanings were simultaneously produced that contended with the often-didactic aims of conversion and demonization (Taylor 2003, 2008).

Persecutions of so-called paganism and the racialized vilification of those assigned the role of 'devils' explicitly sought to eradicate non-Christian religious practices.[5] In Venezuela, José de Oviedo y Baños' editorial account of 1723 refers to black and indigenous peoples as 'barbarians', or 'savages' who worship pagan 'demons or, the devil incarnate' (1723: 35). This perspective in eighteenth-century Venezuela was not unusual in the hemisphere. As Steven T. Newcomb, a Shawnee/Lenape Native American researcher, writes: 'By categorizing our indigenous ancestors as heathens, pagans and infidels, the Christian Europeans were also categorizing our ancestors as less than a human, even akin to monsters' (2008: 108). While major differences certainly existed between black and indigenous groups in fiestas and other performances, often pitting one against the other, the demonization of both indigenous and Afro-descendant peoples in the Americas was part of a relentless strategy of land acquisition and colonial domination (Cañizares-Esguerra 2006; Cervantes 1997). As Newcomb describes, 'This process was not hidden or mysterious, nor was it a conspiracy among judges and priests. It was a long-range planning for the takeover of a continent and a hemisphere. It was the theory that guided colonial practices' (Newcomb 2008: 108). The Catholic Church thus created a troublesome dilemma: they used a promotional 'fiesta' ostensibly to embrace the multiple languages and cultures of the world, in order to damn those it saw as 'infidels' within its expanding enterprise.

Cultural performance, as David Guss suggests, is a battleground for cultural rights (1980: 176). In many ways, the fiesta of Corpus Christi and the Dancing Devils can be considered an example of this battle, which is part of a much larger political, economic, social and ideological war being waged in the Americas. In the case of the devil, the crux of this battle rests on the significations of good, evil and moral authority performed in the events of Corpus Christi in various ways—one of which is the dancing body itself.

The Body: Turns of the Caracol

FIGURES 1-3. The Caracol or Snail Shell dance as performed in Ocumare de la Costa, Venezuela, 2008. All photographs by the author.

The devil's turn is generated through the body. It is, according to most practitioners, devotional and also kinaesthetic—a corporal movement based in weight, positioning and sensations of the body.[6] One of the most exemplary formations of the turn in the devil dances is the Caracol, a signature dance performed in Ocumare de la Costa, a town of 9,000 mostly Afro-descendant residents on the southern coast of the Caribbean in Venezuela (see Figures 1–3). Caracol, which means spiral or snail shell, is a rigorous choreography in which dozens and sometimes hundreds of dancers weave through the shape of a spiral, entering and exiting the eye of a swirling hurricane. From the far corners of the plaza, dancers sweep in with swift, wide circles onto the church portico. One after another, with arms outstretched, looping in on the second round, they pass through the centre in alternating formation.

The spiral dance of the Caracol is known in Ocumare to be one of the oldest and most cherished of the devil-dance choreographies.[7] Stunning to watch, the Caracol requires an acute state of attention as a group dance, for dancers must attune themselves to one another by swiftly interleaving steps between the inner and outer circles. This momentum propels dancers into the spiral. Once inside the centre of the spiral, each dancer tucks in tightly, then alternates an exit from the centre with those approaching the inner ring. It is a practice of dexterity, awareness of others' bodies and, as many dancers describe, total submission to the Holy Sacrament. Diagonals and rotations, spirals, body crossings and switching places are all turns that define the devil's dance. These turns have come to express virtuosity alongside companionship and interdependence in ways that physically position the devil at the heart of a community generated practice. Thus, rather than treating the devil as an outsider to the social body, the dance brings the home-made, fierce, but also humorous and fantastical representation of the devil to the centre of the community and makes it part of a trusted network.

The devil's turn also emphasizes the intergenerational aspect of this network of dancers through the Caracol. The *capataz* of the devil dances in Ocumare, a respected historian and leader the community of Ocumare, José 'Cheché' Echenagucia, stands at the heart of the spiral. Next to him is the youngest dancer—about eight years old—who timidly yet firmly holds his ground at the centre of the cyclone. On his other side is the eldest, most venerated of the 'guardians' of the dance. The young dancers learn the steps, imbibe the energy and the precision of the dance by participating in it and by watching the older adolescents and adults in the performance from the vantage point at the heart of the turn.

If bodies indeed learn through various forms of kinaesthetic memory, then, these young dancers learn from the position of their bodies at the centre of the spiral. At this critical turning point from the inside to the outside, there is a heightened degree of attention. As Thomas J. Csordas has described, these are somatic modes of attention—a state in which paying attention *to* the body accompanies the situatedness of the body in the world, and the 'embodied presence of others' (1993:

138). These turns are swift, complex and interdependent. In other words, the kinaesthetic exchanges between individuals and the group, between participants, between participant and observer, and between observers themselves, produce a network and an 'inter-subjective milieu' within this physical turn. Dancers and other participants are constantly reminded that executing the turn is not a mere function of individual bodies learning a technique. Instead, the Caracol hinges upon a larger interdependent cultural and religious devotion. Once again, rather than outcasts, these devils convey an alternative order and dimension of experience that is integral to the community.

Eventually, the devil dancers of Ocumare dissolve the spiral and move in a second procession to the newly built community centre across the church, then through the streets. Well into the evening, long after the priest has retired, they bless homes of the elderly and infirm and visit other sites such as the cemetery to honour the dead. The devils then reappear the following Sunday in the beach town of Playón, where, again after Mass, they confront the priest who, wielding the monstrance, drives them back into the streets. This time, after blessing the altars, the devils disperse until the following year.

In sum, these are communally integrated networks regenerated and inspired by the devil dancers' turns. These turns are not solo moves—they are group dances that often involve several generations and are choreographed with performers for not just once but in a *repeated* event year after year, thus turning both in time and across time. As an ongoing *practice*, the devil dance engages the collective body in a social, material and physical way, linking generations kinaesthetically in the reproduction of these formal and informal relations.

***

The embodied turn of the Caracol placed next to what scholar and practitioner Leda Martins calls 'spiral time' recalls what Martins refers to as the 'symbolic reversal' in Afro-Brazilian performance of the Congados (2007). These turns are, like other forms of embodiment, in Martins' words, a 'philosophy'. It is a philosophy in which the embodied language of the dance itself is a source of knowledge for practitioners, cultural workers and community members. Movements such as the turn, the spiral and the crossing step hold meaning beyond choreographic device or technique. According to Martins, the idea of a spiral or a turn opens a multi-dimensional space. They are entries into an epistemological understanding of time, space and belief itself, where in spiral time ancestors meet at the crossing between future and past (ibid.).

Martins refers to the 'instrumental attributes and properties of the performances where embodied memories fulfil and create a sign-body that expands itself as cultural

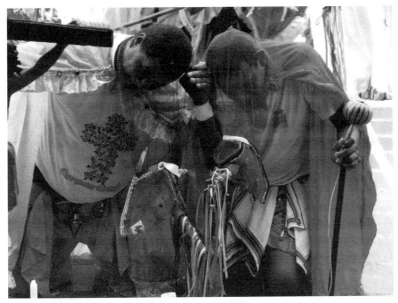

(ABOVE) **FIGURE 4.** Dancers bow in prayer with wire mesh masks in Cata, Venezuela, 2009.
(BELOW) **FIGURE 5** Outside the church during the devil dances in Ocumare de la Costa, Venezuela, 2010.

corpus' (ibid.: 199). For Martins, this sign-body is ultimately conceived kinetically, and, in doing so, the word and its voice make meaning through the body. This kinetic identity is related to motion and the passing of energy, thus creating gestures such as the individual and collective turns in the devil dance. To bow low, (not) to turn one's back, to let the mask fall off the face but not to touch the ground, or to crisscross one's feet are likewise part of this sign-body.

If we accept Martins' sign-body as a part of the devils' dancing bodies and build on her theory that there is a means for the voice and the body to generate an inscription in performance itself, then we see these meanings of the cultural corpus form kinetically. Accordingly, the sign-body and its 'voice' engage, as Martins describes, in an 'expressive contiguous syntax', connecting ancestral memory and the present through movement in the body. In short, what Martins proposes is a language of embodiment and, crucially, a means by which that language conveys its own documentation, historiography and epistemology. Thus, the devil dances kinaesthetically create and restore this space from within.

As an embodied and also socially produced act, the devil's turn refers to a transformation of the devils from that which is purged into a protector of the community, or at least the capability to shift who defines the boundaries of the community. Therefore the devil's turn is a force of collective power, one that has proven extremely effective at disarming a history of violence and demonization.

The devil's turn is an extension of this embodied language, where the turn, according to Martins, opens up spaces for an epistemological reorientation.[8] The town of Ocumare during Corpus Christi is jammed with devils from dawn to dusk. Together, in order, fanning themselves with capes in the pre-monsoon heat, the devils skip among houses and shops and crisscross the narrow mud-packed streets. Individually, the devils cross one leg over the other and even turn their feet outward as they skip into diagonal lines. At times they jump and turn. At other times, the devil dancers pause in lines and then switch places along the processional route, turning inward before the altars. They cross over between lines, turning their bodies to the ground and to one another. As the mid-morning sun rises, several women bring water pitchers for the dancers. A mother steps out and ties a young dancer's shoelaces. Musicians sometimes switch off through the long day of incessant strumming. People sit outside in their lawn chairs to watch the procession pass. Friends and relatives of dancers gather at the street corners and take pictures alongside an occasional tourist. Oral historians share the stories of real devils that have appeared in the dance. Mask and costume makers watch their creations or dance in them. Now, and increasingly over the past 10 years, school groups from Maracay and other nearby cities also visit during the day of the Diablos of Ocumare.

At first glance, the metanarrative of the event suggests that those playing the role of devils surrender unconditionally to the Church. From this perspective, the dance affirms submission to the authority of the Church, despite the Church's disreputable past and the present inclination of the archdiocese to censor the dance. However, this reading obscures the complexity of a practice that opens up a space—kinaesthetically, sociopolitically and symbolically—for reconstituting the collective power of the devils outside of, and also alongside, the Church. In many ways, the dance continues to affirm the act of submission to the symbol of Christ in the Sacrament. Yet, who and what this body of Christ represents, and how the Sacrament is, or is not, symbolically adhered to the Church's disreputable past remains contested ground. It is also the case that many devotees nowadays join these events in order to regenerate African and Caribe-centred cultural and spiritual integrity that this scenario of conversion ostensibly sought to eliminate.

As the procession moves from the church and around the central plaza of Ocumare, the crowds gather in tighter groups while the priest and his devotees remain in tow in order to fulfil their obligatory role in this people's production to bless the altars. The devils then approach in pairs to surrender themselves before each of the nine altars, offering their own blessings and prayers. Then off again and back into the streets, bowing low, crossing themselves, the devils take the lead.

Relations within the dance, between dancers and other practitioners, such as altar makers and historians, become sites for the production of what I've called the devil's turn. Together, like extended nets, these systems, or networks, widen collective authorship beyond the Church, and far beyond the face-value submission of the devils, and equally beyond the notion of pure evil or pagan idolatry that the Church had hoped to eradicate. It is also this level of widespread production that is capable of *turning* the 'absence of solemnity' that Sister Juliana imagined as the black stain on the moon—a sign of waning faith—into a reaffirmation of both the Holy Sacrament *and* Afro-descendant cultural production. Here, the dance exercises a different configuration than the so-called Manichaean divide that the devil dance and the devil were initially conceived to enforce. Although descriptions of the devil dance often refer to it as a timeless struggle between good and evil, the performance of the devil dance complicates this interpretation. Beyond good versus evil, the devil's turn is about spiral time, interdependence and the wider networks of participation that sustain this dance through generations.

Notes

Among the authorities of the devil dances of Ocumare, I wish to acknowledge José 'Cheché' Echegunacia and his extended family, Clemis García and her daughter Rosa García, Luisa García and family, Luisa Rodríguez and family, Jorman Valera and the many dancers, altar makers, mask makers and other producers and coordinators of the dance.

1 Catholic parishioners receive or embody Christ upon consuming the Eucharist at Mass—a form of unleavened bread administered during the religious service.

2 For more on Corpus Christi performances, see Carolyn Dean (1999).

3 As in the Diablos Danzantes de Yare, in Venezuela.

4 For this account, see also Rafael Strauss (2004).

5 See *La extirpación de la Idolatría en el Perú* (1621) by Father Pablo Joseph de Arriaga, and an extensive literature that followed on the extirpations of the Catholic Church in the American hemisphere.

6 Leda Martins references Joseph Roach's 'kinesthetic imagination' as an influence on her ideas on 'spiral time' (2013).

7 Many residents of Ocumare that I spoke to referred to the possible indigenous origins of the Caracol choreography.

8 See Sally Ann Ness' discussion of Gregory Bateson's 'iconic' forms in Ness (2007). See also Pierre Nora (1989).

Northern Devils

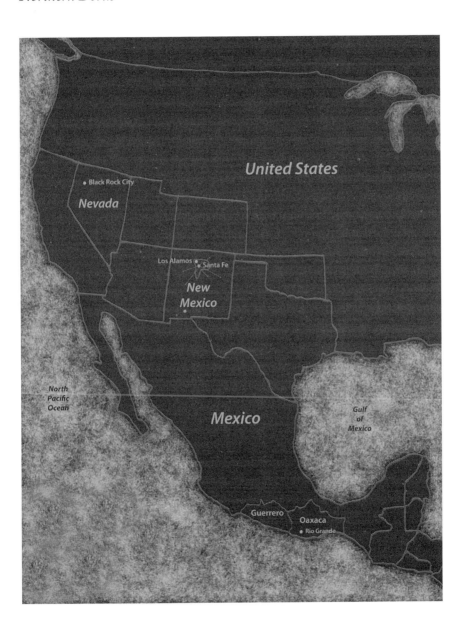

Pancho and Minga
Devilish Renegades Of Mexico

ANITA GONZALEZ

Dance Display

Pancho leaps in the air and lands with a decisive foot fall that calls attention. His followers—a troupe of male dancers clothed in tattered shirts and raggedy pants. As Pancho takes the lead, the grating sound of a *bote*—a large friction drum with a protruding stick—propels the ruffians forward. The deep, squeaking sound, coupled with the chatter of animal teeth produced by a jawbone, creates a sonic environment of chaotic disunity. Within the Afro-Mexican Devil Dance, devil disguise allows Mexican coastal residents to act out theatrical scenarios that include aggressive attacks, public whippings, sexual overtures and other disreputable acts. These black dance artists recreate terrifying scenarios of subordination and control in order to demonstrate the ongoing virility of Afro-Mexican culture.

Mexico is a country where notions of *mestizaje* as national cultural identity predominate. Governmental policies instated after the Mexican Revolution of the early twentieth century inculcated a populist belief in the mixed-race Spanish/Indian identity of all citizens. Native American and Spanish cultures were presumed to be the backbone of a liberated society rooted in histories of Indigenous empires and Spanish nobility. Afro-Mexicans, descendants of enslaved workers and free domestics or soldiers, were not imagined within the Mexican national consciousness. Rather, their communities were subsumed by a general acknowledgement that the 'dark-skinned' *morenos* somehow came to live on the country's coasts as arrivals from an unnamed 'other place'. Between 1500 and 1800, large communities of Afro-descendant people gathered on Mexico's eastern coast, where sugarcane plantations flourished, and on the western coast, where enslaved Africans fled as renegades to develop agricultural and fishing communities. Festival performances of Mexico's western coast repeatedly flaunt the character of the Pancho, a social outcast who assumes a position of authority in popular dances like the Turtle Dance, the Straw Bull Dance and the Devil Dance.[1]

In the west coast Devil Dances, Pancho appears as a poorly dressed man who wears ragged clothing and masks himself with the furry face of an animal. Dressed in *chaparreras* or leather chaps, he carries a whip that he uses to skillfully manage a

FIGURE 1. Pancho is a featured character in a cross section of Afro-Mexican dances including the Devil Dance. This Pancho wears a full-face human mask and his dress identifies him as the head rancher of the Toro de Petate or Straw Bull Dance rather than as a Devil Dancer. Photographer José Manuell Pellicer took this photograph in 2007 at a dance festival in Santiago Llano Grande that brought together festival dance practitioners from the Oaxaca coastal area. All photographs in this essay by José Manuel Pellicer.

double file of masked dancers who follow him through the streets. While some Afro-Mexican dances such as the Toro de Petate, present Pancho as an authoritative rancher or an empowered horseman, the Devil dances of Oaxaca and Guerrero present Pancho as a working member of the lower class. Even though he is a poor man, Pancho controls underlings in a total and unforgiving manner. Whips and shouts enable him to maintain authority over his theatrical community, reaffirming self-sufficiency within a broader landscape of political impotency.

Pancho's biggest challenge is his wife La Minga. When she enters the performance area walking at his side, she performs sexuality and disobedience, taunting her husband by flirting and cavorting with the audience. While Pancho and his minions wear horned masks covered with animal fur, La Minga's face is covered with a human mask. Her normalized facial features demonstrate that she is not a fiend, even if she behaves monstrously. She is never in sync with her husband; instead, she parades out into the crowd, and tantalizes onlookers while challenging his control. It is always a man who enacts the role of this colorful character; and dancers consider the Minga to be one of the most difficult roles to perform because of the extreme, expressive physicality that is required to complete her actions. She must roll, chase, flirt, shake, flaunt, and improvise throughout the entire dance.[2] Sometimes she is childlike and seductive, at other times aggressive and confrontational. And her outfits are outlandish. She may wear a tight pink dress with overstuffed breasts and buttocks or, perhaps, a revealing mini-skirt. The intertextual play of a male body performing

FIGURE 2. Here Pancho appears with his wife La Minga (usually played by a female impersonator) on the street in La Boquilla, Oaxaca (2005). His mask and attire identify him as a lowly commoner who gains power by leading a raggedy team of disruptive followers. Mexican Devil Dancers metaphorically represent the Afro-Mexican renegade who gains respect by rebelling against society.

female sexuality adds a complex layer of innuendos to each gesture that the character makes. For example, when the male Minga walks with mincing steps and then waggles his buttocks, he plays the female, parodying feminine wiles through his gestures. When, however, the Minga aggressively chases and attacks the male Pancho, the physical threat of the 'male dancer dressed as female' appears real and dangerous. His strength and size are a formidable challenge to the dancing Pancho.

Mexican Historical Resistances

These two characters, Minga and Pancho, encapsulate mythologies and histories of Afro-Mexico. Pancho conjures up a sense of disorderly confrontation. Concepts of the black resistor may have originated in historical events connected with slave escape and insurrection. Yet they also support regional ideals of revolutionary action that have developed within the states of Guerrero and Oaxaca. These two Mexican states have always been separated from administrative governing bodies in central Mexico by a series of high mountains. The mountains are difficult to cross. They make travel and communication between the country's capital and the coastal areas difficult. As a result, the western region has always been associated with renegades who take advantage of the remote and dangerous geography. In both the War of Independence (1810–21) and the Mexican Revolution (1910–20), Oaxaca and Guerrero were strategically used to initiate military actions and in contemporary context the two provinces have resurfaced as primary locations for rival narco factions. The name of the state, Guerrero, means 'warrior' in Spanish and rebellious folk characters like Pancho underscore this ideal.

Overseer- and rancher-dance images are also connected to actual labour categories that were filled with Afro-Mexicans. During the colonial period, Afro-descendants served as cow herders or overseers on sugar and cacao plantations. With their knowledge of horsemanship, they easily moved into positions as ranchers, either in charge of their own estates or working on those of others. When a dance character dons chaps, or carries a whip, the character's dress alludes to occupations associated with farm work and animals. Even today agricultural trade is a prime activity for Afro-Mexican labourers on the Costa Chica of Guerrero. The construction of the overseer character is also grounded in historical realities of African cruelties against Native American and *mestizo* workers. Peter Stern (1994) describes specific instances of gangs of black people pilfering villages (1573) or forcing Native Americans into day labour (1663). When black people were placed in positions above local labourers, relationships were antagonistic. On the other hand, in places where Africans laboured alongside the Afro-Mexicans (the Pancho figure), they could be regarded as collaborators.

Pancho generally encapsulates one of three metaphoric ideas that are linked to histories of Afro-Mexican presence: the valiant resistor, the vicious overseer or the skilled rancher. Each of these character traits is associated with a historical archetype; however, the types are not self-contained. By this I mean that the resistor may also be the overseer, or the skilled rancher may perform resistant actions. Pancho's role— his intention—is to keep others in line. When he dances as the lead devil, he gains a small amount of control over the others who surround him, even though they also represent the disempowered. The manner in which Pancho rebels, his corporeal use of the body, is linked to ideals of resistance. As a performer he embodies a lack of *respeto* or respectful restraint. Disrespect (within the context of contemporary community dance) may be interpreted as a deliberate attempt to demonstrate rebellion against mainstream norms or mores.

Steve Stern writes about the concept of *respeto* and its importance within Spanish colonial society. 'The contested meaning of *respeto* condenses the conflictual dynamics of culture. [. . . A]t the core of the term was not only an idea of restraint, deep and varied in its cultural and historical roots [. . . but also] culture as a language of argument in the exercise of power' (1995: 212–13). While Native American and Spanish colonial dances observed deference to a sense of order, place and legitimacy, Afro-Mexican populations, like African diasporic people in many different locations, value a sense of imbalance, disorder and/or rebellion. But the lack of *respeto* is also related to core qualities of African performance that cannot be disregarded. African aesthetics valorize the articulation of the torso and the movement of fertility zones (as well as the arms, legs and head) to communicate. Colonial systems in both Africa and the Americas have repeatedly interpreted the polycentric movements of the torso within African diasporic dance forms as lascivious or immoral. Sterling Stuckey writes: 'A repulsive yet desirable object to many whites, the black body posed problems of a psychological nature for them. This was unavoidable for those who associated blackness with din and lasciviousness and evil as did many white Americans' (2002: 39).

Afro-descendants, dancing within their own cultural aesthetics—using the hips, buttocks, torso and breasts as communicative instruments—would repeatedly be judged as immoral. Yet, in moments of disruptive performance, the movements are embraced and flaunted. Both violence and sexuality can be mobilized to assert presences in an otherwise restrained society. This 'dissing' of the restraint distinguishes Afro-Mexican dancing from the Native American and Euro-American dancing that surrounds it. Francisco Camero Rodríguez graciously describes this artistic proclivity as *El arte de la rebeldía* or the Art of Rebellion (2006: 37).

What is unique about the Devil Dance is that the acts of rebellion, performed as disrespect of mainstream norms, also reify the solidarity of the community that dances together when the devils emerge as a festival act. The process of staging the dance reaffirms local alliances within the community and effectively articulates Afro-Mexican identities as something different from dominant *mestizo* and Catholic ideologies. Because the dance is often performed on the Day of the Dead (*c.*31 October–2 November), it represents an alternative community response to both Native American celebrations of Indigenous ancestors and Catholic celebrations of the Resurrection. At the same time, the corporeal procession of unified black bodies creates a fraternity of the like-minded.

FIGURE 3. A white mask adorns the face of this Minga who appears more feminine and less aggressive. At the 2007 Santiago Llano Grande festival local communities presented diverse interpretations of the Minga character. Dance sponsorship, during festival occasions or otherwise, allows for innovation in characters, dance forms and presentation styles.

La Minga differs from Pancho and the unified procession of Devil Dancers because she has the privilege of 'dancing apart'. Origins of Mexican Mingas can be ascribed to multiple sources. Some representations depict her as a mulatta, or mixed-race black woman. When she appears like this, her mask is red or black or brown. In this representation, her features are chiselled and imply anger. The mulatta Minga may demonstrate male fears about female impropriety. She is clearly out of control and her personage usually reflects this. The white-faced Minga is her counterpoint. Her mask is very white or very pink and has a porcelain veneer. The frailty of the mask provides a contrast to the voluptuous physical frame of the body beneath the mask. I have seen only one interpretation of the Minga where the dancer's body is petite and demure. The white-faced Minga is like a paradox—two culturally distinct bodies merged into a single archetypal character. The impossibility of the combination is perhaps the social commentary. Two seemingly incompatible cultural types thrust into the same corpus.

Pancho's Minga can attack the audience, or her husband, and force her victims to roll around with her on the ground. Whether she is seductive or aggressive depends upon the performer's interpretation of her character. A seductive Minga will approach audience members, show them her child and encourage them to dance with her or to touch her body. When she acts out in this manner, the devil disciplines her and 'teaches' her to control her sexuality. As he maintains his machismo as her male partner, he protects his wife, claims her and brings her under his control. This aspect of their relationship reinforces mainstream social standards of correct comportment. La Minga's sexualized approaches unmask her uncontrolled libido. The Pancho must learn to manage her. In contrast, an aggressive Minga will chase and attack both the Pancho and the crowd. In this instance, her character is still sexual but much more threatening. Rather than depending upon feminine wiles to draw her object of desire to her, the aggressive Minga attacks, forcing compliance to her will.

Most Mingas carry a child—a white baby that is evidence of La Minga's inappropriate copulations. This facet of the character uniquely speaks to social fears about miscegenation and its products. Sometimes the Minga baby is cared for like a baby, although the child can also be a weapon. I have seen dance performances where the 'baby' is worn at the waist and waggled as if it were a penis. More often, the child is 'shared' with the audience as a way of demonstrating the mother's compassionate presence. La Minga's flaunting of the white baby can be interpreted in several ways. In some ways, the character is similar to the Indigenous translator Malinche who slept with Hernando Cortés,[3] betraying her alliances by sleeping with the enemy. Jean Franco, in her book about gender and representation in Mexico argues that: 'orally transmitted narratives, such as folk tale and romance, have their roots in a community where treachery means threatening the very existence of the community to which storyteller and listener belong' (1989: 132). Both Malinche and La Minga touch on cultural anxieties about interracial mixing in Mexico. Literary writings by authors like Octavio Paz (2002) investigate the cultural enigma of La Malinche. La Minga, conversely, may be a performed counterpart to the traitorous character. Re-enactment of social fears (through performance) is thought to allow communities to release collective cultural anxieties. If this is the case, then repeated appearances of La Minga indicate a collective re-imagining of African and Creole identities.

Some scholars maintain that the Malinche character is a direct re-enactment of Cortés' mistress. Max Harris (1996) and Nancy H. Saldaña (1966) both offer a contrasting interpretation of the Malinche character. They ascertain that the figure represents an earth goddess who, for Aztec, Maya and Hopi populations, was a wifely partner to the sun god Huitzilopochtli. Harris and Saldaña believe that the Mexican Malinche is also called La Maraguilla and that she is an extension of these sexualized pre-Columbian deities. They see continuities of this belief system in Maranguilla figures depicted in the Matachines and Moriscas dances of central Mexico. There are instances within these dances when the iconography references the sun; however, symbolic images of the rain god Tlaloc, like the snake, are also included in Tontonac dances. In both instances, the wife/mother character would represent fertility. Of course, the fertile and sexual Mother Earth figure surfaces in theologies of many world cultures. Yemaya from the Yoruba culture, for example, embodies ideals of fertility and sensuality. The Afro-Mexican Minga could, and probably does, originate from several sources. Once again, New World mixtures of religious and metaphysical belief systems continually result in unique, local expressions of cultural mythologies. La Minga is but one of the cultural amalgams that has developed from complex histories of social interactions.

At the same time, there are clear historical referents within Mexico to the mixed-race mulatta woman who carries an illegitimate child. Nicole Von Germeten writes about seventeenth-century provincial towns where Afro-Mexican women appear frequently in church baptismal records. She refers to records that demonstrate that between 1597 and 1670, roughly 75 per cent of the babies baptized had *padre desconocidos* or unknown fathers.[4] These babies were born within slave masters' households and 'the majority of these children were the illegitimate result of sexual relationships between women and their masters, or with their peers' (2006: 128). Over the course of 200 years, more and more Afro-Mexican babies were baptized; however, their fathers also accepted more children as legitimate offspring. These statistics, while inconclusive, provide a historical case study that helps to explain popular cultural associations of Afro-Mexican women with illegitimate babies. La Minga's dance with her half-breed child reflects a past reality of Afro-Mexican illicit sexual activity with *padres desconocidos*. Clearly, evidence of the origins of the Malinche character is somewhat contradictory. What we do know, however, is that her danced public performances defy categorization. La Minga shape shifts into nightmarish representations of the black Mexican woman. Like La Malinche, she is the inevitable, unpredictable result of racial mixing in the Americas.

Collectively, the characters of Pancho and Minga use performance to investigate the status of the Afro-Mexican communities within the wider social constructs of Mexican society. They represent a challenge to officially established order. As socially abominable agents, they restore a sense of valour to destructive, devilish behaviour. Their spectacular dance reconsiders and enacts aggression and sexuality as an ideal of valour. Through the mechanism of dance, the two Devil Dance characters push mythologies about the African diaspora to their limits. Public, in-your-face Pancho and Minga performances of black stereotypes reify and contradict expectations about who and what the black people are.

Community Perspectives

Sitting in a one-room flat in the village of Rio Grande, I listen to Maestro Oscar Jimenez Terrazas, a dance instructor at the local COBAO High School, describe how dancing the devil informs his teaching of Mexican folklore. Jimenez Terrazas dances the devil and participates in ceremonies, but he also teaches high-school students the basics of social dance, folkloric dance and modern dance skills in his daily after-school rehearsals. Staring at the television screen, we review his compilation of Devil Dance videotapes, an archive of images collected from numerous excursions to the smaller villages that surround the town of Rio Grande on the Oaxacan coast. This teacher is neither archivist nor anthropologist but, rather, a dance enthusiast in search of tools to help him interpret culture, history and ultimately how to re-present the patterns and meaning of devil and other dances.

Oscar's viewing and archiving practices point to the importance of community preservation of festival dance activities. Dancing the devil is just one part of an interwoven network of public performances designed to recognize and maintain community culture. In Mexico, where government sponsorship encourages traditional ethnic performances, knowing culture is a way to acquire currency. Dancers compete for awards at local events where government agents distribute prizes and offer touring possibilities. Festival practices privilege conventional folklore—performances where dancers are clad in uniform outfits (pants for the men and dresses for the women) and work with partners to create intricate spatial floor patterns. Money moves to artists and companies who are able to professionalize codified folklore for festivals such as the Gueleguetza, an annual gathering held in the mountain city of Oaxaca, which draws thousands of visitors from around the world who are interested in seeing regional dances on stage. Dancers and their companies travel throughout the states of Guerrero and Oaxaca to participate in the festival. The event includes some couple dances from the Costa Chica, although masked dances, such as the Afro-Mexican Devil Dance or the Toro de Petate, are generally not included. Instead, the festival promotes, as the representative form of the region, the Chilena, a partner dance that is sometimes performed with percussive foot beats on a raised wooden platform called the *artesa*. In its most conventional form, heterosexual couples circle flirt and twirl around each other. Devil Dance, with its fierce attacks and its flamboyant cross-dressing of the Minga character, is a contrasting example of coastal dance. Even though Oscar knows and participates in the Devil Dance, he prefers the Chilena with its billowy dresses. From his perspective, Devil Dance is a local, colourful, community practice of the villages, but only Chilena dance can be entered in the competitions at the Gueleguetza.

Sponsorship impacts greatly upon the meanings and purpose of festival dance performance. Local patrons, often associated with municipal agencies or cultural houses, may choose to sponsor a Devil Dance. Often the occasion is a pre-existing celebration such as the Day of the Dead or a patron saint day. The dance leader is generally responsible for a how the dance is staged; he is familiar with the steps, the patterns and the symbolic hierarchies of that particular dance. Sometimes particular groups of dancers gain notoriety for the humour or uniqueness of their performances. For example, the dancers of La Boquilla are known for their unique tattered costumes, while the dancers of Santiago Llano Grande have a polished unity in the antics of the ensemble corps. To create the outfits and accoutrements for the performance, the dance leader may work with a mask maker or create them in his own studio. Musicians work separately. If they know the songs and rhythms that accompany a certain dance, they will be asked to play once the dance leader agrees to bring out the dance. 'Knowing the music' is to have social status, because song is fundamental to the successful staging of a festival event.

Some dances, like the Devil Dance, include spoken text that is recited to the audience. If this additional element is necessary, then the dance leader is the person who teaches the text to the performers. There is a generational component to festival dance. Communities want to ensure that specific local dances thrive. Consequently, they make certain that younger dancers are included each time that a dance is 'brought out'.[5] Sometimes, to accomplish this, each character will have a young apprentice following along. At other times, an entire troupe of young performers will learn the patterns and sequences of the dance.

The impact of Devil Dancing is primarily on the local community that participates in the staging of the dance. Village members can show off their talents, entertain one another, laugh at the foibles of their neighbours, marvel at transformations of the characters—in short, participate in all of the elements that disguise and performance contribute to human expression. At the same time, because Devil Dancing is a fairly unique cultural expression of the Costa Chica, dancers and audience members use their dance events to acknowledge their membership in a local cultural community.

Afro-Mexican Inversions

In myth and legend, devils are the antithesis of virtue. In the Catholic tradition, they represent evil; they are known to torture human souls, or to mischievously encourage good men to do bad deeds. These qualities of the devil are turned on end in the Afro-Mexican Devil Dance—evil is venerated. The dance is associated with the Day of the Dead or the Dia de los Muertos. It is said to have originated as a ritual to honour the god Rua who represents the bad. *Tenangos*, or runaway day labourers prayed to Rua to liberate them from conditions of hard labour. In the historical context, it is easy to see how Afro-Mexicans, after enduring the injustices of the Spanish slavery system, might choose to embrace the devil—the figure that symbolically represents the opposite of Spanish 'charity'. If the god of the Catholic conquistadors caused pain and suffering for the Afro-Mexicans, then it is natural that underdogs would call to the opposite power, to the devil, for sustenance (Rodríguez 2006: 46). Cultural theorist Mikhail Bahktin writes about this type of performance inversion. Festivities that allowed for public indiscretions were common during the feast days of mediaeval Europe. The carnival and festival dances of the Middle Ages liberated town citizens 'from the prevailing truth[s] and from the established order; it marked the suspension of all hierarchical rank, privileges, norms, and prohibitions' (1984b: 10). In a similar way, Afro-Mexican Devil Dances create a kind of freedom that is achieved through each dancer's impersonation of an antithetical Christian being, a being that is more powerful than the human dancer.

This strategy is even more relevant for African descendants who, under colonial systems, were often associated with barbarism or primitivism. Church clerics and Inquisition officials labelled African religions barbaric even when Africans were striving for social recognition within the burgeoning Mexican colonies. 'Racial-ethnic ideology, which originally evolved in close relation with the discourses of Christian/pagan conflict and encounter, tainted the honor of the colored descendants of "pagan" and "barbarian" bloodline, even for social climbers whose wealth and acquired culture lifted them to an otherwise honorable status' (Stern 1995: 16).

Afro-descendant Mexicans who wished to maintain religious or healing practices were subject to being labelled as witches who might be working in collaboration with the devil. Joan Cameron Bristol describes how Inquisition processes led Afro-Mexicans to renounce the Christian God in an attempt to comply with Church laws against blasphemy: 'Renunciations were probably done deliberately so that the person being beaten might get a hearing in court' (2007: 117). Some enslaved people would attempt to bypass the owner's power by appealing to inquisition authorities. By appearing in court, the servile individual would be able to bring plantation or household injustices to a different court. Beatings and emotionally charged situations could also lead servants to deny the colonial gods. In such a situation, with the offending servant under pressure, the devil could be called upon as an equally powerful entity. Bristol specifically describes the 1614 case of an 18-year-old mulatto named Diego de Cervantes who 'gave his soul to the devil in exchange for aid' (ibid.). Ideas for the Devil Dance traditions may have initiated from *cofradía* or religious groups following this trade-for-aid schema.

Traditional African religions are grounded in recognition of ancestral connections through ceremony and dance rites. Another perspective on the emergence of Devil Dances might reference the ceremonial traditions of West Africa. The Garifuna people of Central America and the Caribbean traditions of Vodún or Santería are religions based upon recognition of African Yoruba deities. Adherents honour the dead, as well as the living, through dance and drum events. Transformation of being and spiritual possession are important components of these religious ceremonies. Because the Devil Dance processions often coincide with indigenous Day of the Dead celebrations, it is tempting to draw parallels between African ancestral ancestor celebrations and the Devil Dance.

After Native American and Afro-Mexican populations were supressed in the coastal provinces of Mexico, honouring the dead may have become a substitute for honouring an Afro-Mexican god Rua. Most Afro-Mexican villages now perform Devil Dances during the Day of the Dead ceremonies, or just before the Christmas holidays. The relationship with the dead is established through a trip to the cemetery before the dance begins. In some communities, dancers choose a particular ancestor to guide them on their journey through the Devil Dance. The spirit inhabits the body of the dancer and, through her or him, communicates with the observing public.

Spatial Controls

Devil Dances, in some settings, begin after the dance group has travelled to the cemetery for a pre-dance ritual. On other occasions, they may simply initiate at the dance leader or sponsor's home. The company of dancers parade through the streets and at intervals they stop to perform a clog-like step with their pounding boots, reminding audience members of their ferocity. Dancers may suddenly lie down on the ground where they roll and growl until the lead Pancho forces them to move on. He raises his whip, and may beat them to prove his power. The use of the whip directly evokes images of ranchers collecting cattle to move them towards a ranch or a field. It also alludes to slavery: 'The gun and whip, prominent features of the apparatus of control in rounding up Africans, were used during the Atlantic voyages' (Stuckey 2002: 39). Pancho literally 'rounds up' his dancers and forces them to move through the town's public areas. Pancho's interactions with the dancers can also be humorous. The monstrous threat of his personage is easily alleviated with humour. He may trip and fall, or succumb to an audience prank. Certainly, there is fun in the way that his wife can scold the fearsome bully to bring him back in line. The interplay of the monstrous and the comedic help to quell emotions of fear: if Pancho can be managed, then adversities of daily life can also, surely, be overcome.

Spatial configurations of the Devil Dance are primarily processional. When the devils are 'brought out', the dancers, in festival style, transverse village streets in double file that moves from location to location with Pancho preceding, following or intertwining between the two lines. With the Pancho urging them on, Devil Dancers demand payment or tribute from bystanders as they roam through the streets. There is an element of the performance that is somewhat like the 'trick or treat' played during Halloween in the United States. After threatening other dancers or street observers, they repeat a chant about Rua that asks the audience to give money, drinks or treats on behalf of the god.[6] If the audience refuses, they are chased or threatened. To avoid this punishment, the crowd gives token gifts to the performers. The performances last all day and into the night. Dancers stop to drink alcohol, either on the streets or in supporters' homes. The drinks refresh the dancers and ease the pain of constantly moving and dancing. Festival dance performance is not easy. The costumes are heavy, scratchy and warm. The streets are hard and uneven, sometimes strewn with garbage or broken glass. Audiences keep a respectful distance but sometimes also taunt and throw things. The will of the dancers keeps them moving through the streets, while the Pancho with his whip, and the Minga with her antics, add variety to the long dance day. Of course, the Devil Dance is never the same. Not only are there differences in the way that the dance is performed each time based upon patronage or performance dates, but there are also noticeable variations across Afro-Mexican villages. Some leaders emphasize costumes; others, mask work; and others, the uniformity and synchronization of the dance steps. A particularly active Minga, for example, can overwhelm the artistry of the other characters.

The actual dance steps of the Devil Dance involve a clog like beating of the feet on the ground. After a heavy rhythmic first hit of the foot, there is a pause, followed by a rapid succession of four quick foot beats. Dancers hold their bodies loose and limber, raising their knees and letting their arms swing from side to side as they amble forward while keeping the rhythm. Each performer carries his weight heavily in the lower body, usually bending slightly forward from the waist. The dance is performed in parallel lines that progress and regress through the streets. On occasions, usually before or after the chant, the dancers lie down on the street and roll around ferociously. The Pancho calms their temper by cracking his whip, he then urges them to stand and continue on with the dance. When the Minga appears, there may be more heated interactions. The open sexuality of the Devil Dancers is not typical of Native American dances of the region. Neither is the intense audience interaction that occurs during the dance. Musicologist Alex Stewart describes these components of the Devil Dance as uniquely Afro-Mexican (personal interview 2007). I would contend that the posture of bent body and the looseness of the upper body also point to the African aesthetics of the dance.

The music that accompanies the Devil Dance is strident but lilting. Musical tempos counterpoint the percussion of the dancer's feet. Three instruments, the *bote* or friction drum, the harmonica and the jawbone of a cow create the sound. The friction drum holds the cadence and sets the tempo for the dancers. It consists of a wooden dowel placed within a piece of rawhide that is wrapped to cover a large gourd. Tar is placed on the stick to create friction, and the tar must be warmed with the hand before the drum will emit a sound. It creates a deep intermittent rasping sound, which, when played rhythmically, sounds like the deep call of an animal. The harmonica plays a simple melody line that replicates the rhythm of the dancer's feet. Finally, the jawbone is scraped with a wooden stick so that the teeth chatter. The collective sound of the musical accompaniment is eerie, rhythmic and guttural. Images evoked by the instruments of the dance are of death, subversion and rebellious rage.

Afro-Mexican Devil Dances encapsulate unique Mexican histories of social plays between overseers and enslaved Africans or Native Americans. The dances, when performed in public settings represent a political disruption in Mexican ideology because they negate the notion that Mexico is a country of solely Native American and Spanish *mestizaje*. Masked characters re-enacted in public performances by black male dancers restage aggression, containment, violence and sexuality as narrative themes. At the same time, the dances reclaim public spaces as sites for the re-enactment of familiar human foibles and behaviours. The masked representations are at times exotic and violent archetypes of the Afro-Mexican. However, they are also community rites that affirm the humanity of the participants who expend time and money to reconnect with a unique cultural history. When Afro-Mexicans impersonate devils, they temporarily escape into a world of corporeal expression in which they can take charge of their physical and social surroundings. Citizens use the dances to create a fantastical order and to re-enact a sense of power. Isolated from the mainstream of Mexican colonialism, African peoples have been able to reclaim traditional religions and incorporate them in communal lifestyles. The beauty of this artful subversion lies in its infinite variety.

Notes

1   In contrast, the Afro-Mexican dances of Mexico's eastern coast generally conform to the traditional codes of folkloric dance performance where the women wear dresses and the men wear variations on peasant trousers and shirts. East-coast Afro-Mexican renditions of folklore feature couple partner dances where percussive foot beats and patterns of circular movement define the form.

2   Information about the challenges of performing the steps and the music comes from interviews with the Bautista and Perez Bautista family of Oaxaca (Argelia, Octavio and Viviana) who represent three generations of Devil Dancers.

3   An Indigenous woman called first La Malinche, and later Doña Marina aided Hernando Cortes, in his conquest of Mexico. She translated for Cortes and became his mistress and concubine.

4   The records are specifically from Valladolid in Morelia, central Mexico.

5   'Bringing out' a dance is my translation of the concept of *sacar la danza*.

6   Musicologist Alex Stewart of the University on Vermont describes the chant as saying, 'Give me a tribute or I will hurt you.' Oaxaca dance teacher Argelia Bautista Torres says that there are multiple versions of the chant and the lyrics generally say, 'Somos los diablos. Vienen a bailar' (We are the devils. Come and dance). After the chant, the devils call out the god's name Rua (personal interview 2007).

From Kiva *to* Fandango *to* Casino
Demonic Admonitions for Changing Times

ENRIQUE R. LAMADRID

Ese Coludo antes iba mucho
a los bailes en todas partes,
pero una vez que encontró
los casinos, de allí no ha salido
[That Longtail used to go a lot / to the dances all around, / but once he
found the casinos / he hasn't come back out]

Charles Aguilar, Bernalillo, New Mexico, 2002

Foundational Legends of Nuevo México[1]

From the first *crónicas, relaciones* and *memoriales* of Spanish colonial times to the
Mexican and American eras, *milagros y portentos*, miracles and signs and the preter-
natural intervention of saints (as well as devils), continue to be a key component of
the dialogues of power and resistance in Nuevo México. Exemplary and cautionary
legends are transmitted through inscription and oral tradition, and memorialized
into what amounts to foundational discourse, situated at both beginning and end
times, continually emergent and current as times change. As they articulate and
amend a social and moral charter for emerging and evolving societies, foundational
legends are set in sharp relief against the chaotic forces that surround and potentially
negate them. Cultural tradition and identity are affirmed and endowed with value
and prestige by tracing the origins of the group back to a loftier, often supernatural
vision of initial events (Bakhtin 1981: 45). Thus are the foundational stories of Nuevo
México linked to miracles as well as diabolic vexations through the hagiographic narrative practices so deeply rooted in the Iberian imagination (DeMarco 2000: 163).

The identification and survey of foundational legends in the region, as inscribed
in collective memory and articulated in performance, verse and text, lead to an aston-
ishing repertory of parables of old saints in a new landscape. Miraculous narratives
explain both extraordinary and everyday events by means of divine intervention. The
dialogical is also dialectical, and the sacred easily inverts into the demonic. At
key junctures in history, as modes of economic and cultural production change and
overlap, bizarre devil tales emerge from zones of social contradiction and cultural

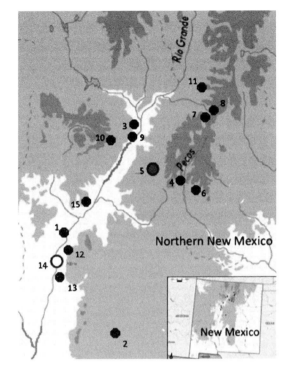

FIGURE 1. Diabolical Visitations in New Mexico, 1598–1998:

1. Bernalillo
2. Las Jumanas Pueblo
3. Ohkay Owingeh Pueblo
4. Pecos Pueblo
5. Santa Fe
6. San Isidiro Norte
7. Chamisal
8. Picurís Pueblo
9. Española
10. Los Alamos
11. Taos
12. Sandía Pueblo
13. Isleta Pueblo
14. Albuquerque
15. San Felipe Pueblo

contestation. Through the symbolic action of narrative, a moral economy is imagined and realized (Jameson 1981).

Provincias Del Demonio: *On the Edges of Empire*

The brothers of San Francisco were the first to promulgate both theological and folk demonology with the Spanish conquest and colonization. Franciscan theologians speculated that when Prince Lucifer fell from grace and was banished from Heaven, he landed in the Americas, where he established his dominions unopposed (Campagne 2004: 7). At the far northern edge of Nueva España—'El Reyno Ultimo de el Mundo y remoto sin igual' (The Last Kingdom of the World and remote beyond compare) in the words of Governor don Diego de Vargas—Nuevo México was well beyond the scrutiny of militant Christianity until the seventeenth century (Kessell 1989: 375; 1987: 92–3).

In his 1630 *Memorial* or report on Nuevo México and its missions, Fray Alonso de Benavides confirms it is '. . . a land where it seems the demon has corrupted the air with his presence, and made it uninhabitable . . .' (1630: 46; my translation). The Franciscans interpreted and condemned native religion as devil worship and did everything possible to eradicate it and destroy its temples, the underground *kivas*—

round or square-walled, underground rooms used for pueblo religious rituals, which Benavides termed '*estufas* (hot rooms) of idolatry' because of the sacred fires tended there (ibid.). The head Franciscan curate or 'Custos' of the province, Benavides attributes tremendous psychological and telluric powers to 'el Demonio' (the demon), and credits him with causing droughts and fouling the air itself to discourage the Tompiro Indians who lived at the edge of the eastern plains from obtaining the spiritual protection of his friars in the 1620s.[2] What he fails to mention is that their distress is not only drought but also Apache attacks. These pueblos were perceived as Spanish allies by plains Apaches who wanted revenge for their losses in the booming Spanish slave trade, which supplied unwilling workers to the great silver mines to the south in Nueva Vizcaya (present-day Chihuahua, Durango and Zacatecas—located in northern and central Mexico).

In the first episodes of her famous bi-locations, Sor María de Ágreda reportedly travelled in trance from her convent of Claritas Descalzas (Discalced Clares) in Soria, Spain, to the valley of the Río Grande to preach Christianity and prepare the natives of the Jumano tribe for baptism. Their homeland was centered at the confluence of the Río Grande and the Río Conchos but their trading expeditions ventured north to the Tompiro Pueblo the Spanish nick-named Las Jumanas, since they were often seen there. When Fray Benavides sent two friars to the Jumano homeland, they were greeted by crowds of people crossing themselves, carrying handmade crosses, and asking for baptism. The natives reported a mysterious lady in a blue-and-grey habit who had appeared to them in the desert, spoke to them in their own language, taught them to fashion the little crosses, and encouraged them to ask for the sacraments and a mission. In 1630, Fray Benavides travelled to Ágreda to meet with Sor María who totally convinced him of her miraculous visitations. The 1634 revision of his *Memorial* added only a few details plus the certainty of all that happened:[3]

> The demon, enemy of souls, seeing that those friars were about to free from his claws souls which he was enjoying, wanted to defend himself, and used one of his customary wiles, which was to dry up the water in the lakes they drank from, which caused the flight of the great numbers of buffalo living there, by which all these nations sustained themselves from; then, by means of Indian sorcerers, he spread the word that they should move away to seek food, and that the friars that were sent for would not come, for in the six years they had waited for them, they did not come, and this time they were so delayed that they should not wait for them, and so ordered the Captains, to strike their tents to leave the next morning; and at daybreak the woman Saint spoke to each one of them individually, and told them that they should not go; for already the friars whom they had sent for were drawing near (ibid.: 85–6).

When Father Benavides goes in person to Las Xumanas Pueblo to preach to the neophytes and dedicate the church they were building, he is challenged on the plaza by a 'sorcerer', undoubtedly an Indian elder or priest, who ridicules the Spanish devotional practice of penitential flagellation as total madness. Convinced that he is possessed by el Demonio, Benavides humiliates him publicly, causing him to sulk away in defeat, to the peals of laughter of his own people. Despite this apparent victory, the drought worsens, Apache attacks intensify and the pueblo is abandoned forever by 1672.

To the Franciscans, el Demonio was a theological adversary whose opposition gave meaning to a Manichaean struggle in which redemption only functions against a field of perdition. In their attempt to teach the Christian concept of evil to the Indians, they ascribed both human and bestial characteristics to him to make him less abstract and more easily comprehended as a real antagonist. In gratitude to the king for his support of missionary programmes, Benavides lauds the achievements of three decades of militant evangelization to give el Demonio some competition in Nuevo México, boasting that 'we snatched so many thousands of souls from the claws of the demon, a thing which would have never come about without a miracle' (ibid.: 46). Even for the theologian or missionary, the powers of evil must be personified to be understood. Benavides and his cohorts imagined el Demonio as a monstrous personage *con garras*, with his hideous claws.

El Diablo: Foundational Folk Legends

No es más que una persona
lo mismo que yo, yo y tú.
Le gusta juegar [sic.] a la baraja,
le gustan las mujeres,
le gusta umm . . .
le gusta el trago.
[He is no more than a person / the same as me, me and you. / He likes to play cards, / he likes women, / he likes umm . . . / he likes to drink.]
Ed Martínez, San Isidro Norte, New Mexico, 1987

Even though he is a fallen angel, Lucifer or Satan, the arch-Demon of Christian theology has few redeeming qualities beyond his own wit. He is the representation of pure evil and the vicious opponent of everything good, an abstraction difficult to imagine. Despite its evangelical zeal, Christianity most successfully replicates itself not through the formal teaching of doctrine and sacrament but, rather, through oral stories and parables, ritual performance and the colourful and captivating paraliturgies of folk Catholicism.

From the first days of the colony of the Españoles Mexicanos[4] or Spanish Mexicans on the upper Río Grande, another kind of anthropoid devil makes his presence known. A *pícaro* trickster with goat, bovine or reptilian characteristics, el Diablo is a folkloric devil who takes up tenure at the sites of cultural negotiation and contestation (Russell 1986; Galeano 1970; Peñalosa 1970; Harmeyer 1947). His physical characteristics are cross-culturally ambivalent or dissonant. Animal traits seen as bestial signs of evil in a Christian perspective can be signs of the sacred in many Indigenous traditions. Just as Christ is distinguished by his humanity, so this Antichrist takes human form to enhance the rivalry. He is dangerous and evil, but his very humanity makes him somehow less malign.

El Diablo makes his first documented appearance in early September of 1598 after a Náhuatl-speaking Tlaxcalan Indian named Jusepe suddenly appeared at Ohkay Owingeh Pueblo, just weeks after the arrival of don Juan de Oñate's colonizing expedition which named it San Juan (Simmons 1991: 124). Jusepe had travelled north with the illegal Leyba de Bonilla expedition in 1593. He took up with Apaches after Bonilla was killed by Antonio Gutiérrez de Humaña, one of the dangerous troublemakers of the group. After giving glowing reports of the buffalo or 'ganados de los llanos de Zíbola', Jusepe convinces Oñate to let his nephew, Vicente de Zaldívar, go with 50 men for a hunt. After passing Pecos Pueblo[5] on their way to the plains, they meet a band of Apaches, preceded by a solitary beastly figure with a fearful snout, huge ears in a red, bloodstained suit with a tail, who tries his best to terrorize them. The encounter is inscribed into the chronicle record as well as the heroic 11-syllable verses of Gaspar Pérez de Villagrá's 1610 epic poem *Verdadera Historia de la Conquista de la Nueva México*:

Por vn repecho vieron que assomaba
Vna figura humana con orejas
De casi media vara y vn hozico
Horrible por extremo y vna cola
Que casi por el suelo le arrastraba,
Bestido con un justo muy manchado
De roja sangre todo bien teñido,
Con vn arco y carax, amenazando
A toda vuestra gente con meneos,
Saltos y con amagos nunca vistos.

[Upon a slope they saw there did appear / A human figure having ears / Almost half a yard long and with a snout / Extremely horrible, and with a tail / That almost dragged upon the ground, / Dressed in a tight garment,

much stained, / And all well-stained with red blood, / With bow and quiver, threatening / All of your folk with gestures, / With leaps and threats as ne'er were seen.]
(Pérez de Villagrá 1992: XVI.189–98)

The intent of this bizarre performance was to frighten the soldiers and cause them to flee. Instead, they feigned fear and tore the Indian's mask off, laughing at the 'barbarian burlesque of that brute'. Two interpretations have been offered of this humorous episode. Since Pecos Pueblo is nearby, it is possible that this might be the first European description of a sacred Pueblo clown whose contestatory lampoons are such a central element of Puebloan rituals (Pérez de Villagrá 1989: 51). Or it may be Villagrá's own parody of the monstrous humans found in contemporary chronicles. On Oñate's desperate trek to the Sea of Cortez in 1605, chronicler Fray Francisco de Escobar mentions some Indians whose ears are so large they drag on the ground and others whose virile members are so long, they fold them up and hang them over their shoulders just so they can walk (Colahan and Rodríguez 1986). I offer a third possibility: Jusepe's prompting of the Apaches to try out the devil impersonation. His theological formation as a neophyte Christian in central Mexico would have saturated him with the demonology the Franciscans devised and translated as part of their missionary teachings (Campagne 2004). Were the Apaches using el Diablo to frighten the settlers and drive them back south? Or was the pantomime part of the satirical response of Indian shamans to contest the first wave of Christian evangelism? In either case, el Diablo is already loose upon the land, alive within the imaginations of Indians and Spanish Mexican settlers alike.

In the next four centuries, el Diablo evolves into a complex and ambivalent figure in the *mestizo* imagination and repertory of legends. He is consistently blamed for promoting idolatry and apostasy among the Indians. Among the settlers, he encourages gluttony, lust and the rest of the capital and venial sins. He is clearly associated with the new forms of production and accumulation that accompany nascent capitalism and which violate the moral economies of culture, tradition and communalism (Scott 1976). Missing from the Nuevomexicano repertory, however, is the classic story of the devil in the mine, lurking around at the site of monetary production. But then, the silver mines in New Mexico were never found until American times.

Although el Diablo is the personification of evil and the adversary of Christians, his functional role is to enforce their traditional code of values and morality, the dark shadow that stands behind and sustains their status quo. If religious obligations, promises and feast days are properly observed, and if parents and neighbours are properly respected, the *buen cristiano* or Good Christian has nothing to fear from el Diablo.

FIGURE 1. 'Angustias del Príncipe Lucifer: The Prince of Light Bemoans His Fate'. Dante Berry of the Gran Pastorela of Belén, New Mexico, 2006. All photographs in this chapter by and courtesy of Miguel Gandert.

One of his chief passions is the temptation of the individual, especially during the two most holy and portentous times of the ritual calendar, Navidad y Cuaresma (Robe 1951). As we will see, Lenten apparitions of el Diablo are unpredictable, although not entirely random. With the introduction of 'La Pastorela', the cycle of Christmas shepherds plays, early in the Franciscan missionary endeavour, they adapted some features of the Diablo as Lucifer, the 'bearer of light', part metaphysical prince, part man of the streets (Campbell 1943). As cosmic angel, he could manipulate celestial events to impress any human who would doubt him:

Mando el sol, mando la luna,
mando ese cielo estrellado.

El sol se verá eclipsado
solo porque yo lo mande.

[I rule the sun, I rule the moon, / I rule that starry sky. / The sun eclipsed will be / only on my orders.]
(Campa 1934: 76)

He does his best to distract the shepherds on their quest to find the manger in Belén and the Holy Child, and successfully tempts Ermitaño, the Hermit monk, only to be defeated and sentenced to return to Hell by his well-armed adversary the archangel San Miguel. The repertory of folk plays draw on the treasure of Spanish Golden Age allegorical plays, the Autos Sacramentales (Campbell 1943: 390), and the poetry of the most famous of Baroque poets, Luis de Góngora. His famous lament from his poem 'La brevedad de las cosas humanas' (The Brevity of Human Affairs) is on the lips of Lucifer and the actors that play him all across New Mexico and Mexico:

Aprended, flores de mí
lo que fue de ayer a hoy.
Que ayer maravilla fui
y hoy sombra de mí no soy.

FIGURE 2. 'Lucifer y el Coro Celestial: Heavenly Rehearsal'. Gran Pastorela de Belén, New Mexico, 2006.

[Flowers, learn from me / what was from yesterday to today. / Yesterday I was marvellous / and today not a shadow of myself.]⁶

The sheer artistry and rhetorical brilliance of Lucifer transmutes to the rowdy Rabelaisian discourse of el Diablo in his improvised quips with the audience. In one of the 2007 performances of *Los Pastores* by the Sangre de Cristo Liturgies group from Taos, he brings down the house in laughter with his praise of the redolent, sulphurous farts of the shepherds and tempts the public with offers of cocaine, heroine and marijuana. He teases audience members individually by name about their sins and *pecadillos*, and pisses and moans about his defeat by San Miguel. In the end, the shepherds in the role of pastoral Everymen prevail over evil. Common sense defeats eloquence, just like Jesus defies Satan in the deserts of Lent.

Lent is the most common setting of the greater part of the Diablo narratives. In a voluminous corpus of legends and memorates compiled by his students in mid-twentieth-century American times, New Mexico Highlands University professor R. D. Jameson documented numerous Diablo stories. Editor and analyst Stanley Robe summarizes the motifs accordingly:

He [el Diablo] appears in a clear pattern which supports the regional system of traditional values, by insisting on the observance of religious feast days, by pressing for the fulfillment of religious obligations, and enforcing respect for one's parents. These values are characteristic of the Hispanic Catholicism of New Mexico, a survival of the militant faith of the sixteenth and seventeenth centuries. The devil is a personification of evil, yet he supports this religious and moral system.

He inspires fear in the members of the community. He can cause fright and shock, inflict corporal injury, cause death, or carry away an evildoer to some infernal place. He covers vast distances in an instant. He is capable of assuming a variety of forms, into which he changes by magic (1980: 145).

In these episodes, el Diablo is a dangerous and formidable character with distinctive, sometimes almost sympathetic human qualities who is easily enough thwarted if first recognized and then neutralized with the sign of the cross and a sincere invocation of the *dulces nombres*, the sweet names of the Holy Family, 'Jesús, María y José', upon which he is rendered powerless.

One of the prominent motif clusters in the collection is the Faust legend, the pact between a person and el Diablo in which riches and other desires are exchanged for a human soul.⁷ Robe deploys the Finnish historical-geographic methodology for his analysis of Jameson's trove, which the English professor had already decontextualized and translated from Spanish into English. Although a distinct grammar and syntax of motifs can be identified with the Aarne–Thompson motif index, folklore studies have more recently embraced performance theory for a more profound and situated insight into folk narrative (Bauman 1977; 1986). With the linguistic tools of ethnopoetic analysis, even a single performance has much to reveal.

Set east of Pecos Pueblo (now in ruins), in the same geographical area as Jusepe's late-sixteenth-century charade, the following story by the late priest and Christian brother Ed Martínez of San Isidro Norte features a distant relative who makes the classic Faustian deal with el Diablo. The performance is heavily embroidered with the two meta-narrative strategies which most contribute to narrative authority— credible references to kin (marked with †) and a very specific topography of places in the upper Pecos valley (marked with ◊) (Briggs and Vigil 1990: 187). The narra-tor's relative, don Miguel, who makes a deal to see him, survives by pronouncing the holy names in time, although the fright gives him *empacho*, a folk malady of the diges-tive system caused by overeating or by psychological trauma. His curious cousin who accompanied him is not so lucky. He is found later, dead and covered with deep scratches.[8]

The narrative is transcribed here to reveal its ethnopoetic structure (Briggs 1988: 55–8).[9]

'El primo que vendió el alma al Diablo'
[*The Cousin Who Sold His Soul to the Devil*]
(Ed Martínez, San Isidro Norte, New Mexico, 1987)

EM: Porque mi mamá† . . .
    Yo no sé si viene siendo parentela† de mi *Dad*†
    o parentela† de mi mamá†,
    pero allí vivía en Rowe◊.
        Y el hombre era muy bien parecido,
        y muy bien vestido . . .
Y y la HISTORIA era
    que se había vendido al diablo.
Y um, platicaban que
    juega a la baraja con el diablo.
    Y él tenía un primo†
Se me hace que todavía está Don Miguel vivo,
se me hace que se llama Miguel,
    que era muy TRAVIESO.
Ese sí.
    Es que le dijo una vez, es que le dijo,

    —¿Oyes si es verdad que fueras con el diablo?

Dijo,   —Sí.

Y le dijo.

    —¿Qué tenía que hacer para ver uno?

Y es que le dijo su primo†,

Eran primos hermanos†,

    Es que le dijo, pues,

        —El que quiera ver.

Que le dijo,

        —¿Cómo que quiera el que quiera ver?

Y le dice,

        —Pues, ¿quiere ver el chiquito o el grande?

Le dice,

        —. . . vale más que mandes el grandolón.

Se le dijo,

        —Bueno, tiene que esperar allí en la,

        en su ranchito. Y luego como a las doce,

        vienes y te introduces.

Y le dice,

        —pos qué HAGO que me vaya a ver al diablo?

        —No, no,

dice él, pos,

        —luego no es más que una persona lo mismo que

        yo, yo y tú.

        Le gusta juegar a la baraja, le gustan las mujeres,

        le gusta umm . . . le gusta el trago.

Y le dice uh un hombre

        —¿qué es de eso?

He went and sat there y está de medio 'frun frun'.

So, abrió la puerta.Tocó la puerta,

        —Que entra.

Y dice él que no más vido,

        —Bueno.

It's probably a gross exaggeration 'cause you know how,

how small the doors are in in in those houses◊ those old houses, pero.

        Es que estaba este amigo grandolón,

        tapado todo lo que era el marco de la puerta.

Y dice,

    —Yo le vide la cara.Muy bien parecido el señor y ya.

    Era moreno con bigotito y muy bien vestido.

    Y le vide a los pies, y dos pezuñas.

Y no más,

    —A alabar los dulces nombres, dije,

    y ¡DIOS ME LIBRE! y un TRAQUIDO

    (*slaps hands*)

    Y olía a puro, puro, sss, azufre.

    Y se desapareció el hombre de la puerta.

Y luego de allí se empachó, de empacho *so* tuvo que ir a

    decirle a

yo creo que a su tía† que,

    —¡¡POR QUÉ TE EMPACHATES!?

You know, the tía† *wanted to know, she was, was, they always wanted*

    to know,

You know, I mean there's no prevention in those old ladies . . .

    —¿Por qué te espantaste?

So allí tuvo que decirle él pa' que diera la sobada del empacho.

Pero la, la risa que se reía en el es que es muy *brave.*

Es que le dice, pues,

    —Si bajas traeme trae el grandolón.

    Cuando vi al grandolón no más las pezuñas le

        vide y, *POOF.*

Y luego después cuando lo hallaron al uh . . .

Yo no sé qué era, primo†, Mi *Mom*† le dice primo†, yo creo o le

    dirá primo†.

Pero lo hallaron muerto. Y, y bien cortado,

parece que lo habían cortado con cuchillos.

Y dizque que el CABALLO lo había corrido

entre, por el cerco de puyas.

EL: Um hm.

EM: *You know, barbed wire fence.*

    Es que lo había arrastrado.

Pero, *you know, that was one theory.* Pero los RASGUÑOS

wouldn't have been that, that . . . Probably maybe they would have been,

who knows, you know, 'cause that barbed wire.

    Y luego la noche que lo VELARON.

Los santos se caiban de las paredes.

No pudieron poner un crucifijo en el cajón.

El padre que venía a bendecir a decirle misa se le quebró
el carro.

Y no pudo venir, y lo enterraron.

He is one of the few people that platican que

un tiro de seis caballos no pudía jalar el cajón pa'l, pa'l campo
santo,

pa' la tierra bendita. *So,* llegaron con el tiro bien cansado . . .

We're talking about less than a quarter mile from the church◊.

Si vas alguna vez te enseñaba.

They just took that sucker down and uh . . .

Lo enterraron ah ah, en tierra sin bendecir.

[EM: Because my mom† . . . / Im not sure if he is a relative† of my dad† / or a relative† of my mom†, but there he lived in Rowe◊. / And the man was very good-looking, / and very well dressed . . . / and the STORY was / that he had sold himself to the devil. / And um, they say that / he plays cards with the devil. / And he had a cousin† / It seems to me that Don Miguel is still alive, / it seems to me he is named Miguel, / who was very PLAYFUL / That one for sure. / He said to him once, he told him, / —Hey is it true that you go out with the devil? / He said, —Yes. / And he told him. / — How did one go about seeing one? / And his cousin told him†, / They were first cousins†, / He told him, well, / —Whoever wants to see. / He told him, / —What do you mean whoever wants to see? / And he tells him, / —Well do you want to see the little one or the big one? / He tells him, / — . . . better that you send the big guy. / He told him, / —Well you have to wait there in, / in your ranch. And then about 12, / you come and introduce yourself. / And he tells him, / —well what do I DO so the devil will see me? / —No, no, / he says, well / —you know he is no more than a person the same as me, me and you. / He likes to play cards, he likes women, / he likes umm . . . he likes to drink. / And a man tells him / —what of it? / *He went and sat there* y and was a bit 'frun frun' / So, he opened the door. Knocked at the door. / —Come in. / And he says that then he saw, / — Well. / *It's probably a gross exaggeration 'cause you know how,* / how small the doors are in in in those houses◊ those old houses, but / This great big guy was there, / blocking that which was the doorframe. / And he says, / —I saw his face. Very good-looking the guy, that's it. / He was dark with a little moustache and very well dressed. / And I saw his feet, and two hooves. /

And then only / —Praise be to the sweet names, I said, / and GOD FREE ME! and a SNAP (*slaps hands*). / And it smelt like pure, / pure, sss, sulphur. / And the man disappeared from the doorway. / And after that he got sick with *empacho*, from empacho, so he had to tell / I think it was his aunt that, / —WHY DID YOU GET EMPACHO!? / *You know, the tía† wanted to know, she was, was, they always wanted to know, / You know, I mean there's no prevention in those old ladies* ... / Why did you take such a fright? / So there he had to tell her to give him the massage for empacho. / But the, the laughter laughed in the it is that he is very brave. / That's what he told him, well, / —If you come down, bring me the big one. / When I saw the big one I just saw the hooves and, POOF. / And then when they found him the ... / I don't know what it was, cousin†, My mom† calls him cousin†, I think or she will call him cousin†. / But they found him dead. And, and all cut up, / it looks like they had cut him with knives. / And it is said that his HORSE had dragged him / between, along the barbed-wire fence. / EL: Um hm. / EM: *You know, barbed-wire fence.* / It is that it had dragged him. / But, *you know, that was one theory.* But the SCRATCHES / *wouldn't have been that, that ... Probably maybe they would have been, / who knows, you know, 'cause that barbed wire.* / And then the night of the WAKE. / The saints were falling down from the walls. / They couldn't put a crucifix on the coffin. / The priest that was coming to bless to say Mass his car broke / And he couldn't come, and they buried him. / *He is one of the few people that* they say / that a team of six horses couldn't haul the coffin to, to the cemetery, / to the blessed ground. *So,* they arrived with the team exhausted ... / *We're talking about less than a quarter mile from the church◊.* / If you go there some time I'll show you. / *They just took that sucker down and uh* ... / They buried him ah ah, in unblessed earth.]

In the two-minute performance excerpted here, kinship references (†) proliferate, almost half to parents and grandparents and the rest to cousins, first cousins, and aunts and uncles. Anyone familiar with the upper Pecos valley east of Santa Fe will quickly recognize places, roads, churches and houses where the action takes place (◊). Where belief is in serious doubt, as in these paranormal events, it is persuasively negotiated between the speaker and the interlocutor (Briggs 1988: 277–84).

In life, the main advantage that the good-looking, well-dressed man derived from his pact was his luck and skill at gambling and the pleasure of consorting with el Diablo over an occasional game of cards. Gambling is perceived as a demonic pursuit that devalues the common good and subverts the moral economy, a late-twentieth-century topic to which we will soon return (Scott 1976).

Inexplicably, el Diablo punishes his young cousin, scratches him with his claws and snatches away his life and soul, apparently in punishment for inviting Miguel who recited the Holy Names and made him disappear. An example to all who would listen, the cursed young man is denied a Christian burial, not by his fellow villagers but because his coffin will not be brought to holy ground or allow itself to be blessed by a crucifix. The miracle with its lesson here is the deliverance of Don Miguel by remembering the proper blessing at the proper time, even though his curiosity almost got the most of him. Being the namesake of the Archangel San Miguel had also worked to his advantage.

Diablos Bailando: Devils at the Fandango

Although he appears in a number of circumstances to stalk or make pacts with his victims, el Diablo's favourite venue in the landmark Jameson collection is the dance hall, and almost half (38 of 97) of the narratives either take place there or make reference to dancing (Robe 1980: 146–90).

> [H]is favorite form in the legend is that of a handsome, well-dressed young man, especially when he escorts an errant young lady to a forbidden dance. Some physical feature betrays him to those who are present, a long tail, feet like those of a chicken, or horns protruding from his forehead. Once his presence is known, he vanishes amid a cloud of sulfurous smoke (ibid.: 145)

Although the stories in this collection have lost their original texture to English translation, another suggestive cluster of Aarne–Thompson motif types emerges (Aarne and Thompson 1973).[10] But the question remains: Why the fascination with dancing? There is something disturbingly dynamic, irrepressible and unpredictable in social dance. In the familiar words of witnesses of demonic apparitions at dances, 'anything can happen at a dance', that ludic and liminal space where society luridly scrutinizes itself in motion (Wallrich 1950a; 1950b; Ostriker 1987; Herrera-Sobek 1988). The unfolding spirals of stylized movement and gesture, writhing knots of bodies intertwined, symbolic social interactions, barely sublimated sexuality are all unified by the rhythm of the human heartbeat, codified in the music that both animates and governs the chaos.

From the earliest accounts of Anglo-American travellers and traders dating from the 1820s, the passion of the Nuevomexicanos for dance was nothing short of an obsession. Dancing was the major pastime and diversion (Gregg 1954: 170). Even in the smallest villages, generations would gather for the weekly social display. Entire families were in attendance; babies were bundled and stashed in every corner. New and old alliances were enacted in the salón or dance hall, the secular centre space of towns and villages. Enmities were taken outside.

In a game called the *baile* or *valse chiquiado* (spoilers dance or waltz), the dance was suddenly called to a halt by the *bastonero*, literally the 'canesman', the master of ceremonies and bouncer combination named for his cane or symbol of authority (Cobos 1956). A randomly, or not so randomly, selected couple would be chosen to face off in verse, in front of the undivided attention of the group. One partner, often the woman, was seated in a chair in the middle of the dance floor. Her partner would then recite or sometimes even compose a *versito* on the spot to coax her out of the chair so the dancing could resume. Some verses just indicated a desire to dance. Others expressed admiration or budding affection for the partner. This poetic coaxing was indicated with the verb *chiquear*, which means to cajole or spoil. Flattery could be returned with flattery or comic disdain, sometimes bordering on the scatological, as in the following implied or actual fart.[11]

Te dije que te quería
te lo dije así no más,
el amor que te tenía
se me salió por atrás.

[I told you that I loved you / I told you just that way, / the love that I had for you / left me from behind.]

(Lamadrid 1984: 18)

Other verses let everyone know that whatever might have existed between the couple was over. This cruel farewell was laced with alcohol, the greatest social anesthetic and enabler of all:

Te dije que te quería
lo hice por entretenerte,
el amor que te tenía
me lo bebí en aguardiente.

[I told you that I loved you / I did it to entertain you, / the love that I had for you / I drank it up in liquor.]

(ibid.)

With such open declarations of affinity or scorn, gossip and speculation about the private lives of the community were put to rest. On occasion, even marriage plans would be announced on the dance floor to the entire community to synchronize rumour and truth:

Qué bonita te vas creciendo
como una espiga de trigo,
ya me estoy apreviniendo
para casarme contigo.

[How beautifully you grow / like a sprig of wheat, / I'm getting ready / to get married to you.]
(Cobos 1956: 99)

Those dancers who could not compose one on the spot in the heat of the moment needed a repertory of at least half a dozen just to manoeuvre through all the social situations leading to adulthood, marriage and maturity.

With a fascination with dance that borders on collective cultural obsession, excess is an inevitable outcome. The same early Anglo-American observers who enjoyed the frequent *fandangos* of Santa Fe were amazed and scandalized at seeing the same all-night revellers of the dance halls bright and early at Mass the next day (Horgan 1975: 122; Gregg 1954: 51). Their Puritan sensibilities ultimately over-whelmed their fascination for the regional pastime. For Nuevomexicano elders, dance has also served as a marker of cultural and economic change. In what Charles Briggs defines as a distinctive oral pedagogical genre of 'historical discourse', speakers con-struct a dialogical critique of the present (*ahora*) by contrasting it with the world of the past (*antes*) (1988: 82–3). José Limón notices an analogous discourse in Texas, where elders also develop in their talk and choreography 'a moral economy based on a number of moral principles and an etiquette, both of which were in evident display at the dances they remember. For all its hardship era *bonita la vida* (life was lovely), and the dance is always used as a signifier of this illustration' (1994: 181).

In the following narrative from the village of Chamisal, New Mexico Evangelina Abeyta uses two metaphorical indexes for changing times—the state of agriculture and the community dance. Shared with the nearby Pueblo of Picurís, the 10 August fiesta of San Lorenzo features feasting as well as ritual and social dancing. She recalls the exuberant agriculture of the past, when people virtuously reaped what they sowed and lived from the fruit of their labour. They threshed with the wind and took wheat to the mill to make flour for tortillas. Nowadays, the fields lie fallow and not even flowers bloom as they used to. And the nobility of the dance has also declined into violence and drug abuse.

'*Memorias de las fiestas y los bailes de San Lorenzo*'
[*Memories of Fiestas and Dances of San Lorenzo*]
(Evangelina Abeyta, Chamisal, New Mexico,1984)
EA: OH SÍ,
más antes bailábanos con unas VELITAS
no más hacían unas VELAS asina o FAROLES.
Con eso bailábanos y VIOLÍN y GUITARRA y
y todo es muy SERIO y

ahora, pos,

    muchas LUCES, mucha BORRACHERA,

    muchos de todos DROGAS, de toda clase de DROGAS y

    PELEÁNDOSE y todo eso

    ya cuasi no puede uno GUSTAR muchas veces

    a gusto porque siempre hay PELEAS pa' allí y pa' acá.

Que eso que yo miro.

[EA: OH YES, / before they danced with little CANDLES / they just made some CANDLES that way or LANTERNS. / With that we danced, and VIOLIN AND GUITARRA and / everything is very SERIOUS and / well, now, / many LIGHTS, much drunkenness, / a lot of all the DRUGS, of every kind of DRUGS and / FIGHTING among themselves and all that / it is almost like you can't ENJOY many times / with pleasure because there are always FIGHTS here and there. / That is what I see.]

All has changed in Abeyta's lifetime, the agrarian economy—the community celebrations and the customs and manners of the people. Dances of the past were lit by candlelight and the traditional music of guitars and violins was the norm, along with the dignity and respect of the dancers. Nowadays, there are blaring lights, alcohol, drugs and conflict. The erosion of the moral economy as recalled in this manner leads to the oral genre of what can be termed 'apocalyptic discourse', where the discrepancies between *antes y ahora* make it obvious to the teller that humanity is approaching *la finación* or the end times, with all of the initial signs and portents (Briggs 1988: 94). Satan is, of course, a major player in the Christian drama of the apocalypse. There is no devil in Mrs Abeyta's story but the scene is set for his impending appearance. As Limón reiterates: 'As more drugs, alcohol, opportunistic sexuality, and violence begin to mark the dance scene as a site of cultural contradiction, the devil also enters the dance to mark this contradiction' (1994: 180).

The timely appearance of a well-dressed, good-looking Diablo who sweeps the young souls off their feet as they follow him across the dance floor comes as some shock but little surprise to the Nuevomexicano. Literally hundreds of sightings have happened over the years. The 'Diablo en el baile' story is so universal that writers such as Fray Angélico Chávez have projected it backwards in time with no problem. His story 'The Ardent Commandant' features the thwarted appearance of a fiery young officer at a dance of the Santa Fe Presidio in the eighteenth century (Chávez 1987). Little does it matter that there is no documentary mention of such apparitions before the twentieth century. They seem to be such a paranormal part of the culture as to seem perfectly naturalized to any particular time period.

The last documented appearance of el Diablo at a dance in northern New Mexico was at Red's Steak House on Riverside Drive in Española on a Lenten Friday night in 1984.[12]

With plenty of employment available up the hill in menial and lower-level positions at the National Laboratory in Los Alamos, times were fairly good for Río Arriba County, one of the poorest counties in one of the poorest states in the US. Work as a security guard, a typist or hazardous-waste fire-fighter at the Labs could provide enough money for payments on a mobile home but left precious little time to build the adobe houses that everyone really wanted. The deep nuclear shadow upon northern New Mexico had eroded the metaphors of apocalyptic talk into a stark and menacing discourse of reality.

In those days, the ominous effects of international politics were deeply felt in Río Arriba County. Since most jobs were connected to the nuclear industry, the anti-nuke movement sweeping the country had less resonance. But everyone was worried about the nuclear-waste container trucks travelling down Main Street to the new dumpsite in Carlsbad. Democratic governor Toney Anaya voiced his opposition to President Ronald Reagan's obsessive wars in Central America, refused to send the state National Guard to provocative war games in Honduras and declared New Mexico to be a sanctuary state for Central American refugees. An annual peace pilgrimage began at the shrine of Chimayó, where sacred earth was gathered and carried 32 kilometres by runners to be deposited at the foot of a tree at Fuller Lodge, the oldest building in Los Alamos (Fox 1994: 35–6). Runners (myself included) were blessed by the archbishop of Santa Fe at one end of the journey and photographed by the FBI on the other. To the Reagan administration, the sanctuary movement and religious groups opposing his Contra wars were declared public domestic enemy number one, and preparations were made for the conspiracy show trials that would follow over the next few years.[13]

Back at Red's, a *ranchera* band was playing to a full and lively house. The hometown crowd noticed a well-dressed stranger who began to ask all the single women, even some with dates, to dance. Well towards closing time, the singles had begun pairing off and the band started playing slow ones. The stranger had paired off with his favourite partner as well, who put her head on his shoulder. Exhausted from a night of polkas and country, she relaxed and then noticed a long lump in his pants where a lump shouldn't be for a man, *la cola*, although the tail was hidden. Startled, she looked down and saw *las pezuñas*, split hooves, somewhere between those of a goat and a cow. Realizing what the score was at that instant, she screamed for her life and her soul—the lights went out and complete confusion reigned for a good five minutes. When the breakers were reset and the lights came on, the stranger was gone, but everyone noticed a strong burning smell. People left in a hurry, leaving half-full beer bottles on the tables. By Monday, talk of the events of Friday night was on the lips of everyone in Española. No one had heard of anything like this in a long time. Did it really happen? If it was true, what could it possibly mean? The article in the weekly newspaper, the *Río Grande Sun*, made light of the incident but most people paid it more mind than they would admit. Something was definitely amiss (O'Brien 2007).

In his fiendish analysis of the rash of devil sightings in the working-class dance halls of south Texas in the same decade, Limón listens to the ambivalent testimonials of women and fully contextualizes the events, linking them to the tough economic times and the cultural penetration of the postmodern:

> But in southern Texas at the edge of late capitalism, the well-dressed, good-looking, sometimes blond figure dances in multiple signification in the dance halls spawned by the collision of tradition and post-modernity. In this respect he is less a folk figure [. . .] yet again, like the dancing, a modernist figure indebted to the past but open and available, a flexible and critical tool for reading and critically evaluating a threatening present (1994: 180).

In the villages of northern New Mexico in the 1920s, the appearance of el Diablo at dances also marked the initial penetration of the modern—and its handmaiden: cash economy. Elders like Abeyta can remember a world that centred on agriculture and pastoralism. Communal values and traditional notions of piety, filial respect and the pre-eminence of family were the norm. The unity and values of the past have been forever changed. The concepts of *respeto* (respect) and *unidad* (unity) have been supplanted by an individualist culture based on the alienated and competitive values of late capitalist society. The psychologist philosopher Norman O. Brown links the advent of cultural and personal devils with the development of the economic system of capitalism:

> Through the archetype of the Devil mankind has said something about the psychological forces, inside man himself, sustaining the economic activity that ultimately flowered into capitalism. The Devil is the lineal descendant of the Trickster and Culture-hero type in primitive mythologies. The

Trickster is a projection of the psychological forces sustaining the economic activity of primitive peoples; and the evolution of the Trickster, through such intermediary figures as the classical Hermes, into the Christian devil, paralleled the changing forms of human economic (especially commercial) activity (1959: 220).

Such tricksters are especially rampant in the landscape of New Mexico, whose economy sprang from the pre-industrial directly to the post-industrial in the space of one generation. A new cash economy with jobs in the nuclear industry just 'up the hill' in Los Alamos created leisure time and disposable income enough to meet the Diablo on his own terms, dancing.

Diablos y Diablas: *Engendering and Confronting Evil*

Since Lucifer is an angel, just like San Miguel, and since angels are by definition gender neutral, productions of the Pastorela occasionally feature female actors to play the parts.[14] In the script, gendered adjectives adjust to reflect the female devil:

Que fui ángel no lo niego
que de Dios fui muy querido / (querida),
hoy por mi vana altivez
soy del reino desposeído / (desposeída).

[I do not deny I was an angel / much beloved of God, / today for my vain pride / I am dispossessed of the kingdom.][15]

In the scenes of the play, there are numerous occasions for dramatic irony and erotic overtone when humanity's fate is the hands of a female Lucifer. In the tales of demonic apparitions, one of which follows later in this essay, the spirit of evil is often gender neutral when it is called 'La Cosa Mala' or the bad thing, the noun of which is female-gendered.

Most narrators reflexively assign masculine gender to demonic tales, associating bullish and goat-like animal traits, strength, cunning and sexual predation to males. Male Diablos sweep vulnerable women off their feet on the dance floor in 30 of 34 or 88 per cent of the Jameson Devil at the Dance tales. Female Diablas appear in only 4 tales, of which #232 is typical:

It was a very beautiful girl who could dance magnificently. Men would go wild over her. One night when the dance was over, a boy wanted to escort her home. When they were a little ways from the house, she started to kick him and scratch him. The boy claimed that she had nails like a rooster and feet like a mule and that she wasn't pretty any more. The conclusion was that she was the devil (Robe 1980: 195–6).

Devils in disguise are betrayed by hooves, long nails or stubs of horns hidden in curly hair. But the tell-tale serpentine bulge in the pants is inevitably along the small of the back, storytellers insist with a wink.

Some of the most compelling and powerful female-gendered diabolical narratives belong to the cycle of Llorona or weeping women tales. In a few variants of the most prevalent motif cluster featuring infanticide by drowning, the grieving mother commits the crime when she is possessed by a demon or is a Diabla, a female incarnation of the devil. A secondary motif cluster serves as both admonition against and retribution for male sexual predation, which is dealt out as an *espanto*, a severe fright.[16] In summary, one or more usually young males who are out drinking notice and follow an attractive woman to an isolated place, often by the water. As hands are laid upon her, she turns a demonic gaze upon her attacker(s), with a terrifying skeletal or bestial face. In the folk imagination, *espanto* can cause the soul to leave the body if the trauma is great. Unbridled male sexuality has demonic qualities and is contested with serious demonic consequences (Robe 1980: 457–65).

El Diablo en el Casino: *Cultural Economies of Indian Gaming*

So the last shall be first, and the first last.

Matthew 20:16

Symbolic inversion is the trope of the sacred clowns in Pueblo Indian public rituals. They have free rein and free licence on the plaza. They may speak backwards, walk backwards or satirize anything in sight, sacred or profane, priest or president. Subversion is their creed, slapstick is their devotion and verbal play their trademark. They respond to many names in the world of the pueblos and their Hispano neighbours: *koshare, chufunetes, abuelos*. They are transgressors and healers. They cross boundaries and borders. In colonial times through burlesque of priests and masses, they and their people survived Christian evangelization with their own beliefs intact (Babcock 1978; Hieb 1975).

What has happened in New Mexico since the 1990s and the passage of the Indian Gaming Act is more understandable, perhaps, through their eyes. Who would have thought that the research of historian Alvin Josephy on the American Indians' fight for freedom and sovereignty would lead in court deliberations to the largest peaceful transfer of wealth in American history? (Josephy, Nagel and Johnson 1999: 168–71). No one could have predicted that Sandía Pueblo, the smallest and poorest of all the Río Grande pueblos would become the wealthiest in a few short years. Economic, social and cultural impacts are huge nationally and locally, and always several steps ahead of the research to quantify or qualify them.

Within months of the conversion of Indian bingo halls into full-fledged casinos, the devil stories began. Previously seen only now and then at dances during Lent, this folkloric but dangerous figure has begun his rounds of the casinos. He typically comes in the guise of a good-looking young man who shows up to tempt or taunt righteous people into a lapse of judgment or worse. Not as metaphysical or awesome as Lucifer, his older brother, this Diablo loves to patrol moral and cultural boundaries. He is attracted to the *baile* because people negotiate their personal affairs and intimate relations as they spin and wiggle on the dance floor. In the intercultural space of the Indian casino, they also stake their fortunes as well as futures.

The accounts of demonic sightings begin in approximately 1996 at Ohkay Owingeh, former San Juan Pueblo, host of the first Spanish colonial settlement in 1598. The following transcript is based on breath groups, since back-channel cueing was entirely non-verbal:

'*La Cosa Mala llega a San Juan*'
[*The Bad Thing Arrives in San Juan*]
(Alfredo García, Española, New Mexico, 1996)
AG: En el casino de San Juan
se dejó ver el diablo.
Fue una noche de entre semana
cuando no había mucha gente allí.
Una señora fue con sus comadres
para jugar con las máquinas bandidas
Ella se apartó de las otras
y quedó en un rincón medio oscuro
porque pensaba que la máquina
que jugaba iba a pegar.
Estaba tan ocupada que casi no sintió
una mano en su hombro.
Dio la vuelta y vio un hombre joven
y muy bien parecido y muy bien vestido.
No dijo nada, solo la miraba sonriendo.
La señora tampoco dijo nada
pero de repente bajó la vista
y vio que el hombre tenía pezuñas.
Pegó un grito tan fuerte
que sus comadres pensaron
que había sacado el jackpot y se arrimaron.

Siguió gritando y llega el security guard.
El diablo salió por la puerta de emergencia
al estacionamiento y el guardia lo siguió,
pero desapareció y no hallaron más
que un fuerte olor a azufre.
Ese fin de semana el casino
estaba cerrado porque tuvieron que traer
al padre para hacer una bendición al edificio.
[AG: In San Juan casino / the devil allowed himself to be seen. / It was a week night / when there weren't many people there. / A lady went with her friends / to play with the one-arm bandits. / She separated from the others / and stayed in a dark corner / becaue she thought the machine / she was playing was going to hit. / She was so preoccupied she hardly felt / a hand on her shoulder. / She turned around and saw a young man / very good-looking and well dressed. / He said nothing, and watched her, smiling. / The lady didn't say anything either / but suddenly looked down / and saw that the man had hooves. / She screamed so loud / that her friends thought / she had hit the jackpot and went over to her. / She kept on yelling and the security guard arrives. / The devil left through the emergency exit / to the parking lot and the guard followed, / but he disappeared and they didn't find anything / but a strong odor of sulphur. / That weekend the casino / was closed because they had to bring / the priest to bless the building.]

Next was Isleta Pueblo, where some of the first sightings of Mary de Ágreda, the Lady in Blue, were reported in 1629. The people of Isleta allied themselves with the Spanish Mexicans in the 1680 Pueblo Revolt and fled south with them into exile to El Paso del Norte. More devil stories have been collected from Isleta than from any other casino, a proliferation yet to be explained. In the familiar guise of a well-dressed young man, el Diablo frequents the slot-machine areas, where more patrons of colour congregate than around the more sophisticated table games. His mysteriously blurry and luminescent image has been captured on surveillance cameras inside the gaming hall as well as in the parking lot. Sightings have been reported in local newspapers (Fletcher 1996), as well as in pulp-style mystery books (Brunvand 1999: 248–50; O'Brien 2007: 139).

In 1998, with a $20 research budget (in quarters), spent over two evenings, several graduate students and I collected six short anecdotes[17] and one extensive, sustained narrative.[18] A well-articulated repertory of rhetorical layering, back-channel cueing, quotatives, kinship authorizations and references to common places was deployed to frame the longer story. Its transcript shares techniques and structures seen in 'El primo que vendió el alma al Diablo' analysed above. In summary, it is the pathetic tale of a middle-aged woman, complete with a name, who gets carried away on a Good Friday casino visit and spends her entire retirement cheque on the slots. As she attempts to leave, a mysterious English-speaking young man appears and offers her three quarters, which he advises her to play all at once in adjacent machines. She does as he commands and hits a $1,000 jackpot. After she cashes out, she rushes to the parking lot to offer him a tip and sees him crouch to enter his fancy white car. There is a lump in his pants she recognizes as a tail. She screams, faints and is taken into long-term intensive care at St Joseph's Hospital in Alburquerque. She remains there today, wasting away, in a foetal position with three distinct red spots on her withered hand from the three cursed coins:

> 'El Diablo en el Casino del Pueblo de Isleta'
> [The Devil at Isleta Pueblo Casino]
> (Theresa Sandoval, Alburquerque, New Mexico, 24 April 1998)
>
> TS: Al otro día la comadre Helen fue a visitar
> a la comadre Eloisa, pero esta estaba
> en coma, no abría los ojos, no se movía,
> no hacía nada. Y ahora mismo si vas
> al hospital ella está ahí, con las máquinas
> puestas y con la mano cerrada. Cuando
> supe de esta historia, se lo dije a mi mama
> y ella me dijo que eso es cierto, ya que
> eso fue en Semana Santa, y Nuevo México,
> aunque es un Pueblo muy católico,
> había que enviarles un castigo y lo hizo.
> Y nunca se supo del señor, del Diablo.
> Pero yo recuerdo, que yo vi en la tele
> que cerraron el casino por dos días
> y mandaron a los medicine men a rezar,
> y el casino estuvo cerrado por dos días . . .
> Y la comadre Helen llora todos los días . . .
> Y en la Semana Santa parece
> que el Diablo está en muchos lugares.
>
> [TS: And the next day co-mother Helen visited / her co-mother Eloisa, but she was in a coma, / she didn't open her eyes or move, / she didn't do anything. And now if you go / to the hospital, she's there with the machines on

/ and with her hand closed. When I found out / about this story, I told it to my mother / and she told me it must be true, since / it happened in NM, and during Holy Week, / even though it is a very Catholic Pueblo, / a punishment must be sent to them and it happened. / Nothing more was learnt about the man, the Devil. / But I remember that I saw on television / that they closed the casino for two days and / sent in the medicine men to pray, / and the casino was closed for two days . . . / And co-mother Helen cries every day. . . / And for Holy Week it seems / that the Devil is in many places.]

By the turn of the millennium, similar tales emerged in virtually every tribal gaming establishment in New Mexico according to story and rumour,[19] a sobering thought for promoters, boosters and the Chamber of Commerce. The first devil stories emerged in Nuevo México by the autumn of 1598 with the coming of Christianity. By the autumn of 1998, four centuries and many miracles and anti-miracles later, the descendants of the same Spanish Mexican settlers negotiate their fortunes and cultural survival in the simultaneously real and metaphorical setting of the Indian casino, where the distinction between chance and destiny is mediated by a fallen angel, el Diablo himself. Dangerous and cunning, he is still easily defeated with the recitation of the Holy Names and the prudent avoidance of casinos, especially during Lent and other holy times. Gamblers who disregard these admonitions and fall into trouble have found help from San Cayetano, the patron saint of gamblers who responds not to promises but to bets (Steele 1994).[20]

From *kiva* to *fandango* to casino, the dramatic shifts of venue for Diablo tales in New Mexico mark transitions between cultural eras or, in Marxist terms, 'modes of production'. In his discussion of Diablo tales from economically depressed south Texas in the era just prior to tribal casinos, Limón quotes Frederic Jameson's appraisal of narrative as symbolic action:

A narrative read at this wider horizon may express, though in a deeply disguised and quite indirect way, the conflict between wholly different cultural periods or modes of production; a narrative may evidence 'that moment in which the coexistence of various modes of production becomes visibly antagonistic, their contradictions moving the very center of political, social and historic life' (Jameson 1981: 84, quoted in Limón 1994: 181).

Demonic narratives are never static; they are continuously emergent, containing overtly moralizing Christian transcripts, as well as hidden transcripts of cultural resistance in constant dialogue with the master hegemonic narratives of our own troubled times. The metaphor of gambling was often used in reference to Wall Street, the 'satanic mills' where America's moral economy was ground to dust. Our national 'casino' is the stock market, where corporate greed and losing bets on the housing market caused the great financial meltdown of 2008–09.[21]

Just north of metropolitan Alburquerque, the town of Bernalillo lies on the campsite where Francisco Vásquez de Coronado and his expedition spent the winter of 1540–41. In close proximity to Sandía, Santa Ana and San Felipe Pueblos, the three casinos are a major employer for Bernalillo. Robert Aguilar has been working at Sandía casino since it was a bingo parlour and he was a teenager selling pull-tabs. After one of the last sightings of 'el Coludo', or the Long-tailed One, at San Felipe casino back in 2002, he excitedly called his parents Charles and Barbara after getting off work. They drove up together to investigate and see what they could see. El Coludo had been spotted prowling the dumpsters where the gourmet restaurant garbage is thrown out. They drove round and round the parking lot and the truck stop and the dumpster area with no luck. *Nada.* 'We took our time looking around the parking lot but never saw anybody.'[22] Disappointed, they drove back home. Years later, they still talk about it with intense fascination . . .

Notes

This essay is the last in series on foundational *milagro* narratives in Nuevo México from 1598 to 2002 (Lamadrid 2007). Fieldwork for this survey was supported with a research grant from the Recovering the U.S. Hispanic Literary Heritage Project, based at the University of Houston.

1 Nuevo México is the Spanish colonial place name which refers to an area much larger than the modern state of New Mexico which is referenced in this essay in English.

2 Tompiro was a language closely related to Piro, two languages spoken in colonial times in central New Mexico. Now extinct, linguists believe they belonged to the Tanoan family.

3 Published in Madrid in 1630, Fray Alonso's *Memorial* was written for Fray Juan de Santander, Commissary General of the Franciscan Order of the Indies to be presented to King Felipe IV. The 1634 revision was written for Pope Urban VIII and never printed.

4 By 1696 and the foundation of New Mexico's second *villa* at Santa Cruz de la Cañada, settlers were referring to themselves as Españoles Mexicanos, Spanish Mexicans (Kessell 1998: 603).

5 Two Puebloan language families are present in modern New Mexico—Keresan and Tanoan. *Keres* is spoken in the Río Grande Pueblos of Kewa (formerly Santo Domingo), Cochití, San Felipe, and Santa Ana, plus Laguna and Ácoma to the west. Three Tanoan languages are spoken at Río Grande Pueblos—*Tiwa* at Taos, Picurís, Sandía and Isleta; *Tewa* at Ohkay Owingeh (formerly San Juan), Santa Clara, San

Ildefonso, Nambé, Pojoaque and Tesuque; and *Towa* at Jémez. Zuni is an isolate Puebloan language spoken at one pueblo in western New Mexico. The Athabascan family in New Mexico is represented by the Ndé or Apache and Diné or Navajo.

6 Arsenio and Theresa Córdova, performance of *Los Pastores* (Santuario de Guadalupe, Santa Fe, New Mexico, 6 January 2007).

7 Motif types are the analytic tool of the historic-geographical method of folkloristics, introduced by Finnish folklorists (Aarne and Thompson 1973). Two main areas of focus were origins and transmission of legend motifs. These are some of the key motifs in the order in which they appear in the Faust legend cluster:

> G303.6.1.2 Devil comes when called upon.
> G303.3.1 The devil in human form.
> N4 Devil as gambler.
> G224.4 Person sells soul to devil in exchange for witch powers.
> G303.16.18 Devil leaves at mention of God's name.

8 Eduardo Martínez, interviewed by the author, Alburquerque, New Mexico, 15 May 1987.

9 The ethnopoetic transcription templates are drawn from semantically based transcriptions of Dell Hymes and the breath-based transcriptions of Dennis Tedlock (Briggs 1988: 10). The rhetorical layering begins at the far left margin with the frame of the two speakers, regularly monitored with back-channel cues in English and Spanish to maximize communicative efficacy. The story itself is laced with imbedded dialogue supported with quotatives and speakers who are all kin including the neighbour who traded his soul. The narrative frame is the first indentation and direct dialogue is indented into a third column. Increased volume is indicated in CAPS and code switches to English in *italics*. EM=Ed Martínez and EL=Enrique Lamadrid.

10 These are the Aarne–Thompson (1973) motif types and the order in which they occur in the New Mexican Devil at the Dance narratives:

> C58 Tabu: Profaning sacred day.
> G303.3.1 Devil in human form.
> G303.3.1.2 Devil as a well-dressed gentleman.
> G303.4.1.6 Devil has horns.
> G303.4.5.4 Devil has goat feet.
> G303.4.5.4.1 Devil is betrayed by his goat hooves.
> G303.4.6.1 A girl recognizes the devil by his tail.
> G303.4.8.1 Devil has sulphurous odour.
> G303.10.4.0.1 Devil haunts dance halls.
> G303.17.2.8 Devil disappears amid stench.

11 These particular *versos chiquiados* were collected and compiled at the Senior Center in El Rancho, New Mexico, by the author (Lamadrid 1984).

12 These field notes date to 1984 when I was teaching at Northern New Mexico Community College in Española, New Mexico. No interviews were conducted at

the time but sensational reports came out in the local newspaper, the *Río Grande Sun*, and later in the pulp press (O'Brien 2007: 137–8).

13 None of the sanctuary movement conspiracy trials in Tucson, Arizona, or the sanctuary trial of famed Chicana writer Demetria Martínez resulted in any convictions (Torres 2007: 315–24).

14 Linda Ronstadt played San Miguel in Luis Valdez and Teatro Campesino's 1991 film and television production of *La Pastorela: A Shepherd's Tale*. For several seasons in the late 1980s, the *Compañía de Teatro de Alburquerque* featured a femme fatale Lucifer named 'Lucy Fer' in the scenes of Los Pastores embedded in the theatre production of Rudolfo Anaya's children's book *Farolitos of Christmas* (1987). The traditional Sangre de Cristo Liturgies of Taos production of Los Pastores features a female Lucifer every third season on average.

15 Córdova, *Los Pastores* (2007).

16 The key Aarne–Thompson (1973) motif in this story is G303.3.1.12.2 Devil in form of woman lures man.

17 Gina Morales and Marcos X, interviewed by the author, Beth Epstein and Marcos Romero, Isleta Casino, Isleta Pueblo, New Mexico, 21 November 1998.

18 Teresa Sandoval, interviewed by the author, Alburquerque, New Mexico, 24 April 1998.

19 Charles and Barbara Aguilar, interviewed by the author, Bernalillo, New Mexico, 5 November 2002.

20 A saint for lawyers and gamblers popular in New Spain and New Mexico, San Cayetano was a sixteenth-century Venetian nobleman who studied law but dedicated his life to helping the sick and the poor. He founded a bank to help the poor and protect them from predatory lenders. In exchange for his favours, instead of making holy vows or promises, the devoted will bet him a Mass or a rosary. His iconographic attributes include the cross and Arma Christi, the tools of the crucifixion or weapons of Christ (Steele 1994).

21 In an online *Counterpunch* article entitled 'Wall Street Gamblers', consumer advocate Ralph Nader warns: 'Move over Las Vegas. The big time gamblers are on Wall Street and they are gambling with your money, your pensions, and your livelihoods' (available at: http://www.counterpunch.org/ader06112008.html; last accessed on 12 May 2010). 'Satanic mills' is a metaphor that visionary British poet William Blake used to refer to factories and the rapacious capitalism of the Industrial Revolution.

22 Charles and Barbara Aguilar, 2002.

The Inferno
Burning Man and the Tipping Point

RACHEL BOWDITCH

FIGURE 1. Festive Devil in a wandering in a dust storm, 2001. Photograph courtesy of Stuart Harvey.

Through me you enter into the city of woes,
Through me you enter into eternal pain,
Through me you enter the population of loss,
Abandon all hope, you who enter here.

Dante Alighieri, *The Inferno*, Canto 3.

An unlikely place to find a festive devil is the scorching desert of northwestern Nevada—apart from the swirling dirt devils that spin across the endless expanses of desert.[1] However, festive devils of all shapes and sizes converge in the Black Rock Desert for a week each year at an annual event known as Burning Man. Occurring for seven days preceding Labor Day weekend, over 65,000 participants converge like pilgrims to build Black Rock City on the ancient lakebed of Lake Lahontan—a semi-circular city of concentric rings modelled from two o'clock to ten o'clock with radial streets dilating from a central focal point—a 12-metre wooden effigy of a 'Man'.

This playa, or beach, entirely devoid of vegetation, is one of the largest in the United States. Desolate, yes, but far from devoid of people. Humans have been present for 12,000 years; this area is part of the Paiute tribal homeland.[2] Within this 'second world' separated from the everyday by five miles of boundary fence shaped like a pentagon, participants build theme camps, villages, art installations, art cars and engage in performances and carnivalesque activities of all kinds from travesty, costuming and excessive sexual and consumptive behaviours. At the end of this week of excess, role-playing, art making and community building, the effigy of the Man is burnt. Black Rock City is a city—although on the cusp of perpetual disappearance—simulated in full detail and complexity for one week, then transforming into a online community for the rest of the year via emails, blogs, websites and chat rooms. In 1996, the theme was 'The Inferno', inspired by Dante's *Inferno* and marking an important turning point in Burning Man history, one worth some consideration. Here the concepts of 'devil',[3] 'Satan', and 'hell' acquire new meanings and become metaphors for the complex transition in the event's evolution from a grassroots countercultural 'temporary autonomous zone'[4] to a multimillion-dollar for-profit corporation.

Burning Man began as a personal healing ritual on Baker Beach in San Francisco in 1986 when founder Larry Harvey decided to burn a handcrafted effigy of a Man. According to Burning Man folklore, Harvey's motives were to purge all the possessions from a relationship that had gone wrong. This origin story has been debated yet still holds some resonance within the community that yearns for a mythological beginning. This first improvised beach burn was attended by 10 close friends. The following year, those numbers doubled until 1990 when the event attracted over 800 people. Shut down by the authorities, Harvey was approached by Michael Mikel and John Law, organizers of the San Francisco Cacophony Society,[5] who suggested moving the burning of the Man to the Black Rock Desert of Nevada. In 1990, 80 close friends, mostly artists, caravanned to the Black Rock Desert in Nevada to build art and burn the Man.[6] After 1990, the event exponentially grew, doubling each year until 1996, with 10,000 people converging on the event.

Since 1990, Harvey has designated a theme around which all the art revolves. In 1996, the theme was based on Dante's *Inferno*, a metaphor that extended beyond the art and into everyday life as the free-for-all anarchy of the early days was spiralling out of control. Bruce Sterling's 1996 article about Burning Man in *Wired* magazine, entitled 'Greetings from Burning Man! The New American Holiday', drew even more attention from the budding tech industry. With the advent of the Internet, Burning Man started attracting participants worldwide. The Silicon Valley's dotcom millionaires discovered Burning Man and they poured money and resources into building elaborate theme camps and innovative art installations, often incorporating new technology such as lasers and Tesla coils. The population was a kaleidoscope of subcultures[7] from hippie, punk, hardcore grunge, techno raver, techno pagan, information technology geeks, circus performers, fire performers as well as intellectuals and journalists to name a few.[8]

A counterpoint to this artistic boom was a darker, more apocalyptic edge of a society spinning out of control. Without rules or regulations imposed on participants, the city sprawled like an amoeba without definition or shape. Participants played with guns in drive-by shooting ranges and drove rental cars at high speeds across the playa, often using them as bumper cars and totalling vehicles, having paid for full insurance coverage (see Doherty 2004). It was an arts festivals but it was also a city of decadence and indulgence on many levels.

If we follow Malcolm Gladwell's theory of the 'tipping point', 1996 is the year Burning Man tipped. Gladwell characterizes the tipping point as 'that magic moment when an idea, trend, or social behavior crosses a threshold, tips, and spreads like wild-fire' (2000: back cover). He argues:

The best way to understand the emergence of fashion trends, the ebb and flow of crime waves, or, for that matter, the transformation of unknown books into bestsellers, or the rise of teenage smoking, or the phenomena of word of mouth, or any number of the other mysterious changes that mark everyday life is to think of them as epidemics. Ideas and products and messages and behaviors spread just like viruses do (ibid.: 7).

Three characteristics that cause an event, idea or virus to tip are: contagiousness; little causes having big effects; and change happening not gradually but at one dramatic moment (ibid.: 9). The latter characteristic is particularly germane to what happened with Burning Man in 1996—in one year, the number of participants jumped from 5,000 to 10,000—from a small, unknown event into a massive social phenomenon that was spinning out of control without rules, structure or boundaries. Gladwell emphasizes the concept of the 'Law of the Few' which is also pertinent to the Burning Man phenomenon—how a small group of friends, artists and organizers planted the seeds of a social movement that now includes hundreds of thousands of people world-wide. While today Burning Man is managed and organized by primarily 25 salaried individuals, a volunteer force of thousands generates the bulk of the labour.

The 1996 theme was fitting: the *Inferno* narrative centred on a fictional mega-corporation, Helco, run by Papa Satan, which was attempting to buy Burning Man. The *Black Rock Gazette,* Burning Man's daily newspaper, covered this mock 'impending merger', even as Burning Man founder Harvey firmly stated, 'Burning Man is not for sale!' (Woolridge 1996). The staged tension of the drama about the impending sale of Burning Man to fictional corporate conglomerates was echoed by real tension that simmered between Burning Man organizers Harvey, Mikel and Law. As one Burning Man artist remembers, 'That was an apocalyptic event. Things were going wrong. It felt like we were at war' (quoted in Doherty 2004: 105).

The concept of 'hell' occurred on two planes—one theatrical, the other actual. These two modes of hell spiralled around each other, defining and shaping the history of the event. Earlier that year, the Burning Man organizers presented an event at

SOMArts in San Francisco called 'Hell Yes! Hell No!' as a prelude to the desert theme of Inferno. Burning Man co-opted the Faustian classic narrative—of a man making a deal to sell his soul to the devil in exchange for receiving unlimited knowledge and worldly treasures—to performatively address the real threat of corporate takeover. As Burning Man continued to grow and become economically sustainable and profitable, it became increasingly desirable for corporate interests. In 1996, Burning Man was perched on the precipice between remaining a grassroots countercultural underground event to becoming a large-scale mainstream phenomenon.

In *The Devil and Commodity Fetishism in South America*, Michael Tausig illustrates how the concept of the devil was brought by European imperialism to the New World and how the symbol of the devil was adopted by the workers in the sugar plantations of western Colombia and the Bolivian tin mines who were experiencing capitalism for the first time. The devil became the source of the workers subjugation and was equated with the evils of the capitalist system of inequality (1980: 28). In Taussig's analysis, the image of the devil and capitalist development are inherently linked:

> [The] vast store of mythology in both Western and South American cultures concern [...] the man who sets himself apart from the community to sell his soul to the devil for wealth. [...] The fabled devil contract is an indictment of the economic system which forces men to barter their souls for the destructive powers of commodities [...]. Man's soul cannot be bought or sold, yet under certain historical conditions mankind is threatened by this mode of exchange as a way of making a livelihood (ibid.: xii).

While tongue-in-cheek satire was the spirit of the 1996 Burning Man event, this temptation to 'sell out' and be co-opted by corporate interests was an underlying reality.

As participants entered the SOMArts gallery, they were accosted by performers playing the role of Helco's sales representatives who dressed in red blazers adorned with the Helco logo. The organizers produced an infomercial that played on an endless loop in the background, featuring performance artist Hal Robins as Helco's pitchman scripted by long-time 'burner' Stuart Mangrum, publisher and editor of Black Rock City's newspaper. The premise was that Helco had come to SOMArts to purchase participants' souls. Participants were informed that Helco had recently acquired 'Hell as part of a hostile takeover and was now about to merge with Heaven, creating the first cosmically integrated vertical marketing system' (Harvey 2008). Participants were given contracts titled 'Standard Short Form Contract for Purchase of Soul', typed in nine-point font on legal paper—getting progressively smaller. Upon signing over their soul to the devil, participants then ascended a steep, three-storey staircase to meet Satan played by long-time Burning Man participant Flash. Participants would sit on Satan's lap—as they would on Santa's—and whisper secret wishes and desires in exchange for a fiery cinnamon lollipop. For Harvey, this faux merger highlighted a real principle that was at stake:

Looking around me, I saw other people who hesitated. They seemed to tremble at the brink. These were the thoughtful ones, of course, but many others signed the bottom line. Merrily, they tripped upstairs to meet the Evil One. Interactive performance should provoke such reactions. It should amuse and delight. It should entertain and engage. It should startle folks and make them laugh—but it should also strive to make them think and choose. Though this is farce and Dada, it should have a moral backbone. [...] As part of our satiric scheme, Satan was understood to have lost his position in the midst of corporate reshuffling. No longer CEO of an underworld empire, he now served as a corporate spokesperson. [...] I'd learned that humor is a master solvent in this process. And yet, actually selling one's soul is potentially a very sober proposition—and in our world of mass consumption it's undoubtedly a very crucial one (2008).

While humour and satire were the key mode of expression, it unearthed a deeper, real-life tension simmering beneath the surface. As Burning Man began to tip into and enter mainstream consciousness, so did the desire to commodify Burning Man into a moneymaking venture. Corporations viewed Burning Man as a valuable platform for marketing new products: What better way to market a new brand than to give away free samples of water, soda or any other product as part of the 'gift economy.' However, it was exactly this type of infiltration of corporate viral marketing that the organizers were trying to evade. This mock pending merger, while humorous, ethically positioned Burning Man against the increasing pressures to commodify their ever-growing popular event. Like any other arts festival in the United States, Burning Man organizers could be capitalizing on their logo and brand by selling mass quantities of paraphernalia such as T-shirts, calendars, stickers, pins, mugs and so on. They do sell these things on a small scale on their website but not at the actual desert event where no money is allowed to be exchanged except for ice at Camp Arctica and the Center Camp Café—with all proceeds going to local charities.

In 1996, Helco reappeared in the desert as a final attempt to buy Burning Man. In the annual Burning Man newsletter, Harvey describes this impending merger:

This year in the Black Rock Desert the Burning Man Project presents *The Inferno*—a rendering of Hell in our postmodern age. The place we know as Hell has been portrayed in many ways. It is most frequently an after-world, an abode of the dead, and one's journey through it is a trial or initiation. Our own interpretation is adapted from the Hell of Dante Alighieri as it derives from Hades, the underworld of ancient Greece. Guarded by terrifying monsters—the Furies, Medusa, and Cerberus, the three-headed dog of Hell—it will be a place where every sin and folly of our age is catalogued, held up for public view, and punished. [...] Most fundamentally, throughout successive ages Hell has been a place of banishment. [...] Unlike Heaven, the home of the perfect, Hell is, and will always be, a supremely ironic place. 'Welcome to Hell!' (2008).

In 1996, the event was three days long[9] and on Saturday night, Flash reprised his role as Papa Satan sitting upon his throne, surrounded by corporate conglomerates such as Aunt Jemima, the Jolly Green Giant and Mr Klean. Michael Mikel concurs:

1996 was a pivotal year for Burning Man. It was the first year of a large theatrical performance centered around a cohesive theme. Helco was a parody of consumer culture and with the Devil as its chief executive. It represented all that was evil in the world of commerce. It was a drama between good and evil in which we all became artists and performers. It was the tipping point, which added legitimacy to the festival and set the stage for the elaborate productions to come (personal correspondence 2010).

Structured like a fairy tale, Harvey was seduced three times to sign over the property rights of Burning Man and Black Rock City to Helco and three times he refused. Finally, he exclaimed, 'I can't sign this! I don't own Black Rock City! Burning Man belongs to all of you! You have to decide!' The crowd unanimously supported Harvey's decision not to 'sell out' to corporate America. Satan was then chained to the back of a truck and made to lead the procession through the Gates of Hell created by artist Kal Spelletich. According to Harvey, these gates resembled an array of toll booths on a freeway adorned by a fire-spewing Cerberus, lit by a sign evoking Dante's words 'Abandon all hope, you who enter here.' A landmark feature of Hell was the Helco tower designed by Flynn Mauthe, illuminated by neon letters recycled from a Payless shoe store.

Once Harvey declined the offer to sell out, the Helco tower was ignited and John Law, an original Burning Man organizer and experienced daredevil, flew off the top on a zip line before the tower was engulfed in flames. The celebration culminated at the City of Dis (referencing Dante's *Inferno*) where a performance by the Burning Man Opera titled *The Arrival of the Empress Zoe*, conceived by Pepe Ozan and performed by hundreds, followed the soul's journey from birth to death. This was the first interactive performance of this magnitude and complexity on the playa. Comprising about 50 people—including performers, musicians, sculptors, special-effects technicians and costume designers—the centrepiece of the opera was a series of lingam towers: hollow, phallic tubes constructed out of rebar, mesh and mud, which went up in flames for the finale.

One important theme of carnival, as described by Mikhail Bakhtin, was the underworld and the representation of hell—the vertical conception of the world, with heaven on top and hell below (1984b: 401). According to Bakhtin, in sixteenth-century Roman carnival, as in French carnival, the set that depicted hell was solemnly burnt at the peak of the festivities. It was represented in the form of a globe ejecting flames and was known as the 'jaws of hell' (ibid.: 91). The Burning Man Opera, like carnival, embodied this spirit of creative destruction.

As in the Book of Revelation, Satan is defeated, 'reduced to impotence on a fixed day and will on the final day be hurled into a pool of fire and sulphur' (20:1–3, 10; Boyd 1975: 60). In all accounts, the victory over Satan is a decisive one and good over evil prevails once again (ibid.: 59). The *Black Rock Gazette* performatively celebrated the downfall of Helco and Satan. As Harvey wrote:

Market Debacle! Helco Collapses! Reports of a breakdown in talks between Burning Man and HELCO have sent shock waves through world financial markets. Helco stock, valued at $10,000 per share at the end of yesterday's trading on the New York, Tokyo, and Black Rock exchanges, has plunged to a minus value. Many investors, caught in panic selling, have leapt to their deaths. The long expected acquisition of Burning Man by Helco began to unravel on Saturday night when several thousand playa activists stormed a Helco stockholders' meeting conducted in downtown Black Rock City. Chanting, 'Hell Co! Hell No!' the angry mob overturned Satan's throne, sending Helco's board of directors scurrying for cover. The outraged participants proceeded to storm Hell's Gate. In the ensuing confusion, the City of Dis—Satan's Citadel—was destroyed, and Helco Tower, world headquarters of the supranational conglomerate, was burned to the ground. Property damage totals in the billions. There are no reports of injuries. As a result of Saturday's turmoil, the acquisition of Burning Man by Helco has been canceled and merger talks with Heaven, scheduled to take place later this year, have been indefinitely postponed. The Archangel Gabriel, Heaven's chief negotiator, was unavailable for comment. Sources report, however, that Heaven's higher-ups, alarmed by yesterday's disturbance, fear a public relations backlash. [...] As of this writing, however, it appears that Hell itself will survive the demise of its parent company. Helco has collapsed into a morass of insolvency, but Hell, enriched by a bumper crop of suicides, seems likely to remain with all of us for a very long time (2008).

Parallel to this performed, satirical version of hell was a real-life version of hell unfolding for the organizers.

A major event threatened to shut Burning Man down—the tragic death of Michael Fury and the social drama[10] surrounding the tragedy. Fury was a veteran burner who played in the punk-polka act Polkacide and was known for his wild, reckless behaviour. The first phase of the social drama—that is, breach—came before the event opened. As the story goes, according to long-time burner Chicken John, there were approximately 13 people in the desert helping set up the site. Fury had gone drinking in the nearby town of Gerlach. Returning to the desert on his motorcycle, Fury saw John Law's truck driving in the distance, driven by Burning Man old timers SteveCo and his friend Mark Perez. Fury was playing chicken with the truck, dodging in and out, driving full speed towards it. The accident occurred when, in a too-close pass, Fury's head collided with the truck's driver-side mirror decapitating and instantly killing him. The organizers feared that this incident would shut down the event for good.

The fatal collision was only the beginning. A second crisis occurred late Sunday night or early Monday morning during the event itself, when an apparently drugged-out man driving recklessly cruised out near the rave camp and ran over a woman and then into a tent where two people were sleeping. Everyone lived but the three people were seriously injured, one permanently. The tragedies deeply affected Law, who felt he couldn't control the rising level of destructiveness at Burning Man. Law did not want the event to get any bigger; however, Harvey and Mikel both realized that the event had the potential to exponentially grow and, in order to do that, safety structures had to be implemented. Mikel wanted participants to become active agents in creating their own experience as well as take full responsibility for their actions. It was after the 1996 incidents that Mikel added the terminology on the back of the ticket that reads, 'You accept the responsibility for serious injury or death by attending this event.' It became an unsigned contract—there was a shared sense of participation, but now there is also a shared responsibility. After a huge falling out with Harvey, Law walked away and didn't look back (Doherty 2004: 116). Harvey reportedly then asked Mikel if he was still on board and he said he was. The three former partners established PaperMan LLC in 1997 so that the Burning Man Project could continue without Law. Law left the organization but kept his ownership in the trademark until 2007. Harvey and Mikel, along with four others, created Black Rock City LLC in 1999, the organization that has produced the Burning Man event since 1997.

Over the course of 20 years, the impromptu, chaotic beach burn has evolved into a highly structured 'for-profit' organization that continues to expand and become more sophisticated. The formation of the Black Rock City Limited Liability Company (LLC) was part of the effort to manage the increasingly complex event. The LLC set up by Harvey and Mikel in 1997 protected the individual organizers from legal liability and established Burning Man as a professional 'for-profit' operation in the eyes of financial institutions. Originally, the LLC had nine board members but in 1999 a permanent board of six was formed, with Larry Harvey as the Executive Director, and Michael Mikel, Crimson Rose, Will Roger, Harley K. Dubois and Marian Goodell. This board continues to govern the Burning Man organization, as of 2015. Harvey states:

> We have never imagined that Burning Man is or should be property in any ordinary sense of the term. Everyone feels that the Project should not be treated as a commodity. The idea that any one of us might possess the right to transfer these assets onto the market felt aberrant. We've labored so long in the radically de-commodified world of Burning Man that this agreement represents a form of common sense. Millions of dollars may stream into Burning Man each year, and millions may flow out, but Burning Man is not for sale.[11]

As an example of how commercialization has been resisted, Harvey proudly recalls how the organization sued MTV for an attempt at airing unauthorized footage of the event. MTV had already started running promos that read 'Secret Rites of Burning Man!' focusing on the more Dionysian aspects—the sex, drugs and alcohol. The organization felt MTV was trying to exploit the event and turn it into a mainstream product, violating its integrity and spirit. The filmmaker had signed a media release form that legally prevented MTV from using the footage. The case was settled out of court and the footage was never aired (Larry Harvey, personal interview 2004).

Burning Man represents a radical departure from most US corporate festival models that are structured on profit making. The organization is 100 per cent dependent on ticket sales and has never applied for any grants or sought private investments or commercial sponsorship; and it does not permit any vending on site apart from Center Camp Café and Camp Arctica, which sells coffee and ice. Harvey boasts: 'If anything, we joke—we are more aptly termed a "no-profit".' Harvey is proud of the fact that they have never had investors or commercial sponsorships, the typical sources of income and funding that ensure the potential for turning a profit in a 'regular' business.[12]

Welcome to the Black Rock Café

Robert Kozinets, a professor at the Kellogg School of Management, and John F. Sherry, a professor of anthropology in the Mendoza College at the University of Notre Dame, who together conducted a study of temporary communities such as Burning Man, speculated on the existence of life outside the marketplace (2005: 87). They thought Burning Man would be a perfect place to study life outside the market, but when they first arrived in Black Rock City they observed:

How amazingly ironic it was, then, to walk through Burning Man for the first time, to walk through the vast neon-tubed, electroluminescent-wired, uber-strip mall of the place, the signs competing for attention, the touristic cameras, the elevated RVs on prime real estate, the lowly K-Mart tent shanty-towns. [...] We found a sign that mocked capitalism while also celebrating it—the familiar sign of the Hard Rock Café, that read, 'Welcome to the Black Rock Café'. [...] We had gone a long way to penetrate the anti-marketing zone, only to be once again confronted by popular brands and commodities for sale (ibid.: 88).

Sherry and Kozinets read Burning Man as a demonstration of the powerful lengths to which consumers feel they must go in order to decommodify products, services and even their own identities (ibid.: 101). Products are 'purified' through the acts of decommodification, which include customizing, masking or transforming brand names; burning branded objects; and turning commoditized products into gifts (ibid.: 20). Still brand names are ubiquitous. Upon entering Black Rock City, one sees a vista of Budget and U-Haul rental trucks, RVs and cars, creatively transformed to become a temporary shelter for a week, some disguised but many still boldly displaying the corporate logos. The irony behind covering a logo, on a Pepsi can, for example, is that you are still drinking a Pepsi and that you still bought it at the supermarket before you entered the desert.

(LEFT) **FIGURE 2.** Devil Art Car, 2008. Photograph courtesy of Bryce Hunt. (RIGHT) **FIGURE 3.** Stilting Devil, 2005. Photograph courtesy of John Tzelepis.

Bombarded by the scopic regime of the mainstream, Burning Man attempts to escape into a world without logos and corporate sponsorship, yet the inherent contradiction of attempting to erase a product's surface demonstrates the impossibility of this enterprise. As Louis-Ferdinand Celine accurately remarks, 'There is no escaping American business' (quoted in Hardt and Negri 2000: 370). Burning Man functions as a futile attempt to escape the commodity and the reigns of the global network of exchange, yet inevitably fails. Participants enter into the fated devil contract by participating in the gift economy, transforming gifts into commodity fetishes.

The Ambivalence of the 'Gift Economy'

Unique to Burning Man is the idea of the 'gift economy' prescribed by Harvey, although the idea is filled with contradictions in this context. In a lecture titled 'La Vie Boheme' at the Walker Art Center in Minneapolis in 2000, Harvey proudly asked, 'Have you ever been in a city of thousands of people where you couldn't buy or sell anything?' (Harvey 2000). Harvey draws his philosophy of the gift economy from Lewis Hyde's *The Gift*, in which the author establishes the cardinal difference between gift and commodity exchange: a gift establishes a permanent bond between two people while the sale of a commodity does not necessarily leave a connection (1993: 56). The exchange of gifts creates a series of interconnected relationships which in turn builds community and serves as a vehicle for culture making.

A gift, when given without the promise of anything in return, creates a different kind of expectation. For the gift economy to function, the exchange should contain a minimum of three people rather than the usual one-to-one reciprocal giving. In order to sustain this communal bond, gifts need to keep moving from hand to hand in a circular pattern, which Hyde likens to a river (ibid.: 4). Should the flow of the gift halt, the chain of the gift economy is broken. As Hyde notes, 'when the gift moves in a circle its motion is beyond the control of the personal ego, and so each bearer must be a part of the group and each donation is an act of social faith' (ibid.: 16). The gift is to be used up, consumed or even destroyed, as in the practice of the potlatch in order for it to be efficacious (ibid.: 8).

Harvey believes that burning the Man has always been a gift and that gifting is the tissue that holds the community together (Van Rhey 2002). When I asked Harvey how the concept of the gift economy emerged, he said it evolved organically, with no plan or theory attached. At first, there were sporadic attempts to sell things but those failed because no one bought anything; everyone came over prepared with food, water and other necessities: 'It was an environment where sales didn't make sense. Originally, of course, it would have been gauche, and in the worst possible form. It would be like going to a family picnic or a picnic of friends and trying to sell someone your stuffed olives. No one would do that! It would disrespect the relation-ships—the implied social contracts' (personal interview 2004).

As the event grew, further attempts at commerce were made, but they too failed. In 1997, the Black Rock City LLC realized that this failure was in fact a blessing and the organization incorporated a 'no-vending' policy into their by-laws. The no-vending policy went hand-in-hand with the adoption of the gift-economy philosophy and has had a major impact on the formation and development of Burning Man cul-ture and ethos. Harvey states, 'If you are living in a gift economy, it means you give without expectation of returns. It is an unconditional relationship. When those kinds of interactions happen on a sufficient scale within any society it leads to a kind of general sense of cohesiveness—of belonging together.'[13] However, Marcel Mauss would strongly disagree, arguing that there is no such thing as a 'free gift', that the exchange of a gift is actually an archaic form of contract that leaves the recipient in debt to the gift giver. By accepting a gift, one is committing oneself to a binding con-tract with a burden attached (Mauss 1967: 41).

While Harvey holds that the gift is 'unconditional', among burners there is an unspoken contract that their participation in the community is an obligation to give and receive gifts. Theme camps, art installations, workshops, free food and drink—all could be considered forms of gifts. In exchange for roaming Black Rock City and benefitting from acts of unconditional gift giving, it is expected that one will give something in exchange, similar to a barter system. Over time, Harvey has shifted his view of the gift economy. Originally, gift giving was an organic exchange of items of some value to the giver but, increasingly, gifts are store-bought trinkets without value or meaning ordered in mass quantity to be distributed ad hoc. 'That's because people don't really care about them. [...] Simply do someone a kindness or contribute to the life of our city instead of passing out so many tangible souvenirs' (Van Rhey 2002). The gift becomes a fetish object that is inherently linked to commodification and the exchange of global capital. As Taussig notes, this commodity exchange is likened to the contract with the devil, one that is inherently fraught with ambiguity (1980).

The devil contract of the commodity fetish, in many ways, functions like the Native American potlatch and many parallels can be drawn between the two. Mauss translated 'potlatch' in terms of nourishment; however, more commonly, the word is taken to mean 'gift' or 'giving'. A potlatch is a form of gift economy practised tradi-tionally by northwest coast Native Americans. It assumes a social contract in which one tribe gives gifts of blankets, whale oil and other valuable and symbolic items with the expectation that these gifts will be returned twofold the following year—what Philip Drucker and Robert F. Heizer call a 'double return', as they have noted in their study of the southern Kwakiutl potlatch (1967: 53). Often the gifts are destroyed and burnt as a symbolic gesture of status, wealth and power.[14] This form of contract is both symbolic and functional, serving to bind the community. Yet many societies have been ruined by the practice of potlatch. Burning Man participants sometimes go too far, exerting themselves financially beyond their means.

At Burning Man, items of value take months to fabricate and construct, only to be destroyed on a vast scale. But, unlike in the potlatch system, at Burning Man the giver and the destroyer are one and the same. The display of one theme camp's assets is a form of gift to the others in attendance and creates a binding network of exchange. This reciprocal relationship carries over from year to year and builds in momentum and scale. The potlatch idea of 'double return' can be seen in the community's commitment to double the ambition and scale of the year before, and the theme camps, art installations and costumes to grow exponentially more elaborate and complex each year.[15] Consequently, each year the level of destruction increases twofold, as the community outdoes itself, competing with levels of generosity followed by competitive destruction. The wholesale destruction, often through fire, of art and the Man are symbolic acts that demonstrate the ability to let go of material possessions, yet are interwoven with global capital—a commodity exchange occurred before participants arrived at the desert event. The essential difference between a potlatch and what goes on at Burning Man is that in most cases participants return to their lives in the same economic bracket as when they arrived. However, some Burning Man participants are ruined financially, having poured their life's savings into an installation or artwork that is eventually burnt. What is at stake in the potlatch and at Burning Man is honour and prestige.

The Devil Returns

After the hellish crisis of 1996 and the establishment of the Black Rock City LLC, the event stabilized until 2007. Then the devil returned, wreaking havoc and mischief —this time as a form of protest against what Burning Man had become. On Tuesday, 28 August 2007, at approximately 2.58 a.m., old-time burner Paul Addis, a 35-year-old San Francisco playwright torched the Man as an act of rebellion against the Burning Man organization. Addis climbed up the shade-cloth installation surrounding the Man before anyone saw him and set the Man ablaze. Black Rock City LLC board member Crimson Rose, who has known Addis for about 15 years, said, 'He was totally pissed off that we had sold out and it was not like the good old days' (Crimson Rose, personal interview 2008). Addis was arrested and jailed by Pershing County on felony charges of arson and destruction of property, as well as with misdemeanour for the possession of fireworks and resisting a police officer. He posted a US$25,632 bond and was released. Addis' arraignment on these charges was

(LEFT) **FIGURE 3.** Blue Devil, 2003. Photograph courtesy of Michael Leach. (CENTRE) **FIGURE 4.** Bike Devil, 2002. Photograph courtesy of Matt Freedman. (RIGHT) **FIGURE 5.** Festive Devil in full red body paint, 2005. Photograph courtesy of George Post.

scheduled for 25 September 2007, at the Pershing County courthouse where he was charged with first-degree arson, destruction of property and the reckless endangerment of human life.

The irony is that the Man is built to be burnt but not by anyone at any time. Addis defended his action in an interview with *Wired* magazine's Miyoko Ohtake, saying it was a 'badly needed reality check for the desert art festival' (cited in Ohtake 2007: n.p.). Addis ultimately claimed full responsibility: 'Burning Man has turned into an "Alterna-Disney"', and the act was a protest against the Man's increasing commercialization' (ibid.). The early burn was premeditated and planned well in advance. Addis felt that Burning Man had lost all spontaneity: 'The Burning Man organization doesn't have any sense of humor anymore and that streams and trickles down to the participants themselves' (ibid.).

Addis had attended the event in 1996, 1997 and 1998 but didn't go again until 2007 because he felt that Burning Man was 'only advocating social impact and responsibility in the name of its own self-preservation, survival and expansion' (ibid.), and he was not willing to be a part of that. The 2007 early burn, according to Addis, was his attempt to recapture the original anarchistic spirit of the event. Addis felt his act of arson was a reminder of why the event started in the first place, an act of radical self-expression, which he believes is no longer possible at the event because it has become too large and regulated. People had been talking about pulling this prank for years before Addis finally succeeded. For setting fire to the Man, Addis served two years in a Nevada prison and in 2012 tragically took his own life.

The toll exacted by Addis' act was emotional as well as financial. Participants' responses varied. Some supported Addis, shouting, 'Burn the Man!' Others saw the act as disrespectful of the event and the organizers. The incident was an important moment in the history of the event because it again called into the question the tenuous relationship between the increasing commercialization of the festival and the yearning to remain an anti-establishment countercultural event. This was a difficult lesson to learn, as Rose realized:

> It kind of woke us up out of being a little bit innocent and naïve—that we would allow someone to take advantage of us (The Burning Man Organization). However, this is just a little glitch. I think we need to protect things a little better. It just means we need to be more on the ball. I think we will be better prepared for it in the future. . . . This is not something I want to repeat (personal interview 2008).

At any moment, whether it is an accidental death of a participant, the early burning of the Man or some other unpredictable event, the future of the event is continuously at stake. Analysing several pivotal moments in Burning Man's history from the Inferno and mock takeover by the fictional conglomerate Helco and Papa Satan in 1996 to the early burn in 2007 reveals that, ultimately, Burning Man is like any other business; the only difference is that the product is affective and ephemeral—'experience', 'participation' and 'community'—rather than a tangible commodity. To this day, the streets of Black Rock City are paraded by festive devils of all shapes and sizes as a constant reminder of the delicate balance between chaos and order, commodity fetishism and the gift economy. Adorned in colourful, elaborate costumes that include body paint, horns, faux fur and other accessories, these festive devils run amok causing mischief and havoc in playful, performative ways—a symbol for the ambiguity inherently present within the everyday life of the desert festival.

Notes

1   The playa, one of the largest in the United States, is 43 kilometres long and 19 kilometres wide, bordered on the west by the Calico Mountains and on the east by the Black Rock Range, with elevations from 1,450 to 2,500 metres. The entire Black

Rock Desert and its associated wilderness areas encompass 4,810 square kilometres in which there are no paved roads; it is surrounded by Washoe County, Pershing County and Humboldt County (Bureau of Land Management 2000). According to the Nevada Bureau of Land Management (BLM), three historic trails traverse the playa and traces of these crossings have been found from wagon-wheel ruts, historic carvings and axle-grease markings on rocks. The most famous being the 1848 California gold rush which saw a surge of pioneers trekking through the brutal desert to discover their fortunes on the West Coast (ibid.). In the summer, the playa consists of fine clay silt that is a smooth surface to drive on, and, in 1997, the official land-speed record of 1,228 kmph was set on the Black Rock playa by the British SSC Thrust jet car. In winter, the playa is wet and largely impassable.

2   Today the Paiute live on reservations in Arizona, California, Nevada and Oregon. In a 2000 census, the Pyramid Lake Paiute tribe had a population of 1,734. Paiute reservations in the area include: to the north, the Summit Lake Reservation; to the northeast, the Fort McDermitt Reservation; and to the southwest, the Pyramid Lake Reservation (Bureau of Land Management 2000). The area also contains paleontological and archaeological resources of national importance, such as the remains of woolly mammoths, sabre-tooth tigers and other Pleistocene animals that were trapped there along the marshy shores of ancient Lake Lahontan. At present, the alkali left in the soil when the lake dried up prevents anything from growing. Sometimes you find seashells as a reminder of the distant past, or a scorpion from today, but not much else. The Black Rock Desert is a national conservation area managed by the BLM and the US Department of the Interior.

3   James Boyd notes the term 'Satan', predominantly used in the New Testament, is a 'Hebrew name derived from the root *sâtan* which means "to oppose" or "to act as an adversary". The term 'Devil', which comes from the Greek word *diabolos* was used in the Septuagint (LXX) to translate the Hebrew *sâtan*' (1975: 13). Historically, by the end of the first century, the terms 'Devil' and 'Satan' had become dominant terms for the embodiment of an evil adversary and were treated as synonyms (ibid.: 13, 17). According to Boyd, 'It is through his activities that the Devil is best known and a glimpse of his character ascertained. The idea of Satan as a fallen angel who is chief among a class of fallen angels, is an idea which appears frequently in apocalyptic literature. [. . .] Satan appears to be an angel who, together with his followers, has been cast from heaven' (ibid.: 28). 'The activities of Satan or the Devil are many, but for the most part fall into the following categories: temptation, deception, obstruction, and torment, possession and instigation, and destruction' (ibid.: 19). The devil evokes a sense of 'corruption' and 'ruin', as well as a figurative sense of spiritual death (ibid.: 37).

4   The early days of Burning Man could be billed as what anarchist writer Hakim Bey calls a Temporary Autonomous Zone (TAZ)—a spontaneous yet intentional community (or festival) living outside the boundaries of everyday life. A TAZ operates clandestinely, beneath the law, for brief moments in time. Bey notes, 'The TAZ is like an uprising which does not engage directly with the State, a guerilla operation which liberates an area (of land, of time, of imagination) and then dissolves itself to

re-form elsewhere before the State can crush it' (1985: 3). While Burning Man began as a TAZ, there has been an increased presence of police and surveillance over time. In order for the event to survive, the Burning Man organization needed to comply with the authorities and the law, forever changing what was originally a true anarchist temporary autonomous zone.

5   The Cacophony Society was founded in 1986. It was inspired by the playful and subversive anti-art aesthetic of Dada and the surrealists. Cacophonists called themselves 'a randomly gathered network of free spirits united in the pursuit of experiences beyond the pale of mainstream society' (Cacophony Society website, available at: http://www.cacophony.org; last accessed on 28 April 2015). Cacophonists not only recycled culture, they precycled it—that is, they would grab anything that wasn't nailed down, combed through the industrial detritus of society, recycled it as art, and invested it with new meaning. In its heyday between 1986 and 1996, the Cacophony Society threw over 200 mischievous events that included guerrilla theatre, themed parties, public spectacles, pranks, hoaxes, billboard alterations and 'zone trips'. The first trip to the Black Rock Desert was a Cacophony 'zone trip'.

6   See Brian Doherty (2004) and Rachel Bowditch (2010) for full history of Burning Man.

7   Among sociologists and anthropologists, 'subculture' is a contested term. Sociologist Mike Brake gives a clear definition: 'Subcultures exist where there is some form of organized and recognized constellation of values, behaviour and action which are responded to as different from the prevailing set of norms' (1985: 8–9).

8   An annual census of the Black Rock City population conducted by the Burning Man organization began in 2001. Over four years, the data has remained remarkably consistent. I have selected 2004 as a sample year. While the data represents only 13 per cent of the population, they paint a rough portrait of the demographics of the Burning Man community. When asked why they attend Burning Man, 37 per cent of the people surveyed by the Burning Man organization responded 'fire'; 23 per cent responded 'community'; and 13 per cent responded 'personal quest'. Their motives are frequently mixed: personal transformation, the desire to build community, to party like never before or even to watch others perform and party. The census results indicate that 57 per cent are male, 41 per cent female and 1 per cent transgender. The largest age group is 31–40, the second-largest being 21–30-year-olds. Only 4 per cent are under 21 and 2 per cent over the age of 60. Those who responded to the census indicated that the event is predominantly heterosexual (70 per cent), with 18 per cent being bisexual and 8 per cent homosexual. The majority of those attending the event are from urban areas, followed by suburban residents, and only 15 per cent from rural areas. The survey also indicates that 40 per cent have a college degree and 16 per cent have a graduate degree. Only 3 per cent did not graduate from high school. In 2004, 40 per cent of the participants were single, 17 per cent married and 17 per cent were in a serious relationship. Twenty-four per cent of the population earned between $25,000 and $50,000; the rest are equally

distributed between $15,000 to over $100,000. It is interesting to note that the census did not include a racial demographic. Without collecting questionnaires and data, one can deduce at a glance that Burning Man is a predominantly white, middle-class event. While Latinos, African Americans, Native Americans and Asian Americans are present, they represent a minority of the population (Bowditch 2010).

9 In the early days, the event was three-days and in 1997 it moved to a week-long event.

10 The term social drama is developed by Victor Turner and divided into four phases: breach; crisis; redressive action; and reintegration or schism (see Turner 1969).

11 'Financial Structure', Burning Man website. Available at: http://burningman.org/-culture/history/brc-history/afterburn/04-2/financial_structure/ (last accessed on 10 April 2015).

12 'AfterBurn Report 2005'.

13 Ibid.

14 Mauss argues: 'To refuse to give, to fail to invite, just as to refuse to accept, is tantamount to declaring war; it is to reject the bond of alliance and commonality. [...] All the forms of potlatch in the American northwest know this theme of destruction. [...] Material and moral life, and exchange, function within it in a form that is both disinterested and obligatory (1967: 13–16).

15 According to Helen Codere, who conducted a study on the Kwakiutl potlatch, the potlatch is a public giving and destruction of what she calls 'surplus economy' of goods (1950: 63); it produces a vast network of 'debtor–creditor' relations based on accumulations that double each time. It is the distribution as well as destruction of property (ibid.: 77). As John W. Adams observed in the Gitksan potlatch, gifting is a sign of social status and prestige (1973: *iii*).

PART 3

Crossings/Encrucijades

Matters of the Spirit
Rendering Festive Devils unto Various Gods

MILLA COZART RIGGIO

Render unto Caesar that which is Caesar's and unto God that which is His.

Matthew 22:21

I don't do nuance.

President George W. Bush to Senator Joe Biden,
as quoted in *Time*, 15 February 2004

In a probably apocryphal story, Soviet filmmaker Sergei Eisenstein is said to have been asked in the late 1930s why he had trouble with the authorities in Stalinist Russia. His purported answer—'I always want to kiss arse, but at the last moment I can never resist taking a bite'—speaks to the essence of the festive devil. Generated historically as part of a mechanism for maintaining religious control through rituals of submission, penitence and abjection, the festive devil has emerged throughout the Americas as a force of resistance, as one who bites when s/he should obediently bow. Affirming as well as resisting, this frequently scatological, witty character—whether diablo or diabla—often dances (at times obscenely) on the bones of a despised or rejected religious orthodoxy, thus claiming power for the nether regions: of the physical body, the body politic and the mythically defined cosmos. At other times, these creatures play within at least the nominal colonial/neocolonial structures or reflect the syncretic assimilation that inevitably accompanies centuries of cohabitation, even within the asymmetrical parameters of inequality, social isolation and rigid gender definition.

Though, as Angela Marino affirms, the devil was born in the cauldron of political necessity and though both politics and religion are imbedded in the economic realities that Paolo Vignolo discusses in the final essay of this volume, the devil is a religious figure. Bred of a worldview that, like Hugo Chávez's 'devil' Bush, does not 'do nuance', the devil's very existence presumes a binomial opposition between good and evil. That moral dichotomy has in this volume repeatedly—for instance, by Angela Marino, Paolo Vignolo and Thomas Abercrombie—been called Manichaean. But what, exactly, is Manichaeism? And how accurately does that concept define the battle between good and evil, light and darkness that the devil was born to wage and that the festive devils of the Americas complicate?

As defined by Abercrombie:

Manichaeanism, named after a third-century Persian [Mani], propagated the idea that humanity was created as a result of a cosmological struggle between the independent principles of good (purely spiritual, embodied in light) and evil (material, embodied in darkness), which continue to war with each other. It resembles the orthodox Christian dichotomy between light and dark, good and evil [. . .]. By extension, the terms—especially Manichaean—are often applied to those who believe in absolute, opposing principles of good and evil without reference to the specific cosmology that produced the Manichaean beliefs. Perhaps qualifying as Manichaean are Orureño appeals to the devil/indigenous deities for material prosperity alongside penitential bodily offerings to the Virgin for spiritual well being (see p. 92, note 10, in this volume).

The online *Catholic Encyclopedia* expands this idea:

Manichaeism[1] [. . .] purported to be the true synthesis of all the religious systems then known, and actually consisted of Zoroastrian Dualism, Babylonian folklore, Buddhist ethics, and some small and superficial additions of Christian elements. As the theory of two eternal principles, good and evil, is predominant in this fusion of ideas and gives color to the whole, Manichaeism is classified as a form of religious Dualism. It spread with extraordinary rapidity in both East and West and maintained a sporadic and intermittent existence in the West (Africa, Spain, France, North Italy, the Balkans) for a thousand years, but it flourished mainly in the land of its birth (Mesopotamia, Babylonia, Turkestan) and even further East in Northern India, Western China, and Tibet, where, *c.* AD 1000, the bulk of the population professed its tenets and where it died out at an uncertain date.[2]

That is to say, Manichaeism does specify the principles of good (as light) and evil (as darkness) at war in the universe. Unlike orthodox Christianity, however, as Abercrombie notes, these principles do not emanate from one central, powerful, omnipotent and omniscient God who rules over the universe. From the Manichaean perspective, the principles of good and evil are independent cosmic forces. Indeed, because chaos preceded creation, evil existed earlier. As in orthodox Christianity, the evil force initiated the cosmic battle. Good and evil might have cohabited peacefully had the 'Prince of Darkness' (probably named after the Christian devil) not chosen to invade the region of light. Though orthodox Christianity put forward a similarly dualistic principle, Manichaeism was consistently rejected as heretical.[3] To the Manichaeans, evil was invasive, contaminating and destructive, but it was a separate cosmological force. Thus, it could never be absolutely rejected.

What Manichaeism illustrates that is crucial to understanding the development of festive devils is how the religions of Africa, Asia and Europe were interwoven, how close finally are the cosmologies of the Zoroastrian, the Hindu, the Buddhist and the Yoruban, and, yet, despite some 'small and superficial' Christian similarities, how fundamentally distinctive was the Christian binary of good and evil. Basic to many of these cosmologies was the integrative notion of cosmic energy as generated from the perpetual, inevitable interplay between creation and 'destruction',[4] life and death, seen as sustaining the essential balance of the universe. That the festive devil can be a protective figure, as in *El Tio* (the Uncle) in the mines of Bolivia, to which Abercrombie refers, reinforces the stabilizing balance of universal forces.

Though Christianity was the hegemonic and nominally controlling religion of colonization, it was by no means the only religion imported into the Americas. Asian and African religions were brought largely by enslaved and indentured labourers. Varieties of African perspectives—chief among which is the Yoruba—and, as represented in this volume, Hindu points of view stand out.[5] Both the Yoruba and Hindu believe in a supreme deity (the Yoruba Olorun or 'King of the Sky' and the Hindu Brahman), in relationship to which other deities (African orishas, Hindu avatars, devas and devis) find their place.[6] They privilege the ancestral in analogous but different ways, but most centrally, they share a sense that, in Rawle Gibbons' terms, 'the universe is entirely interconnected, multi-faceted and finely balanced' (personal correspondence, 2014). Within this set of religious constructs, 'play' is an essential feature of the universal creative process. In the form of 'lila', it is, from the Hindu perspective, the play of Brahman (through the triune aspects of Brahma the creator, Vishnu the stabilizer and Shiva the destroyer/dancer/transformer) that creates and sustains the universe itself. Within lila, 'destructive' play is crucial to the continuity of existence, as death and transformation are crucial to life.[7] Though there is no true analogue in either Yoruba or Hindu cosmology for the cosmic battle of universal forces or for 'evil' in the form of an outcast devil, it is within this sphere that the festive devil's performance finds its threatening but also mischievous and, as represented by the Yoruba god Eshu, ultimately transformative place.

Analogous versions of what may superficially resemble the universal battle between creation and destruction, often linked to light and darkness, permeate a variety of indigenous American cosmologies which, likewise, stress the interpenetration of various regions and forces. As in African religions, there is no singular indigenous cosmology: to name only some of the diverse groups in the Andean area alone, for instance, there are the 'Chimú, Chanca, Nazca, Huanca, Yarowilca and Canaris,' along with the 'Lampatos and Chanas' who lived beyond the equator, or the 'Quechua and Aymara' (cited by Miguel Rubio Zapata, p. 52 in this volume); or the Tompiro and Apache and others in the arid north (cited by Enrique R. Lamadrid, p. 272 in this volume). Throughout the extensive regions of the Americas, such diversity 'giv[es] way to a vast diversity of dress and culinary forms and traditions, and of costumes and dances, many of which are now extinct or in the process of extinction' (Rubio in this volume, p. 50). To generalize within this context of diversity is dangerous. But most indigenous cosmologies presume the need to 'work out the equilibrium between both forces in order to live well' (ibid.) as, for instance:

> In the Aymara language, the Alaj papa is the kingdom of light, of good and kindness, and it is located in the higher regions of the world, where God resides. On the opposite side lies the Manqha pacha, kingdom of darkness and of evil, situated in the lower regions of the world. In-between these two realities live the Aymara, inhabitants of the Aka pacha, which represents 'the reality in which we live'. Whoever lives in the Aka pacha must know how to work out the equilibrium between both forces in order to live well (Rubio, p. 54 in this volume).

The region that Rubio defines as 'the kingdom of darkness and of evil' is alternatively described by Silvia Rivera Cusicanqui as the 'space-time of the ancestors', into which the deities and forces of the earth, water and sky were all 'hurled' together—a place misnamed as 'hell' (2014: n.p.; see also Introduction, p. 6 in this volume).

At stake here are two important ideas: first, how one relates to the earth itself and to the body as part of the earth—signified by emblems of fertility and sexuality in their seasonal and physical, sometimes grotesquely scatological or phallic, embodiments; second, and related, how 'festival space and time' enhance and expand the finite limitations of material space and time to create what in Trinidad is called a 'third path', a path that integrates past, present and future as it enfolds the 'space-time of the ancestors' both kinesthetically and through personal and cultural memory (see Riggio and Gibbons, p. 216 in this volume).

The body itself is central for many reasons, one of which is that it allies fertility with ancestral memory. Within the festival world, one reaches the spirit not—as Christianity suggests—by discarding or mutilating the body, but directly *through* the body. The imperfect flesh provides access to the spirit. Thus, festival practices are at once embodied and, paradoxically, anti-material. The body is the conduit, the medium of expression and the gateway to the spirit—the ancestors with which that spirit links it and the rites of fertility that ensure continuity. Thus it is that the sometimes grotesquely or obscenely evoked bodily functions do more than impudently undermine the conventions of polite society. They flamboyantly ally the physical to the immaterial, the sacred to the profane, reminding us that, in the terms of the Irish poet W. B. Yeats, 'love has pitched his tent / in the place of excrement' (1997: 263).

As we collectively argue in the Introduction to this volume, the 'festive body' was one of the few joyous bodies celebrated in Christianity. Though half the Christian year was keyed to the movements of the sun and the moon (which determine all moveable feasts built around Easter, including Corpus Christi and Carnival, central sites for festive devil appearances), its negation of the body in favour of the spirit gave this religion a basic sense of immateriality, removing it from the nature cults that were powerful in its origins.

The other religions and cosmologies that have influenced essays in this volume also frequently distinguish between the material and the immaterial or the body and the spirit. But, generally, the varied African, Hindu and indigenous cosmologies tend to ally the body with the spirit and, often, to revere the Earth itself, as mother (Pachamama) or protector, with respect for both the creative and destructive powers of the universe. From these perspectives, the boundaries between the material and the immaterial are porous and may be transgressed, the spirit world most often manifesting itself in the physical.

This speaks to the 'obeah' or magically transforming nature of Carnival—and by extension other fiestas. As defined by Gibbons in this volume, obeah is a term to signify a special kind of spiritual power, often called magic, derived from West African sources. Like other forms of folk magic, obeah can be either harmful or helpful. In this context, to say that Carnival (or fiesta) is 'obeah' is to acknowledge its capacity to transform both the space and the people who celebrate in that space in ways that, though often unacknowledged, are spiritual and cosmic. That is to say, the fiesta alters its 'space'—often familiar, ordinary streets, urban parks, village greens—beyond the moment of the festival itself. It defamiliarizes the familiar venue and claims it for the festive function, marking it even when the celebration is over. It becomes in this sense what might be called an Eshu space (see essays by Ligiéro and Riggio and Gibbons in this volume)—a playful space, evocative of the ancestors, filled with mischief and some danger that is ultimately transformative.

Festival space is implicitly allied with time. Bringing the past into the present, festive 'space' evokes—even when unacknowledged—the 'space-time of the ancestors'. Lowell Fiet defines the role of the *vejigante* in the Fiestas of Santiago Apóstol on the west coast of Puerto Rico:

The specific and local Hispanic-Afro-Creole mythology also projects general and universal themes of the relationship of the dead to the living, rebirth and renovation, liminal spaces that allow for the rehearsal of physical, geographical, and social transformations, and pasts and presents that fuse the gaps of the unresolved 'social drama' [citing Turner 1982] that accompanies the African experience in Puerto Rico and the Americas in general (p. 172 in this volume).

The 'pasts and presents' (and, as I will argue, futures) of festival time are, as described by Miguel Gandert in this volume, 'circular' rather than 'linear'—belonging to the ancestral past: '[We] discuss good metaphors for the Andean world—agriculture representing the indigenous past and circular time, contrasted by mining as linear time and the symbol of European oppression. Although there was mining prior to Spanish conquest of the Americas, gold and silver were the driving force for the earliest conquerors' (p. 97 in this volume).

Festive time as thus defined in agrarian terms is measured not by the clock but by the turning of the seasons, the coming and going of the sun and the birth and death of those who live beneath it. Time expands and contracts; it embraces play and pauses for the celebration. The fiesta may begin 'late' but it is always on—or in—time, moving to the beat and rhythm of time itself, musically, percussively and cosmically. It can, in this sense, be regarded as liminal, except that its rhythm and energy are not merely temporary or escapist. Substituting the pulsing energy of the heartbeat for the monotony of the ticking clock, they pose an alternative to relentless linearity.

Carnival and its festive cousins represent and ritually re-enact the cosmic dramas of existence, which are encoded in the movements of festival devils. The cosmos is neither created nor does it revolve in a linear pattern. Its movements are winding, circular, cyclical and organic. The temporal fluidity and the movements of festive devils echo this cosmic reality. Eschewing the linear path that is at once the directional pattern both of moral self-righteousness and of tightly administered hierarchy, festive devils move in winding, circular, sometimes weaving patterns that echo their rejection of the 'straight and narrow', both literal and ethical.

Though the concept of 'organic', circular time might seem static, locked in unchanging, recurrent patterns, and thus smacking of nostalgic primitivism, fiestas evolve. Thus, their time scheme may be more accurately described as spiral, that is, the circle that expands as it moves through time, linked to an epistemology that I have elsewhere associated with the festival world (see Riggio 2004). In an embodied, ancestrally based epistemology of spiral time, Leda Martins (quoted by Angela

Marino in this volume) similarly describes the movements of festive characters in the Americas as an Afro-based 'philosophy'. As Marino summarizes:

It is a philosophy in which the embodied language of the dance itself is a source of knowledge for practitioners, cultural workers, and community members. Movements such as the turn, the spiral and crossing steps hold meaning beyond choreographic device or technique. They are entries into an epistemological understanding of time, space and belief itself, where, for example, in spiral time, ancestors meet at the crossing between future and past (p. 248 in this volume).

From this perspective, time and space centrally link the physical (that which can be perceived through the senses) to the metaphysical (the non-material, the ancestral, the imaginative) and the past not only to the present but also, partly through their educative function, to the future. One of the striking features of popular fiestas and carnivals is that—despite the tendency to excess (in drink, food and, at least in Carnival, sex)—they often engage children, trained by adults in what looks like a kind of festival school.

It is largely through the children that the festive past moves forward to the future. At this point, theology intersects modern neuroscience, allying festival time with what Endel Tulving called 'episodic memory' (1983). The ability to recall the past and to project from the past into the future, a particularly human capacity, is linked to the survival and development of the human race, as Dan Falk explains:

The capacity for mental time travel gave our ancestors an invaluable edge in the struggle for survival. [Psychologists Thomas Suddendorf and Michael Caballis] believe there is a profound link between remembering the past and imagining the future. The very act of remembering, they argue, gives one the 'raw material' needed to construct plausible scenarios of future events and act accordingly. Mental time travel 'provides increased behavioral flexibility to act in the present to increase future survival chances.' If this argument is correct, then mental time travel into the past—remembering— 'is subsidiary to our ability to imagine future scenarios.' Tulving agrees: [. . .] 'Perhaps the evolutionary advantage has to do with the future rather than the past.' [. . .] Modern neuroscience appears to confirm that line of reasoning: as far as your brain is concerned, the act of remembering is indeed very similar to the act of imagining the future (2008: 101).

In our world of cyber-magic, where we regularly communicate 'wirelessly' through media that transmit across unseen airwaves, the festive function of connecting the ancestral with both the present and the future finds confirmation in scientific theories of the brain. What seemed to be grounded in traditional forms of faith turns out to correspond to verifiably modern (albeit also contested) science. Though popular festivals belong in other ways to the 'modern world' with their own complex organizational structures, which often have internal hierarchies and can be profit-making entities, they do not—as Benito Irady affirms elsewhere in this volume—*primarily* reflect 'market interests':

> Th[e Devil Dance] represents another victory for the ancestral traditions of the peoples of the Americas whose marvels and revelations show us, amidst the continent's landscape, part of the path of our cultural diversity, of our values, of [. . .] communities [. . .] profoundly elevating their own elements of creation [. . .] centuries-old expressions, to be carried out by local communities and communal representatives, in order to counteract the impact generated by market interests and globalizing trends (p. 236 in this volume).

Thus, though as Vignolo describes in the essay that concludes this volume, fiestas and festive devils belong to the economic orders of society, they finally engage economics, politics and media of exchange in a larger system of values. If the balancing rhythm of the festive—and the traditions that it represents—is removed, the basic standard of measurement becomes work, defined by the industrializing norms of modernity; both the fiesta and the nation lose their soul. The beauty and the power and the productivity of the festive, then, lies in a 'work ethic' that also privileges leisure, that understands that its strengths lie partly in the way it sees the release from work as equal to the work itself. To insist only on the economic 'modernity' of the mode is to seriously undermine that balance, crucial to various cosmologies that inform the play of festive devils. Played out not only in individual lives but in social choices, the balance between 'work' and 'play'—echoing the balance of the universe itself—is crucial to personal and cultural health. Transforming time as well as space, engaging the ancestral and using the human capacity to remember the past and to imagine the future are not only at the essence of popular fiestas; they arguably provide keys to cultural survival. And, in a study like this one, they move us beyond the religion of the colonizers to the myriad cosmologies that interpenetrated one another in festive celebrations throughout the Americas.

The cosmologies that underlie balance in the fiestas of the Americas were not essentially Christian but in their evolution they permeated and influenced Christian celebrations. Rubio provides one example of the way in which the identification of the Christian Virgin—in whose processions festive devils frequently make their appearance—has been impacted by indigenous cosmology:

According to the Quechua and Aymara cosmogonies, the Festival of the Virgin of Candelaria, or Mamita Kanticha, is deeply linked to the agricultural cycles of sowing and harvest, and its purpose is to serve as an offering to Pachamama, or Earth Mother. As a consequence of the postcolonial cultural juxtaposition, Candelaria is the one who intercedes in the face of natural forces, as she is the Christian and mestiza representation of the Virgin and of the Pachamama (p. 52 in this volume).

In this conjunction lie two central principles that implicitly guide the festive devil's dance: first, the syncretism that allows Candelaria simultaneously to 'represent' the Christian Virgin and the Pachamama, the maternal-Earth presence who figures throughout the essays of Abercrombie, Vignolo, Ligiéro, Rubio, and is implicitly invoked as the spirit of the Earth in other essays; second, the importance of the point at which popular celebration and mythology meet, merge with and displace the official Christian narrative, even in festivals as large and as municipally authorized as the pre-Carnival celebration of Candelaria, Peru.

Christianity came to the Americas as a conquering religion—its aim essentially to colonize and control both the land and the people in a region thought to be the place Lucifer landed when he fell from Heaven, as noted by Lamadrid or described by Abercrombie in this volume: 'The story's [that of the Virgin of the Mineshaft first appearing in the days before the Spanish Conquest in the form of a beautiful Inca princess] basic theme echoes that, portrayed in the Diablada dance, of the Archangel's banishment from Heaven of Lucifer and his minions, who have been recast as the evil inspirers of Indians' original pagan religion' (p. 87 in this volume).

Though not literally Hell, the Americas thus were often seen as the abode of the Devil, the eradication of whom was one of the primary aims of the European colonizers (see Cañizares-Esguerra 2006: Chapters 1–3). The nature of Christianity—and particularly Roman Catholicism—as it evolved from its humble origins to its position as the religion of the conqueror was thus to rule, subdue and subjugate. In this context, it was obviously Christ, rather than the devil, who provided the primary model of obedience: As Max Harris explains, "Christ's agony on the cross [was] offered as an example to the enslaved" to obey even the harshest of masters (see p. 142 in this volume).

Nevertheless, as the example of the Virgin of Candelaria illustrates, among the multiple tools Christianity employed in the process of colonial subjugation was the appropriation of pre-existing sacred locations and parallel religious forms and figures. Thus, from the fourth century CE, when Emperor Constantine first placed a Christian cross over the chariot of the Roman sun god, Roman Catholicism has cleverly used the potential for assimilative syncretism as an active tool for conversion.[8] The

Christian devil offered a convenient repository for virtually all aspects of indigenous and imported non-Christian cosmologies that were deemed undesirable. Catholicism was particularly susceptible to a subtle interweaving of the demonic into the realm of the sanctified—the profane penetrating the sacred. As explained by Dexter Brereton, a Catholic priest exploring why devout Catholics in the mountain area of Paramin in Trinidad could so easily become devils in Carnival, the answer lies partly in Catholicism's penchant for generating devils: 'One of the side effects of Catholicism is that it is a religion of demons and devils; it generates a whole world of devils and a hierarchy of angels' (personal interview 2011).

Though Protestants (particularly Puritans) also believed in the central seductive power of the Devil, only the Catholic devil was, from the European Middle Ages forward, in some manifestations comic—and, thus, by extension festive. Indeed, the events in which festive devils appear are largely Catholic in origin. Even in Trinidad, where the pre-Lenten Carnival has spawned a variety of devil-masquerade forms, Carnival as an evolving festival was associated more directly with French Catholic cultural presence than with English rule. By impudently challenging the 'message of patient suffering' that Christ himself embodied, festive devils not only provide a counternarrative, they also build on the degree to which imperial Catholicism was an 'absorbing' religion given to syncretism:

> In comparison to a more Protestant understanding of the faith, Catholicism absorbs and purifies. It finds some degree of official sanction [...]. Though Catholicism was a conquering religion in a pejorative sense requiring first peoples and others to accept Catholicism, [... it was also a religion that depended on] inculturation: harmonizing the gospel message with local people, without compromising the integrity of the gospel, making it understandable to local people. Syncretism would have enjoyed the benevolent approval of the Church (Brereton, personal interview 2011).

Throughout the Americas, African religions were noted for the ways in which they adapted to Christianity, partly by disguising their orishas behind the masks of Christian saints, which at times they also worshipped. The festive devil figures in this formula, partly through analogies with Eshu, a prankster figure in the pantheon of orishas. As described by Ligiéro: 'In Candomblé, Eshu is central to the African resistance in Brazil, while in Umbanda, this same figure has absorbed most of the characteristics traditionally attributed to the Catholic Devil. In fact, Umbanda religion has also incorporated Catholic saints and the ideas of Christian charity' (p. 155 in this volume).

The absorption of one set of religious figures within another religion, such as the use of religious processions, presents possibilities for both resistance and affirmation, and can play ambiguous roles by establishing visibility within the context of existing authority. Early fiestas in the Americas, particularly of Spanish colonizers, for instance, often involved 'Indian' participants in a way that at least superficially reaffirmed, rather than challenged, the colonial hierarchy. As described by Abercrombie, the Feast of Corpus Christi was one such event (p. 76 in this volume).

Monica Rojas similarly describes her participation in the Son de los Diablos (Dance of the Devil) in Lima, Peru, but, instead of 'Indian' participation, she tracks her own ancestry through the participation of 'Afro-descendents' in this dance, further complicating the issue of ethnicity, ancestry and identity influenced in part by urban and rural distinctions that are reflected in festive traditions discussed throughout this book (pp. 107–26 in this volume).

Such affirmations are not always subversive. Processions and devil dances may still be used to assert official claims to power and authority. Seven hundred and fifty members of the Peruvian army have begun to dance the Diablada in Puno, Peru, partly as a way of claiming the rights of Peru itself to a diablo that in the name of national self-interest Bolivia is attempting to deny them (see Rubio, pp. 50–61 in this volume). It is often in and through such formal or officially sanctioned fiestas that devils intervene from below, or from outside the privileged centre, to manifest their own concepts of identity, which are often local, hybrid, stabilizing yet also subtly destabilizing of the institutional norm.

We have elsewhere in this volume described this as a function of the festive devil's capacity, in systems of popular production, to establish alternative forms of governance within the official narrative (see, for instance, Marino and Harris in this volume). The primary point to be made here, however, is that religion is not merely the blindly subverted, unaware progenitor of popular festive subversion. The symbiosis between religion and popular 'para-liturgies' sets the stage for the festive devil's dance. As described by Enrique Lamadrid in this volume: 'Despite all of its evangelical zeal, Christianity most successfully replicates itself not through the formal teaching of doctrine and sacrament, but rather through oral stories and parables, ritual performance and the colourful and captivating para-liturgies of folk Catholicism' (p. 273 in this volume).

Abercrombie further defines the 'dual nature' of the pageantry that empowers the 'dark forces' in the 'arena' established by nominally Christian festive settings:

> Devotees routinely engage in a variety of magical practices—coded as 'Indian'—in the context of Bolivia's miracle-saint shrines. [. . .] Yet these forces—and practices—are intelligible only through their articulation with the Christian powers, and more canonically Christian practices, that

domesticate them in a cosmological struggle [. . .]. It is this dual nature of pilgrimage pageantry that makes it a favoured arena for working on the vexed issue of national identity (p. 71 in this volume).

Locally organized festivals further complicate issues of 'national identity', both with reference to the subversion of ritual occasions and the relationship of the local community to the larger national entity. One of the striking features of the fiestas described throughout Part Two of this volume is the degree to which the occasion for the appearance of festive devils is most often provided by the liturgical calendar of the Catholic Church. Saints' Day processions, the Feast of Corpus Christi, pre-Lenten Carnival and the celebrations of Holy Week provide many of the venues in which festive devils perform.

Within this context, the organizing community, primarily local, emerges in a way that is—as has already been affirmed—at once traditional and entirely modern. A world that has grown increasingly transnational and global, challenging the notion of 'nationhood', has simultaneously become more conscious of the power of the local, privileging and encouraging the reclamation of real and mythically imagined ancestral heritages (see Gilroy 2004; Ashcroft 2009). This process facilitates what Abercrombie calls finding 'the Indian within' or promotes the celebration of African legacies, as in Rojas' Dance of the Devil or the Umbanda, Condomblé and Orisha festivals described by Ligiéro, Riggio and Gibbons and others in this volume. Thus, contemporary performance serves the purposes of mediation and subtle transformation, incorporating ancestral legacies and encompassing participants and observers alike within the central circle—all as a by-product of celebrating and having a good time within the community.

The process of affirming identity within the construct of the local community brings together festive traditions that appear in different 'regions' of this volume. Fiet's description of *vejigantes*, thus, may be seen in the context of festive-devil performances in the Andes, where Saint's Days serve as a major site of festivity, as well as in comparison with Harris' analysis of Holy Week celebrations in the Dominican Republic. (Indeed, Harris in this volume makes the comparison with the *vejigantes* of Loiza, about which he has himself elsewhere written. See Harris 2001.) Compare, for instance, the devil dances described by Anita Gonzalez in the states of Oaxaca and Guerrero on the Pacific coast of Mexico with those discussed by Marino in Ocumare on the southern Caribbean coast of Venezuela. Both events take place in remote regions; both manifest Afro-descendant communal identities.

According to Gonzalez:

MATTERS OF THE SPIRIT | 331

These two Mexican states have always been separated from administrative governing bodies in central Mexico by a series of high mountains. The mountains are difficult to cross. They make travel and communication between the country's capital and the coastal areas difficult. As a result, the coastal region has always been considered a remote and dangerous area populated by renegades. It is viewed as an escape zone for rebels (p. 258 in this volume).

Similarly, Ocumare is remote from the industrial areas of Venezuela, effectively marginalized from the centres of power. Though marginal cultures often play symbolically central roles in what Benito Irady in this volume calls the 'sense of belonging to a homeland', the *cofradías* that organize the Corpus Christi fiesta in Ocumare claim local power and help to affirm diasporic African ancestral identities within the community. In this sense, Gonzalez's work echoes that of Marino. However, these comparable fiestas differ in relationship to the religious occasions on which they occur.

The Ocumare devil's dance occurs in the Feast of Corpus Christi, during which, as Marino defines it, the 'metanarrative' leads the dancing devils finally to apparent submission to the authority of the Church. The religious occasion provides the opportunity for a community to assert its own power indirectly and obliquely:

In many ways, the dance continues to affirm the act of submission to the symbol of Christ in the Sacrament, but who and what this body of Christ represents, and how the Sacrament is, or is not, symbolically adhered to the Church's disreputable past remain contested ground. It's also the case that many devotees today join these events in order to regenerate Afro- and Indigenous-centred cultural and spiritual integrity that this scenario of conversion ostensibly sought to eliminate (p. 251 in this volume).

The syncretic and assimilative process allows a community to pay homage and respect to its past through the implicit doubling of the 'body' of Christ with the submerged 'body' of the community itself. The local, grassroots organizing and owning of the event empower the community while also engaging them respectfully in the ceremony of the Church. Though subversive, the Ocumare fiesta celebrates the ancestral, accepts the 'black stain' on the moon associated with the origins of the Feast of Corpus Christi (see Marino "The Devil's Turn" in this volume), and manifests communal identity through organization and a ritualized process of performance (also identified by Irady, as quoted earlier in this essay).

Gonzalez describes a similar affirmation of localized communal identity on Mexico's western Costa Chica (pp. 253–69 in this volume). However, in the dances she describes the two individual figures of Pancho and his disorderly wife Minga manifest a very different set of identities associated with aggressive disorder in the Pacific coastal Mexican states of Oaxaca and Guerrero. These manifestations do subvert subordination into power. However, the dancers in Ocumare dance together, with precise cross-over steps that regulate the rhythm of their performance. Though clearly directed and choreographed, the dances submerge the individual within the communal. It is true that there is a dance master in the Ocumare, Venezuela, Corpus Christi dance and that the Mexican Pancho does lead a group of dancers whose steps are synchronized. Nevertheless, Pancho is an aggressive individual who establishes power in terms of 'virility' that might recall the whip-cracking warrior Jab Jabs or transgressive Jab Molassi of Trinidad Carnival (see Riggio and Gibbons in this volume) or the whip-cracking, Judas-burning Cachúas of the Holy Week celebrations in the Dominican Republic (see Harris in this volume) more than the Corpus Christi devil dancers of Ocumare.

> Within the Afro-Mexican devil dance, devil disguise allows Mexican coastal residents to act out theatrical scenarios that include aggressive attacks, public whippings, sexual overtures and other disreputable acts. These black dance artists recreate terrifying scenarios of subordination and control in order to demonstrate the ongoing virility of Afro-Mexican culture (Gonzalez, p. 255 in this volume).

Moreover, Pancho performs not only resistance but also Afro-complicity, as one of the 'metaphoric ideas' he 'encapsulates' is that of the 'vicious overseer'.[9] Pancho has options and choices of character not relevant to the Ocumare Corpus Christi dancers. In non-devil dances, he can, for instance, assume the character of a wealthy rancher. When he dances the devil dance, however, he does assume power from below. His attire and demeanour is of the 'lower class' but his power is invested not so much in a performed sense of community as in his claim to 'authority' and 'self-sufficiency': 'Even though he is a poor man, he has a sector of dancers beneath him whom he controls; and his control is total and unforgiving. As a disempowered individual he maintains authority within his community. This aspect of Devil Dance performance reaffirms an ideal of self-sufficiency within a broader landscape of political impotency' (Gonzalez, p. 256 in this volume).

The ritual of the occasion in tandem with the character of the region distinguishes these two Afro-based devil dances. Pancho does not appear alone. He is accompanied by his cross-dressing wife Minga (played by a man) who brings into discussion questions of gender as well as cultural identity that might link Gonzalez's analysis with that of Paolo Vignolo who describes the entry of a Diabla as an aggressively uninvited companion for King Diablo in the Carnival of Riosucio, Colombia.

Minga is both grotesquely seductive and monstrously controlling. Like the Riosucio Diabla, 'she' is, among other things, a companion for the male Diablo. Together, these female devil figures raise issues of gender representation within carnivalized celebrations. In some instances (as described by Abercrombie in this volume), dark, seductive female bodies are imagined within the European Christian construct as demonic temptations, at times to be resisted, at other times to be yielded to and then discarded in ways that echo horrifying colonial realities.

However, the Riosucio Diabla, like the Jamettes (those who live 'beyond the boundaries') of Trinidad, who helped to wrest Trinidad Carnival from the control of the creolized French Catholics in the late nineteenth century, is an emblem of empowerment rather than victimization. She belongs to those at the margins of the public sphere (street artisans as well as hoodlums and prostitutes) and embodies urban power, in opposition to the attempts to generate an 'Indian carnival' in the rural space: 'The Diabla, built and wheeled through the streets in a procession by a group of persons at the margins of the public sphere became a symbol of recovery/ empowerment and participation for city dwellers. In contrast to other processes of heritage promotion related to this festivity, such as the attempts to generate an 'Indian carnival' in the rural space similar to the Carnaval del Diablo, or Devil's Carnival, the appearance of the *Diabla* in the town's public space has signified a successful exercise in active citizenship, arising from its reclaiming of a right to festive performance' (Vignolo, pp. 338–54 in this volume).

There is no doubt that the issues of reclamation, 'active citizenship' and rights that Vignolo examines have both political and economic significance. However, they are in essence metaphysical. They frequently bear on one of the distinctions that has been implied throughout this analysis but not precisely defined: that between urban and rural fiestas. In the context of syncretized festivities in the Americas, where the strong maternal-Earth presence of the Pachamama may be represented by a Christian Virgin, such as the Virgin of Candelaria, the Diabla exemplifies ways in which the female power associated with the Earth in rural and agrarian festivities and mythologies may in a different form be asserted in an urban context, even when that challenges rural traditions.[10]

Often, in costume as well as music, dance and festive styles, the urban manifestations of both male and female devils modernize and complicate festive forms.[11] Such modernization is characteristic of other festive events in differing ways, as, for instance, in the female figure of Pomba-Gira in Brazilian Afro-based celebrations: 'There are few images of this deity as a black woman. In the ritual of the People of the Street, Eshu and Pomba-Gira recreate a ballroom in the yard, where they dance entwined and change partners according to their temperaments and musical tastes, which range from samba, bolero and tango rhythms to other lesser-known forms of music (Ligiéro, p. 163 in this volume). Rejected by some as inauthentic, the modernizing of the fiesta in an urban setting provides, according to Ligiéro, a way of sustaining both the culture and the religions of Africa for contemporary Brazilian youths:

> The Eshus are also associated with the so-called *malandros*, typical characters in Brazilian culture. The best known of such characters is Zé Pelintra, from Lapa district, in Rio de Janeiro, a sort of symbol of the bohemian behaviour of men who dwelt between the hills and the city, where radio and theatre artists could be found in the casinos and dancing houses playing the tango and the samba in the early twentieth century (p. 162 in this volume).

As described by Lamadrid in this volume and discussed by Vignolo in the essay that concludes this book, casinos have provided modern venues for devil appearances throughout the southwestern United States. However, the intrusion of the modern into the traditional or, more aptly, the appropriation within a modern setting of traditional devil figures is most clearly illustrated in this volume by Rachel Bowditch's study of the annual Burning Man phenomenon in Nevada, an appropriation that intriguingly re-routes the subversive path of the festive devil, shifting the notion of worship into the metaphorical contexts of consumerism which may function as if it were a religion but which finally reflects the absence of a sustaining faith.[12]

Festive devils may gamble, drink, carouse and manifest their power by flamboyantly thumbing their noses or, more often, farting in the face of middle-class respectability and its ethics-based code of morality. But one significant aspect of their power particularly implicated in the history of the devil is their intelligence, their scepticism and their link to language. As resisters, festive devils frequently boast of their prowess in powerful speeches or sing of them in chants (as in the case of the Jab Jabs or other characters in Trinidad carnival). Vignolo makes the case for their relationship to language: 'In a celebration that is, above all, a feast of the word, where the lyrical, critical and satirical potential of language is celebrated, *matachines* and poets compete with one another, in verses and stanzas, so that their Satan will soon re-emerge among his followers' (p. 24 in this volume).

Festive devils are not only wily, subversive and shape-shifting tricksters. They are also often intelligent sceptics[13] and at times well-bred, cultured gentlemen (as in the case of the gownmen in Trinidad). In this sense, along with associations with figures in many other religions, they echo the role of Lucifer in the drama and mythology of late mediaeval Europe. Particularly in the fifteenth century—and echoed throughout the Protestant Reformation of the sixteenth century—performing devils styled themselves as both intelligent and sophisticated,[14] reflecting a concept of intelligence that was associated with *scientia* rather than *sapientia*, that is, with logic and scientific reasoning rather than the received wisdom embodied in Lady Sapientia who was at times identified directly with the Virgin Mary herself.[15] An orthodox Christianity that could reject doctrines that it regarded as gnostic, partly for encouraging sceptical reasoning, favoured wisdom over scientific logic.

The wit and sceptical intelligence that are among the festive devil's strongest features also quintessentially define the opposition to the *hierarchy* of received wisdom. This moves the character beyond the European parameters, allying them with figures such as the African Eshu whose scepticism, along with playfulness, is at once intelligent and subversive. The devil's identification with language and ability to use words effectively derive from and reflect the breadth of this character's ancestry and its reach. Moreover, that language—which is sometimes monolingual and easily understandable and at other times an imaginative invention of chants and sounds from varied linguistic sources (as in the Black Indian masquerades of Trinidad)—not only characterizes some of the festive devils in the Americas but also has broader currency linked to the survival strategies of colonial subjects. As West Indian poet and playwright Derek Walcott expressed it in his Nobel Prize Laureate acceptance speech:

> Deprived of their original language, the captured and indentured tribes create their own, accreting and secreting fragments of an old, an epic vocabulary, from Asia and from Africa, but to an ancestral [...] rhythm in the blood that cannot be subdued by slavery or indenture [...]. The stripped man is driven back to that self-astonishing, elemental force, his mind (1992).

The devil as wild creature—as bestial, animalistic, bearing horns, carrying pitchforks, burning in a pit of fire or claiming destructive fire as his own element—is a familiar figure who recurs throughout the images and festivities chronicled in this book. Festive devils also have props, such as accompanying serpents, that Christians see as infernal but that in other mythologies and religions signify fertility and creative life forces. The sacrificial devil, who in Vignolo's terms at times has a Via Crucis of his own, paralleling the Passion of Christ with the 'passion of the burning fire pit', embodies the mourning, often tragic elements of life in the Americas. But the festive devil who taunts listeners into thinking or who tricks them with the nuances of language, or charms them with his or her sophistication and beauty is an equally powerful reminder of the complex and far-reaching spiritual as well as political and economic implications of the festive-devil performances. Unlike ex-president Bush, the festive devil does 'do nuance', and those nuances follow this creature on the wandering paths of the Americas.

Notes

1   Manichaeism and Manichaeanism are variants of the same term.

2   'Manichaeism' in *New Advent: Catholic Encyclopedia* (available at: http://www.-newadvent.org/cathen/09591a.htm; last accessed on 7 February 2015).

3   Manichaeism was rejected essentially as a Gnostic religion, akin to many other heresies. And it has, of course, a complex history. The important point for the analysis of the festive devil is that, for orthodox Christianity, evil is not a separate cosmological force but generated through rebellion against the supreme good.

4   Neither Hindu nor Yoruba cosmology allows for 'destruction' as a concept in itself, since the universe is perpetual and all is incorporated into the ongoing balance of universal forces. Nothing can be 'destroyed'. Even using a term like 'destruction' or finding analogues to 'devils' in theologies that allow for neither shows the degree to which Christianity, in Raviji's terms, 'bedevils' other theologies.

5   In Trinidad, where the Indo-descended population outnumbers all others (roughly 41 per cent of the population), there is a significant Muslim as well as Hindu presence. And, of course, Islam has been present throughout the Americas, as have other Asian religions. But in this volume, it is the Hindu perspective that has so far informed our study, primarily in reference to Trinidad (see Milla Riggio and Rawle Gibbons, pp. 189–220 in this volume).

6   In the descriptions that follow, I am once again indebted to Rawle Gibbons and Raviji, my co-authors of the essay in this volume.

7   In comparison, 'From the Yoruba point of view, the "ajogun" aspect of existence (disaster, tragedy, wanton destruction) manifests an absence of balance in some other aspect or condition (individual, social environment, etc.) [...whereas] Eshu's mischief [. . .] reflects man's own folly and self-delusion, especially at critical moments of choice' (Gibbons, personal correspondence 2014).

8   Those who spread Christianity through Northern Europe were urged in early Christian Roman imperial edicts specifically to find and use locations sacred to the people of each region in establishing their Christian places of worship, thus making it easier for the local people to accept the sites as sacred. The African practice throughout the Americas (echoed also in indigenous religious ceremonies) of disguising orishas or other sacred figures behind the masks of Christian saints, thus paying homage simultaneously to two different religions, turns this practice upside down and is allied with the power and presence of festive devils in the Americas.

9   Harris in this volume also discusses the notion of Afro-complicity, as reflected in festive devil performances in the Dominican Republic, linking it to the whipping of the Cachúas in Holy Week processions in Cabral (pp. 127–50 in this volume).

10 Such coded and symbolical uses of gender within the festive context have broader religious implications as well, particularly in terms of the history of authority and control that in the Catholic Church was for so long—and, to a large extent, still is—dominated by men.

11 To 'modernize' in this sense means, generally, either to be more aggressively satirical or to engage performers in modern, often Latinized, dances which have a greater appeal to adolescents and young adults than some more traditional performance modes. This is not to say, however, that 'urban' representations of the female are more powerful than rural, where the maternal-Earth presence is often overwhelming. Representations of authority and submission are complicated in various festive forms, the precise analysis of which is beyond the scope of this essay.

12 It is not that there are no powerful manifestations of spiritual awakening or forms both of parodic and serious reverence present in Burning Man, though not directly associated with the Devil. The final burning event of the annual gathering is of a temple built in Black Rock City, behind the Man, which is burnt on Sunday night in a much more solemn ceremony than the burning of the Man the previous night and which, through the week, is a centre for personal reveries and meditations (see Bowditch 2010: 223–44) And, of course, consumerism and economics do play a significant role in the manifestations of festive devils elsewhere (see Vignolo, 'Who Owns the Devil?' in this volume).

13 In the annual Fiesta del Virgen del Carmen in the Andean village of Paucartamba, Peru, the *comparsa* that represents devils among the festival's presenters includes many teachers, educators and intellectuals.

14 See, for example, Lucifer in *The Play of Wisdom* (Riggio 1998). A clear echo of this demonic figure is heard and seen in William Shakespeare's development of the intelligent 'demi-devil' Iago in *Othello*, where the demonic is identified directly with the accumulation of money ('Put money in the purse') and, thus, with the nascent growth of a capital-driven economy.

15 The Sapiential Virgin, always seated with a book, was known as the Virgin of Wisdom. For information on this aspect of learning and of the Devil's link to knowledge and to reasoned logic, as well as his disguising of himself as a gentlemen, see Riggio (1998).

Who Owns the Devil?

PAOLO VIGNOLO

Relations between Bolivia and Peru are already strained due to the tension between Presidents Evo Morales and Alan García, but now the Devil has stepped in. Bolivia has threatened to sue Peru in the International Court of Justice to defend its cultural rights to the traditional *Diablada*, or Devil's Dance, performed at the Oruro Carnival, which Peru also claims as its own. The controversy arose at the Miss Universe pageant on Aug. 23 where, according to [the Bolivian newspaper] *Opinión*, Peruvian contestant Karen Schwarz wore the traditional devil's outfit.[1]

News of the dispute between Peru and Bolivia reached us while we were holding our first workshop dedicated to festive devils of the Americas during the Seventh Hemispheric Encounter on Performance and Politics, which took place in Bogotá in 2009. The debate held at that Encounter among the members of our research group 'Play, Fiesta and Power' was serious and at the same time humorous, and it was the seed that gave life to this collective book.

Where does he come from, this devil whose attire inspires so much enthusiasm and yet sows so much discord in the Andean Altiplano? What economic system of production, exchange, and consumption does the Diablada belong to? What interests lie behind the border disputes between the two South American governments? Who can claim property rights over the devil himself? The thread that ties these queries together is the ambivalent relationship between festive devils and an expanding capitalist modernity.

The Production of the Devil

Where does the Oruro devil come from? In *The Devil and Commodity Fetishism in South America*, Michael Taussig poses the problem within two broader research questions: 'What is the relationship between the image of the devil and capitalist development?' and 'What contradictions in social experience does the spirit of evil mediate?' (1980: xii) His argument is that 'devil-beliefs' are intensified along the borders of capitalist expansion, or more specifically, along the edges of that particular form of capitalist production that characterizes mining and monoculture as established at the time of the Spanish conquest and which to this day marks the history of the Americas.

In other words, the devil isn't so much an expression of precapitalist societies, as is maintained implicitly or explicitly in many studies of folklore, but, rather, an expression of resistance, resilience and adaptation to the imposition of a capitalist mode of production. Devils emerge and are socially reproduced in the liminal condition of proletarianization, the brutal integration of indigenous, African and mestizo peoples to conditions of labour exploitation typical of the mode of production brought to the New World by Europeans. The devil becomes a mediator between processes of accumulation that are typical of modernity/coloniality (Quijano 1992; Mignolo 1995: 39), and forms of 'moral economy' (Thompson 1971) that are alien to the logic of *Homo economicus* and to governing techniques typical of liberalism and neoliberalism. 'The fetishization of evil, in the image of the devil, is an image which mediates the conflict between precapitalist and capitalist modes of objectivizing the human condition' (Taussig 1980: *xii*).

Many of the studies compiled in this volume take this interpretation as a starting point in one way or another. From the relationship established by miners in Bolivia and Peru with a devilish image called El Tío de la Mina, to the tribute paid to the devil by the inhabitants of Riosucio in Colombia and the steel drum bands of Trinidad whose instruments were originally made from recycled oil barrels, there is ample evidence of the relationship between the presence of devils and extractive industries. Taussig's work comparing the Oruro region to the Alto Cauca in Colombia's Pacific region also leads us take a comparative perspective in relation to sugar plantations on the Venezuelan coast, in Puerto Rico, and in the Dominican Republic, as well as to the Pacific coastal regions of Mexico and Peru, marked as they are by analogous labour conditions and surprisingly similar representations of the devil.

As a research group, however, we are interested in focusing not so much on the already widely studied sphere of the demonic in general, but more specifically on the devil as a character in celebrations and festivals.[2] The emphasis on a reading of the phenomena through the lens of performance studies and through the theories and practices of the fiesta provide a fruitful approach to the debate. Taussig's intuition of seeing the devil as an expression of the proletarianization process in relation to *campesinos* and miners displaced from their means of subsistence and thrown into the vertigo of the capitalist machine remains inspiring, but our approach to the problem provides an unprecedented heuristic potential to work at the intersection of social liminality and the ritual liminality of the fiesta.

As I point out in my contribution in this volume about the Carnaval of Riosucio, there is no doubt that telluric and chthonian powers evoked in this celebration of the devil are intimately connected with mining production in nearby Marmato. The underlying tensions, sometimes dating back to colonial times, have produced a treacherous armed conflict, the strong repression of trade union activity, and a struggle over land and mining rights. The local population, which depends for its livelihood on landowners and mining companies, re-enacts ancient rituals connected with fertility cults and creates new ritualistic practices as an expression of the traumatic changes they have experienced after the imposition of new economic practices that uprooted existing social relations.

In Riosucio, both the Indian Carnival and the Carnival de la Diabla are examples of invented tradition, 'a set of practices, normally governed by overtly or tacitly accepted rules and of a ritual or symbolic nature' (Hobsbawm and Ranger 1983: 8). This set of reiterated practices, which Richard Schechner calls 'twice behaved behaviors', brings the staging of competing representations of tradition into the public sphere (Schechner 2002; Taylor 2008). In Foucauldian terms, these devices are endowed with a certain degree of rationality, which answers to an emergency or a crisis (Castro Gómez 2011), the growing struggle over land in the case of the Indian Carnival, and the exclusion of marginalized urban sectors in the case of the Diabla. New collective subjectivities are forged out of these practices, not the other way around. It is through the recovery of traditional dances, music, and rituals in rural areas, for example, that a growing number of campesinos have begun to identify with what is considered indigenous.

The festive devil does not emerge so much as a subject of historical events as he does as their symptom, in Warburg's sense of the term (Didi-Huberman 2002). Beyond seeing the devil as an agent of capitalism (whether harmful or benign), or celebrating him/her as an expression of resistance, our interest lies in the exploration of that complex of festive practices (gestural, corporal, iconic, oral, musical . . .), which in specific local contexts bring about the creation of this extraordinary character. The mobilization of hundreds of musicians, dancers, mask makers, costume tailors, clergy, confraternity members, oral historians and musicians, to name a few of those involved in the production of festivals, shows that while the power of these performances does stem to some extent from what the devil does, it stems even more from what people do as they deal with the devil.

For example, in reference to the dancing devils of Ocumare, on the Caribbean coast of Venezuela, Angela Marino writes:

> At first glance, the metanarrative of the event suggests that those playing the role of devils surrender unconditionally to the Church. From this perspective, the dance affirms submission to the authority of the Church, despite the Church's disreputable past and the present inclination of the archdiocese to censor the dance. However, this reading obscures the complexity of a practice that opens up a space—kinaesthetically, sociopolitically

and symbolically—for reconstituting the collective power of the devils out-side of, and also alongside, the Church (pp. 249–50 in this volume).

Marino's analysis allows us to understand the approach to asymmetric power relations and the unequal application of social prerogatives that is inherent to the fiesta, allowing the moral dichotomies upon which the pre-established order is founded to be disrupted through what she calls 'the Devil's turn'. As an embodied and also socially produced act, the devil's turn refers to a transformation of the devils from that which is purged into a protector of the community, or at least the capability to shift who defines the boundaries of the community. Therefore the devil's turn is a force of collective power, one that has proven extremely effective at disarming a his-tory of violence and demonization. This 'devil's turn' functions as a combinatorial play that, through multiple transgressions, inversions, and subversions, opens up new and unexpected thresholds of meaning and potential routes to emancipation or escape from established structures.

Only by understanding the Diablada in the broader context of the Andean festive system is it possible to gain an awareness of what lies behind the dispute around the Miss Universe diabla costume. Miguel Rubio reminds us that the Diablada is not exclusive to Oruro:

It has been in existence throughout the Altiplano region where Peru and Bolivia meet around Lake Titicaca since pre-Hispanic times, so we can say that it predates the current territorial configurations of both countries. [. . .] According to the Quechua and Aymara cosmogonies, the Festival of the Virgin of Candelaria, or Mamita Kanticha, is deeply linked to the agri-cultural cycles of planting and harvesting, and its purpose is to serve as an offering to Pachamama, the Earth Mother. As a consequence of the post-colonial cultural juxtaposition, it is the Virgin of Candelaria who intercedes with natural forces, as she is the Christian and mestiza representation of the Virgin and of Pachamama (p. 52 in this volume).

Thomas Abercrombie complicates and provides a nuanced reading of the varied relationships different social sectors establish with the image of the devil. As he makes clear from the very beginning of his chapter, the devil image can in no way be reduced to a simple mediator for recently proletarianized sectors facing exogenous forces of production: 'Every year during Carnival in Oruro, Bolivia, the city's elites forgo their usual disdain for the customs, superstitions, and dress of indigenous peoples and the poor in order to dance in the streets in "Indian" attire, performing "indigenous" dramas in a complex spectacle that includes dancers of both sexes' (1992: 279). He describes a 'postcolonial paradox', the many contradictions and ambivalences of which include members of the white elite who self-identify as 'decent people' and at carnival time engage with their own 'Indian within'; mestizo-cholo[3] urban sectors attempting to rescue an alleged cultural authenticity of their indigenous roots; and Aymara or Quechua *campesinos* who emulate the manners of the model patriotic citizen (ibid.: 280).

Abercrombie also offers us assistance in understanding the dispute over the devil costume worn by Karen Schwarz:

[M]ore than any other indicator in Bolivia, it is a person's dress that marks ethnicity and social class. 'Traditional Indian dress' covers a wide variety of 'fashion mandates' that distinguish members of different ethnic groups from others. None of these, however, reflect pre-Columbian styles of dress. Since the Conquest, Spanish influence (at times imposed by decree) has meant that 'indigenous dress' has loosely conformed to urban styles of previous eras' (1992: 290).

Thus we see that the social distinction between *campesinos* and urban dwellers, between criollos (Spanish-descended Latin Americans), mestizos and Indians, between classes, ethnic groups and generations depends greatly on the style of dress. The white creole (*criollo*) elites dress up as Asku with homemade costumes during Carnival, while middle-class mestizo sectors seek out the 'primitive' and 'indigenous' look by appropriating the *pollera* costume (whose broad pleated skirt, however, is associated with urban cholos). *Campesinos*, in turn, 'civilize' themselves when entering the city by camouflaging their origins with cosmopolitan and western industrial production attire, setting aside the 'traditional' clothing that distinguishes them from other ethnic groups.

Style of dress also plays a crucial role in the construction of gender. As Judith Butler asks: 'How are the contours of the body clearly marked as the taken-for-granted ground or surface upon which gender significations are inscribed, a mere facticity devoid of value, prior to significance?' (1990: 129). This happens in the context of beauty pageants, for example, where behavioural norms, quantifiable standards, 'certificates of quality' with regard to women's physical and social position are established. If the reason for the quarrel between Peru and Bolivia is seemingly a folkloric costume, this is but a pretext for a symbolic struggle to control the female body. Two state apparatuses are disputing their foundational fictions (Sommer 1991) in order to acquire the spoils of victory in the form of a garment worn on a woman's body reduced to a battlefield.

Gambling with the Devil

Analysing the fiesta as a rhetorical and material device allows us to understand social confrontations that mark race, class and gender relations, modes of production and geographies of dwelling based on its practices in constant metamorphosis. The festive devil emerges onto this stage from a backdrop of sacred colonial mysteries, under the control of ecclesiastic authorities, to assume his proper role as protagonist of the social drama in the Americas.

All the devil figures studied in this book have one thing in common. Their mystical or historical origins are in rituals associated with non-capitalist societies. As José Morales Serruto and Ana Isabel Morales Aguirre explain, the Diablada has evolved from an event for pleading and expressing gratitude to Pachamama for good harvests. It dates back to many years before the arrival of the Spanish. In fact, more important than the presence of the devil is that of El Tío, [also known as] El Marcari or Huywiri, master of underground riches in Aymara mythology (Rubio, pp. 57–8 in this volume). This is also true with regard to the figure of the *palhaço* (clown) in the Folia de Reies (Three Kings Festival) of northeastern Brazil, the town crier of Lima's black carnival, Port of Spain's Bookman, the *vejigantes* of Loiza, Puerto Rico, and Minga and Pancho of Mexico's Costa Chica, to mention just a few of the cases presented in this volume.

The modern Mephistopheles is an analogous phenomenon in the traditions of Western Christianity. He 'who eternally wills evil and eternally does good' is a direct descendant of diabolical figures who animated medieval Christian celebrations. Moreover, in Goethe's *Faust*, the devil functions as the demiurge of nascent capitalism. He is not just any devil, though, but a festive devil. In Part II, Act I of the tragedy, the emperor, surrounded by his court, eagerly awaits the coming carnival. One after the other, his chancellor, military commander, and treasurer burst onto the scene, bringing ill-fated news: chaos, corruption and injustice prevail across the empire. There is devastation and fratricidal war everywhere, anarchy is growing and the imperial coffers are empty. Finally, the steward arrives and announces that even the store of wine is exhausted.

At a loss for what to do, the Emperor seeks the advice of the juggler, that is, Mephistopheles disguised as the juggler. In a parody of the wedding at Cana, where Jesus turned water into wine so that the wedding could be properly celebrated, Mephistopheles performs a miracle. He has a brilliant solution to offer the Emperor: The earth holds immense treasures, he says, vestiges of past splendours, and all of it belongs to him by imperial decree. One need not, however, excavate these treasures, for that would require too much effort. It should suffice to produce a 'paper worth gold or pearls', a paper whose warranty lies upon the riches buried beneath his territorial holdings. This is the invention of paper money, of the *Zauberblätter*, that is: charmed notes, easy money—easy because it is produced not by the sweat of the brow with which man must earn his living, charmed because it is the fruit of magic, of a demonic spell. Capitalism, it turns out, is the work of a devil, one who dressed for a festival mortgages the entrails of the earth, Hell itself, in exchange for man's soul. This is a myth deeply rooted in the Western imaginary, whose poetic power exerts its enchantment on American soil. Taussig notes:

> Of its plethora of interconnected and often contradictory meanings, the devil contract is outstanding in this regard: man's soul cannot be bought or sold, yet under certain historical conditions mankind is threatened by this mode of exchange as a way to make a livelihood. In recounting this fable of the devil, the righteous man confronts the struggle of good and evil market economies. The individual is dislocated from the community. Wealth exists alongside crushing poverty. Economic laws triumph over ethical ones. Production, not man, is the aim of the economy, and commodities rule their creators (1980: p. *xii*).

If we turn our attention from the sphere of production to that of exchange, we can point to other festive embodiments of Mephistopheles, associated in this sense with trafficking and gambling rather than mines or plantations. Zeca Ligiéro, for example, tells us that divinities of African origin such as Eshu are incorporated into the image of the *malandro*, a characteristic figure in early twentieth century of Rio de Janeiro. He frequents dance halls and casinos leading a bohemian life on the porous border between crime and lawfulness. ' . . . lord of the crossroads, the master of time and space, the master of communication. He embodies all of human life in its Eshu aspects, for he not only governs the genitals but, in relationship to economic concerns, he is also the patron of those who want to accumulate energy in the form of money' (Ligiéro, p. 159 in this volume). The *malandro* is the expression of a rapidly accelerating capitalism where the Faustian image of a pact with the devil accounts for uninhibited lifestyles and consumption, and the magical enrichment of a new social class whose power depends upon rackets, questionable doings and easy money.

There is a similar figure in the southwestern United States, where, according to Enrique Lamadrid, since the 1920s, the emergence of an elegant and seductive dancing devil is directly related to the penetration of the market economy as opposed to moral economies embodied in culture, tradition and communitarianism (Scott 1976, quoted by Lamadrid in this volume). The perception of *la dolce vita* associated with gambling and open sensuality as a 'demonic pursuit that devalues the common good and subverts the moral economy' (p. 283 in this volume) picks up steam in the late twentieth century, when impoverished Indian reservations of the region experience

WHO OWNS THE DEVIL? | 345

an unexpected bonanza with the establishment of Las Vegas–style casinos. Once again, the Trickster of New Mexico's indigenous mythology, which mobilizes a person's psychic energy and channels it into the economic sphere, is re-embodied in the swindler devil, the conjuror devil, the gambler devil, who offers inequitable exchange, trafficking in souls for material rewards, and the merger of moral and commercial spheres (Brown 1959: 220). 'The first Devil stories appear in New Mexico along with arrival of Catholicism in the autumn of 1598,' writes Lamadrid (p. 295 in this volume). By the fall of 1998, after four centuries and many miracles and anti-miracles, the descendants of the Spanish-Mexican colonizers secure their fortune and cultural survival in the simultaneously real and metaphoric space of the Indian casino, where the difference between luck and fate is mediated by the fallen angel, the Devil in person.

The festive devil's habitat may change, but not his habits. The warmth of community festivities with musically induced euphoria, alcohol fumes, and bodies united in a vertigo of dance no longer appeal to him. Nor does the 'frigid carnival' of Eco's emphatic intellectual irony, proposed as the only antidote to the abuse of power. Rather, he is at ease now in the sterile, perpetually air conditioned fiesta of the casino under video surveillance, where a lonely crowd wanders amid coin-devouring slot machines and ubiquitous advertising, in search of the obscene enchantment of commodities.

Stories of festive devils of the Americas tell us of capitalism's unstoppable penetration into spaces previously closed off to the market economy. Devils disguised as jugglers or clowns invent paper money, signalling the transition from the Middle Ages to modernity. Other street-smart and seductive devils engage in illicit hustles at the margins of modernity. And a high-rolling devil at the roulette table, where betting is with plastic money, introduces us to a new era of finance capitalism. As Lamadrid reminds us: 'The metaphor of gambling was often used in reference to Wall Street, the 'satanic mills' where America's moral economy was ground to dust. Our national 'casino' is the stock market, where corporate greed and losing bets on the housing market caused the great financial meltdown of 2008–09' (pp. 295–6 in this volume).

Activists and artists of underground countercultures have been creatively appropriating this association. From the carnivalization of student protests in Chile, Mexico and Colombia to the performed citizenship of the *indignados* and the masked-hacker activism of Anonymous, as well as the Occupy Wall Street movement and its avatars all around the globe, varied contemporary personifications of the festive devil rebel against the infernal forces of finance and corporate capitalism.

In her research on Burning Man, Rachel Bowditch explains with great clarity how 'the concepts of "devil", "Satan", and "hell" acquire new meanings that become metaphors for the event's complex evolution from a grass roots countercultural *temporary autonomous zone* to a multimillion-dollar for-profit corporation' (pp. 299–316 in this volume). By virtue of the performative sale of Burning Man to the mega-corporation Helco, run by Papa Satan, the 1996 version of the festival was turned into a dramatic *mise-en-scéne* of its own inner contradictions. 'Participants were informed that Helco had recently acquired "Hell as part of a hostile takeover and was now about to merge with Heaven, creating the first cosmically integrated vertical marketing system"' (Harvey, quoted in Bowditch, p. 304 in this volume). In this case, though, the tensions between a devil who embodies both the malignant icon of finance capitalism and the totem of an utopian world independent of market logic are not felt by those at the lowest rungs of a production pyramid associated with extractive industries or agro-exports. Those affected belong to a middle class that is itself alienated and in search of a way out, or at least a respite from a system where commodification seems to dominate mind, body and soul.

In examining the theories of Mauss (1967), Bowditch reveals the paradox of the gifting and counter-gifting economy set in place exclusively in the liminal space of the fiesta. The more Burning Man attempts to present itself as a space liberated from the tyranny of commodity fetishism and the relentless expansion of marketing, the more it actually highlights the impossibility of escaping logo penetration and the power relations of late capitalist society. 'Originally, gift giving was an organic exchange of items of some value to the giver, but increasingly gifts are store-bought trinkets without value or meaning, ordered in mass quantity to be distributed ad hoc. [. . .] The gift becomes a fetish object that is inherently linked to commodification and the exchange of global capital' (Bowditch, p. 310 in this volume).

The desire for a renewed sense of community through a simulation of reciprocal gift giving ultimately exposes the profound mechanisms that characterize any construction of community. Roberto Esposito traces the etymology of this term and argues that 'From here it emerges that *communitas* is the totality of persons united not by "property" but precisely by an obligation or a debt; not by an "addition" but by a "substration": by a lack, a limit that is configured as an onus' (2010: 6) . Thus there is a double contradiction in Burning Man. A group of individuals set out to create *communitas* only to discover that they are more than ever a lonely multitude, dedicated to a frivolous and solipsistic fiesta where in contrast to the potlatch, 'the giver and the destroyer are one and the same' (Bowditch, p. 311 in this volume). And a *communitas* always comes together with *immunitas*, or immunity, intended as the bio-political defense of life through the incorporation of what menaces life itself. In Burning Man, this immunity turns out to be as fictitious as the sense of community. Despite the restricted access enforced by exorbitant registration fees, in the case of an accident such as one that occurred in 1996, the Sherriff's Department takes immediate control of the area, dispelling the anarchist and libertarian illusion of a Temporary Autonomous Zone (TAZ).

Beyond its spectacular nature and the originality of creative expression to which it gives rise, the massive collective exorcism is merely an act of ritual purification from the sins of consumer culture, an ablution on the shifting sands of counterculture, a tempting mirage of the devil in the desert. In the cultural panorama of the United States, Burning Man is to Christmas—that other huge potlatch dedicated to mass consumption—as Carnival is to Easter on the Catholic religious calendar. Paradoxically, it transgresses and at the same time ironically or comically reinforces established norms of the social drama (Eco: 1989). In this paradoxical sense, the expression 'Burning man is not for sale' is the most seductive slogan for marketing the event's commercial value.

The Devil's Heritage

The issue of borders between Peru and Bolivia may have generated the most discussion among our research group. How is it possible that in the name of old and new nationalisms, states assume the right to designate borders between the here and the beyond, between Earth, Heaven and Hell, or in this case between Kay Pacha, Uko Pacha and Hanan Pacha, the 'Three Worlds' of Andean cosmogony? What is at stake in the imposition of artificial limits on cultural phenomena that are inevitably transnational, nomadic and intimately linked to migratory movements, diasporas and displacements? We can say that this is an attempt to symbolically and materially take possession of the imaginary pertaining to festive devils. We see a contemporary variant of the old question of political control of the fiesta, or, to paraphrase the work of Enrique Gil Calvo (1991) and David Guss (2000), attempts to imbue the 'state of the fiesta' with the logic of the 'State fiesta'.

Jesuit anthropologist Xavier Albó sums up the August 2009 contretemps over the Diablada in this way:

> The only hindrance now in all of these celebrations shared by Oruro, Puno, and Iquique are the borders that make us feel different from each other and even enemies due to different economic and political interests, first polarizing Chile vs. Bolivia and Peru, and now Bolivia vs. Peru, with the presidents of the latter countries hurling epithets at each other. This polarization has proven to be more diabolic than the dancing devils, who in fact are rather seductive and endearing. Were it not for these tensions, we would obviously be happy to share this common historical, cultural, and religious

tradition that could do so much to bring western Bolivia together with southern Peru and northern Chile (2009: n.p.).

In the final analysis, we are facing a battle for the appropriation of tradition. But what are the practices, who are the actors, what are the strategies in this conflict?

We can begin by describing practices for appropriating festival heritage. Whether motivated by counter-hegemonic intentions, to uphold the status quo or for any other reason, anyone who wants to get gain access to the political as well as the economic potential of the fiesta must control the mechanisms of epistemological validation and the inter-generational transmission of the performative repertoire associated with the celebration. In her essay on the carnival of Tepoztlán, Mexico, Diana Taylor writes:

> The repertoire, this often underappreciated cultural repository, makes these resources of the past available for use over time, both through annual repetitions and in moments of crisis. Performances reactivate historical events and scenarios that provide contemporary solutions. They 'quote' and reinsert fragments of the past (what Schechner calls 'strips of behavior' [1985: 35]) to supply historical antecedents for present claims or practices. They also *make history* by using lessons and attitudes derived from previous experience to produce change in the present (2006: 72).

As Miguel Rubio notes, based on his experience as a man of the theatre, 'When the performer dances, tradition is renewed and interrogates the contemporary world' (personal communication).

Let us take, for example, the whip, a central element in many festive devil performances (the Jab Jabs of Trinidad, the Cachúas and Juás of the Dominican Republic, the Pachos and Mingas of Afro-Mexican tradition, and Puerto Rico's *vejigantes*, among others discussed in this book). Milla Cozart Riggio and Rawle Gibbons invite us to discern three levels of the phenomenon: social, mythical and cosmic. At the social level, 'Whipping was the regular form of punishment passed down from slave plantation to indentured estates to prisons, schools and, indeed, homes. The whip—in any of its forms—was thus a powerful symbol of authority and an instrument of fear' (Riggio and Gibbons, p. 197 in this volume). Max Harris adds:

> As devils, armed with whips, they represent 'the enslaver, the colonizer'. As cojos, they represent those abused by slavery. At the same time, as festive maskers, they are free to burlesque the oppressor. The whip is a means of exploitative torture and a sign of 'the submission, the suffering resistance [. . .] of the enslaved', but in the hands of the Cachúas it is also a sign of resistance and freedom (pp. 140-1 in this volume).

According to Harris, the performance of the Dominican Republic's festive devils would thus maintain a relationship with the atavistic memory of the overseer in slavery days as well as the much more recent memory of the Caliés, a popular name for the secret police of the 1930–61 Trujillo dictatorship: 'Under the circumstances, it is perhaps not surprising that the Cachúas' mutual whippings and their final immolation of the calié Judas seemed to me to bear witness less to festive freedom than to unresolved trauma' (p. 148 in this volume).

To reject these kinds of repertoires and privilege positivist historiographical attitudes and archives as the only authorized research resources prevents us from understanding these other forms of making history. Nevertheless, the point is not to claim a direct, univocal and transparent connection between gestural performance and past traumas as a certain essentializing folklorism would. What is of interest to us here is to examine 'strips of behavior' specific to the traditions relevant to particular historical moments and highlight their political and poetic relevance. In the words of Riggio and Gibbons, 'the chains with which an imp will restrain the king or other blue devil may not consciously symbolize enslavement but without question they evoke that aura in their performance. ' (p. 206 in this volume).

The 'auratic' nature (in the sense that Walter Benjamin applied to the term *auratisch*) of the antagonistic, seemingly contradictory relationship established in certain aesthetic experiences between an 'infinite remoteness' and an 'infinite proximity' leads us into the mythical level of the performative act.

As devils, then, the Cachúas represent abusive power, whether that of Roman or Jewish authorities in biblical times, plantation owners in the days of plantation slavery, or Trujillo and his collaborators during the dictatorship. As those who bear the cross, they represent all who follow Christ's example of suffering and resignation under slavery or any more recent forms of oppression and torture. With even greater dramatic power, they both conceal and expose the deep cultural scars of betrayal and complicity (Harris, p. 149 in this volume).

Similarly, the extraordinarily powerful stage production of *Los Santos Inocentes* (Innocent Saints) by Bogota's Mapa Teatro (2010) homes in on the paramilitary violence that has overtaken the Guapi region of Colombia's Pacific coast through a portrayal of the mythical violence of Herod's Massacre of the Innocents, transformed not only by the experience of slavery and the African diaspora but also by the festive rituals of the urban middle class. In both cases, the whipping of street devils points not only to Catholic mythology but also to what Ligiéro (in this volume) calls the driving sociocultural forces, centred in the powerful trio of drumming-singing-dancing, which provides the nerve centre for African performance traditions rooted in the sacred (p. 155 in this volume).

Lowell Fiet similarly taking up some of Gibbons' reflections on Trinidad, notes that the *vejigantes* of Loiza and Ponce in Puerto Rico become sacred intermediaries for maintaining contact with the world of the dead in African mythologies, where ancestral spirits are incorporated into earthly pleasures thorough the medium of trickster-devils functioning as substitutes or living surrogates (Roach 1996):

> Even if the identity, function and significance of the *vejigante* cannot be defined with absolute precision, it continues to serve as a metaphor for the encounter of conditions that coincide and interconnect in the search for possible transformations within the inequalities of the Afro–Puerto Rican experience: the past and the present, the ancestors and the living, Africa and the diaspora, slavery and freedom, the sacred and the secular, and the 'foreign' and the 'traditional' that 'interact' like 'a ray of light with a prism' (Fiet, p. 185 in this volume, quoting Rojo 1989: *xxvii*).

The festive devil thus reminds us of Benjamin's dialectical image of lightning, which grants us access to memories thought to be irretrievably lost, whose salvation can be consummated only in the performative act: 'The past can be seized only as an image which flashes up at the instant when it can be recognized and is never seen again' (1940: n.p.). This presents us with a third level for understanding the phenomenon, going beyond not only specific sociohistorical junctures but also great mythical meta-narratives. As Riggio and Gibbons argue: 'In this instance, the "devil" is not a horned, pitchforked infernal being, but a process of becoming, the outward climax to an inner drama—a manifestation . . . . There is another level, a shared ancestral cosmology' (p. 194 in this volume), in which through carnivalistic expression the Jab Jabs of Trinidad integrate deities such as the Yoruba Eshu, the Hindu Kali Ma, and the Christian Devil in personifications of disturbance and chaos that transcend the categories of good and evil as understood by Catholicism.

Civil and religious authorities have always taken great advantage of the powerful reserves of social energy concentrated in fiestas to promote the construction of imagined communities. The struggle for political control of the Diablada is recorded in a long history of manipulation, abuse and exploitation in the name of patriotic sentiment, regional pride and religious values. Spectres of old and new fundamentalisms are in motion across the hemisphere and are evident throughout this book. That is why we decided to begin our introduction with Venezuelan president Hugo Chávez's well-known attack against the 'imperialist devil' George Bush, consistent with a narrative that represents the Bolivarian republic's president as Saint George slaying the

Gringo dragon. Lamadrid, in turn, associates the devil's appearance in New Mexico with the Reagan administration's demonization of the movement against US wars in Central America, while Ligiéro denounces the growing wave of religious intolerance by Brazil's charismatic churches, which undertake crusades against African religions that they consider Satanic.

Mónica Rojas and Anita Gonzalez write of efforts for inclusion by Afro-descendant communities in the national narratives of Peru and Mexico respectively. With respect to the Danza de los Diablos (Dance of the Devils) of Mexico's Pacific coast, Gonzalez underscores its 1–2 November performance, which affirms the importance of the African presence in the country's history. It is a day that coincides with the Day of the Dead—of Indigenous tradition—and with Halloween, celebrated due to the influence of the United States. This affirmation of African presence forces us to reconfigure the dominant rhetoric of *mestizaje*: 'The dances, when performed in public settings, represent a political disruption in Mexican ideology because they negate the notion that Mexico is a country of solely Native American and Spanish *mestizaje*' (Gonzalez, p. 268 in this volume).

Silvia Rivera Cusicanqui and Miguel Rubio share similar positions with regard to the Diablada. Rivera Cusicanqui reminds us that as a border space where the State seeks to underscore its control, the space of the fiesta is disputed:

> One must not forget that in Bolivia, the Virgen de la Candelaria (Our Lady of Candelaria) in Copacabana was crowned and declared 'Queen of the Nation' in 1925. Her appropriation by the Peruvian Army relates to the 1995 victory over Shining Path, but also to disputes with Bolivia. There is an attempt to impose an official dance without variants, in direct contrast to the varied Aymara practices on the Altiplano.[4]

Rubio adds: 'Since Puno is a border province and a zone of armed conflict against subversive groups, the main function of the armed forces until the 1990s was limited to one of security' (p. 53 in this volume). In recent years, though, the armed forces have begun participating actively in the festival. The devils' troupe, made up of members of the Peruvian Army, consists of 750 dancers, accompanied by five musical bands that play 'militarized' *diabladas*. The parade of worship becomes a devilish military march . . . (p. 52 in this volume).

However, there is more. Despite their efforts to overlay cultural expressions with nationalistic rationales, governments now function within a globalized context, where the rules of the game are often set by international entities. The tensions surrounding Miss Peru's outfit, for example, came about because of a superimposition of criteria between two worldwide devices: the Miss Universe pageant on the one hand and the

2003 UNESCO Convention for the Safeguarding of Intangible Cultural Heritage on the other. Both devices legitimate cultural practices and policies at the national and local levels in Peru and Bolivia, throughout each nation's territory. By turning to the repertoire of 'traditional', which is to say, folkloric dress, the Miss Universe pageant adds a touch of multiculturalism to its attempt at imposing a universalist aesthetic canon upon the image of women. The UNESCO convention, on the other hand, takes it upon itself to designate what cultural expressions are worthy of safeguarding from the threat of globalization, that is, which of them belong to 'humanity's cultural heritage'.

Despite beauty pageants and UNESCO statutes having only symbolic value, their political, economic and even legal impacts are far-reaching. In the game of politics, those folkloric-heritage acknowledgements function as 'seals of authenticity' to certify a group's cultural belonging. From an economic perspective, they function as a 'quality brand name' for promoting a city, a region or a collectivity's territorial marketing. In legal terms, they serve as 'registered trademarks' in the jungle of modern copyright and intellectual property legislation (Vignolo 2011; Chaves, Montenegro and Zambrano 2014).

Despite its seemingly trivial nature, the dispute over the Diabla costume of Peru's candidate for Miss Universe is revealing of how new strategies for appropriating the festive repertoire are being developed under the label of 'cultural heritage'. The entry for 'Diablada' in *Wikipedia* includes the following text:

> It is the opinion of Bolivian cultural organizations and the Bolivian government that if other countries include this dance as part of their cultural heritage, they would be incurring in an 'unlawful cultural heritage appropriation' and hold that the designation [by UNESCO] of the Carnaval de Oruro as a Masterpiece of the Oral and Intangible Heritage of Humanity supports the position of Bolivia and the city of Oruro.[5]

Peruvian authorities, however, cite academics and experts on culture to argue that 'culture has no borders', and that no country has exclusive rights to the cultural heritage of the Andean Altiplano. They also point out that UNESCO has no jurisdiction over intellectual property. 'The Convention focuses,' they say, 'on safeguarding the intangible cultural heritage—that is on ensuring its continuous recreation and transmission by identifying and defining the heritage itself—rather than on legally protecting specific manifestations through intellectual property rights, which at the international level falls mainly within the field of competence of World Intellectual Property Organizations'.[6]

Once again, our festive devil becomes a symptom of the deep contradictions of a system of cultural promotion in the era of globalized capitalism. According to the *Wall Street Journal*, which published an extensive article on the issue:

Bolivia's Culture Minister Pablo Groux said what's really fiendish about the costume is that it's a rip-off of Bolivian culture. He maintains *La Diablada* originated in the 12,000-foot-high Bolivian city of Oruro and that Peru's imitation is threatening the national brand—and the tourist industry [...]. Oruro is an economically hard-pressed city which depends on the carnival celebration for survival. That's why, he says, the Miss Universe complaint isn't a superficial defense of a dress or a dance, but of a true patrimony and source of tourist development (Moffett and Kozak 2009: 3).

Claiming rights to the Diablada as a way of increasing the country's weight in the global geopolitics of the fiesta is also a way of generating and protecting new markets for cultural commodities associated with tourism, cultural entrepreneurship and territorial marketing, building upon the symbolic capital associated with the celebration. As a Bolivian official said during a UNESCO meeting, 'We don't have any cultural industries, but we have the Oruro carnival!' (Lacarreu 2014: 389).

The valorization of some forms of cultural expression by organizations as diverse as the Miss Universe pageant and UNESCO produces complex paradoxes. In the commodities market of globalized culture, hyper-identities (sexual, racial and social) sell a great deal more than do fluid, transitional identities that are in constant metamorphosis and negotiation. And, of course, there is nothing 'sexier' or more attractive on the market of symbolic goods than the millennial image of the festival devil, or, in the case of Miss Universe, its female version interpreted by Karen Schwarz. The price to pay for this is to transition from the condition of cultural subjects to that of cultural objects. Cultural heritage, reifying the magma-like flow of cultural phenomena, allows them to be operationalized, normativized and naturalized (Vignolo 2011). Anita Gonzalez reminds us that the case of Mexico, 'Festival practices privilege conventional folklore—performances where dancers are clad in uniform outfits (pants for the men and dresses for the women) and work with partners to create intricate spatial floor patterns. Money moves to artists and companies who are able to professionalize codified folklore for festivals . . .' (p. 263 in this volume).

Finally, although national constitutions explicitly recognize the limit to private property inherent in cultural heritage, the current wave of declarations designating cultural practices as expressions of a heritage to be protected extends the field of private property to unforeseen frontiers. While cultural rights are considered collective rights, the absence of an international normative system to protect them allows for the appropriation by a few (natural or legal) persons of the profits generated thanks to cultural heritage (Vignolo 2011; Taylor 2008).

Just a decade ago, any threat to lodge a complaint before the International Court of Justice for the use of a folkloric outfit would have seemed ludicrous, as would the claim by national authorities to property rights over the devil himself! Now, however, this kind of legal strategy is coming to be considered a legitimate way to demand property rights over the intangible, the immaterial, and the symbolic, that is to say over the frontiers of capitalist expansion in the twenty-first century.

In light of this new colonization of imaginaries, which expands the capitalist dynamic to the most intimate practices embodied in the fiesta, festival devils once again prove capable of producing alternative proposals and forms of protest. We all agreed with our colleague Rivera Cusicanqui when at the end of our encounter on performance and politics she suggested that if the governments of the region insist upon claiming ownership of His Majesty the Devil, we may have to call a conclave of devils without borders to let them take a vote on the matter. It is a supreme (and devilish) irony that we may be forced to defend the very symbol of evil as a 'common good'.

Notes

1   Pastor Landívar, quoted in 'The Devil ensnares Bolivia and Peru' (available at: www.diablosfestivos.org; last accessed on 1 April 2015).
2   For an approach to the figure of the devil in the Americas, see Jaime Humberto Borja Gómez (1998); Serge Gruzinski (1992); Jorge Cañizares-Esguerra (2006); Félix Báez-Jorge (2003).
3   'Cholo' is a complex term but as usually understood it refers to a person of mixed European and Amerindian ancestry, often having migrated from a predominantly indigenous Andean region to a more diverse city or town.
4   Comment made during editorial retreat on festive devils in San Cristobal de las Casas, Chiapas, Mexico, in August 2010.
5   'Diablada', Wikipedia (available at: https://es.wikipedia.org/wiki/Diablada; last accessed on 1 June 2015).
6   UNESCO, 'Frequently Asked Questions' (available at: http://www.unesco.org/culture/ich/index.php?pg=00021; last accessed on 1 April 2015).

Works Cited

AARNE, Antti and Stith Thompson. 1973. *The Types of the Folk-Tale: A Classification and Bibliography.* Helsinki: Suomalainen Tiedeakatemiu Academia Scientiarum Fennica.

ABERCROMBIE, Thomas. 1991. 'To Be Indian, To Be Bolivian: Ethnic and National Discourses of Identity' in Joel Sherzer and Greg Urban (eds), *Indian and Nation-State in Latin America.* Austin: University of Texas Press, pp. 95–130.

———. 1992. 'La fiesta del carnaval postcolonial de Oruro: Clase, etnicidad y nacionalismo en la danza folkórica' (The Postcolonial Festival of the Oruro Carnival: Class, Ethnicity and Nationalism in Folk Dance). *Revista Andina* 20(2): 279–352.

———. 1996. 'Q'aqchas and the Plebe in Rebellion: Carnival vs. Lent in 18th-Century Potosí'. *Journal of Latin American Anthropology* 2(1): 62–111.

———. 1998. *Pathways of Memory and Power: Ethnography and History among an Andean People.* Madison: University of Wisconsin Press.

———. 2003. 'Mothers and Mistresses of the Urban Bolivian Public Sphere: Postcolonial Predicament and National Imaginary in Oruro's Carnival' in Andres Guerrero and Mark Thurner (eds), *After Spanish Rule: Postcolonial Predicaments of the Americas.* Durham, NC: Duke University Press, pp. 176–221.

ABSI, Pascale. 2005. *Los ministros del diablo: el trabajo y sus representaciones en las minas de Potosí* (The Devil's Ministers: Work and Its Representations in the Mines of Potosi). La Paz: PIEB.

ADAM, Adolf. 1981. *The Liturgical Year: Its History and Its Meaning after the Reform of the Liturgy* (Matthew J. O'Connell trans.). Collegeville, MN: Liturgical Press.

ADAMS, John W. 1973. *The Gitskan Potlatch: Population Flux, Resource Ownership and Reciprocity.* Austin, TX: Holt Rinehart & Winston.

AIYEJINA, Funso and Rawle Gibbons. 2000. *Orisa (Orisha) Tradition in Trinidad.* St Augustine: Research and Working Papers Series, Faculty of Social Sciences, University of West Indies.

ALBÓ, Xavier. 1987. 'From MNRistas to Kataristas to Katari' in Steve J. Stern (ed.), *Resistance, Rebellion, and Consciousness in the Andean Peasant World: 18th to 20th Centuries.* Madison: University of Wisconsin Press, pp. 379–419.

———. 1991. 'El retorno del indio' (Return of the Indian). *Revista Andina* 9(2): 290–366.

————. 2009. 'Fronteras endiabladas' (Devilish Borders). *Lamalapalabra*, 26 August. Available at: http://revistalamalapalabra.blogspot.com/ (last accessed on 12 December 2014).

———— and Matías Preiswerk. 1986. *Los Señores del Gran Poder* (Lords of Great Power) La Paz: Centro de Teología Popular.

ALBRO, Robert. 1998. 'Neoliberal Ritualists of Urkupiña: Bedeviling Patrimonial Identity in a Bolivian Patronal Fiesta'. *Ethnology* 37(2): 133–64.

————. 2000. 'The Populist Chola: Cultural Mediation and the Political Imagination in Quillacollo, Bolivia'. *Journal of Latin American Anthropology* 5(2): 30–88.

ALEGRÍA, Ricardo E. 1956. 'The Fiesta of Santiago Apóstol (St James the Apostle) in Loíza, Puerto Rico'. *Journal of American Folklore* 69: 123–34.

ALEMÁN, Carmen Elena. 1997. *Corpus Christi y San Juan Bautista: Dos Manifestaciones Rituales en la Comunidad Afrovenezolana De Chuao* (Corpus Christi and San Juan Bautista: Two Ritual Manifestations in the AfroVenezuelan Community of Chuao). Caracas, Venezuela: Fundación Bigott.

ALEXANDER, Elizabeth. 1994. 'Can You Be BLACK and Look at This? Reading the Rodney King Video(s)' in Thelma Golden (ed.), *Black Male: Representations of Masculinity in Contemporary American Art*. New York: Whitney Museum of American Art, pp. 91–100.

ALLEYNE, Mervyn. 2002. *The Construction and Representation of Race and Ethnicity in the Caribbean and the World*. Kingston: University of West Indies Press.

ALONSO, Ana Maria. 1990. 'Men in "Rags" and the Devil on the Throne: A Study of Protest and Inversion'. *Plantation Society in the Americas: An Interdisciplinary Journal of Tropical and Subtropical History and Culture*: 73–120.

ALVA, Antônio de. 1987. *O Livro dos exus* (Book of Eshus). Rio de Janeiro: Eco.

ANAYA, Rudolfo. 1987. *The Farolitos of Christmas: A New Mexico Christmas Story*. Santa Fe: New Mexico Magazine.

ANDERSON, Mark. 2009. *Black and Indigenous: Garifuna Activism and Consumer Culture in Honduras*. Minneapolis: University of Minnesota Press.

APPELBAUM, Nancy P. 2003. *Muddied Waters: Race, Region, and Local History in Colombia, 1846–1948*. Durham, NC: Duke University Press.

ARCINIEGAS, Germán. 1990. 'Carta a Otto Morales Benítez'. Paper presented at the Eighth Encuentro de la Palabra, Riosucio, Colombia, August.

ARGUEDAS, José María. 1967. 'Puno, la otra capital del Perú' (Puno, the Other Capital of Peru). El Dominical (Sunday supplement), *El Comercio*, 12 March, n.p.

AROSEMENA MORENO, Julio. 1984. *Danzas folkloricas de la villa de Los Santos* (Folk Dances of La Villa de los Santos), 2nd EDN. Panamá: Banco Nacional de Panamá.

ARRIAGA, Pablo Joseph de. 1621. *La extirpación de la idolatría en el Perú*. Available at: http://www.biblioteca.org.ar/libros/155230.pdf (last accessed on 9 April 2015).

ARRIVÍ, Francisco. 1970[1957]. *Vejigantes*. Río Piedras: Editorial Cultural. Available in English as: Francisco Arriví. 1976. *Masquerade* (Gabriel Coulthard trans.) in Errol Hill (ed.), ... *a time and a season* ... : *8 Caribbean Plays*. Trinidad and Tobago: School of Continuing Studies, University of West Indies, pp. 101–64.

ARROM, José Juan. 1967. *Historia del teatro hispanoamericano (época colonial)* (History of Latin American Theatre: Colonial Period). Mexico City: Eds de Andrea.

ARROM, Silvia Marina. 1985. *The Women of Mexico City, 1790–1857*. Stanford, CA: Stanford University Press.

ARZÁNS DE ORZUA Y VELA, Bartolomé. 1965[1702–35]. *Historia de la Villa Imperial de Potosí* (History of the Imperial Villa of Potosí) (Lewis Hanke and Gunnar Mendoza eds), 3 VOLS. Providence, RI: Brown University Press.

ASHCROFT, Bill. 2009. 'Beyond the Nation: Post-Colonial Hope'. *The Journal of the European Association of Studies on Australia* 1(1): 12–21.

BABCOCK, Barbara A. 1978. 'Liberty's a Whore: Inversions, Marginalia, and Picaresque Narrative' in Barbara A. Babcock (ed.), *Forms of Symbolic Inversion Symposium in Art and Society*. Ithaca, NY: Cornell University Press, pp. 95–116.

BÁEZ-JORGE, Félix. 2003. *Los disfraces del diablo: Ensayo sobre la reinterpretación de la noción cristiana del Mal en Mesoamérica* (Devil Costumes: Essay on the Reinterpretation of the Christian Notion of Evil in Middle America). Xalapa Enríquez: Universidad Veracruzana.

——, and Luis Millones. 2014. *Avatares del Demonio in Mesoamérica y en los Andes* (Demon Avatars in Mesoamerica and the Andes). Lima: Librería Amazon (e-book).

BAKEWELL, Peter. 1984. *Miners of the Red Mountain: Indian Labor in Potosí, 1545–1650*. Albuquerque: University of New Mexico Press.

——. 1988. *Silver and Entrepreneurship in Seventeenth-Century Potosí: The Life and Times of Antonio Lopéz de Quiroga*. Albuquerque: University of New Mexico Press.

BAKHTIN, Mikhail M. 1981. *The Dialogic Imagination: Four Essays* (Michael Holquist ed.; Caryl Emerson and Michael Holquist trans). Austin: University of Texas Press.

——. 1984a. *Problems of Dostoyevsky's Poetics* (Caryl Emerson trans). Minneapolis: University of Minnesota Press.

——. 1984b. *Rabelais and His World* (Helene Iswolsky trans.). Bloomington: Indiana University Press.

BALAGUER, Alejandro. 2010. 'Celebrations in Harmony with Nature'. *Américas* 62(2) (2010): 20–7.

BARRAGAN, Rossana. 1997. 'Entre polleras, ñañacas y llicllas: los mestizos y cholas en la conformación de la "Tercera República"' (Between Polleras, Ñañacas and Lliclllas: Mestizos and Cholas in the Formation of the 'Third Republic') in Henrique Urbano (eds), *Tradición y Modernidad en los Andes* (Tradition and Modernity in the Andes). Cusco: Centro Bartolomé de las Casas, pp. 43–73.

BONFIL BATALLA, Guillermo. 1996. *México Profundo: Reclaiming a Civilization* (Philip A. Dennis trans.). Austin: University of Texas Press.

BAUDIN, Louis. 1928. *L'empire socialiste des Inkas* (The Socialist Empire of the Incas). Paris: Institut d'Ethnologie.

BAUMAN, Richard. 1977. *Verbal Art as Performance*. Rowley, MA: Newbury House Publishers.

——. 1986. *Story, Performance, and Event: Contextual Studies of Oral Narrative*. New York: Cambridge University Press.

BAYLE, Constantino. 1951. *El Culto del Santissimo en Indias* (The Cult of the Santissimo in Indians). Madrid: Consejo Superior de Investigaciones Científicas, Instituto Santo Toribio de Mogrovejo.

BEHAR, Ruth. 1989. 'Sexual Witchcraft, Colonialism, and Women's Powers: Views from the Mexican Inquisition' in Asunción Lavrin (ed.), *Sexuality and Marriage in Colonial Latin America*. Lincoln: University of Nebraska Press, pp. 178–206.

BELTRÁN HEREDIA, Augusto. 1956. *Carnaval de Oruro*. Oruro: Editorial Universitaria.

BENAVIDES, Alonso de. 1630. *Memorial qve fray Ivan de Santander de la orden de San Francisco, comissario general de Indias, presenta a la Magestad catolica del rey Don Felipe Qvarto nuestro señor / hecho por el padre fray Alonso de Benauides comissario del Santo Oficio, y custodio que ha sido de las prouincias, y conuersiones del Nueuo-Mexico; tratase en el de los tesoros espirituales, y temporales, que la Diuina Magestad ha manifestado en aquellas conuersiones, y nueuos descubrimientos, por medio de los padres desta serafica religion: con licencia* (Memorial that friar Juan de Santander of the order of Saint Francis, commissary general or the Indies, presented to his catholic Majesty King don Phillip IV our lord / made by father fray Alonso de Benavides, commissioner of the Holy Office, and custodian which he has been of the provinces, and conversions of New Mexico; treated therein the treasures spiritual and temporal, that the Divine Majesty has manifested in those conversions, and new discoveries). Madrid: Imprenta Real.

BENÍTEZ ROJO, Antonio. 1989. *La isla que se repite: El Caribe y la perspectiva posmoderna* (The Repeating Island: The Caribbean and the Postmodern Perspective). Hanover, NH: Ediciones del Norte.

BENJAMIN, Walter. 1999. *The Arcades Project* (Rolf Tiedemann ed., Howard Eiland and Kevin McLaughlin trans). Cambridge, MA: Harvard University Press.

BERNARDES, Ausonia. 2004. *O palhaço da folia de reis: Dança e performance Afro-Brasileira* (The Clown of Folia de Reis: Dance and Afro-Brazilian Performance). Rio de Janeiro: UNIRIO.

BEY, Hakim. 1985. *The Temporary Autonomous Zone, Ontological Anarchy, Poetic Terrorism.* New York: Autonomedia.

BEYERSDORFF, Margot. 1997. *Historia y drama ritual en Los Andes Bolivianos* (*siglos XVI–XX*) (History and Ritual Drama in the Bolivian Andes, Sixteenth to Twentieth Centuries). La Paz: Editorial Plural / Universidad Mayor de San Andrés.

Boletín Histórico de Puerto Rico. 1925. 'Relación veridica en la que se da noticia de lo acaecido en la isla de Puerto Rico a fines del año de 45 y principios de el 47 con el motivo de llorar la muerte de N. Rey y Señor don Phelipe quinto . . .' (True Account in Which Is Given News of What Happened on the Island of Puerto Rico in late 45 and early 47 to Mourn the Death of King Philip V . . .). *Boletín Histórico de Puerto Rico* 12: 148–93.

BORJA GÓMEZ, Jaime Humberto. 1998. *Rostros y rastros del demonio en la Nueva Granada: indios, negros, judíos, mujeres y otras huestes de Satanás* (Faces and Traces of the Devil in New Granada: Indians, Blacks, Jews, Women and Other Followers of Satan). Bogotá: Editorial Ariel.

BOWDITCH, Rachel. 2010. *On the Edge of Utopia: Performance and Ritual at Burning Man.* London: Seagull Books.

BOWSER, Frederic. 1974. *The African Slave in Colonial Peru, 1524–1650.* Stanford, CA: Stanford University Press.

BOYD, James W. 1975. *Satan and Māra: Christian and Buddhist Symbols of Evil.* London: E. J. Brill.

BRAKE, Mike. 1985. *Comparative Youth Culture: The Sociology of Youth Cultures and Youth Subcultures in America, Britain, and Canada.* London: Routledge & Keegan Paul.

BRANDES, Stanley. 1981. 'Like Wounded Stags: Male Sexual Ideology in an Andalusian Town' in Sherry B. Ortner and Harriet Whitehead (eds), *Sexual Meanings: The Cultural Construction of Gender and Sexuality.* New York: Cambridge University Press, pp. 216–39.

BRIGGS, Charles L. 1988. *Competence in Performance: the Creativity of Tradition in Mexicano Verbal Art.* Philadelphia: University of Pennsylvania Press.

———— and Julián Josué Vigil (eds). 1990. *The Lost Gold Mine of Juan Mondragón: A Legend from New Mexico Performed by Melaquías Romero.* Tucson: University of Arizona Press.

BRISTOL, Joan Cameron. 2007. *Christians, Blasphemers, and Witches: Afro-Mexican Ritual Practice in the Seventeenth Century.* Albuquerque: University of New Mexico Press.

BROWN, David H. 2003. *Santeria Enthroned: Art, Ritual and Innovation in an Afro-Cuban Religion*. Chicago: University of Chicago Press.

BROWN, Norman O. 1959. *Life against Death: The Psychoanalytical Meaning of History*. New York: Random House.

BRUNVAND, Jan Harold. 1999. *Too Good to Be True: The Colossal Book of Urban Legends*. New York: W. W. Norton.

BUREAU OF LAND MANAGEMENT. 2000. *Black Rock Desert Visitors Guide*. Reno, NV: National Conservation Area and US Department of the Interior.

BURGA, Manuel. 1988. *Nacimiento de una utopía* (Birth of a Utopia). Lima: Instituto de Apoyo Agrario.

BURKE, Peter. 1978. *Popular Culture in Early Modern Europe*. New York: Harper and Row.

BUTLER, Judith. 1990. *Gender Trouble: Feminism and the Subversion of Identity*. New York: Routledge.

CAJÍAS DE LA VEGA, Fernando. 1983. 'Los objetivos de la revolución indígena de 1781: el caso de Oruro' (The Objectives of the Indigenous Revolution of 1781: The Case of Oruro). *Revista Andina* 1(2): 407–28.

———. 1987. 'La sublevación tupacamarista de 1781 en Oruro y las provincias aledanas: sublevación de indios y revuelta criolla' (The Tupac Amaru Uprising in Oruro and Nearby Provinces: Indian Uprising and Creole Revolt). PhD dissertation, Universidad de Sevilla.

———. 2004. *Oruro 1781: Sublevación de indios y rebelión criolla* (Oruro, 1781: Revolt of the Indians and the Creole Rebellion). La Paz: Instituto de Estudios Bolivianos / ASDI / Instituto Francés de Estudios Andinos.

CAMPA, Arthuro L. 1934. *Spanish Religious Folk Theatre of the Southwest*. Albuquerque: University of New Mexico Press.

CAMPAGNE, Fabián Alejandro. 2004. 'Witches, Idolaters, and Franciscans: An American Translation of European Radical Demonology (Logroño, 1529–Hueytlalpan, 1533)'. *History of Religions* 44(1) (August): 1–35.

CAMPBELL, Thelma. 1943. 'Satanás Diablo Demonio Lucifer: Hero of *Los Pastores*'. *Hispania* 26(4): 387–96.

CAMPOS, Mario. 1987. 'José Durand al Son de los Diablos'. *Ilustracion Peruana Caretas*, 26 October.

CANAVESI DE SAHONERO, M. Lissette. 1987. *El traje de la chola paceña* (Dress of the La Paz Chola) La Paz: Amigos del Libro.

CANESSA, Andrew. 2005. *Natives Making Nation: Gender, Indigeneity, and the State in the Andes*. Tucson: University of Arizona Press.

CAÑIZARES-ESGUERRA, Jorge. 2006. *Puritan Conquistadors: Iberianizing the Atlantic, 1550–1700*. Palo Alto, CA: Stanford University Press.

CARR, Andrew T. 1988. 'Pierrot Grenade' in Gerard A. Besson (ed.), *Trinidad Carnival*. Port of Spain: Paria, pp. 197–207.

CASTRO GÓMEZ, Santiago. 2011. *Historia de la gubernamentalidad* (History of Governmentality). Bogotá: Siglo del Hombre.

CERECEDA, Verónica. 1986. 'The Semiology of Andean Textiles: The Talegas of Isluga' in John V. Murra, Nathan Wachtel and Jacques Revel (eds), *Anthropological History of Andean Polities*. New York: Cambridge University Press, pp. 149–73.

CERVANTES DE SAAVEDRA, Miguel. 1949. *The Ingenious Gentleman Don Quixote de la Mancha* (Samuel Putnam trans.). New York: Viking.

———. 2003. *Don Quixote* (Edith Grossman trans.). New York: HarperCollins.

———. 2004. *Don Quixote de la Mancha*. 2 VOLS. Puebla: Santillana Ediciones.

CERVANTES, Fernando. 1997. *The Devil in the New World: The Impact of Diabolism in New Spain*. New Haven, CT: Yale University Press.

CÉSAIRE, Aimé. 2002[1969]. *A Tempest* (Richard Miller trans.). New York: Theatre Communications Group.

CHÁVEZ, Fray Angélico. 1987. 'The Ardent Commandant' in *Short Stories of Fray Angélico Chávez* (Genaro M. Padilla ed.). Albuquerque: University of New Mexico Press, pp. 75–89.

CHRISTOPHER, Emma. 2013. 'How Cuban Villagers Learned They Descended from Sierra Leone Slaves'. *Atlantic*, 22 April. Available at: http://www.theatlantic.com/-international/archive/2013/04/how-cuban-villagers-learned-they-descended-from-sierra-leone-slaves/275067/ (last accessed on 3 September 2014).

COBOS, Rubén. 1956. 'The New Mexican Game of Valse Chiquiao'. *Western Folklore* 15(2): 95–101.

CODERE, Helen. 1950. *Fighting with Property: A Study of Kwakiutl Potlatching and Warfare, 1792–1930*, VOL. 18. New York: J. J. Augustin.

COLAHAN, Clark, and Alfred Rodriguez. 1986. 'Relacion de Fray Francisco de Escobar del Viaje Desde el Reyno de Nuevo Mexico Hasta el Mar del Sur' (Report of Friar Francisco de Escobar of the Journey from the Kingdom of New Mexico to the Southern Sea). *Missionalia Hispanica* 43: 373–94.

COMITÉ CÍVICO PRODEFENSA DE MARMATO. 2011. 'El comportamiento del gobierno nacional en Marmato y las declaraciones del primo del Presidente Santos' (The Behaviour of the National Government in Marmato and Statements by the Cousin of President Santos). *Marmato Vive*, 14 July. Available at: http://marmato-vive.blogspot.com/2011_07_01_archive.html (last accessed on 2 February 2012).

CORNBLIT, Oscar. 1995. *Power and Violence in the Colonial City*. Cambridge: Cambridge University Press.

COWLEY, John. 1996. *Carnival, Canboulay, and Calypso: Traditions in the Making*. Cambridge: Cambridge University Press.

CRASSWELLER, Robert D. 1966. *Trujillo: The Life and Times of a Caribbean Dictator*. New York: Macmillan.

CRESPO, Alberto. 1967. 'La fundación de la villa de San Felipe de Austria y asiento de minas de Oruro' (The Foundation of the Town of San Felipe of Austria and Seat of Mines of Oruro). *Revista Histórica* 29: 3–25.

CROWLEY, Daniel J. 1988 [1956]. 'The Traditional Masques of Carnival' in Gerard A. Besson (ed.), *Trinidad Carnival*. Port of Spain: Paria, pp. 42–90.

CSORDAS, Thomas J. 1993. 'Somatic Modes of Attention'. *Cultural Anthropology* 8(2): 135–56.

CUENTAS ORMAECHEA, Enrique. 1986. 'La Diablada: una expresión de coreografía mestiza del altiplano del Collao' (The Diablada: An Expression of Racially Mixed Choreography of the Collao Plateau). *Boletín de Lima* 44 (March): 31–48.

DALHAUS, Carl. 1980. 'Nationalism and Music' in Carl Dalhaus (ed.), *Between Romanticism and Modernism: Four Studies in the Music of the Later Nineteenth Century*. Berkeley: University of California Press, pp. 79–101.

DE LA CADENA, Marisol. 2000. *Indigenous Mestizos: The Politics of Race and Culture in Cuzco, Peru, 1919–1991*. Durham, NC: Duke University Press.

DEMARCO, Barbara. 2000. 'Cantaron la Victoria: Spanish Literary Tradition and the 1680 Pueblo Revolt' in María Herrera-Sobek and Virginia Sánchez Korrol (eds), *Recovering the US Hispanic Literary Heritage*, VOL. 3. Houston, TX: Arte Público Press, pp. 163–72.

DE MESA, José and Teresa Gisbert. 1970. 'Oruro: origen de una villa minera' (Oruro: Origin of a Mining Town') in *La minería hispana e iberoamericana, contribución a su investigación histórica: Ponencias del I Coloquio Internacional sobre Historia de la Minería* (Spanish and Iberoamerican Mining, Contribution to Its Historical Investigation: Papers of the First International Congress on the History of Mining), VOL. 1. León: Cátedra San Isidoro, pp. 559–90.

DEAN, Carolyn. 1999. *Inka Bodies and the Body of Christ: Corpus Christi in Colonial Cuzco, Peru*. Durham, NC: Duke University Press.

DEBRET, Jean-Baptiste. 1834–39. *Voyage pittoresque et historique au Brasil* (A Pictorial and Historical Account of Travels to Brazil), 3 VOLS. Paris: Firmin Didot Frères.

DEIVE, Carlos Esteban. 1980. *La esclavitud del negro en Santo Domingo, 1492–1844* (*Black Slavery in Santo Domingo, 1492-1844*). 2 VOLS. Santo Domingo: Museo del Hombre Dominicano.

———. 1989. *Los guerrilleros negros: esclavos fugitivos y cimarrones en Santo Domingo* (Black Gueriillas: Fugitive and Runaway Slaves in Santo Domingo). Santo Domingo: Fundación Cultural Dominicana.

DIDI-HUBERMAN, Georges. 2002. *L'image survivante: Histoire de l'art et temps des fantômes selon Aby Warburg* (The Surviving Picture: Art History and Phantoms of Time according to Aby Warburg). Paris: Minuit.

DOHERTY, Brian. 2004. *This is Burning Man: The Rise of a New American Underground*. New York: Little, Brown.

DOUGLAS, Mary. 1966. *Purity and Danger: An Analysis of the Concepts of Pollution and Taboo*. London: Routledge and Keegan Paul.

DRUCKER, Philip and Robert F. Heizer. 1967. *To Make My Name Good: A Reexamination of the Southern Kwakiutl Potlatch*. Berkeley: University of California Press.

DURÁN, Diego. 1994. *History of the Indies of New Spain* (Doris Heyden trans.). Norman: University of Oklahoma Press.

DURAND, José. 1988. *Son de los Diablos*. TV Cultura, Lima. Video.

ECO, Umberto. 1984. 'The Frames of Comic "Freedom"' in Umberto Eco, V. V. Ivanov and Monica Rector, *Carnival!* (Thomas A. Sebeok ed.). Berlin, New York and Amsterdam: Mouton.

ERICKSON, Ivan. 2014. 'The Carnival Masks of the Dominican Republic'. Available at: http://www.dominicanmasks.com/ (last accessed on 9 December 2014).

ESPOSITO, Roberto. 2010. *Communitas: The Origin and Destiny of Community* (Timothy Campbell trans.). Standford, CA: Stanford University Press.

ESTENSSORO, Juan Carlos. 1991. 'Modernismo, estética, musica y fiesta: élites y cambio de actitud frente a la cultura popular, Perú, 1750–1850' (Modernism, Aesthetics, Music and Celebration: The Elites and the Change of Attitude towards Popular Culture, Peru, 1750–1850) in Henrique Urbano (ed.), *Tradicion y Modernidad en los Andes* (Tradition and Modernity in the Andes). Cusco: Centro Bartolomé de las Casas, pp. 181–96.

FALK, Dan. 2008. *In Search of Time: The History, Physics, and Philosophy of Time*. New York: Thomas Dunn Books.

FANON, Frantz. 2008. *Black Skin, White Masks* (Richard Philcox trans.). New York: Grove Press.

FELDMAN, Heidi. 2000. *Black Rhythms of Peru: Staging Memory Through Music and Dance, 1956–2000*. PhD dissertation, University of California, Los Angeles.

FÉLIZ, Werner. 2003. 'Las Cachúas, origen y evolución' (The Origin and Evolution of the Cachúas). Paper delivered at a conference at the Museo del Hombre Dominicano, Santo Domingo, 2 April.

FERNANDEZ, Donald. n.d. 'Mask-Making: Carnival-Costuming and I'. Unpublished manuscript.

Ferris, Elizabeth. 2012. 'Good News from Chiapas—But a Larger Challenge for Mexico'. *Brookings*, 17 February. Available at: http://www.brookings.edu/blogs/up-front/posts/2012/02/17-mexico-idp-law-ferris (last accessed on 8 May 2015).

FIET, Lowell. 2006–07. 'Re/Visions: Why Re-examine the Fiestas of Santiago Apóstol'. *Sargasso* (Re/Visions of Santiago Apóstol: Art, History, and Cultural Criticism): *ix–xviii*.

———. 2007. *Caballeros, vejigantes, locas y viejos: Santiago apóstol y los performeros afro-puertorriqueños* (Spanish Gentlemen, Trickster/Diablos, Mad Women, and Old Men: St James and Afro-Puerto Rican Performers). San Juan: Terranova Editores.

FLETCHER, Harrison. 1996. 'Something Evil is on the Prowl in our Casinos'. *Albuquerque Tribune*, 9 May.

FONTANA, Bernard. 1979. *Tarahumara: Where Night Is the Day of the Moon*. Flagstaff, AZ: Northland Press.

FORTÚN, Julia Elena. 1961. *La danza de los diablos* (The Dance of the Devil). La Paz: Ministerio de Educación y Bellas Artes.

FOX, Steve. 1994. 'Sacred Pedestrians: The Many Faces of Southwest Pilgrimage'. *Journal of the Southwest* 36(1) (Spring): 33–53.

FRANCO, Jean. 1989. *Plotting Women: Gender and Representation in Mexico*. New York: Columbia University Press.

GALEANO, Eduardo. 1970. 'El diablo entre los marginados'. *Víspera* 4(17): 235.

GÄRTNER POSADA, Alvaro. 1994. 'Tras la huella del Padre Bonafont en el Archivo Central del Cauca (Elementos para una nueva visión de la fundación de Riosucio)' (On the Trail of Father Bonafont in the Central Archive of Cauca: Elements for a New Vision of the Founding of Riosucio). Paper presented at the Twelfth Encuentro de la Palabra, Riosucio, Colombia, August.

GERMETEN, Nicole von. 2006. *Black Blood Brothers: Confraternities and Social Mobility for Afro-Mexicans*. Gainesville: University Press of Florida.

GIL CALVO, Enrique. 1991. *Estado de Fiesta*. Madrid: Espasa-Calpe.

GILL, Leslie. 1994. *Precarious Dependencies: Gender, Class, and Domestic Service in Bolivia*. New York: Columbia University Press.

GILROY, Paul. 1993. *The Black Atlantic*. Cambridge, MA: Harvard University Press.

———. 2004. *After Empire: Melancholia or Convivial Culture?* Abingdon: Routledge.

GIRARD, Raphael. 1978. 'Historia de las civilizaciones antiguas de América desde sus orígenes' (History of the Old Civilizations of America from Its Origins). Barcelona: Hispanoamérica / Editores Mexicanos Unidos.

GIRARD, René. 1972. *La violence et le sacrè* (Violence and the Sacred). Paris: Grasset.

GISBERT, Teresa, Silvia Arze and Martha Cajías. 1987. *Arte textíl y mundo andino* (Textile Art and the Andean World). La Paz: Gisbert y Cía.

GLADWELL, Malcolm. 2000. *The Tipping Point: How Little Things Can Make a Big Difference.* New York: Little, Brown.

GOLDSTEIN, Daniel M. 2004. *The Spectacular City: Violence and Performance in Urban Bolivia.* Durham, NC: Duke University Press.

GOSE, Peter. 1987. 'Sacrifice and the Commodity Form in the Andes'. *Man* 21: 296–310.

GOTKOWITZ, Laura. 2007. *A Revolution for Our Rights: Indigenous Struggles for Land and Justice in Bolivia, 1880–1952.* Durham, NC: Duke University Press.

GREENBLATT, Stephen. 2004. *Will in the World: How Shakespeare Became Shakespeare.* New York: W. W. Norton.

GREGG, Josiah. 1954. *Commerce of the Prairies* (Max L. Moorhead ed.). Norman: University of Oklahoma Press.

GRUZINSKI, Serge. 1992. *The Aztecs: Rise and Fall of an Empire.* New York: Harry N. Abrams.

GUERRA Gutierrez, Alberto. 1970. *Antología del carnaval de Oruro* (Anthology of the Carnival of Oruro), 3 VOLS. Oruro: Imprenta Quelco.

———. 1984. *Oruro, realidad socio-cultural* (Oruro: Sociocultural Reality). Oruro: Editora Lilial (Cordeor).

GUSS, David. 1980. *The Festive State: Race, Ethnicity and Nationalism as Cultural Performance.* Berkeley: University of California Press.

GUTIÉRREZ, Gustavo. 1988. *A Theology of Liberation*, REVD EDN. Maryknoll, NY: Orbis.

HALE, Charles. 1997. 'Cultural Politics of Identity in Latin America'. *Annual Review of Anthropology* 26: 567–90.

HALL, Gwendolyn Midlo. 1971. *Social Control in Slave Plantation Societies: A Comparison of St. Domingue and Cuba.* Baltimore, MD: Johns Hopkins University Press.

HANDLER, Jerome S. and Michael L. Tuite Jr. 2008. *The Atlantic Slave Trade and Slave Life in the Americas: A Visual Record.* Charlottesvile: Virginia Foundation for the Humanities / University of Virginia. Available at: http://www.slaveryimages.org (last accessed on 9 December 2014).

HANKE, Lewis. 1956–57. 'The 1608 Fiestas in Potosí'. *Boletín del Instituto Riva-Agüero* 3:107–28.

HARDT, Michael and Antonio Negri. 2000. *Empire*. Cambridge, MA: Harvard University Press.

———. 2004. *Multitude: War and Democracy in the Age of Empire*. Cambridge, MA: Harvard University Press.

HARMEYER, Alice J. 1947. 'Devil Stories from Las Vegas, New Mexico'. *Hoosier Folklore* 6: 37–9.

HARRIS, Max. 1993. *The Dialogical Theatre*. New York: St Martin's Press.

———. 1996. 'Moctezuma's Daughter: The Role of La Malinche in Mesoamerican Dance'. *The Journal of American Folklore* 109(432): 149–77.

———. 2000. *Aztecs, Moors, and Christians: Festivals of Reconquest in Mexico and Spain*. Austin: University of Texas Press.

———. 2001. 'Masking the Site: The Fiestas of Santiago Apóstol in Loíza, Puerto Rico'. *Journal of American Folklore* 114: 358–69.

———. 2002. 'A Bolivian Morality Play: Saint Michael and the Sins of the Carnival Virgin'. *European Medieval Drama* 5: 83–98.

———. 2003. *Carnival and Other Christian Festivals: Folk Theology and Folk Performance*. Austin: University of Texas Press.

HARVEY, Larry. 2000. 'La Vie Boheme: A History of the Burning Man'. Lecture delivered at The Walker Art Center, Minneapolis, MN, 24 February. Transcript available at: http://burningman.org/culture/philosophical-center/founders-voices/larry-harveys-writings/la-vie-boheme/ (last accessed on 10 April 2015).

———. 2008. 'The Early Years: Reflections on Interactive Performance'. Burning Man website. Available at: http://burningman.org/culture/history/art-history/perspectives-on-playa-art/early-years/ (last accessed on 10 April 2015).

HENDRICKSON, Carol. 1990. *Weaving Identities: Construction of Dress and Self in a Highland Guatemala Town*. Austin: University of Texas Press.

HERRERA-SOBEK, María. 1988. 'The Devil in the Discotheque: A Semiotic Analysis of a Contemporary Legend' in Gillian Bennett and Paul Smith (eds), *Monsters with Iron Teeth: Perspectives on Contemporary Legend*. Sheffield: Sheffield Academic Press, pp. 147–58.

HERSKOVITS, Melville J. 1940. 'Dramatic Expression Among Primitive Peoples'. *Yale Review* 33 (1940): 683–98.

HIEB, Louis A. 1975. 'Meaning and Mismeaning: The Ritual Clown' in Alfonso Ortiz (ed.), *New Perspectives on the Pueblos*. Albuquerque: University of New Mexico Press, pp. 163–95.

HILL, Errol. 1972. *The Trinidad Carnival*. Austin: University of Texas Press.

HOBSBAWM, Eric and Terence Ranger. 1983. *The Invention of the Tradition*. Cambridge: Cambridge University Press.

HORGAN, Paul. 1975. *Lamy of Santa Fe*. Middletown, CT: Wesleyan University Press.

HÜNEFELDT, Christine. 1994. *Paying the Price of Freedom: Family and Labor Among Lima's Slaves, 1800–1854* (Alexandra Sterns trans.). Berkeley: University of California Press.

HYDE, Lewis. 1993. *The Gift: Imagination and the Erotic Life of Property*. New York: Random House.

IM THURN, E. F. 1901. 'Games of the Red-men of Guiana'. *Folklore* 12: 132–61.

JACQUOT, Jean (ed.). 1975. *Les Fêtes de la Renaissance* (Renaissance Festivals), 3 VOLS. Paris: CNRS.

JAMESON, Frederic. 1981. *The Political Unconscious: Narrative as a Socially Symbolic Act*. Ithaca, NY: Cornell University Press.

JOSEPHY, Alvin M., Joane Nagel and Troy R. Johnson. 1999. *Red Power: The American Indians' Fight for Freedom*. Lincoln: University of Nebraska Press.

JUAN, Jorge and Antonio de Ulloa. 1978a[1749]. *Discourse and Political Reflections on the Kingdoms of Peru* (John J. TePaske and Besse A. Clement trans, John J. TePaske ed.). Norman: University of Oklahoma Press.

———. 1978b[1748]. *Relación histórica del viaje a la America meridional* (A Historical Account of Travels to South America), 2 VOLS. Madrid: Fundación Universitaria Española.

KAMEN, Henry. 1983. *Spain in the Later Seventeenth Century, 1665–1700*. London: Longman.

KELLERT, Stephen H. 1993. *In the Wake of Chaos: Unpredictable Order in Dynamical Systems*. Chicago: University of Chicago Press.

KESSELL, John L. (ed.). 1989. *Remote Beyond Compare: Letters of Don Diego de Vargas to his Family from New Spain and New Mexico, 1675–1706*. Alburquerque: University of New Mexico Press.

———. 1987. *Kiva, Cross and Crown: The Pecos Indians and New Mexico, 1540–1840*. Alburquerque: University of New Mexico Press.

———. 1998. *Blood on the Boulders: the Journals of don Diego de Vargas, New Mexico, 1694–97*. Albuquerque: University of New Mexico Press.

KOZINETS, Robert V. and John F. Sherry. 2005. 'Welcome to the Black Rock Café' in Lee Gilmore and Mark van Proyen (eds), *AfterBurn: Reflections on Burning Man*. Albuquerque: University of New Mexico Press, pp. 87–106.

LACARREU, Monica. 2014. 'Fiesta si, coca, yajé y conflicto armado, ¿también? El patrimonio inmaterial entre valoraciones económicas, culturales, sociales y políticas' in Margarita Chaves, Mauricio Montenegro and Marta Zambrano (eds), *El valor del patrimonio: mercado, políticas culturales y agenciamientos sociales*. Bogotá: Instituto Colombiano de Antropología e Historia, pp. 389–441.

LAMADRID, Enrique R. 2007. 'From Santiago at Ácoma to the Diablo in the Casinos: Four Centuries of Foundational *Milagro* Narratives in New Mexico' in Phillip B. Gonzales (ed.), *Expressing Culture, Expressing Place: Nuevomexicana/o Creativity, Everyday Ritual, and Collective Remembrance*. Tucson: University of Arizona Press, pp. 41–60.

——— and Arthur Sze. 1984. *Cuentos: Telling Our Stories*, VOL. 3. Santa Fe, NM: Open Hands.

LAVRIN, Asunción. 1989. 'Introduction: The Scenario, the Actors, and the Issues' in Asunción Lavrin (ed.), *Sexuality and Marriage in Colonial Latin America*. Lincoln: University of Nebraska Press, pp. 1–44.

LEON, Javier. 2003. *The Aestheticization of Tradition: Professional Afroperuvian Musicians, Cultural Reclamation, and Artistic Interpretation*. PhD dissertation, University of Texas, Austin, 2003.

LIGIÉRO, Zeca. 1993. 'Candomblé is Religion–Life–Art' in Phyllis Galembo (ed.), *Divine Inspiration from Benin to Bahia*. Albuquerque: University of New Mexico Press, pp. 97–120.

———. 2004. *Malandro divino: a vida e a lenda de Zé Pelintra, personagem típico da Lapa Carioca* (Divine Rogue: The Life and Legend of Zé Pelintra, a Typical Character from Carioca Lapa). Rio de Janeiro: Nova Era.

———. 2011. *Corpo a corpo: Estudos das performances Brasileiras* (Melee: Brazilian Performamance Studies). Rio de Janeiro: Garamond.

———. 2014. *Initiation into Candomblé: Introduction to African Brazilian Religion*. New York: Diasporic Africa Press.

——— and Dandara. 1998. *Umbanda: paz, liberdade e cura* (Umbanda: Peace, Freedom and Healing). Rio de Janeiro: Editora Record.

LIMÓN, José E. 1994. *Dancing with the Devil: Society and Cultural Poetics in Mexican-American South Texas*. Madison: University of Wisconsin Press.

LIND, Samuel. 2005. 'El vejigante de Loíza'. *Claridad*, 25–31 August, p. 23.

LINK, Luther. 1996. *The Devil: The Archfiend in Art from the Sixth to the Sixteenth Century*. New York: Harry N. Abrams.

LIZARDO, Fradique. 1974. *Danzas y bailes folklóricos Dominicanos* (Folk Dances of the Dominican Republic). Santo Domingo: Taller.

LÓPEZ CANTOS, Angel. 1990. *Fiestas y juegos en Puerto Rico* (*siglo XVIII*) (Fiestas and Games in Puerto Rico in the Eighteenth Century). San Juan: Centro de Estudios Avanzados de Puerto Rico y el Caribe.

LUNA, Lisandro. 1975. *Zampoñas del Collao* (Zampoñas of Collao). Puno: Editorial Los Andes.

MARAVALL, José Antonio. 1979. *Poder, honor y élites en el siglo XVII* (Power, Honour and Elites in the Seventeenth Century) Madrid: Siglo Veintiuno.

———. 1984. 'Trabajo y exclusión: el trabajador manual en el sistema social de la primera modernidad' in *Estudios de historia del pensamiento español* (Work and Exclusion: The Manual Worker in the Social System of the First Modernity). Madrid: Ediciones Cultura Hispanica, pp. 363–92.

MARTÍ, José. 1991. *Obras completas* (Complete Works), 27 VOLS. Havana: Editorial de Ciencias Sociales.

MARTINS, Leda. 2007. 'Performances of Spiral Time' in Alyshia Galvez (ed.), *Performing Religion in the Americas: Media, Politics and Devotional Practices of the Twenty-First Century*. London: Seagull Books, pp. 173–208.

———. 2013. 'Spiral Time: An Approach to African-Brasilian Ritual Cosmovision'. Lecture presented at the conference 'Spiraling Time: Intermedial Conversations in Latin American Art', Arts Research Center, University of California, Berkeley, 16 March.

MAUSS, Marcel. 1967. *The Gift: Forms and Functions of Exchange in Archaic Societies*. New York: Norton.

MCKENZIE, Jon. 2001. *Perform or Else: From Discipline to Performance*. London: Routledge, 2001.

MEDINACELI, Carlos. 1978. *La Chaskañawi: novela de costumbres bolivianas*, 10th EDN. La Paz: Amigos del Libro.

MEDLIN, Mary Ann. 1983. 'Awayaqa Sumaj Calchapi: Weaving, Social Organization and Identity in Calcha, Bolivia'. PhD dissertation. University of North Carolina, Chapel Hill.

MEISCH, Lynn Ann. 1986. 'Weaving Styles in Tarabuco, Bolivia' in Ann Pollard Rowe (ed.), *The Junius B. Bird Conference on Andean Textiles, April 7 and 8, 1984*. Washington, DC: The Textile Museum, pp. 243–74.

Memorias de Yuyachkani. 1987. Archived material. Casa Cultural Yuyachkani archives, Lima.

MENDEZ, Cecilia G. 1991. 'República sin indios: la comunidad imaginada del Perú' (Republic without Indians: The Imagined Community of Peru) in Henrique Urbano (ed.), *Tradicion y Modernidad en los Andes* (Tradition and Modernity in the Andes). Cusco: Centro Bartolomé de las Casas, pp. 15–41.

MENDOZA, Zoila S. 1999. 'Genuine but Marginal: The Embodiment of Indigenous Identity through Public Performance in Peru'. *Journal of Latin American Anthropology* 3(2): 86–117.

———. 2000. *Shaping Society through Dance: Mestizo Ritual Performance in the Peruvian Andes*. Chicago: University of Chicago Press.

MESSADIÈ, Gérald. 1997. *A History of the Devil*. New York: Kodansha America.

MIGNOLO, Walter. 1995. *The Darker Side of the Renaissance: Literacy, Territoriality, and Colonization*. Ann Arbor: The University of Michigan Press.

MILLONES, Luís. 1988. *El Inca por la Coya: Historia de un drama popular en los Andes peruanos* (The Inca for the Coya: History of a Popular Drama in the Peruvian Andes). Lima: Editorial Hipatia, S. A. (Fundación Friedrich Ebert).

MILLS, Charles W. 1998. *Blackness Visible: Essays on Philosophy and Race*. Ithaca, NY: Cornell University Press.

MITCHELL, Timothy. 1988. *Colonizing Egypt*. Berkeley: University of California Press.

MOFFETT, Matt, and Kozak, Robert. 2009. 'This Spat Between Bolivia and Peru, the Details Are in the Devils'. *The Wall Street Journal*, 21 August, p. 3. Available at: http://online.wsj.com/article/SB125081309502848049.html (last accessed on 12 December 2014).

MOLANO BRAVO, Alfredo. 2008. 'Contrastes'. *El Espectador*, 23 August 2008. Available at: http://www.elespectador.com/node/33870/print?q=node/33870/print (last accessed on 2 February 2012).

———. 2008. 'Rutina'. *El Espectador*. 2008. Available at: <http://www.elespectador.com/opinion/columnistasdelimpreso/alfredo-molano-bravo/columna43230-rutina> (last accessed on 2 February 2012).

MOLINIÉ, Antoinette. 1995. 'Dos celebraciones de Corpus Christi, en los Andes y en La Mancha' (Two Celebrations of Corpus Christi, in the Andes and La Mancha). *Antropología* 10: 41–72.

MONTES CAMACHO, Niver. 1986. *Proceso intimo del carnaval de Oruro* (Intimate Process of the Carnival of Oruro). Oruro: Editorial Universitaria.

MORALES SERRUTO, José Morales and Ana Isabel Aguirre. 2009. 'Historia de la Diablada'.

MOSQUERA, Daniel O. 2004. 'Nahuatl Catechistic Drama: New Translaions, Old Preoccupations' in Barry D. Sell and Louise M. Burkhart (eds), *Nahuatl Theater, Volume 1: Death and Life in Colonial Nahua Mexico*. Norman: University of Oklahoma Press, pp. 55–84.

MOTOLINÍA, Toribio. 1950. *Motolinía's History of the Indians of New Spain* (Elizabeth Andros Foster trans.). Berkeley: The Cortés Society (Bancroft Library).

MURRA, John V. 1978[1956]. *La organización económica del estado Inca* (The Economic Organization of the Inca State). Mexico City: Siglo Veintiuno.

NASH, June. 1979. *We Eat the Mines and the Mines Eat Us: Dependency and Exploitation in Bolivian Tin Mines*. New York: Columbia University Press.

NESS, Sally Ann. 2007. 'Going Back to Bateson' in Mark Franco (ed.), *Ritual and Event: Interdisciplinary Perspectives*. New York: Routledge, pp. 13–30.

NEWCOMB, Steven T. 2008. *Pagans in the Promised Land: Decoding the Doctrine of Christian Discovery*. Golden, CO: Fulcrum.

Newcomb, Steven T. 2008. *Pagans in the Promised Land: Decoding the Doctrine of Christian Discovery*. Golden, CO: Fulcrum.

NORA, Pierre. 1989. 'Between Memory and History'. *Representations* 26 (Spring) (Special Issue: Memory and Counter-Memory): 7–24.

O'BRIEN, Christopher. 2007. *Secrets of the Mysterious Valley*. Kempton, IL: Adventures Unlimited Press.

OBOLER, Suzanne. 2005. 'The Foreigness of Racism: Pride and Prejudice among Peru's Limeños in the 1990s' in Anani Dzidzienyo and Suzanne Oboler (eds), *Neither Enemies nor Friends: Latinos, Blacks, Afro-Latinos*. New York: Palgrave Macmillan, pp. 75–100.

OHTAKE, Miyoko. 2007. 'A Fiery Q&A With the Prankster Accused of Burning the Man'. *San Francisco Chronicle*, 1 September.

OLMOS, Andrés de. 2008. *Final Judgment* (1521) (John J. Cornyn and Byron McAfee trans) in Diana Taylor and Sarah J. Townsend (eds), *Stages of Conflict: A Critical Anthology of Latin American Theater and Performance*. Ann Arbor: University of Michigan Press, pp. 53–8.

ORLOVE, Benjamin. 1994. 'Sticks and Stones: Ritual Battles and Play in the Southern Peruvian Andes' in Deborah Poole (ed.), *Unruly Order: Violence, Power, and Cultural Identity in the High Provinces of Southern Peru*. Boulder, CO: Westview Press, pp. 133–64.

ORTIZ, Diego F. 2007. 'Riosucio: ¿Una metáfora de la nueva República de Colombia?' (Riosucio: A Metaphor for the New Republic of Colombia?). Paper presented at the Fifteenth Congreso de Colombianistas, Universidad Nacional, Bogota, 1–4 August.

ORTIZ, Fernando. 1981[1951]. *Los bailes y el teatro de los negros en el folklore de Cuba* (The Dances and Theatre of the Blacks in the Folklore of Cuba), 2nd EDN. Havana: Letras Cubanas.

———. 2002. *Contrapunteo cubano del tabaco y el azúcar* (Cuban Counterpoint: Tobacco and Sugar). Madrid: Catedra.

OSTRIKER, Alicia. 1987. 'Dancing at the Devil's Party: Some Notes on Politics and Poetry' in Robert von Hallberg (ed.), *Politics and Poetic Value*. Chicago: University of Chicago Press, pp. 207–24.

OVIEDO Y BAÑOS, Jose de. 1723. *Historia de la conquista y poblacion de la Provinca de Venezuela* (History of the Conquest and Population of the Province of Venezuela). Madrid: D. Gregorio Hermosilla.

PAZ, Octavio. 2002. 'The Sons of La Malinche' in Gilbert Joseph and Timothy Henderson (eds), *The Mexico Reader*. Durham, NC: Duke University Press, pp. 20–7.

PEARSE, Andrew. 1988[1956]. 'Mitto Sampson on Calypso Legends of the Nineteenth Century' in Gerard Besson (ed.), *Trinidad Carnival*. Port-of-Spain: Paria Press, pp. 140–63.

PEÑA RIVERA, Victor A. 1977. *Trujillo: historia oculta de un dictador* (Trujillo: The Secret History of a Dictator). New York: Plus Ultra.

PEÑALOSA, Joaquín Antonio. 1970. *El diablo en México*. México City: Seminario de Cultura Mexicana.

PENNYBACKER, Susan. 2009. *From Scottsboro to Munich: Race and Political Culture in 1930s Britain*. Princeton, NJ: Princeton University Press.

PÉREZ, Xiomarita (ed.). 2008. *Consultorio folklórico* (The Information Office for Folklore). Santo Domingo: Dirección Nacional de Folklore, Secretaría de Estado de Cultura, República Dominicana.

PERRY, Mary Elizabeth. 1980. *Crime and Society in Early Modern Seville*. Hanover, NH: University Press of New England.

PETERSON, Frank Loris. 1934[?]. *Hope of the Race*. Nashville, TN: Southern Publishing Company.

PLATT, Tristan. 1983. 'Identidad andina y conciencia proletaria: Qhuyaruna y ayllu en el norte de Potosí' (Andean Identity and Proletarian Consciousness: Qhuyaruna and Ayllu in the North of Potosi). *HISLA, Revista Latinoamericana de Historia Economica y Social* 2: 47–73.

PORT OF SPAIN GAZETTE. 1908. 'The Teacher's Journal'. *Port of Spain Gazette*, 25 February, n.p.

PROCOPE, Bruce. 1988[1956]. 'The Dragon Band or Devil Band' in Gerard Besson (ed.), *Trinidad Carnival*. Port-of-Spain: Paria Press, pp. 186–96.

QUIJANO, Anibal. 1992. 'Colonialidad y Modernidad/Racionalidad' (Colonialism and Modernity/Rationality) in *Los Conquistados: 1492 y la población indígena de las*

Américas (The Conquered: 1492 and the Indigenous Population of the Americas) (Heraclio Bonilla comp.). Quito: FLACSO / Ediciones Libri Mundi, pp. 437–49.

RADCLIFFE, Sarah and Sallie Westwood. 1996. *Remaking the Nation: Place, Identity and Politics in Latin America*. London: Routledge.

RAMOS GAVILÁN, Fray Alonso. 1976[1621]. *Historia de Nuestra Señora de Copacabana* (The History of Our Lady of Copacabana). La Paz: Empresa Editora Universo.

RAMOS SMITH, Maya. 2010. *Censura y teatro novohispano* (Censorship and Theatre in New Spain). Mexico D.F.: Escenología.

REU, Tobias. 2009. 'Folkloric Dance, Civil Society, and the Public Sphere in the Bolivian Saint's Festival of the Virgin of Urqupina'. PhD dissertation. New York: New York University.

RICE, Timothy. 1994. *May It Fill Your Soul: Experiencing Bulgarian Music*. Chicago: University of Chicago Press.

RIGGIO, Milla Cozart. 1998. *The Play of Wisdom: Its Texts and Contexts*. New York: AMS Press.

—— (ed.). 2004. *Carnival: Culture in Action—The Trinidad Experience*. London: Routledge.

RIOS DA SILVEIRA, Aressa Egly. 2009. *A performance do palhaço e da folia de reis no Vale do Paraíba: jogo e ritual—a tradição em transformação*. Dissertação de Mestrado defendida no PPGAC em, 2009 (The Performance of the Clown and the Group of Folia de Rein in the Valley of Paraiba: Play and Ritual—A Tradition in Transformation). MA dissertation, Federal University of the State of Rio de Janeiro, Rio de Janeiro. Available at: http://www.portalabrace.org/vicongresso/estudosper-formance/Aressa%20Egly%20Rios%20da%20Silveira%20-%20O%20palha-%E7o%20de%20Folia%20de%20Reis%20e%20o%20diabo%20festivo%20na%20A m%E9rica%20Latina%20-%20representatividade,%20teatralidade%20e%20religio-sidade.pdf (last accessed on 1 April 2015).

RIVAS, Roberto. 2002. 'Danzantes negros en el Corpus Christi de Lima, 1756 "Vos estis Corpus Christi"' (Black Dancers in the Corpus Christi of Lima, 1756) in *Tomo I: Etnicidad y discriminación racial en la historia del Perú* (Volume 1: Ethnicity and Racial Discrimination in the History of Peru). Lima: Instituto Riva Agüero, Pontificia Universidad Católica, Programa Sociedad Civil Banco Mundial, pp. 35–6.

RIVERA CUSICANQUI, Silvia. 1996. *Ser mujer indígena, chola o birlocha en la Bolivia post-colonial de los años 90* (To Be an Indigenous, Chola or Birlocha Woman in the Postcolonial Bolivia of the 1990s). La Paz: Ministerio de Desarrollo Humano, Subsecretaria de Asuntos de Género, Plural Editores.

————. 2009. 'Sociology of the Image: A View from Andean History'. Unpublished keynote lecture for 'Staging Citizenship: Cultural Rights in the Americas', Hemispheric Institute of Performance and Politics Encuentro, Bogotá. Colombia.

————. 2014. 'The Potosí Principle: Another View of Totality'. *e-misférica* 11(1). Available at: http://hemisphericinstitute.org/hemi/en/emisferica-111-decolonial-gesture/-e111-essay-the-potosi-principle- another-view-of-totality (last accessed on 6 August 2014).

ROACH, Joseph R. 1996. *Cities of the Dead: Circum-Atlantic Performance*. New York: Columbia University Press.

ROBE, Stanley L. 1951. 'Four Mexican Exempla about the Devil'. *Western Folklore* 10: 310–15.

————. 1980. *Hispanic Legends from New Mexico: Narratives from the R. D. Jameson Collection*. Berkeley: University of California Press.

ROCKEFELLER, Stuart Alexander. 1998. '"There Is a Culture Here": Spectacle and the Inculcation of Folklore in Highland Bolivia'. *Journal of Latin American Anthropology* 3(2): 118–49.

RODRÍGUEZ-BOBB, Arturo. 2004. *At the Other Side of the Atlantic: Ensayo sobre la esclavitud del negro; Razón, violencia estructural y racismo institucional en el discurso de los intelectuales colombianos del siglo XVI al siglo XIX* (Essays on Black Slavery; Reason, Structural Violence and Institutional Racism in the Discourse of Colombians in the Sixteenth to the Nineteenth Centurie). Berlin: Wissenschaftlicher Verlag.

RODRÍGUEZ, Francisco Camero. 2006. *Canto a la Costa Chica: El mundo poético de Alvaro Carrillo* (Song of the Costa Chica: The Poetic World of Alvaro Carrillo). Estado de México: Universidad Autónoma Chapingo.

ROJAS, Monica. 2007. *Docile Devils: Performing Activism through Afro-Peruvian Dance*. PhD dissertation, University of Washington, Seattle.

ROMERO, Fernando. 1988. *El son de los diablos* (An Afro-Peruvian Dance). TV Cultura, Lima. Video.

————. 1994. *Safari africano y compraventa de esclavos para el Peru, 1412–1818* (African Safari and the Sale of Slaves to Peru, 1412–1818). Ayacucho: San Cristóbal of Huamanga University.

ROSENBLAT, Angel. 1954. *La población indígena y el mestizaje en América* (The Indigenous Population and the Mestization in America). Buenos Aires: Editorial Nova.

RUSSELL, Jeffrey Burton. 1977. *The Devil: Perceptions of Evil from Antiquity to Primitive Christianity*. Ithaca, NY: Cornell University Press.

————. 1986. *Mephistopheles: The Devil in the Modern World*. Ithaca, NY: Cornell University Press.

SAHAGÚN, Bernardino de. 1577. *Florentine Codex: The Universal History of the Things of New Spain*, BK 1. Available at: http://www.wdl.org/en/item/10096/ (last accessed on 5 August 2014).

SALDAÑA, Nancy H. 1966. 'La Malinche: Her Representation in Dances of Mexico and the Unite States'. *Ethnomusicology* 10(3): 298–309.

SALMÓN, Josefa. 1997. *El espejo indígena: El discurso indigenista en Bolivia, 1900–1956* (The Indigenous Mirror: The *Indigenista* Discourse in Bolivia, 1900–56). La Paz: Plural Editores.

SÁNCHEZ, María Ángeles. 1991. *Fiestas de España* (Spanish Fiestas). Madrid: El País / Aguilar.

SANTA CRUZ, Nicomedes. 1974. *Socabón: Introducción al folklore musical y danzario de la Costa Peruana* (Socabon: Introduction to the Peruvian Coastal Music and Dance Folkloric Forms). Lima: El Virrey Industrias Musicales S.A.

SCHECHNER, Richard. 1985. *Between Theater and Anthropology*. Philadelphia: University of Pennsylvania Press.

———. 1988. *Performance Theory*. London: Routledge.

———. 2002. *Performance Studies: An Introduction*. New York: Routledge.

——— and Willa Appel (eds). 1990. *By Means of Performance: Intercultural Studies of Theatre and Ritual*. Cambridge: Cambridge University Press.

SCOLIERI, Paul A. 2013. *Dancing the New World: Aztecs, Spaniards, and the Choreography of the Conquest*. Austin: University of Texas Press.

SCOTT, James C. 1976. *The Moral Economy of the Peasant: Rebellion and Subsistence in Southeast Asia*. New Haven, CT: Yale University Press.

SCRUGGS, T. M. 1999. '"Let's Enjoy as Nicaraguans": The Use of Music in the Construction of a Nicaraguan National Consciousness'. *Ethnomusicology* 43(2): 297–321.

SEED, Patricia. 1988. *To Love, Honor, and Obey in Colonial Mexico: Conflicts over Marriage Choice, 1574–1821*. Stanford, CA: Stanford University Press.

SELIGMANN, Linda J. 1989. 'To Be In-Between: Cholas as Market Women'. *Comparative Studies in Society and History* 31(4): 694–721.

SHAKESPEARE, William. 1999. *King Henry VI, Part II* (Ronald Knowles ed.). London: The Arden Shakespeare.

SILVERBLATT, Irene. 1988. *Moon, Sun, and Witches: Gender Ideologies and Class in Inca and Colonial Peru*. Princeton, NJ: Princeton University Press.

SIMMONS, Marc. 1991. *The Last Conquistador: Juan de Oñate and the Settling of the Far Southwest*. Norman: University of Oklahoma Press.

SKURSKI, Julie. 1994. 'The Ambiguities of Authenticity in Latin America: Doña Bárbara and the Construction of National Identity'. *Poetics Today* 15(4): 605–42.

SOMMER, Doris. 1991. *Foundational Fictions: The National Romances of Latin America*. Berkeley: University of California Press.

SPALDING, Karen. 1984. *Huarochirí: An Andean Society Under Inca and Spanish Rule*. Stanford, CA: Stanford University Press.

SPIVAK, Gayatri Chakravorty. 1993. 'An Interview with Gayatri Chakravorty Spivak' by Sara Danius and Stefan Jonsson. *Boundary* 20(2) (Summer): 24–50.

STEELE, Thomas J. 1994. *Santos and Saints: The Religious Folk Art of Hispanic New Mexico*. Santa Fe, NM: Ancient City Press.

STERN, Peter A. 1994. 'Gente De Color Quebrado: Africans and Afromestizos in Colonial Mexico'. *Colonial Latin American Historical Review* 3(2) (Spring): 183–205.

STERN, Steve. 1995. *The Secret History of Gender: Women, Men, and Power in Late Colonial Mexico*. Chapel Hill: University of North Carolina Press.

STRAUSS, Rafael. 2004. *El Diablo en Venezuela: Certezas, Comentarios, Preguntas* (The Devil in Venezuela: Certainties, Comments, Questions). Caracas: Fundación Bigott.

STRESSER-PÉAN, Guy. 2009. *The Sun God and the Savior: The Christianization of the Nahua and Totonac in the Sierra Norte de Puebla*. Boulder: University Press of Colorado.

STUCKEY, P. Sterling. 2002. 'Christian Conversion and the Challenge of Dance' in Thomas DeFrantz (ed.), *Dancing Many Drums: Excavations in African American Dance*. Madison: University of Wisconsin Press, pp. 39–58.

SUPAY: LEYENDA DE WARI (Supay: Legend of Wari). 1981. Oruro: n.p.

TABARES, Vivian Martínez. 2004–05. 'The Freedom of the Mask: An Interview with Deborah Hunt'. *Sargasso* (Special Issue: Caribbean Theater and Cultural Performance): 97–110.

Tamayo, Franz. 1910. *Creación de una pedagogía nacional* (Creation of a National Education). La Paz: Librería Editorial.

TANDETER, Enrique. 1981. 'La producción como actividad popular: "Ladrones de minas" en Potosí' (Production as Popular Activity: 'Mineral Thives' in Potosí). *Nova Americana* 4: 43–65.

———. 1993. *Coercion and Market: Silver Mining in Colonial Potosí, 1692–1826*. Albuquerque: University of New Mexico Press.

TAUSSIG, Michael. 1980. *The Devil and Commodity Fetishism in South America*. Chapter Hill: The University of North Carolina Press.

——. 1987. *Shamanism, Colonialism, and the Wild Man: A Study in Terror and Healing.* Chicago: University of Chicago Press.

TAYLOR, Diana. 2003. *The Archive and the Repertoire.* Durham, NC: Duke University Press.

——. 2006. 'Performance and/as History'. *The Drama Review* 50(1) (Spring): 67–86.

——. 2008. 'Performance and Intangible Cultural Heritage' in Tracy C. Davis (ed.), *The Cambridge Companion of Performance Studies.* Cambridge: Cambridge University Press, 2008, pp. 91–104.

—— and Sarah J. Townsend (eds). 2008. *Stages of Conflict: A Critical Anthology of Latin American Theatre and Performance.* Ann Arbor: The University of Michigan Press.

TAYLOR, Gerald. 1980. 'Supay'. *Amerindia* 5: 47–63.

TEJEDA ORTIZ, Dagoberto. 1998. *Cultura popular e identidad nacional* (Popular Culture and National Identity), 2 VOLS. Santo Domingo: Consejo Presidencial de Cultura / Instituto Dominicano de Folklore.

——. 2003. *Atlas folklórico de la República Dominicana* (Folkloric Atlas of the Dominican Republic). Santo Domingo: Santillana.

——. 2008. *El carnaval Dominicano: antecedentes, tendencias y perspectivas* (The Dominican Carnival: Antecedents, Trends and Perspectives). Santo Domingo: Instituto Panamericano de Geografía e Historia, Sección Nacional de Dominicana.

—— and Odalis Rosado. 2010. *Máscara e identidad: Imágenes del carnaval Dominicano* (Mask and Identity: Images of the Dominican Carnival). Santo Domingo: Ediciones de la Secretaría de Cultura.

TEMPLE, Edmond. 1830. *Travels in Various Parts of Peru, Including a Year's Residence in Potosi, Knight of the Royal and Distinguished Order of Charles III*, 2 VOLS. London: Henry Colburn and Richard Bentley.

THOMPSON, E. P. 1971. 'The Moral Economy of the English Crowd in the 18th Century'. *Past & Present* 50: 76–136.

TOMPKINS, William. 1981. *The Musical Traditions of Blacks of Coastal Peru.* PhD dissertation, University of California, Los Angeles.

TORRES, Héctor A. 2007. *Conversations with Contemporary Chicana and Chicano Writers.* Albuquerque: University of New Mexico Press.

TORRES PÉREZ, Misael 'Misa'. 1998. *Trilogía del diablo.* Bogota: Magisterio.

TREXLER, Richard C. 1984. 'We Think, They Act: Clerical Readings of Missionary Theater in 16th Century New Spain' in Steven L. Kaplan (ed.), *Understanding Popular Culture.* New York: Mouton, pp. 189–228.

——. 2003. *Reliving Golgotha: The Passion Play of Itztapalapa*. Cambridge, MA: Harvard University Press.

Tujibikile, Pedro Muamba. 1993. *Las Cachúas: revelación de una historia encubierta* (The Cachúas: Disclosure of a Hidden History). Santo Domingo: Museo del Hombre Dominicano / Ediciones CEPAE.

Tulving, Endel. 1983. *Elements of Episodic Memory*. Oxford: Oxford University Press.

Turino, Thomas. 1991. 'The State and Andean Musical Production in Peru' in Greg and Joel Sherzer Urban (eds), *Nation States and Indians in Latin America*. Austin: University of Texas Press, pp. 259–85.

——. 2000. *Nationalists, Cosmopolitans, and Popular Music in Zimbabwe*. Chicago: University of Chicago Press.

Turner, Terence S. 1980. 'The Social Skin' in Jeremy Cherfas and Roger Lewin (eds), *Not Work Alone: A Cross-cultural View of Activities Superfluous to Survival*. London: Temple Smith, pp. 112–42.

Turner, Victor W. 1969. *The Ritual Process: Structure and Anti-structure*. New York: Aldine de Gruyter.

Turner, Victor. 1982. *From Ritual to Theatre: The Human Seriousness of Play*. New York: PAJ.

Valdez, Pedro Antonio. 1995. *Historia del carnaval vegano* (History of the Carnival in La Vega). La Vega: Ediciones Hojarasca.

Van Rhey, Darryl. 2002. 'An Economy of Gifts: Interview with Larry Harvey'. Burning Man website. Available at: http://burningman.org/event/preparation/ (last accessed on 28 April 2015).

Vargas Llosa, Mario. 2000. *The Feast of the Goat* (Edith Grossman trans.). New York: Farrar, Straus and Giroux.

Vélez de Guevara, Luis. 1968. *El diablo cojuelo* (The Limping Devil). Madrid: Ediciones Alcalá.

Very, Francis George. 1962. *The Spanish Corpus Christi Procession: A Literary and Folkloric Study*. Valencia: Tipografía Moderna.

Vignolo, Paolo (director). 2009. *Una cita con el diablo* (A Date with the Devil). Bogota: Universidad Nacional de Colombia-Unimedios. Audiovisual documentary.

——. 2011. 'Paradojas de la patrimonialización' (Paradoxes of Patrimonialization) in *La Cultura: Identidad, Economía y Políticas Públicas* (Culture: Identity, Economics and Public Policy). Bogota: Organización de Estados Iberoamericanos OEI, Corporación Escenarios de Colombia, Departamento Nacional de Planeación, Fundación Universitaria Politécnico Grancolombiano, pp. 144–55. Available at:. http://www.poligran.edu.co/comunica/paipa_2010_html/index.html (last accessed on 2 February 2012).

VILLAGRÁ, Gaspar Pérez de. 1989. *Historia de la Nueva México* (Mercedes Junquera Gómez ed.). Madrid: Historia 16.

——. 1992. *Historia de la Nueva México, 1610* (Miguel Encinias, Alfred Rodríguez and Joaeph P. Sánchez eds and trans). Alburquerque: University of New Mexico Press.

VIQUIERA ALBÁN, Juan Pedro. 2004. *Propriety and Permissiveness in Bourbon Mexico* (Sonya Lipsett-Rivera and Sergio Rivera Ayala trans). Wilmington, DE: SR Books.

VIVEROS, Mara. 2009. 'Mestizaje y occidentalización' (Miscegenation and Westernization) in Paolo Vignolo (ed.) *Ciudadanías en escena: performance y derechos culturales en Colombia* (Staging Citizenship: Performance and Cultural Rights in Colombia). Bogota: Editorial Universidad Nacional de Colombia, pp. 381–3.

WACHTEL, Nathan. 1977. *The Vision of the Vanquished.* New York: Barnes & Noble.

WADE, Peter. 1997. *Gente negra, nación mestiza: dinámicas de las identidades raciales en Colombia* (Black People, Mestizo Nation: Dynamics of Racial Identities in Colombia). Medellin-Bogota: Universidad de Antioquia, ICANH, Uniandes, Siglo del Hombre.

WALCOTT, Derek. 1970. 'What the Twilight Says: An Overture' in *Dream on Monkey Mountain and Other Plays.* New York: Farrar, Straus, and Giroux, pp. 3–40.

——. 1992. 'The Antilles: Fragments of Epic Memory'. Nobel Lecture, Oslo, Norway, 7 December 7. Available at: http://www.nobelprize.org/nobel_prizes/literature/-laureates/1992/walcott-lecture.html (last accessed on 7 February 2015).

WALLRICH, William Jones. 1950a. 'The Demon Dancer'. *Southwestern Lore* 16: 34–5.

——. 1950b. 'Some Variants of the "Demon Dancer"'. *Western Folklore* 9: 144–6.

WEBSTER, Susan Verdi. 1998. *Art and Ritual in Golden-Age Spain: Sevillian Confraternities and the Processional Sculpture of Holy Week.* Princeton, NJ: Princeton University Press.

WEIGLE, Marta. 2007[1976]. *Brothers of Light, Brothers of Blood: The Penitentes of the Southwest.* Santa Fe, CA: Sunstone Press.

WEISMANTEL, Mary. 2001. *Cholas and Pishtacos: Stories of Race and Sex in the Andes.* Chicago: University of Chicago Press.

WHITE, Hayden. 1978. *Tropics of Discourse: Essays in Cultural Criticism.* Baltimore, MD: Johns Hopkins University Press.

WOOLRIDGE, Mike. 1996. 'Organizers Deny Takeover Rumors'. *Black Rock Gazette*, 29 August, n.p.

YANCY, George (ed.). 2012. *Reframing the Practice of Philosophy: Bodies of Color, Bodies of Knowledge.* Albany: State University Press of New York.

YEATS, William Butler. 1997. 'Crazy Jane Talks with the Bishop'. *The Collected Works of William Butler Yeats*, VOL. 1: *Poems*. New York: Scribner, p. 263.

ZULAWSKI, Ann. 1995. *They Eat from Their Labor: Work and Social Change in Colonial Bolivia.* Pittsburgh, PA: Pittsburgh University Press.

Notes on Contributors

Thomas Abercrombie is an associate professor of anthropology at New York University. He has attended Oruro's carnival several times since carrying out a year's fieldwork there in 1987–88. His work on the history of popular performance and social memory practices in Bolivia's cities and towns has taken him repeatedly into the mines of Oruro and Potosí as well as the folkloric festivals and archives of Bolivia. He is author of *Pathways of Memory and Power: Ethnography and History among an Andean People* (1998) and numerous articles on carnival and the carnivalesque in the South American past and present.

Rachel Bowditch is a theatre director, performance studies scholar and associate professor in the School of Film, Dance and Theater at Arizona State University. Her book *On the Edge of Utopia: Performance and Ritual at Burning Man* was published in 2010. From 2009–10, she was an Institute for Humanities Research Fellow at Arizona State University to develop the forthcoming title *Performing Utopias*, co-edited with Pegge Vissicaro. She has presented papers at conferences in the US, Singapore, Argentina, Colombia, Brazil and the UK.

Amiel Cayo was born in Puno, Peru, in 1969. Being involved with the group Escena Inka, he developed a career in theatre. He founded the group Yatiri which was later converted into a theatre workshop. After adapting the Andean fable 'The Fox and the Cuy' for stage, he joined the group Yuyachkani in 1990, where he currently serves as a mask maker.

Lowell Fiet is a professor of English, drama and performance at the University of Puerto Rico-Río Piedras, where he currently directs the Institute of Caribbean Studies. He has directed the *Taller de Imágenes* performance collective (1988–95) and currently coordinates the *másTaller* mask-making workshop. Widely published as a theatre critic and scholar, he is the founding editor of *Sargasso* (1983 to the present), the theatre critic of the weekly newspaper *Claridad* (since 1992), the author of *El teatro puertorriqueño reimaginado: Notas críticas sobre la creación dramática y el performance* (2004) and *Caballeros, Vejigantes, Locas y Viejos: Santiago Apóstol y los performeros afro-puertorriqueños* (2007) and is at work on a broader study of Caribbean and Latin American masks.

Miguel Gandert, an award-winning photographer, is distinguished professor of Communication and Journalism and director of the Interdisciplinary Film and Digital Media Program at the University of New Mexico. Gandert, who works primarily in black-and-white photography, sees his work as both an art form with a strong capacity for expression and a way of telling stories and understanding complex cultural relationships. A primary focus of this work is *mestizo* heritage and the fusion and tension of the relationship between colonial Spain and the native cultures of the Americas. Gandert's photographs have been exhibited and are archived in numerous museums and libraries throughout the world.

Rawle Gibbons, a prize-winning Trinidad playwright, director and educator, is the founder and former head and a senior lecturer in the Department of Creative and Festival Arts, University of West Indies, St Augustine. Gibbons has a master of philosophy degree on 'Theatrical Enactments in Trinidad'. His publications include *No Surrender*: *A Biography of the Growling Tiger* (1994), *A Calypso Trilogy* (1999), *Towards 2000: Models for Multi-cultural Education* (1999) and *Love Trilogy* (2012). He has written and spoken on pan-African aesthetics, the Orisha tradition and its influence on popular arts in Trinidad and Tobago and the relevance of African religion today. In 2002, he delivered the Philip Sherlock Centre's 36th Anniversary Lecture Series in Mona, Jamaica, in honour of Errol Hill.

Anita Gonzalez is a professor of theatre and drama at the University of Michigan. Her research and publication interests are in the fields of intercultural performance and ethnic studies, particularly the way in which performance reveals histories and identities in the Americas and in transnational contexts. Her books include a co-edited anthology with Tommy DeFrantz, *Black Performance Theory* (2014), *Afro-Mexico: Dancing Between Myth and Reality* (2010) and *Jarocho's Soul: Cultural Identity and Afro-Mexican Dance* (2004). Other publications include articles about cruise-ship culture ('Maritime Scenography and the Spectacle of Cruising', 2013), utopia in urban bush-women performance (2004), archetypes of African identity in Central America ('Mambo and the Maya', 2004), and the pedagogy of teaching African American drama (2009). Gonzalez is also a theatre director who has staged more than 50 productions during the course of her career.

David M. Guss is a professor of anthropology at Tufts University. He has participated in and written about festivals throughout Latin America and the US for more than three decades. He has also danced for several years as a devil with the Diablada Internacional Juventud Relámpago del Gran Poder, one of the oldest dance fraternities in La Paz, Bolivia. Among his numerous publications is *The Festive State: Race, Ethnicity and Nationalism as Cultural Performance* (2000).

Max Harris is executive director emeritus of the Wisconsin Humanities Council, University of Wisconsin–Madison. He has also taught at Yale University and the University of Virginia, and served as president of the Medieval and Renaissance Drama Society. He is the author five books, including *Aztecs, Moors, and Christians: Festivals of Reconquest in Mexico and Spain* (2000), *Carnival and Other Christian Festivals: Folk Theology and Folk Performance* (2003) and *Sacred Folly: A New History of the Feast of Fools* (2011). He has studied festive devils in the Dominican Republic, Puerto Rico, Trinidad, Bolivia, Peru, Mexico, Louisiana and New Mexico as well as in many parts of Europe.

Benito Irady is the president of Venezuela's Centro de la Diversidad Cultural and, until recently, was the vice-minister of culture. He was born in the city of El Tigre in the state of Anzoátegui, Venezuela. He is the author of two collections of short stories (*Fabulaciones*, 1990, and *Zona de Tolerancia*, 2012) and has received more than a dozen literary prizes. He is also the author of numerous ethnographic studies, films and recordings carried out throughout Venezuela and the Caribbean.

Enrique R. Lamadrid is distinguished professor emeritus of Spanish and former chair of the University of New Mexico's Department of Spanish and Portuguese, where he taught folklore, literature and cultural history. He currently edits the Querencias series at University of New Mexico Press. His research interests include ethnopoetics, folklore and music, Chicano literature, contemporary Mexican poetry and literary translation. His field work is centred in New Mexico but ranges as well into Mexico, Spain, the Andes and the Caribbean. His research on the Indo-Hispanic traditions of New Mexico charts the influence of Indigenous cultures on the Spanish language and imagination. His literary writings explore the borderlands between cultures, their natural environments and between popular traditions and literary expression. Lamadrid was awarded the Chicago Folklore Prize for his 2003 ethnography *Hermanitos Comanchitos: Indo-Hispano Rituals of Captivity and Redemption* and the Américo Paredes Prize for his cultural activism and museum-curatorial projects.

Zeca Ligiéro is a writer, visual artist and director. He has a PhD from New York University and a post-doctorate in art history from Yale University. He coordinates the Center for Study of Afro-Amerindian Performances (NEPAA) in Universidade Federal do Estado do Rio de Janeiro and was the curator of Augusto Boal's Archive in Rio from 2009 to 2011. He has adapted for the stage and directed *The Third Bank of the River*, based on the novel by Guimaraes Rosa, and *Elegba Crossings, Journey* in the US; directed *Noticias de las cosas pasadas*, based on the work of Augusto Boal, in Colombia; and, with Barbara Santos, directed *Mama Africa* for the Third Festival of Black Art in Senegal. He has published books in Portuguese, English and Spanish including *Divine Inspiration from Benin to Bahia* (1998), *Iniciación al Candomblé* (1995), 'Inititation in Candomblé: Introduction to Africa Brazilian Religion' (2014). He has directed several videos including 'Samba Tap Dance' and 'Zé Pelintra's Interactive Altar'.

Angela Marino is an assistant professor at the University of California, Berkeley working in the areas of performance studies, fiesta and carnival, and social movements in Latin/o America. She is curator and editor of the site festivedevils.org, and is currently working on a research project on fiesta and governance. Her book *Populism and Performance: Fiesta Politics in the Bolivarian Revolution of Venezuela* is forthcoming from Northwestern University Press.

Raviji (Ravindranath Maharaj) is a community worker who was raised in the sugarcane village of Caparo in Central Trinidad and Tobago. He served as a primary-school teacher before leaving for India where he pursued studies in Hinduism. Returning to Trinidad after 10 years, he was drawn into community work at several Hindu temples, organizations and youth camps. He grounds the Hindu imagination and strives to create a voice of the

Hindu Caribbean through discourses, radio broadcasts, weekly columns, poems, drama, songs and experiments in Hindu festivals. He also works with students from local and foreign universities. For the past twelve years, he has been experimenting on community development through children in a system combining Dharmik heritage, performance (of Ramdilla) and service learning. He is the interim chairman of Astrel that works with Hindu, Amerindian and African traditional religious communities.

Milla Cozart Riggio, James J. Goodwin Professor of English, Trinity College, Hartford, Connecticut, received her PhD from Harvard University. Since 1995, she has focused on Trinidad Carnival and culture. Among her edited books and monographs are *Ta`ziyeh: Ritual and Drama in Iran* (1988), *The Play of Wisdom: Its Text and Contexts* (1990), a special issue of *TDR: The Drama Review* on Trinidad and Tobago Carnival (1998), *Teaching Shakespeare through Performance* (1999), and *Carnival: Culture in Action—the Trinidad Experience* (2004). She co-edited *Medieval and Early Renaissance Drama: Reconsiderations* (special issue of *Mediaevalia*, 1995), *Renegades: The History of the Renegades Steel Orchestra* (2002) and *In Trinidad: Photographs by Pablo Delano* (2008). She has also written on Hindu Ramleela/Ramdilla performances in Trinidad.

Monica Rojas earned her PhD in cultural anthropology from the University of Washington with her dissertation 'Docile Devils: Performing Activism through Afro-Peruvian Dance'. Rojas is a recognized community artist and activist and has contributed as choreographer, cultural consultant, dance and music instructor, guest artist and scholar to multiple organizations both in Peru and the US. She recently combined her academic and artistic skills to launch and direct two community-wide arts education organizations called DE CAJóN Project and MÁS—Movimiento Afrolatino Seattle, both dedicated to promoting and educating people about the cultural contributions of Afro-descendants in Peru and Latin America respectively. Rojas is currently Assistant Director, African Studies and Latin American and Caribbean Studies Programs, Jackson School of International Studies, University of Washington.

Miguel Rubio Zapata is the co-founder and director of Grupo Cultural Yuyachkani, Peru's most important theater collective. Yuyachkani (which is a Quechua word that means 'I am thinking, I am remembering') has been working since 1971 at the forefront of theatrical experimentation, political performance and collective creation, devoting itself to the collective exploration of embodied social memory, particularly in relation to questions of ethnicity, violence and memory in Peru. Yuyachkani won Peru's National Human Rights Award in 2000. Known for its creative embrace of both Indigenous performance forms and cosmopolitan theatrical forms, Yuyachkani offers insight into Peruvian and Latin American theatre and to broader issues of postcolonial social aesthetics.

Rafael Salvatore was born in Lavello, Italy, in 1946. In 1979, he moved to the city of Cumana, Venezuela, where he came in contact with the popular customs and traditions that are a fundamental part of his photographic repertoire. He has had more than 10 exhibitions and received various prizes. He has served as the still photographer in more than 30 Venezuelan and foreign films. The Cinemateca Nacional de Venezuela published his two books *Fijaciones Que Una Foto Fija* (1997) and *Rafael Salvatore: Foto Fija . . . ma non troppo* (2008).

Paolo Vignolo is associate professor of history and humanities at the National University of Colombia, Bogota. His fields of research and creation deal with public history, cultural heritage and memory studies with a focus on live arts, play and performance. He holds a PhD in history at the EHESS (School for Advanced Studies in the Social Sciences) of Paris, and has been 2012–13 Santo Domingo Visiting Scholar of the David Rockefeller Center for Latin American Studies (DRCLAS) at Harvard University. He is director and co-founder of the research group 'Play, Fiesta and Power' of the Hemispheric Institute of Performance and Politics (New York University) and co-founder of the Colombian chapter of the Cultural Agents Initiative (Harvard University). Among his forthcoming publications are 'A Place for the Dead in the City of the Living: the Central Cemetery of Bogota' in Grindle M. S. (ed.), *Reflections on Memory and Democracy* (Cambridge. DRCLAS book series, Harvard University Press); and 'The Dark Side of Mooning: Antanas Mockus's Transgressive Bet' in Tognato C. (ed.), *Cultural Agents Reloaded: the Legacy of Antanas Mockus* (Cambridge. Harvard University Press). For more details, please visit, http://unal.academia.edu/PaoloVignolo

diablesse 191

diablo, diabla

 chinas diabla 54

 diablo cojuelo 139–41, 143, 150n15

 danzante diablos 252n3

 diablito 131, 181

 diablico 67, 115, 129, 130, 149n2

Dickinson, John 233

Didi-Huberman, Georges 340

Dionysus 186; *see also* Bacchus

disguise 63, 131, 136, 137, 138, 143, 168–9, 185, 191, 255, 291, 332, 343, 345

dithyramb 186

dobalê 157

Doherty, Brian 301, 306, 315

Dominican Republic 14, 129–50, 175, 330, 332, 336n9, 339, 348–9

Douglas, Mary 17, 205

dragon 3, 5, 13, 56, 84, 88, 193, 197, 201, 351

 dragon bands 193, 197, 201, 207–16, 219n27, 219n28

dress 10, 33, 50, 70, 73, 74, 75, 76, 82, 93n13, 94n22, 95n38, 112, 121, 152, 163, 218n7, 256, 257, 258, 263, 264, 269n1, 322, 341, 342, 352, 353

Drucker, Philip 310

drum 7, 22, 121, 154, 155, 156, 157, 187n4, 190, 221, 222, 235, 255, 266, 268, 339

Durand, José 108, 110, 115, 125

Earth 323, 327, 333, 337n11, 347

Earth Mother 46, 51, 55, 79, 262, 327, 341; *see also* Pachamama

Easter 77, 134, 137, 142, 144, 150n13, 150n18, 191, 222, 328, 347

Echenagucia, José 'Cheché' 247

Eco, Umberto 345, 347

egungun 172, 215

Eisenstein, Sergei 319

El Cholo Portales 80

El Dorado 25

Elías Piña (Dominican Republic) 129, 130, 149n1, 150n12

Emberá-Chamí 33

enemy 3, 96n43, 146, 189, 261, 272, 288

Erickson, Ivan 150n15

Espanto 291

Eshu 8–9, 153–4, 159–61, 162–5, 200, 217, 321, 323, 328, 333, 334, 335, 336n7, 344, 350

Esposito, Roberto 28, 346

Estenssoro, Juan Carlos 91n1

Eucharist 28, 82, 92n10, 244, 245, 252n1

Europe 77, 92n10, 97, 108, 132, 176, 188n10, 200, 245, 265, 321, 334, 336n8

European 3–4, 5, 25, 29, 48n7, 55, 56, 72, 84, 94n28, 97, 108, 115, 125n2, 143, 151–67, 168, 173, 176, 184, 185, 188n10, 190, 193, 213, 215, 235, 246, 275, 302, 324, 327, 328, 333, 335, 339, 354n3

 Eurocentric 156

Evangelical 154, 166n4, *176*, 273, 329

Evil 60, 290–1

Falangist 80

Falk, Dan 325

fang 56

Wachtel, Nathan 35n35

Wade, Peter 28

Walcott, Derek 177, 335

Wallrich, William Jones 284

Wall Street 295, 298n21, 345
  Occupy Wall Street 345
  Wall Street Journal 353

war 3, 8, 28, 79, 80, 92n10, 109, 141, 146,
  148, 181, 188n11, 214, 246, 258, 288,
  301, 316n14, 320, 343

Warburg, Aby 340

Wari 52, 86–7, 88

Webster, Susan Verdi 134

Weigle, Marta 134

Weismantel, Mary 91n1

Wenner-Gren Foundation 91n1

Westwood, Sallie 91n1

whip(s) 14, 69, 115, 129–50, 174, 175,
  192, 194, 195, 196, 197, 199, 200,
  218n7, 218n12, 218n13, 255, 256, 258,
  267–8, 332, 336n9, 348–9

White, Hayden 89

wig 55, 60, 61

witchcraft 3, 153, 164

Woolridge, Mike 301

World Intellectual Property Organization
  352

xirê 161, 166n9

Yancy, George 217n3

yatiris 57

Yeats, William Butler 323

Yoruba 8, 159–61, 162, 183, 188n13, 200,
  215, 262, 266, 321, 336n4, 336n7, 350

Yuyachkani, Grupo Cultural 9, 14, 107,
  117, 118–9, 120, 122, 126n6

Zambrano, Marta 352

zampoña 54

Zé Pelintra 162, 163, 334

Zulawski, Ann 91n1, 95n34